Capitalism Takes Command

Branden Adams

CAPITALISM
Takes Command

The Social Transformation of Nineteenth-Century America

Edited by
Michael Zakim *and* Gary J. Kornblith

The University of Chicago Press
Chicago and London

Michael Zakim is associate professor of history at Tel Aviv University. He is the author of *Ready-Made Democracy: A History of Men's Dress in the American Republic, 1760–1860*, also published by the University of Chicago Press. **Gary J. Kornblith** is professor of history at Oberlin College and the author of *Slavery and Sectional Strife in the Early American Republic, 1776–1821*.

The University of Chicago Press, Chicago 60637
The University of Chicago Press, Ltd., London
© 2012 by The University of Chicago
All rights reserved. Published 2012.
Printed in the United States of America

21 20 19 18 17 16 15 14 13 12   1 2 3 4 5

ISBN-13: 978-0-226-45109-1 (cloth)
ISBN-13: 978-0-226-45110-7 (paper)
ISBN-10: 0-226-45109-7 (cloth)
ISBN-10: 0-226-45110-0 (paper)

Library of Congress Cataloging-in-Publication Data

Capitalism takes command : the social transformation of nineteenth-century America / edited by Michael Zakim and Gary J. Kornblith.
    p. cm.
Includes index.
ISBN-13: 978-0-226-45109-1 (cloth : alk. paper)
ISBN-10: 0-226-45109-7 (cloth : alk. paper)
ISBN-13: 978-0-226-45110-7 (pbk. : alk. paper)
ISBN-10: 0-226-45110-0 (pbk. : alk. paper)
    1. Capitalism—United States—History—19th century. 2. Capitalism—Social aspects—United States. 3. United States—Economic conditions—19th century. 4. United States—Social conditions—19th century. I. Zakim, Michael. II. Kornblith, Gary John.
HC105.C24 2012
330.973'05—dc23

                                                                2011023776

Contents

v

Editors' Acknowledgments

This book's creation testifies to the persistence of "the community of scholars" not only as an academic ideal but as a lived reality in the early twenty-first century. The editors are deeply grateful to all the contributors who signed onto the project at its inception in 2007–2008, read and "workshopped" the first drafts of one another's papers at a two-day mini-conference in June 2009, and then proceeded to revise their essays for inclusion in the present volume. We sincerely thank Robert E. Wright for hosting the June 2009 meeting at New York University's Stern School of Business and for arranging the necessary funding for this event with the generous assistance of Richard Sylla. We also thank James Livingston for his critically important participation in that gathering and Eli Cook for creating a transcript of our conversations.

Robert P. Devens of the University of Chicago Press has guided this project from its germinal stage through to its final publication. We thank him for his steady application of good sense as well as for his dedication to the highest standards of history writing. We also thank the anonymous outside reviewers recruited by Robert for their support and constructive criticism of the enterprise as it developed. And we thank Anne Summers Goldberg, Therese Boyd, Ryan Li, and Jim O'Brien for their essential labor in transforming the manuscript into a beautiful book.

Finally, we thank Zivya Seligman-Pinchover and Carol Lasser for the intellectual and emotional inspiration they have supplied for all our projects. They make everything possible.

Introduction

An American Revolutionary Tradition

Michael Zakim and Gary J. Kornblith

The essays in this volume explore capitalism's rise to economic
and cultural supremacy in the United States during the nineteenth century. This was when buying and selling became so urgent and prevalent, and efficient, that the exchange relationship
emerged as a dominant form of social intercourse as well as an
equally dominant form of social thought. That dominance was
no foregone conclusion, however. It was far from obvious, for
instance, that a system of profitmaking based on the perpetual
movement of goods and persons could possibly serve as the
foundation of public order and stable government. For that to
happen, some of the most basic tenets of American life needed
to be recast, if not redefined.

This ambitious program found incisive expression in an ety-
mological detail: capital's transformation into an "ism." There
was no better indication that the specific exigencies of doing
business had acquired a general application to human affairs.
Capitalism, that is to say, reached far beyond the purview of

1

capital, and even of the economy, and offered a comprehensive vision of the social order that prescribed new roles for government, family, and the individual while declaring that they now applied to everyone. That same universality also provoked furious debates over access to money and credit and the state's responsibility in regulating that access, over the place of moral constraint in a system based on maximization and risk, and over the proper relationship between public welfare and private interest, and between wages and work.

The history of capitalism is not, then, just an account of transaction costs, economies of scale, and diminishing returns, but of social habits, cultural logics, and the conditions of system-building as well. All were now harnessed to the engines of change, which contemporaries increasingly referred to as "progress" and which economists would eventually call, ironically using an agrarian metaphor, "growth." But nature had been decisively subjugated by an integrated circuit of "steam-navigation, railways, electric telegraphs, clearing of whole continents for cultivation, canalization of rivers, [and] whole populations conjured out of the ground" that far exceeded anything "all preceding generations together" had ever experienced, as the *Communist Manifesto* breathlessly pronounced in a survey of the great transformation in 1848. Americans were equally impressed, and concerned, with the unprecedented scope and scale of industrial change. A "crazing, unobservant, lightning-like speed" had taken control of their lives, a New York memoirist noted in 1843. "General fermentation and excitement of matter and of mind" was the result, which threatened "our great political and civil institutions and the social and moral principles upon which they depend for their existence and perpetuity." The danger was born of capitalism's systematic disregard for custom and convention once these lost their utility. Longstanding hierarchies and traditional forms of authority were subsequently, and unsentimentally, discarded. Capitalism, it could be said—although few have said it—became America's revolutionary tradition.[1]

Nor was this revolution confined to the destruction of an agrarian past. Its subversive energies were no less manifest in relation toward the new, that is, toward itself. That was because business kept revising its own premises and practices in a ceaseless effort to negotiate a better deal. Citizens of the commercial republic found themselves participating in a dizzying array of property transactions that reflected the ever-shifting conditions of making money in the nineteenth century. Mercantile capitalism, market capitalism, family capitalism, laissez-faire capitalism, industrial capitalism, corporate capitalism, and finance capitalism, to name just a few of the better-known rubrics, variously mobilized a "disorganized" demographic of private bankers, insurance brokers, wholesale importers, start-up manufacturers, plantation owners, western yeomen, investors in government securities, and artisanal sweaters whose world diverged from older commercial systems. The profit incentive had once been assigned to a narrower segment of society which practiced a more repetitive and prolonged form of trade. Capitalism, in contrast, pursued "fast property" that dissolved obligations upon the completion of each transaction. This allowed contracting parties to resume their former autonomy without further regard to each other. Such "freedom" of action—freedom, that is, from "noneconomic," or unprofitable, commitments as a just price and equity, not to mention family obligations and the common weal—was essential to the rational calculation of one's best interests. The result was highly dynamic and generated considerable amounts of new wealth. That dynamism also meant that whoever succeeded in securing his or her interests was, by the same token, in a position to lose them. "They clutch everything but hold nothing fast," as Tocqueville observed of the consequent restlessness of the times.[2]

Capitalism was a Promethean event for it at once marked the acme of humanity's command over nature as well as the deluge which then ensued. "Capital must go forth like a mighty genius, bidding the mountains to bow their heads, and the valleys to rise, the crooked places to be straight, and the rough places plain." Thus Edward Everett conjured the supernatural effects of modern commercial practice in the premiere issue of *Hunt's Merchant's Magazine*. But "the life of a merchant is, necessarily, a life of peril," Joseph Hopkinson no less acutely, and precisely, observed in his "Lecture upon the Principles of Commercial Integrity." "He can scarcely move without danger. He is beset on all sides with disappointments, with fluctuations in the current of business, which sometimes leave him stranded on an unknown bar, and sometimes sweep him helpless into the ocean."[3]

There was no contradiction here between the two characterizations. Rather, the system could not work without such constant threats of collapse. Any talk of perfect competition or equilibrium was no more than that, and a misleading rhetoric at best. In practice, the system would stagnate if it did not continually expand, innovate, exploit "asymmetries," and restlessly move capital, people, information, and goods from here to there and back again in search of higher returns. The workings of credit were a good example of this nervous logic. Credit allowed humanity to reshape time and space—to level "mountains and valleys," as it were—in accordance to one's ambitions. The promise to pay (that is, to assume a debt) thus became the primary medium of exchange in the capitalist system. This then resulted in a double form of "dissociation," for not only was a currency of promises intrinsically separate from the things being traded, but it was also increasingly separated out from any actual relationship between particular persons. This was because debts themselves were soon being bought and sold in their own networks of exchange, which, of course, generated more credit and thus more exchange. In such circumstances, the very possibility of assigning "intrinsic" value to money, or even to goods—of the kind that measured the "fruit of many years' industry, . . . something sacred that is not to be sported with," as Tom Paine had insisted in 1786—became nonsensical.[4]

The American bourgeoisie thus acted like revolutionary classes throughout modern history, both in its struggle to gain a measure of control over the chaos born of its own success, and the willingness to destroy parts of itself in doing so. True, as Max Weber observed, the pursuit of gain was not a capitalist innovation. Markets are likewise to be found throughout history, operating on familiar terms of mutual exchange and often using money to do so. However, only in the nineteenth century did these societies with markets become market societies; that is, only then did exchange transcend the temporal and spatial boundaries to which it had long been confined, either by law or circumstance, and come to characterize all spheres of life. "Man's economy is, as a rule, submerged in his social relations," Karl Polanyi wrote about a traditional political order that subordinated material practices to the general requirements of stable government. "The change from this to a society which was, on the contrary, submerged in the economic system was an entirely novel development." Commerce, in fact, acquired a democratic status in market society as it was reorganized to allow, if not compel, everyone to trade with everyone else, and anything to be traded for anything else, and at any time. Material relations were consequently removed from the closed, parochial context of community, family, and personality and transplanted to an objective economic sphere where membership was open to any and all rational agents.[5]

Theirs was a historically specific, and even historically peculiar, rationality. It found high expression in personal and bureaucratic calculations of risk, and in the consequent utilization of contracts, insurance policies, securities, and bankruptcy laws, among a growing inventory of other market-powered tools, to ameliorate those market-generated dangers, if not to actually take advantage of them. Individuals were in a position to either gain or lose but, in any event, they all became vulnerable to forces beyond their control and, often enough, beyond their perception. The systemic instability of this order has consequently made it an elusive subject of inquiry. The orthodox division of scholarly labor, for instance, while yielding plentiful, discrete studies of the firm, working-class consciousness, technological change, and free-market ideology, among other pertinent subjects, has devoted far less energy to exploring the multidisciplinary intercourse by which capital became an "ism" and business became a political philosophy.

The cliometric habits of economic historians are a case in point, for they consistently flatten the history of market society by "bracketing" whatever proves too difficult to integrate into a quantifiable universe of price series, wage averages, or productivity regressions. Long arcs of development, resting on "data" retrofitted into axiomatic categories of growth or stagnation, invariably result in highly cogent patterns of secular change. The revolutionary disruptions essential to capitalism's reorganization of society—conflicts over the very forms of capital and their legitimacy, or the political negotiation over the boundaries of property rights and contractual obligations, or concern over the effects of competition on the civic life of the polis—are then dismissed as exogenous to the organic logic of exchange, and so irrelevant to a history of the economy. That is why studies in economic history so often reproduce capitalist ideology itself, separating economic activity out from the murky realms of the unmeasurable and assigning it an autonomous operating principle.

Business historians have shown greater sensitivity to the inherent disruptions and extra-economic dynamics of market society's restless drive to innovate and profit. Business studies have effectively traced, for example, the creation of systems for managing the troubled symbiosis between chaos and control that lies at the heart of capitalist praxis. Business historians have recognized that the market does not coordinate economic activity, as Adam Smith presumed it did, as much as it itself requires coordination on the part of economic agents. And yet, scholars of business consistently refuse to follow these activities out of the firm and factory in order to ask how such models permeated industrial society as a whole. How, we are left wondering, did business logic become a general social logic and the "bottom line" emerge as a favorite synonym for the unadulterated truth?

One might try to circumvent such frustrations by approaching the history of capitalism from the opposite direction. The minutiae of everyday life—the genealogy of cooking stoves, mixed cottons, or suburban gardens, for instance—that comprise the subjects of "material culture" present an excellent opportunity for examining the practical foundations of industrial civilization, for exploring the interplay between high and low, abstractions and tangibilities. But while such mechanics offer a commodious peephole for gazing upon a vast field of human experience, scholars too often make them the principal subject of inquiry. The result is a technical focus that ignores the social relations by which things are actually turned into commodities. Meanwhile, the

opposite problem plagues the writing of cultural history, including those studies explicitly concerned with the process of commodification and its effects on
social authority and the production of truth. Historians of privacy, sensibil-
ity, and the self, for instance, ambitiously analyzing the very epistemologies of
social intercourse, rarely think about the movement of prices, contract law, or
bankruptcy proceedings as anything more than the symbolics of power. They
consequently reinscribe the categorical division between materiality and mentality that informs the same liberal gestalt under examination.

No doubt, the most consistent effort in recent decades to broaden our understanding of the contexts and consequences of capitalist revolution has been
undertaken by social and labor historians. Motivated by both scholarly and
ideological opposition to an older historiography that positioned capitalism at
the heart of national consensus (ever since it putatively arrived in America on
"the first ships"), these studies have striven to rescue memories of working-class
resistance, communal mutuality, and proud corporate identities from a Whig-
gish teleology that demonstrated little interest in what was deemed to be social
marginalia best suited to the dustbin. Social and labor historians consequently
recovered a radical dissenting tradition, which they located deep within American republican thought and experience, an authentic, antimarket impulse that
constituted an alternative version of the nation's political origins and, thus, a
new kind of usable past. Unfortunately, however, in describing popular opposition to commercial progress as a radical project, they have reflexively identified
market society as a conservative status quo, thus improbably turning capitalism
into a force of reaction rather than revolution.[6]

The outstanding achievement of Charles Sellers's *Market Revolution: Jacksonian America, 1815–1846*, which attracted the attention of an unusually
broad audience of historians when published twenty years ago, was its emphasis on the subversive, if not revolutionary, effects of commodity exchange in the
American republic.[7] Incisively, often derisively, arguing that the same private
property which had once anchored the country's agrarian way of life ended
up underwriting the industrial progress that destroyed it, Sellers showed how
deeply entrenched cooperative practices and beliefs were dialectically upended
by a new ethos of competition and self-centered ambition. The imperatives of
profit ruthlessly undermined longstanding customs, including a native-born
democracy resting on the modest habits of local yeomen. *The Market Revolution* presented a sweeping social and political jeremiad of the kind not seen
in the profession since Charles Beard, to whom it owed much in style as well
as substance. We thus learn, for instance, that the country's commercial elites
leveraged the federal Constitution's distrust of popular politics into control of

the country's financial, legal, and physical infrastructures, which then allowed them to impose an integrated market on the nation at large. Even when anti-capitalist forces succeeded in electing Jackson to the presidency—who accordingly proceeded to destroy the nation's central bank—the democratic majority was thwarted by a federalism that made it possible for capital to "shop around" and find political protection at the state level.

The Market Revolution thus replaced those hopeful, sometimes even heroic, accounts of popular resistance to a market regime so often preferred by social and labor historians with a tragic, even elegiac, account of loss and destruction. This might at first seem to present a more politically savvy version of events, to be contrasted to celebrations of subaltern agency popular in recent decades, savvy especially in light of the future direction American society was to follow. And yet, Sellers's history of capitalist revolution ultimately reads like a passion play in which a virtuous moral economy succumbed to a nefarious political economy that flooded the pristine land—that "immemorial provider of survival"—with worthless paper, real estate speculation, low wages, and every other manifestation of humanity's worst traits. As a consequence, "capitalist hegemony" verged here on caricature, a *deus ex machina* devouring everything of use value in its path, a spontaneous function of the ascendant Money Power with no history of its own. Sellers's social history of capitalism, in other words, bracketed the more complicated, ambiguous, and ambivalent heart of the story.[8]

This volume consciously seeks to engage those complications and in so doing offers a collective attempt to "bring the economy back" into American social and cultural history. Family farms, general incorporation laws, mortgages, inheritance, images of abundance, filing systems, and the exigencies of risk management constitute our inventory of means by which capitalism took command of society. This is by no means an exhaustive list of capital's transformative effects on the course of human events, or on life in the United States during the industrial century. But it is enough to propose a master narrative that puts the commodity at the center of American experience while arguing that there was nothing natural, preordained, or predictable in that development. The market required an enormous social effort—and provoked intense social conflict—in becoming the basis of the social order.

Land once seemed the surest way of doing this. That was why the young republic founded its economy on an abundance of family farms. These farms actually drove the commercial development of the United States, Christopher Clark argues, commodifying the land, extending trade across the continent, and promoting financial innovation. Ordinary farmers benefited from the system, as did banks, insurers, wholesalers, and investors. But we should not be lulled into complacency. That same mutuality also pushed the sides apart: the homesteader found his proprietary status undermined by new forms of property that promised greater profits. The confrontation that ensued was not, then, between capital and an older, precommercial relationship with the land, but between distinct ways of integrating the soil into the market.

The mortgage was such a "financial instrument" born at the intersection of land and capital. It was not a new invention, Jonathan Levy reminds us. In fact, the mortgage served as a most effective means of achieving the traditional goal of a family homestead. But in so doing, it tied proprietorship to the incomes of distant investors, entangling farms within a system that preferred the financial over the agricultural value of land. Was the mortgage, we soon ask, a means of securing independent proprietorship, or was it a new form of dependency in a market society? The fact that it was both of these—that proprietorship and dependence were now two sides of the same coin, so to speak—is revealing of capitalism's destabilizing role in the history of property rights.

Slavery was another old form of property closely bound to the land. That is why slaveowners considered themselves heirs of the republic's agrarian tradition. But slaves also proved to be a highly instrumental financial asset. Edward E. Baptist describes how they were systematically collateralized in order to raise the operating funds and long-term credit that would enhance their masters' ability to control the plantation economy. This was a pressing goal for cotton growers looking for hedges against the virulent booms and busts of the world market. The bodies of slaves were so effectively capitalized, in fact, that the resulting securities were widely marketed throughout Europe and America. But this success also became a source of great vulnerability during economic crises, such as occurred in the wake of panic in 1837. As Baptist explains, the subsequent failures of Southern banks, together with Jackson's destruction of the Bank of the United States, which had supplied the bulk of its credit to the plantation economy, left slaveholders increasingly dependent on foreign, including Northern, money. This inflamed sectional resentment. It also pushed Southerners toward a search for new means of securing their economic future, which included territorial expansion.

And so land proved to be an erratic form of property and, as such, the root of rampant social conflict. Order and stability would have to be founded on a more transcendent source. The family, Elizabeth Blackmar suggests, was a possible alternative. The transfer of wealth from one generation to another was certainly driven by an ethos of preservation antithetical to the liquidity, risks, and uncertainties of capitalist economy. And yet, as partible inheritance became more common after American independence—advancing republican goals of a wide distribution of property—the direct partitioning of land among heirs was replaced by a distribution of the returns from the land's sale. This proved to be a more equitable way of passing on family property. Certainly, land did not lose its central importance in this practice. However, its value was now measured in monetary terms. What's more, with family farms increasingly enmeshed in market exchanges, they were more likely to carry extra-family debts at the time of the householder's death, complicating the settlement of estates. Blackmar describes how probate courts were consequently charged with overseeing the proper management of family assets, which was interpreted to mean a profitable investment of the property rather than allowing it to lie "idle." Such investments included real estate trusts, which were safer than industrial corporations, and which also meant that the system had come full circle, back to the soil, except that now, of course, land was exclusively an investment value rooted in a commodity structure of liquidity and risk.

The troubled relationship between making profits and protecting families provoked antebellum America's most virulent debate, that over slave breeding. The reproduction of slaves was a signal feature of the chattel system, Amy Dru Stanley observes, but the practical apparatus of sexual compulsion is not the key to understanding its significance in the making of market society. We should focus, instead, on the attendant moral controversy that broke out between abolitionists and slaveholders, one that constituted, in fact, a confrontation over the meaning of love. And so, while scholars have recently argued that the existence of a giant slave market constitutes powerful evidence of the South's essentially capitalist character, Stanley redefines the whole question. Slave breeding for commercial profit, she contends, marked the antithesis of capitalism's social relations. This was because "unfree love" violated the core values of individual will and personal autonomy by which liberals justified— and naturalized—market competition, profit maximization, and the satisfaction of personal desire.

In addition to land, inheritance, and slaves, corporations constituted another well-established economic institution. They were most prevalent in America, Robert E. Wright shows, and in every section of the country. The reasons were obvious enough: incorporation was a particularly effective method for coordinating physical capital, human capital, and money capital, which would make it possible to take advantage of economies of scale and influence prices as well as develop a credit base for financing the market system as a whole. These "economic" gains, however, became a political liability. Such effective control over capital was translated by critics into a dangerous concentration of power and influence. Popular protest brought about a change in the existing rules of incorporation and their replacement with general procedures. This meant that the special privileges traditionally granted corporations would now be available to everyone. That was, of course, a contradiction in terms, and Wright takes note of the resulting rise in competition, which led to a new emphasis on management techniques. These, in turn, insulated the corporation from public oversight and accountability. And so opposition to special incorporation, together with the popular demand for a democratization of economic life, can be said to have ultimately enhanced bureaucratic power.

Such contradictions — dare we say, dialectics — of a society organizing itself around the liquidity, fungibility, and incessant maximizations of the commodity were largely lost on an American gentry anticipating a bright future of material abundance. They were thrilled as well by new technologies for organizing the surfeit of goods, on view at the London and Liverpool docks. These visions of commercial grandeur were so striking that American visitors invoked notions of the Sublime to capture their excitement. What had once been an expression of awe and terror in response to the wonders of the natural world, Tamara Plakins Thornton notes, was now applied to a thoroughly artificial landscape. Such aesthetics balanced the two essential but often incompatible elements of commercial progress, namely, risk and control, which meant that "capitalist sublime" introduced order and security into a reality conventionally associated with adventure and anxiety. A happy transition to a world dominated by profit seemed possible, together with a new self-identity for the propertied classes that would rest on economic and technological innovation rather than ground rents and gentlemanly leisure.

Capitalist sublime impressed William Leggett, the radical journalist and leader of the workingmen's movement in New York City, as a parody at best and a gothic horror at worst. More generally, it heralded the corrupting effects of industrial progress. Leggett himself was no less prone to cast social questions in aesthetic terms, Jeffrey Sklansky points out, although he preferred the Manichean devices of the popular stage for doing so. These allowed Leggett to array "publick credulity" against "soulless corporations," labor against money, and democracy against monopoly, and so cast political economy as a moral clash between grand historical forces of good and evil. In personalizing the abstract and often intangible operations of capital, such melodrama offered the public a grammar for thinking about and debating these questions in an age before they became the professional prerogative of experts. Money redeemable at face value thus embodied values of transparency that would expose the manipulations and misrepresentations of a privileged coterie of specially chartered banks and other sordid monopolists. Leggett, in other words, was no enemy of market logic but rather its champion. His calls for a level playing field were meant to give each citizen an equal, and equally honest, chance to advance him- or herself.

Capitalists were no less anxious to introduce regularity and integrity to what was usually advertised as a free market. They recruited a giant new class of clerks in order to discipline the exploding volume of exchange with ledgers, inventory controls, credit reports, regular communications, and the accelerating circulation of information across ever-expanding networks of time and space. In fact, Michael Zakim argues, these clerks labored on capitalism's most important production project of all, the production of the market, which was no less of an industrial artifice than steam or steel. All their paperwork produced abstract knowledge, which proved no less essential to industrial production than the material surfeit of crops and goods. At the same time, the clerk belonged to a decidedly different kind of laboring class, not comprised of heroic artisans or radicalized factory operatives but of ambitious employees scribbling hard at their desks and hoping to make partner someday.

Regulation of the economy—and the attendant responsibility for the social order—was the traditional prerogative of government. The Civil War, according to Sean Adams, changed that equation forever. Victory did not just save the Union and end slavery. It recast the relationship between political authority and economic practice. This is because mass mobilization had forced Northern legislatures to grant corporations far-reaching protections in hopes of encouraging initiatives that would both bolster the economy and aid the military effort. The state thus ceased to be a regulator of industrial development and became, instead, an active partner in that project. The new corporate charters cemented the rehabilitation of what had once been "monstrous" institutions into engines of national progress. An alliance was born between the government's promotion of general prosperity and industrial capital's unrivaled ability to organize resources, setting the stage for the colossal dimensions of corporate enterprise in the late nineteenth and early twentieth centuries.

And so capitalism took command, doing so through an array of means and methods that no one entirely anticipated, let alone controlled. At the same time, capitalism was a thoroughly manmade system: human agency was one of its organizing principles. Siegfried Giedion addressed this philosophical and political conundrum in his epic study of the techniques of industrial production, *Mechanization Takes Command* (1948), in which he argued that engineering was the defining paradigm of modernity, and had subsequently recast human nature in its own image. We lost control over our humanity, Giedion declared, just as we perfected our control over nature. It was a disastrous paradox, no doubt informed by the dark times of the twentieth century, and Giedion sought to explore its counterintuitive dynamics. He did so by focusing on the "anonymous" forces which shape society, writing a history of tangible experience—of comfort, posture, hygiene, and the built environment—that made these "invisible" practices of everyday life the subject of critical insight, and a key for understanding the more conscious spheres of social existence as well.[9]

Capitalism Takes Command continues Giedion's project. It also strives to illuminate the anonymous, often invisible, workings of a system that has effectively reorganized our humanity. Mechanization, however, is no longer the crux of this story. "Financial engineering," for instance, proves to be no less integral to industrial success than the assembly line, that which Giedion identified as the acme of commodity logic. This is because machines are only powered up if their products can be effectively marketed. And so, rather than ask "Who built America?"—a common query of social and labor historians once hoping to peel away all the brokered layers of mediation in search of the real, labor-driven source of wealth—we find ourselves asking "Who sold America?" or, perhaps more to the point, "Who financed those sales?" The ensuing paper trail keeps leading in circles, and cycles, through a thickening web of interpersonal opportunism that dissolved "stability and absoluteness" into "motions and relations," as Georg Simmel described the fundamental dynamic of market society.[10] It was a nervous basis for social order, no doubt, and a most profitable one.

1

The Agrarian Context of
American Capitalist Development

Christopher Clark

Over the long nineteenth century, from the late colonial period
to the aftermath of World War I, American capitalism established itself with revolutionary force. The United States became
the world's largest economy and in per capita terms one of its
richest, while developing to a marked degree the main facets of
industrial and finance capitalism. Contemporaries marveled at
the speed of the transformations this entailed. By the 1890s the
United States had become the world's biggest manufacturer and
producer of minerals, its largest absorber of mobile international
labor, and one of its chief financial centers. Its most powerful
figures were among the world's wealthiest individuals. Essential
elements of American capitalism—integrated markets in land,
capital, labor, and commodities; large-scale manufacturing; corporate organizations; a substantial wage-earning working class
and salary-earning middle class—all emerged during the period.
     Economic historians once characterized this as a sectoral
shift from "primary" activities, such as agriculture and fisheries,

to "secondary" manufacturing activity, noting the growth of urban societies and the emergence of service ("tertiary") sectors to facilitate and coordinate these. Scholars in the Marxian tradition pointed to the constraints that led working men and women—American-born and immigrants—to enter wage work, providing the labor force on which capitalist industry and finance were built. But the long nineteenth century, in which the United States expanded territorially from seaboard settlements to become a continental empire, was also a period of dramatic growth in agriculture. During the seventy years before 1860 alone this growth was rapid enough: farms and plantations more than quadrupled in number to more than two million. But over the next sixty years, the figure more than trebled again, to nearly six and a half million. Farms and ranches large and small were created across much of the continent, and the United States played a leading part in a global drama of agricultural settlement that involved Canada, Australasia, and parts of South America, Africa, and Asia.[1]

Agriculture and its expansion were deeply involved in many of capitalism's key attributes, and so had profound implications for American capitalist development. Expansion entailed the creation of landed property by the addition of "new" lands to the property system, the emergence of land markets, and the production and distribution of produce that fed growing national and international commodity markets. Agriculture also created markets for wage labor, though here the picture was more complex and ambiguous. The sectional conflict between North and South and the destruction of chattel slavery during the Civil War involved the defeat of one agricultural system based on forced bondage by another based on "free" family and wage labor. But while wage labor in farming grew in specific circumstances, agriculture did not become primarily a locus for waged employment. The continued growth of farming that relied on family-based labor would give American capitalism some of its notable characteristics.

The long nineteenth century marked a distinctive period in the development of US agriculture, and hence American capitalism as well. Rural societies, of course, had dominated early America; in 1790 nine-tenths or more of the population was engaged in or connected with farming. The emergence of other sectors meant that the relative position of farming necessarily declined. By 1820 about 72 percent of the workforce was in agriculture; by 1920 the proportion had fallen to 27 percent, and in that year census enumerators found, for the first time, less than half the population living in settlements defined as "rural" (with fewer than 2,500 inhabitants). Yet the expansion of American farming continued throughout this period. Though its proportion of total employment fell, the absolute size of the farm workforce increased until the 1910s. Only in certain pockets did the number of farms decline before 1900, and the total number was still rising in the 1920s. In many regions, farm households tended to become focused on specific patterns of agricultural production; as household manufacturing declined, farm consumption from markets rose, and specializations emerged.[2]

By 1920, however, agriculture was entering a new phase. Output continued to rise, but farming went into significant demographic and even geographical retreat; farm sizes grew but, except during the Depression, the number of farms fell. Government and agribusiness came to dominate farm policy and investment, and the proportion of the population engaged in farming began to plunge toward its present-day level of around 2 percent.[3] Systematic investment in machinery, artificial fertilizers, hybrid seeds, and other commoditized inputs marked a massive substitution of capital for labor, raising labor productivity in agriculture by a factor of 15 by the early twenty-first century. Previously, by contrast, productivity gains had been more modest and as much attributable to labor as to capital inputs.[4] Nineteenth-century farmers had increased their production for markets, but even the most commercialized often relied on their own or neighborhood resources for such essentials as seeds, fertilizer, and motive power that later in the twentieth century they would purchase in the market.[5] Farm work was organized in ways that limited reliance on wage labor. Large farms and plantations existed in certain circumstances but were not the majority of farms, or often even permanent features of a system dominated by medium- and small-sized units.[6]

What effects did the expansion and sustained importance of agriculture have on American capitalism before 1920? Some influences were complementary: the first part of this chapter considers these. But agricultural expansion was uneven and contested, so the discussion will move on to explore its more problematical influences. Structural conditions guiding the relationships between agriculture and capitalism provoked conflicts among different kinds of producers, between farming and commerce, and between proprietors and labor.

There were numerous evident ways in which agriculture complemented other aspects of America's economic and social transformation:[7] continental expansion; the acquisition and privatization of land; the output of foodstuffs and other produce that became commodities in national and international commerce; the distribution of urban and commercial centers; and connections with manufacturing and with finance. In all these arenas agricultural growth and capitalist development appear to have been mutually reinforcing.

The pursuit of continental expansion was rooted in several contingencies. Several colonies made claim to "western" land, and the Confederation congress succeeded in gaining federal control over these "public lands" outside the already settled regions. Under the 1783 Treaty of Paris and other international agreements from which indigenous people were excluded, Euro-Americans assumed sovereignty over land actually held by Native Americans. Governments used land sales as a source of revenue that avoided political obstacles to direct taxation. Above all there was an inexhaustible supply of citizens and immigrants keen to occupy and cultivate new regions. To Euro-Americans there was a virtuous circle of government and private interest, resulting in expansion.

White settlement divided and commoditized land, creating land markets and setting terms for cultivation by private property-holders. This process helped destroy other kinds of transactions across the zones of intercultural contact between Native Americans and Euro-Americans that Richard White dubbed the "middle ground."[8] Driven by popular demand for landed independence and, in the case of slaveholders, by opportunities for clearing new land with slave labor, the nation's rural regions and rural populations grew rapidly. Though less than a majority of people owned land, the proportion was significantly greater than in much of Europe. So, though rural societies were far from egalitarian—even for whites—freehold farming and the vision of equality that it conjured up underpinned the ideology of expansion. Widespread land ownership, members of Congress claimed in 1796, would create a "free, enlightened, and independent" populace who would "make good Republicans instead of servile tenants."[9]

Agrarian expansion has long been associated with the spirit of American capitalism. A leading Latin American historian remarks that the availability of land for ownership by millions of individual farmers was "the most outstanding product of the American democratic ideal."[10] Commentators were prompt to note the advantages this provided over European societies. In 1871 the *Baltimore Sun* claimed that 100,000 settlers had acquired land under the 1862 Homestead Act, and that this alone exceeded by 70,000 the total number of landowners in Britain.[11] Access to land was interpreted as distinguishing American "farmers" from European "peasants," and as a means by which farmers could turn themselves into capitalist "businessmen." In post-Revolutionary rhetoric the "independent farmer" represented republican virtue and simplicity. In the nineteenth century the farmer stood for the rights of "producers" or for "free labor." By the twentieth, farmers stood as symbols of the private enterprise system and as crucial bulwarks against communism.[12]

European settlement and cultivation in North America can be seen as a process of versatile adaptation to a new environment. Landholders from various origins adopted new methods and crops, learning from the other peoples they encountered. The historian Russell Menard has labeled as "mestizo agriculture" the blend of Native American, African, and European crops and techniques that colonial cultivators passed on to the farmers of the long nineteenth century.[13] Adapted to the new land, this agriculture was productive, feeding a rapidly growing national population and furnishing foodstuffs and raw materials for export. Rising productivity enabled a proportionately shrinking farm population to supply grains, lumber, tobacco, cotton, and other produce to cities, industries, and overseas customers alike.

Patterns of farming and the social structures of agricultural regions shaped the character and distribution of urban commercial centers. The colonial contrast between the scarcity of urban centers in the Chesapeake and the South, and the prominence of port towns in New England and the mid-Atlantic region, was replicated across the eastern half of the continent as farm settlement spread to the Southwest and into the "Old Northwest" in the first half of the nineteenth century. Plantation regions in the South, where slaves labored and practiced various skills year round, gave rise to relatively few, often small, urban centers. Most large Southern towns lay at the region's peripheries, handling the shipping of agricultural produce to distant markets.[14] Nonplantation agriculture in the South was sufficiently marginalized, either socially or geographically, to give it little influence in the forging of urban or commercial systems. Small farmers in plantation districts were often under the thumb of powerful planter neighbors. Nonplantation regions tended to be uplands, or otherwise distant from trading centers; only in specific areas, such as the Northwest Georgia upcountry, did local developments spur significant market activity before the Civil War.[15] Northern agriculture, by contrast, whose production for markets was often diversified and handled by family labor, spawned many commercial centers within farming districts, some of which grew into large commercial or industrial cities. Though in both South and North there were complementary relationships between town and countryside, the consequences for capitalist development differed. Northern farm regions came to support larger commercial and manufacturing populations than did much of the rural South.[16]

Regions with high population densities or wide seasonal variations in demand for field labor became significant nuclei of manufacturing.[17] Though early industry developed in port towns, it also grew in rural areas, where labor and skill could be recruited for seasonal work, for domestic outwork, or to provide labor for workshops and factories. In southern New England alone, rural districts produced textiles, paper, woodenware and furniture, metalwares, clocks, guns, tools, and machines.[18] The combination of rural skills and labor with the development of multiple commercial towns was an important spur to industrial development. A vast triangle, whose base ran from Maine to Maryland and whose apex lay in Illinois, became the principal seat of American manufacturing by the 1850s, and remained so for more than a century. Well into the nineteenth century, most leading US manufactured goods were fashioned from agricultural raw materials: natural-fiber textiles; boots, shoes, and other leather goods; and woodenware and other lumber products. Methods developed to produce these goods were applied to new processes. For example, rolling technology used in wool carding was adapted to printing and ironworking and cloth-dyeing techniques were extended to papermaking and chemicals.[19] One of the great Midwestern growth industries of the second half of the nineteenth century—meatpacking—adopted methods of sequencing, motion, and coordination in the handling of animals and their parts which would in the twentieth century be widely applied to industrial mass production.[20]

Agriculture also underpinned commercial and financial techniques essential to the rise of American capitalism. Land itself, once it was privately owned, was the most acceptable security for lending and capital accumulation, not least because land values tended to rise as farms were cleared and improved, population grew, and market integration proceeded. Mortgages on farmland became important instruments for transferring capital from older to newer regions and for placing the expected future value of farms and crops behind nonagricultural investments. Real estate mortgages became significant in the portfolios of banks, insurance companies, and other institutions, and hence as backing for commercial and industrial credit.[21] Meanwhile, farmers' own periodic and cyclical demands for credit influenced the financial system. The national and international circulation of commercial paper mirrored the shipment of crops and the financing of farming, fostering an urban-hinterland dynamic around commercial centers small and large. New York City's emergence as the nation's largest commercial metropolis reflected both its geographical position at the intersection of continental and Atlantic trade routes and the efficiencies that centralized trading services could offer across widely dispersed rural regions. This fostered New York merchants' influence over the international trade in cotton, even though this commodity was produced hundreds of miles away in the plantation districts of the South.

In time, the growth of farm output called for new commercial and financial

techniques. The bulk marketing of grains, meats, and lumber products, especially in the Midwest, led during the mid-nineteenth century to innovations
along the chain of commerce, including grain elevators, urban commodity exchanges, and futures contracts. These not only facilitated the transformation
of individual farms' produce into standard commodities, but also turned them
into invisible items represented only by paper instruments.[22] As well as Southern plantation districts, large areas of farmland in the rest of the United States
were drawn into the orbits of commodity handling, processing, and financial
metropolises, of which Chicago became the epitome. Whether we interpret
these financial relationships between city and countryside as complementary
or as neocolonial in character, the methods of trading farm commodities over
long distances embraced farm producers in networks over which they had little
oversight or control.

Agriculture also played a central part in America's emergence as a global
economic power.[23] By the 1850s the United States held a unique position:
it was an independent (noncolonialized) polity undergoing rapid economic
transformation that was positioned on both of the world's largest oceans at
a time when Europe's seaborne empires were reaching their zenith. Agriculture's demands helped shape the United States' own early ventures into overseas empire. Proslavery Southerners proposed annexations in Cuba or Central America during the 1850s in hope of expanding American slavery despite
mounting opposition to its spread in the West. The federal Guano Islands Act
of 1856, passed in response to the search for organic fertilizers, enabled the
United States to assert its sovereignty over rocks or small islands in the Atlantic, Caribbean, and Pacific against the likely rival claims of Britain and other
European powers. American interest in Hawaii and the Philippines, first stimulated by whaling or trading, came later in the century to be directed toward
political control and formal annexation by promoters of sugar plantations and
other agricultural projects. All along, agricultural commodities were most
prominent among US exports. First cotton, then grain, became key commodities fueling the industrial and demographic expansion of Europe.[24] American
crops became sufficiently crucial that at the end of World War I US officials
and merchants intervened directly in the provision of food to large areas of
Central and Eastern Europe that had been cut off from trade by the wartime
Allied blockade.

An analysis emphasizing the complementary aspects of agricultural expansion
for broader capitalist development can explain much, but it also glosses over
deep divergences in American agriculture and the degree to which agrarian

issues posed problems and conflicts. Ties between agricultural settlement and the financial system were not always constructive. Frantic booms in public land purchases and speculation, peaking in 1818, 1836, and the mid-1850s, contributed to the panics of 1819, 1837, and 1857. More generally, the very circumstances that made agriculture so significant—the occupation of the continent, the establishment of farms, and the distribution of populations across vast regions—were also sources of abiding tensions. The apparent mutuality between agricultural expansion and capitalism actually contained much variation, while the engagement of farmers with a developing national market system provoked conflicts between producers and traders and between proprietors and laborers. These tensions arose from several structural factors: the role of the state; the existence of different types of regional society and power structure; the influence of local economic practices on farmers' behavior; and the ways labor in agriculture interacted with wider labor markets.

Though agricultural expansion is usually viewed as a vector of private economic action and individuals' independence, rural America was always dependent on the policies and protection of the state. Government granted land and administered land laws; it adjudicated and legitimated the acquisition of Native American lands; and it removed Indian nations seen as obstructing the spread of white agriculture. In the semi-arid West, government became involved in administering water rights.[25] Throughout our period, governments provided military force and conducted warfare against Native Americans to enforce land policies and protect settlements, often at the behest of settlers whose intrusion into Indian country had provoked tensions to begin with. Armies had to be fed, and the demands of military procurement, especially in wartime, forged links between government and farm suppliers that helped develop agricultural markets.[26] The Civil War imposed extraordinary demands on rural areas, which produced many soldiers, as well as most of the supplies, for armies of unprecedented size. Particularly in the North, these demands pressed farmers toward greater reliance on machinery and fostered commercial networks in the handling and processing of agricultural commodities that extended the scope of national markets. Over time government involvement in agriculture evolved from pursuing territorial expansion to promoting farm productivity. In establishing the US Department of Agriculture and making provision for land-grant colleges, the Civil War Congress took initial steps toward greater government engagement with farming that would develop more fully after 1920.

Underlying these patterns of state involvement were political imperatives deriving from both ruling and popular groups' demand for land. The predisposition for access to freehold land, derived from peasant conflicts in Europe, translated into successive phases of settler pressure that drew metropolitan governments into policies of geographical expansion.[27] The colonial pattern of assigning land grants to favored individuals had whetted wealthy colonists' appetite for land speculation. The British administration's attempt to interfere with settlement by controlling movement across the Appalachian Proclamation Line in 1763 sparked outrage among speculators and prospective settlers, helped touch off the Revolution, and reflected the importance of a developing struggle between indigenous peoples and European settlers in the trans-Appalachian West. The migration of settlers westward after the Revolution put irresistible pressure on federal administrations to suppress indigenous rights, for fear of losing the loyalty of settlers and control of the region to other European powers.[28] To harness their land hunger to national ends and to foster their loyalty, Euro-American settlers in the "West" were granted full constitutional incorporation into the national polity, giving them influence over the terms by which land would be distributed. Even at the end of the nineteenth century, when the failure of populism appeared to mark the political defeat of the agrarian West, settler influence remained potent. By 1920, conscious of farming's relative demographic decline, agriculture's advocates had begun to change strategies from relying on its political weight at the polls to forming organizations, such as the Farm Bureau, to lobby legislators.

Yet although settler-agrarian expansion had a powerful influence on government, regions differed in the effectiveness of their claims on government policies. Dispersed settlement and farm-making created a formidable distributional problem that influenced everything from communications and the handling of commodities to identity and political adherence. Between regions, and even within them, there could be marked variations between different crop regimes and their social implications.[29] Cotton and tobacco, grown respectively on large and smaller farms, could support differing social structures and patterns of economic inequality, both under slavery and after emancipation. The skills and work rhythms involved in rice and sugar cultivation produced social patterns that were each distinct from those in cotton. Differences emerged also between the corn and wheat belts of the Midwest.

Landownership was widespread among farmers and planters, who alike venerated their propertied independence. Yet there was a difference between those who controlled only the labor of themselves and their families, and those who had access to the labor of others. While various forms of servanthood and wage-work were common in early America, the biggest distinction was of course associated with slavery. Agricultural development where slavery remained legal and common diverged from that where slavery declined or was prohibited.[30] Apart from the moral questions it posed, contemporaries divided on the consequences of slavery's presence. Advocates in the early 1820s for the legalization of slavery in Indiana and Illinois suggested that "our country would populate in abundance, wealth would be in our country, money would circulate . . . —it would be a new spring to business." The contrary opinion was embedded in portrayals of the two sides of the Ohio River of the kind that Alexis de Tocqueville would report in *Democracy in America*: that "free" Ohio displayed energy, enterprise, and prosperity lacking across the water in "slave" Kentucky. A Louisville lawyer, Richard Clough Anderson Jr., wrote during a visit to Ohio in 1817 that "the rapid improvement of this Country shews the good policy of excluding slaves & . . . the high benefit of dividing land into small parcels." Towns and countryside "Thriving and busy . . . populous and populating," were the result.[31] Distribution, communications, and regional variations sustained a nation of decentralized power structures, shaped on local and regional rather than national lines. Different kinds of class power resulted.

Robin Einhorn has shown, for example, that the influence of slaveholders was such as to shape federal tax policies to protect slavery from interference or destabilization.[32] Access to slave labor meant that the most fertile parts of the South and Southwest were the most important regions in which it was possible to sustain large agricultural estates. In nonslave regions, North or South, farm sizes were smaller, large farms were rarer, and those that were created often did not last long. Accordingly, Southern planters were the largest ruling group to obtain wealth and profits directly from agriculture. In the Southern economy, plantation production was often the most lucrative attraction to investors and proved more attractive than possible alternatives in trade, manufacture, or finance. Nonplantation agriculture gave investors less opportunity to profit directly from the land. Land speculation was risky or expensive, and few who went into it made the fortunes they dreamed of. In the absence of slave labor, farming had to be left mainly to household-based proprietors who could manage small or medium-sized farms with the labor available to them. In the North, therefore, profits were greater from the collection, transportation, processing, and distribution of crops than directly from growing them.

Accordingly, capital for investment became channeled into commerce, urban development, transport, and manufacturing activities that serviced the rural economy. Even speculative profits in land could more often be made in successful towns, where commercial functions concentrated, than in farmland as such. Rising urban property values, reflecting the growth of commercial activities, themselves became an important source of wealth. This concentration of capital in activities indirectly related to farming, as distinct from in farming itself, marked an evolutionary step in capitalist development. It connected the expansion of agriculture to the growth of nonagricultural functions in both old and newer regions of the United States, deepening market connections and fostering further development. It also placed economic and social power in the hands of urban and small-town traders, bankers, and professionals, creating geographically dispersed, provincially oriented ruling groups of different character from those in the South.

The emergence of national markets in agricultural produce was, accordingly, rooted in local patterns of economic activity and exchange. Since the 1970s, historians have noted the significance of locally conducted, often non-monetary exchange networks in rural economies, and of the role of familial ambitions and strategies in shaping economic activity.[33] Contemporary views of local exchange varied. Samuel G. Goodrich, fondly recalling life in a Connecticut town, saw it fostering community peace and stability. The Prince de Talleyrand, observing transactions on the Maine coast in the 1790s, saw it as a "web of reciprocal frauds."[34] As rural production intensified in the context of a growing commerce, Americans acted on both perceptions. Daniel Vickers demonstrated that local and market exchanges were each embedded in social relationships, which altered as farming became more commercialized. He also noted that local dealings themselves, because they varied in character from the customary to the negotiable, might either be insulated from or responsive to price information from outside.[35] Studies of New England, New York's Hudson River Valley, early Ohio and Indiana, northern Virginia, Georgia, and elsewhere have shown both how local exchanges were conducted in different contexts and how market relationships were assimilated into local life.[36] Nonmonetary personal exchanges continued even in localities where commercial agriculture expanded. Community rather than individual decisions could influence the adoption of new machinery or techniques: econometric models of Midwestern farmers' purchases of mechanical reapers failed to explain observable patterns until Alan L. Olmstead and Paul W. Rhode showed that farmers did not act alone, but cooperated with neighbors to acquire equipment.[37] The expansion of market dealings in a growing national economy inevitably affected, and was in turn influenced by, local credit and exchange networks.

Factors conducive to capitalist development were not limited to competition or individual ambition, nor could these factors ensure development in the face of unfavorable social conditions. Many parts of the antebellum South failed to develop diversified rural economies not simply because there was a comparative advantage to producing staple crops, but also because the social structures and conventions of a slave-based society discouraged diversification. Networks of local knowledge and distribution, and opportunities to deploy skills, which fostered development in Northern rural regions, were less adapt- able in the slave South. Here, skills were partly commanded by enslaved people, but interaction and exchange among slaves, and between slaves and whites, were increasingly subject to suspicion and control by authorities fearful of insurrection.[38] Outside the South such fears did not arise, so farm neighbor- hoods and associational networks could foster the creation of social capital. From New England towns that spawned social libraries and supported printing presses, to western New York and Ohio, where social reform and educational organizations sprang up in new farming districts, households' pursuit of famil- ial strategies led to their support of associational activities and to the diversi- fication these could prompt. Schooling and voluntary associations rooted in neighborhood networks formed, alongside growing commercial involvement, a rural "public sphere" that sprang from farm families' needs and ambitions as much as from the demands of the marketplace. This fostered conflicts with professional and commercial families, whose sponsorship of semiprivate acad- emies and then of broader school reform reflected a desire first to sidestep and then to confront rural households' influence over education.[39]

Yet greater engagement with distant markets also imposed new disciplines on farmers.[40] Rural regions underwent subtle, often long, drawn-out, processes by which local networks and exchange practices were adapted to and often ultimately supplanted by the requirements of market trading. This did not necessarily entail conflict. Tony Freyer's concept of "associational market rela- tions" encompasses the social, rather than individualistic, character of many commercial dealings. B. Zorina Khan's research in Maine court records sug- gests that producing for distant markets promoted more cooperation among rural neighbors than conflicts between them.[41] But tensions between social and individual purposes did induce friction. In New York and elsewhere, mar- ket regulations stipulated that traders should treat all buyers equally and deal with the first seeking to be served, but could not easily suppress the habit of favoring particular, personally known customers. Debates over debt and bank- ruptcy laws repeatedly confronted the anxiety that insolvent debtors would settle accounts with their friends at the expense of others.[42] Behavior in the marketplace often followed the dictates of social obligation rather than of ab- stract principle.

Even so, as Vickers noted, local neighborhood ties could restrain as well as support. Local exchange networks that helped nurture commercial and associ- ational links also spurred individuals to make new connections that could free them from family and neighborhood constraints. James Guild set out from his native Tunbridge, Vermont, in 1818 to work as a peddler, leaving behind personal entanglements both of indebtedness and of friendship with neighbors who were "content and happy . . . strongly attached to one another, with 'no ambition to shine.'"[43] Guild's portrayal of his breach of these personal relationships reminds us that rural adaptation to wider markets more often fomented tensions within and between families than overt conflict between groups.

Capitalist institutions emerged subtly in these interstices of older social and economic networks. Merchants and wealthy farmers organized banks, insurance companies, and related organizations both to raise capital and to distance themselves from the kinds of personal obligation that the existing credit system entailed. Richard Clough Anderson had no sooner become a director of a Louisville bank in 1815 than he denied his brother-in-law's loan request, made on the strength of their family connection. Though applauding his kinsman's kindness and benevolence, Anderson concluded that the man was so indebted that he would lose his property, and "that his friends who are assisting him must . . . be materially injured in the Shipwreck." As Naomi Lamoreaux and Tamara Thornton have each shown in different contexts, owners of new institutions could construct and operate within circles of trust that were disconnected from the claims of family or neighborhood.[44] By the 1810s, when the number of banks began to multiply rapidly, such institutions did not remain exclusively the preserve of the wealthy. The establishment of mechanics' banks in cities and efforts to set up farmers' banks in rural areas reflected the wishes of small producers as well as wealthy men to transfer some of their transactions from risky or overburdened local, kinship, and neighborhood credit networks to more impersonal markets for capital and credit.[45]

Finally, in addition to influencing the state, regional social structures, and local exchange patterns, agriculture shaped American capitalism through the character of its labor force. Early America's agrarian economies had used different intermixtures of exploited labor, from hired wage labor by legally free workers at one end of the spectrum to the forced labor of chattel slaves at the other, and with an array of dependent, unfree, or coerced laborers in between: tenants and cottagers, wives and children in families, indentured servants and apprentices, paupers "bound out" to work for others, and convicts and imprisoned debtors. All subordinates, including wage laborers and married women, were nominally subject to the authority of a master or husband. Some four-fifths of the population held one dependent status or another at the end of the colonial period, and many of these conditions survived well into the nineteenth century.[46] Over time, however, the range dwindled. Indentured servitude declined, formal apprenticeship diminished, many states abolished imprisonment for debt, and New York's 1846 constitution significantly modified the status of manorial tenants in the Hudson Valley. By the 1840s most subordinate workers in the United States were slaves, hired laborers, or family members in households. Chattel slavery would be abolished at the end of the Civil War in 1865, so these changes have usually been interpreted as part of the emergence of a "free labor" standard that was itself an index of developing capitalist social relations.

Yet the existence of different forms of labor was attributable not only to historical contingencies but also to structural conditions. Unfree labor had grown in early America because a small population in relation to land area led property owners and household heads to employ coercive means to get work done for them.[47] The expansion of agriculture across the continent in the nineteenth century replicated these conditions, perpetuating the high land–labor ratios of the colonial period even as the nation's population multiplied. Slavery, wage work, and family labor were not so much different forms on a spectrum from coercion to freedom as the remaining available means by which farmers could compel labor from others.

Slaveholders, large and small, defended their entitlement to own and coerce human chattels because the value of being able to do so was high. The monetary value of slaves rose in the 1850s as commodity prices rebounded from the slump of the late 1830s and early 1840s. After their efforts to retain slavery collapsed in defeat in 1865, planters worked to re-create its attributes: trying first to circumscribe freed people's movements, then holding tenants and sharecroppers to contracts that extracted much labor for limited returns. Southern sharecroppers worked in a variety of circumstances: some, for example, were in "squad share" arrangements that partially emulated gang labor. But most worked as single-family units. Interpretations of sharecropping have likened it to each of the types of labor prevalent before the war. Emphasizing the cropping contract and crop lien as mechanisms for "debt peonage" treats it as a close substitute for slavery. Noting the legal designation of sharecroppers as "laborers," and the high annual movement of sharecropper families from farm to farm at the expiration of their terms, stresses its similarities to wage labor. But a focus on male household heads obscures the power these individuals held over members of their own families. "Freedom" often led to the intensification of patriarchal authority in households. Nate Shaw, born to Alabama sharecroppers in 1885, recalled that his father "kept me right under his thumb until the year I was nineteen years old." That year, 1904, he was hired out to a white farmer, but the next year his father refused to do so again and "took me back to work for him so he could go on his way." Whatever its similarities with slavery or with wage work, sharecropping also replicated the power of household heads to control their own families' labor.[48]

Nonslaveholders, North and South, had the more limited options of using hired or family labor. Family discipline could be harsh and demanding. On a Wisconsin farm in the 1850s the young John Muir felt at least as keenly as Nate Shaw would the power of a patriarchal system. Kept by a strict father (who used corporal punishment) at work on the family land during his teenage years, Muir would reflect that "through the vice of over-industry . . . we were all made slaves."[49] In the long run, wage labor on farms became increasingly common, but it was not a straightforward process. The Civil War diminished the availability of labor for hire, obliging many farm families to call on their own resources, and encouraging those with means to invest in machinery. Labor remained sufficiently scarce on the postbellum frontier that legislators dreamed up schemes to supply it; one proposal in 1878 envisaged an Enlisted Labor Association that would recruit 100,000 volunteers for five years' work on a government reservation "for military and agricultural purposes."[50] Though in certain pockets of late nineteenth-century agriculture hired work became common, much farm work continued to be done within households, where paternal authority enforced discipline among women and children whose labor contributed to family strategies. The 1910 Census, for example, found that 72 percent of gainfully employed children were working in agriculture.[51]

The balance between hired and family labor varied with crop regimes and the cycles of settlement and farm-making. Large-scale use of wage labor was to be found on the extensive grain farms of California, and on the "bonanza farms" that sprang up in the western prairies and eastern Great Plains between the 1860s and 1880s. Although later observers such as V. I. Lenin saw a trend toward increasing use of wage labor on farms, the balance of evidence suggests that this was less of a general process than the result of particular conditions.[52] Wage work was most frequent in three sets of circumstances: when farms were being newly created; when farms were large; and when specific crop regimes required large seasonal labor inputs. Wage labor in farm-making was an important but temporary solution to heavy labor demand. Newly settled regions saw declines in wage work once farms became more established. Except in California, large grain farms were themselves impermanent features of a new landscape; many prairie "bonanza" farms were divided and sold after one or two decades for cultivation in smaller parcels by farm households. Wheat and fruit growing, along with crops such as sugar beets, did make heavy labor demands, particularly at harvest time, but the labor required for corn and other crops were more capable of being handled without significant infusions of seasonal labor. So the later nineteenth-century expansion of agriculture tended to reinforce rather than erode the importance of family labor.

In many regions, as we have noted, demand for wage labor was seasonal. In consequence, the populations available to carry out such labor either became dependent on migrating to follow the demand for work, or occupied a marginal status in the farming districts in which they lived. Among the employers of wage labor were California fruit and vegetable growers, including cooperatives like the California Raisin Growers' Association, which proved to be as hard taskmasters as any landowner.[53] As farm expansion in California and the interior West progressed after the Civil War, alarm over the alleged dangers from itinerants ("hoboes") mounted among small town and rural settlers whose need for such workers' labor was seasonal and intermittent. Chinese laborers in California faced increasing prejudice and restrictions before formal curbs on immigration were imposed on them in 1882. Japanese laborers also faced prejudice, but less harsh measures; many of them shifted in time from wage work in fruit and vegetable fields to purchasing and running their own small farms, using family labor, or maintaining a balance between work on their own land and hiring out at busy times to larger growers. Social relations in agriculture therefore differed from those usually associated with manufacturing. Instead of employers and hired workers there was a more complex mix of landowners, family labor, and marginal, migrant, or intermittent wageworkers, some of whom themselves partly subsisted from, or sought to return to, household-based working arrangements.

Varied labor arrangements also emerged in the West as farming spread into more arid regions and confronted problems of water supply. Promoters of irrigated farming sought to rely on migrant or settled seasonal labor; the Newlands Valley project in Nevada, developed from 1905 onwards, attempted to maintain a dependent population of Paiute and Shoshone Indians who had been displaced from tribal lands but assigned small plots just sufficient to enable them to subsist between the seasons when white farmers wanted to hire them for planting and harvest. Advocates of "dry farming" in the High Plains of western North Dakota and Montana, on the other hand, espoused a vision of grain cultivation and livestock raising that would rely primarily on family labor and intermittent hiring among neighboring households.[54]

Market demands and family authority combined to compel more work on farms. Particularly during and after the Civil War, productivity increases were partly attributable to farmers' investment in machinery and new techniques. But recent findings by economic historians have played down the significance of labor-saving capital investments, and instead emphasize the importance of labor inputs as an explanation for late nineteenth-century productivity growth. Men, women, and children on farms worked harder; there is also evidence that they worked more effectively, incrementally improving land-clearing, drainage, cultivation methods, animal breeding and plant selection, and achieving gains over time largely by their own efforts. Compared with their successors, relatively few nineteenth-century farmers systematically employed commercialized methods to raise yields.[55] This again emphasizes the distinction we have drawn between the long nineteenth century and the developments that were to come after 1920.

Such structural conditions—the involvement of the state, regional distributions of social functions and power, the adaptation of local exchange patterns to market demands, and patterns of labor in agriculture—all contributed to divergences in agricultural experience and responses to it. They shaped the conflicts over agricultural issues that arose perennially throughout the long nineteenth century—issues that reached well beyond agriculture itself to touch on political rights, privilege, and power in society generally.

The American Revolution, for instance, provoked struggles about price regulation, property rights, and the terms on which the new nation's finances would be conducted. New states and the federal government offered rural people contradictory lessons on the nature of property, debt, money, and financial obligations. Where the lessons were harshest, as in Massachusetts in the mid-1780s, the consequence was Shays's Rebellion, an armed insurrection that some historians have seen as only the most dramatic of a series of conflicts endemic to rural societies' encounters with governments in the early republic.[56]

Most prolonged were conflicts over the terms for occupying the land itself. Pressures from both elite and popular interests worked to provoke confrontations with Native Americans and to inveigle or force them into ceding their land for white settlement. The issue had been endemic since the earliest European settlements, but the Revolution unleashed white expansion into the trans-Appalachian West on terms that Native Americans were hard-pressed to resist. Along with the white purchase, theft, or confiscation of land and the destruction, removal, or corralling of Native American societies came the first essential precondition for capitalism: the creation of private property in land that had previously been held outside the reach of markets.[57] But this commoditization merely set up new social conflicts.

These were conflicts between those who wanted land for homes and livelihoods and those who sought to control it or extract its wealth for profit.

The colonies had witnessed landlord-tenant conflicts in New York, New Jersey, and elsewhere; the persistence of manorial tenancies in the Hudson River Valley produced perennial "anti-rent" insurgencies between the 1760s and the 1840s. Similarly, there were prolonged contests from Maine to the Southwest between grantees of large tracts of unsettled land and squatters who occupied land without legal title, cleared and cultivated it, claiming rights to it by virtue of their labor over the unearned titles of the nominal holders.[58] Where they could, settlers sought their own titles to land and pressed for rights for smallholders against those of large land claims. Early settlers in Kentucky, finding the law favorable to large landholders, moved into what became Ohio. A North Carolina congressman urged the federal government to sell public lands in 160-acre lots so that the poor would "be put into a situation in which they might exercise their own will, which they would not be at liberty to do if they were obliged to become tenants to others."[59] The claims of those who improved the land against those who merely held paper title to it corresponded to broader contemporary debates about the respective rights of "producers" and "nonproducers." These in turn helped shape state and federal land policies in the antebellum period.

Early federal policy was to sell public land as a source of government revenue. Government interest therefore conflicted with that of actual settlers, and laws of 1804 and 1808 sought to restrict unlawful entry onto public land and to remove squatters. But this proved impracticable and, in time, ideologically objectionable. The continued demand for land, either from speculators or from settlers, population shifts to new regions, and the incorporation of new territories and states all pushed land policy toward favoring actual settlers. Preemption laws, first passed in 1830 and made permanent in 1841, permitted the legal settlement of those who had occupied and improved land—reflecting the "producerist" view that labor earned the right to its product. Successive laws also reduced the price and eased the terms for purchasing public lands. By the 1840s voices were being heard for opening land for free settlement by "homesteaders."

Conflicts over a proposed homestead law, which many Southern leaders opposed as a challenge to the expansion of slavery in the West, threaded the sectional debates of the 1850s. By 1860, when Democratic president James Buchanan vetoed a homestead bill, citing the social inequities and loss of government revenues it would cause, a significant political realignment had been completed. Democrats, once advocates of easy terms for farm settlers, employed arguments once associated with their erstwhile Whig opponents. Former Whigs, now allied with Free Soilers in the new Republican Party, became exponents of an expanding society of small freeholders. As Abraham Lincoln graphically described it, the switch was like "two drunken men fighting each *out* of his own coat, and *into* that of the other."[60]

Meanwhile, land policy also intersected with other tensions arising from the pace of settlement. From the era of Jefferson onward, and in the light of issues ranging from relations with Native Americans to the character of the national economy, commentators debated the merits of agricultural expansion. Should the expansion of farm settlement be encouraged, so as to promote the vision of a republic of independent property-holders, or should it be restrained so as to enable urban settlements, commerce, manufacturing, and the arts to flourish in densely populated regions? Should economic activity be dispersed or concentrated? Among the most explicit critics of expansion was the Philadelphia printer Mathew Carey, who in the 1820s condemned the tendency of westward migrants to purchase what he considered to be excessive amounts of land and so disperse settlement wastefully across the landscape. Better, he argued, that they improve their produce on smaller acreages and "encourage . . . a market at home, by fostering and protecting domestic manufactures." Carey's son, the political economist Henry C. Carey, continued until beyond the Civil War to argue for restraint in national expansion and for the efficiencies to be gained by concentrating, not dispersing, economic activity. Although the Careys' strictures had little practical effect, Henry's arguments did influence subsequent debates about tariffs and currency that arose in the context of simultaneous agricultural and industrial development.[61]

Above all, of course, the simultaneous growth of Northern and Southern agriculture led to the most devastating conflict in American history, between the proponents and opponents of slavery and its expansion. Political compromises mostly muted the rivalry between slave and nonslave regions until the 1840s, but competing claims for rights to expand into newly conquered territory then forced the nation toward civil war.[62] Southern political calculations were rooted in the significance of the South's staple crops (cotton alone accounted for three-fifths of US exports by value in 1860), and planters' wealth and power (the twelve wealthiest counties in the United States were in the plantation belt).[63] The Union defeat of the Confederacy and the abolition of slavery altered this pattern of intersectional rivalry but did not erase the racial divisions on which it had been based. Southern agriculture quickly evolved new forms of race-based subordination to replace slavery, though it was now reduced to neocolonial status in a burgeoning Northern-dominated economy, and continued well into the twentieth century to function largely cut off from national and international labor markets. Though during the later nineteenth century North and South worked out a national reconciliation based on white supremacy and the tolerance of racial segregation in the South, two different models of capitalism continued in tension with one another.[64]

The massive postwar agricultural expansion encountered problems of a different sort. Politicians of the 1860s pondered the vastness of the West and imagined the opportunities available to Easterners and immigrants who could be persuaded to settle and farm new lands. Within three decades, however, commentators were conscious of the limits to expansion, that the continent was filling up, and that the "frontier" dividing open from settled land was "closing."[65] A factor in this shift of perceptions was the reality of pressing settlement into more and more arid regions of the West. There were numerous proposals for overcoming what many feared were undue constraints on settlement, many of them based on the assertion that "civilization" could reverse unfavorable natural conditions. Rain, according to some, would "follow the plow"; others argued that trees should be planted on the plains to reverse the region's aridity. Still others subscribed to elaborate theories of "dry farming" promoted by agriculturalists, land agents, and railroad companies that induced many thousands of families to settle the High Plains between the 1890s and 1917, until soil exhaustion and the return of drought drove many of them into retreat in subsequent years.[66]

Ascendant Republicans in the Civil War Congress quickly brought homestead legislation forward again once secession had removed Southern opponents from the arena. The 1862 Homestead Act, coupled with the building of the transcontinental railroad, other railroad land grants, and provision for agricultural education, sought to inscribe "free labor" ideology on the continent's western half. Granting land free on certain terms, government switched from using public lands for revenue to extending national settlement and providing far-flung homesteaders with links to political and commercial centers. Republicans long celebrated the homestead law's effects; as a Minnesotan put it in 1900, the act "was one of the greatest factors in the marvelous progress that the Republic has made since that time—a progress that has astonished the world." Americans and immigrants had "poured into the fertile, unoccupied regions of the West, and by the labor of their hands . . . transformed the forests into fruitful farms and . . . the . . . prairie grass into billowy fields of waving grain."[67] But settlement under the law encountered limitations and conflicts that echoed those of the previous periods its enactment was supposed to supersede.

Homestead provisions often replicated racial divisions. Though some African Americans, including former slaves, were able to take up homestead claims in the West or in Florida, the law's thrust was to satisfy white demands for farmland and circumscribe black claims for equitable treatment. Early in the Civil War, some Northerners had envisaged a rapid Union conquest of the South and a redistribution of rebels' property not to freed slaves but to white soldiers and settlers who would redeem it from the slave power by the exercise of free labor. Military setbacks and the eventual conquest of the South, in conjunction with the dismantling and then abolition of slavery, diffused these aspirations, which the Homestead Act had in any case redirected westward.[68] Some abolitionists and radical Republicans struggled to redistribute land to former slaves, and a limited Southern Homestead Act was enacted in 1866, restricted to the reallocation of land deemed to have been "abandoned" by its owners. In the name of protecting property rights, many Northerners opposed the redistribution of Southern land to freed people, arguing (despite what Lincoln had called their centuries of "unrequited toil") that they had not earned it. Meanwhile, homesteaders were occupying free land in the West that they presumably had not "earned" either. The outcome of the failure of Southern land reform was to restrict African Americans' access to land of their own and to drive many former slaves back into the arms of their former masters, as tenants and sharecroppers.[69] For Native Americans, meanwhile, homestead policy pointed in the opposite direction. White farm settlement, coupled with railroad building and the destruction of the bison, was a potent threat to their continued use of the land. Government policy favored granting Native Americans homestead privileges, as the best means of inducing them to relinquish huge acreages still under tribal control. The Dawes Allotment Act of 1887 formalized this policy, concerting efforts to turn Plains Indians into farmers of their own small, private properties. While racial policy in the South helped planters to retain both their land and control over formerly enslaved labor, racial policy in the West aimed to dispossess indigenous landholders and place millions of newly commoditized acres in the hands of white ranchers and farmers.

Numerous contradictions beset the implementation of the Homestead Act. Congressional reports reflected a litany of difficulties, as the interests of homesteading families came into conflict with those of other capitalist institutions. Just as they had earlier in the century, politicians and settlers feared the tendency of lands to fall into the hands of speculators. Concern about the creation of landed "monopolies" and large estates surrounded the settlement process and the implementation of land grants to railroad companies. Always there was anxiety that land would be appropriated by other than small proprietor-settlers, that speculators would amass individual entries, or that companies would use preemption and homestead provisions to acquire large amounts of timberland. Homesteaders' claims conflicted with those of claimants under the older preemption laws, with the claims of railroads or other corporations, or—in the case of California—with holders of land under Mexican grants confirmed at the time of annexation in 1848. Railroads surveyed routes, allocated land to settlers on their grants, and then relocated their tracks, leaving farmers with inadequate holdings. Soldiers had difficulty proving occupancy of the land for the prescribed period, or were unable to obtain additional land contiguous with their claims. Officials or imposters provided false information or swindled settlers; frauds and forgeries were persistent complaints.[70]

But the complexities of settling new land paled in comparison to the tensions associated with actually farming it. The unleashing of expansion and settlement into the West initiated further struggles between farmers and ranchers, smallholders and large landholders, rural producers and corporations that shaped American politics into the early twentieth century. Farmers dependent on railroads and merchants to sustain their local economies and move their crops to market voiced dismay at high freight rates and low prices, and at what one contemporary called "the confidence games that, when played on a large scale, pass for commerce."[71] Seen as pitting small producers and laboring people against more powerful and wealthy adversaries, these conflicts appear similar to one another. The widespread adoption, for example, of cooperative organizations to collect and market crops and other commodities was both an attempt to gather collective power and an effort to forge an alternative route to "progress."

Historians have variously interpreted the populist movement and other farm protests of the late nineteenth and early twentieth centuries as backward-looking resistance to change; as manifestations of paranoia among traditionalist social groups raging against modernity; as expressions of the claims of rural producers against urban and metropolitan merchants and bankers, whose nonproducer status and influence over the monetary system they regarded as a moral affront; as the last stand of an agrarian-based popular democracy; and as part of a distinctive agrarian strand in a progressive movement that projected rural society and its ways as central to America's development. Briefly in the 1890s, populism even seemed to bridge a widening racial divide by forging alliances between white and black tenant farmers, and between Southern and Midwestern reform campaigns.[72] The structural conditions we have discussed connect aspects of all these interpretive emphases. The inclusion of large segments of rural America in the patterns of commodity production, and in the institutional arrangements for financing and handling this that have been outlined by William Cronon and others, placed farm households and the goods that they produced in a relationship to one another comparable with that of factory workers and the products of their labor. Although in terms of property, skill, or social capital, farmers largely owned the means of production, their degree of control over the fruits of labor had diminished; in many cases such control was now impersonalized and dispersed across a far-flung commercial system. In addition, adapting to the demands of production for national and international markets could alter or conflict with patterns of local interaction, exchange, or sociability to which many farm households remained committed.

However, these general circumstances were mediated by the scale and regional variety of US agrarian economies and societies, which gave protest movements distinctive characteristics. Farmers struggling against railroads could have a national impact through the introduction of federal regulations in the 1880s, but farmer mortgagors and debtors facing unsympathetic banks were usually dealing with powerful local or regional institutions less susceptible to political protest or restraint. Cooperative efforts succeeded or failed according to different regional conditions. Populism, the most significant manifestation of protest, was both forged and constrained by its deep roots in rural communities. Other farm protest movements, from socialism in Oklahoma and Texas, to the Non-Partisan League on the northern Great Plains in the 1910s, drew their strength as much from regional particularities as from a common political and economic predicament.[73]

Nineteenth-century agriculture shaped American capitalism in ways that made it powerful, distinctive—and not entirely "capitalist." The "rise of big business" in the late nineteenth century was accompanied by a parallel rise of small businesses, many of which owed their existence to the dispersed commercial patterns connected with agriculture. While small businesses multiplied in all sectors of society, agriculture fostered the networks of towns and commercial centers that supported many of them, and—through the persistence of family-based ownership and labor in farming itself—sustained the aspirations to small proprietorship that had long been associated with access to the land. Such patterns also helped explain the relative strength and importance of service-sector activities, which by some calculations have consistently employed more people than manufacturing since 1840, and more than agriculture since 1880. This mix of large and small organizations gave American capitalism a bimodal character for which agrarian expansion was partly responsible.[74]

Although economic and political change helped abolish most forms of "unfree" labor, farming did not rely exclusively on wage labor and would never come to do so. Karl Marx attributed the emergence of wage labor to the processes of "primitive accumulation" that limited ownership or control of land to ruling classes and by denying impoverished workers access to the means of subsistence obliged them to seek employment by others. Capitalist development in North America followed a different path. Here "primitive accumulation" involved the dispossession and displacement not of peasants and smallholders, but of indigenous peoples, whose land was purchased or seized for redistribution to settlers, some of whom were drawn from the very European groups that were subject to displacement back home.

Nevertheless, by indirect means the dispossession and displacement of nonindigenous peoples did play an important role in capitalist development. Enslaved African Americans were forcibly moved, or born, into a state of dispossession. After emancipation, only a small proportion of freed people achieved more than a tentative hold on land; most had to accept exploitative tenancy or sharecropping arrangements. Meanwhile, economic constraints, poverty, and political conditions in Europe impelled millions of migrants overseas during the nineteenth century; though they went to many parts of the globe, the largest numbers of migrants reached the United States, feeding a growing economy's insatiable demand for wage labor. Indeed, these conditions helped make possible the continuous long nineteenth-century expansion of an agricultural system substantially based on independent proprietors and household labor.

But even as it expanded, American agriculture created conditions that would in the long run alter its relationships to capitalist labor markets. Throughout our period, pockets of rural society faced soil exhaustion or competition from new regions, which weakened farmers' ability to wrest livelihoods from their land. Hundreds of thousands emigrated to find or make better farms, and at least as many others moved to nonagricultural occupations, often in the wage-labor market. The burdens of debt, or the threat of repossession by a mortgage lender, drove families and individuals from the land or encouraged farmers' offspring to try their luck elsewhere.

By the early twentieth century a structural change was under way that would in time permanently alter the relationship between farm ownership and the nation. Just as a generation or more previously merchants had inserted themselves into rural exchange networks to increase farmers' market involvement, now agricultural extension agents employed farmers' local connections to have them demonstrate improved methods to neighbors.[75] As more successful farmers increased their investment in new machinery and techniques, they reduced their dependence on the labor of their own family members. New methods and technology enhanced the ability of farm owners to rely principally on their own and on seasonally hired labor, reinforcing the tendency for agricultural wage labor to be drawn from migratory or socially marginal populations. Even as the defeat of populism and anxiety about the decline of farm life spurred attempts like that of the Country Life Commission to diagnose and reverse rural ills, the actual need to "keep the boys down on the farm" was starting to recede.[76]

Between the 1920s and the 1960s, a period in which the United States exercised its most stringent restrictions on immigration, rural areas became the nation's chief "reserve" sources of wage labor. Except during the Great Depression, when nonagricultural employment collapsed and many moved "back to the land," streams of people—black and white—who had grown up on farms moved to cities and industrial areas, entered industrial bi-employments, or took up occupations such as truck-driving that removed them a step or more from farming.[77] Agriculture was increasingly left to agribusiness, and to a dwindling cohort of family farmers whose productivity, but also their capital investment and indebtedness, far outstripped those of their nineteenth-century predecessors.

2

The Mortgage Worked the Hardest

The Fate of Landed Independence in Nineteenth-Century America

Jonathan Levy

After 1870 there emerged an American market in what are now called "mortgage-backed securities." New financial intermediaries purchased mortgages on western farms, guaranteed them, and then mostly passed them on to private and institutional investors in the East, or packaged them together into bonds for public sale. Capital consequently flowed westward while wheat, corn, and other staples flowed eastward.[1] During the 1880s, homesteaders annually mortgaged roughly between 30 and 40 percent of all farm acreage west of the Mississippi River and east of the Rocky Mountains.[2] The "western farm craze" had spread like a fever among the eastern investing public, but after a series of droughts and the financial panic of 1893, the market collapsed. But by then the logic of American farming had been transformed.[3] This chapter examines the significance of that transformation for its participants and for the history of American capitalism.

In the early nineteenth century American farmers commonly

pursued the ideal of "landed independence"—a way of life that rested on freehold ownership, command over household labor, and control over the resources of the farm. Farmers were proprietors. They were not members of the expanding class of dependent wage laborers. Nor did their lives resemble those of the rising urban commercial classes that might gain greater riches, but who were existentially dependent upon the vicissitudes of markets. By practicing "mixed farming," freeholders could both meet their families' baseline subsistence needs and sell their "marketable surplus" for a profit. At mid-century American farming could thus be considered commercially oriented. At the same time, it enjoyed built-in hedges against the fates dispensed by an expanding market system.[4]

After the Civil War, as before, many farmers migrated west in pursuit of the economic and psychological rewards of landed independence. Clearly, some had other goals in mind. There were farmers who put all possible acreage into wheat, for instance, the great western staple, in search of short-term profit rather than economic security. The 1880 western guidebook *Where to Go to Become Rich* devoted a chapter to plains farming, next to another on southwestern gold prospecting.[5] Still, landed independence remained the ideal for a large proportion of western migrants in the 1870s and 1880s.

Take the case of Henry Ise. A German immigrant, Ise earned an outright claim in western Kansas by fighting for the Union Army. In 1873 thirty-year-old Henry and his eighteen-year-old wife, Rosie, settled on their Kansas quarter of 160 acres in the hope of achieving independence.[6] In 1887, needing $363 to pay a quack doctor to care for their youngest son, John, stricken with polio, the couple decided to mortgage their homestead. It was a fateful decision; the Ises subsequently felt that they had lost control over their lives. According to John's memoir, the mortgage became the "relentless master of the family destinies"— commanding their labor, controlling the resources of the farm.[7] The Ises successfully paid off this mortgage, but years later they again found themselves in debt. By his son's account, Henry worried incessantly and was often found sitting in a chair mumbling aloud to himself, counting figures, and wondering if he would have enough cash on hand when the note came due. When Henry died in 1900, his son considered him a broken man. Looking back, Rosie Ise described her husband as a terrific "farmer" but a terrible "business man."[8] The opposition between "farmer" and "business man" (a term that had acquired currency only in the 1820s) was meaningful, suggesting as it did the difference between the pursuit of independence and the pursuit of profit as the core principle in operating a farm.

Although the amount of American farm acreage under mortgage debt increased by 42 percent during the 1880s, while the amount of absolute farm mortgage debt increased by 71 percent, farm mortgage debt was not a new phenomenon.[9] Farmers lamenting their debts was not new either. What was novel, rather, was the financial architecture of the market for western farm mortgages and the systemization of financial risk of which that was a part. Until the middle of the nineteenth century there existed a direct, personal link between many mortgage lenders and borrowers. Most farmers knew who owned their mortgage.[10] With the rise of mortgage-backed securities and new forms of financial intermediation, this was no longer the case. The relationship between lender and borrower became attenuated. Landed wealth became a dematerialized abstraction. The Ises first mortgaged their farm to a local lender, who then sold their mortgage to the Pennsylvania Mortgage Company, a new type of business that bought individual western mortgages, stapled them together, and resold them to private and institutional investors in the East. As farmers worked harder and longer to repay their debts, they became cogs within an increasingly complex financial system. The system allowed a great many people the opportunity to farm, but it also squeezed their labor and pushed them into global commodities markets. Western farmers had difficulty wrapping their minds around how such an impersonal system worked. As Rosie Ise observed of plains farming, "Nobody's responsible."[11]

Ironically, farmers looked to another financial innovation for the economic security that the land directly under their own feet had ceased to provide: life insurance policies. Vigorously marketed to farmers in the 1870s (particularly to those with mortgages), these policies were the ultimate emblem of the inversion of land and labor on the western plains. The same firm that bought a farmer's "life risk" might also, through a network of intermediation, own his mortgage. Indeed, the largest institutional investors in the western mortgage market were life insurance companies. As the mortgage and insurance markets systematized and intersected, western farmers became both agents and objects of a newly abstract power. Not surprisingly, the ever-anxious Henry Ise purchased a life insurance policy.

The Ises' story is worth recounting not only because of the family's failed quest for landed independence in the older sense, but also because, by monetary measures, their farm was a success. The Ises were never in danger of foreclosure. In fact, however complex it became, the western mortgage market had worked to lower western interest rates.[12] Unlike the Ises, many farmers observed their rising incomes and land values, and with access to new financial forms of economic security, they happily proclaimed themselves "independent."[13] Yet Henry Ise kept sitting in his chair, worriedly counting figures. Others would voice their anxieties in the populist revolt, demanding that the federal government ensure them the economic security that a landed independence had once provided.[14] But financial systematization sealed the fate of landed independence. It also created the very conditions for the collapse of the first market in mortgage-backed securities.

A crucial agent of enclosure in early modern England, the mortgage traveled with European colonizers to the New World.[15] William Penn even mortgaged the entire colony of Pennsylvania in the early 1700s. By the mid-eighteenth century, legislatures in the New England and Middle colonies had created loan offices that issued paper money to farmers against their lands as collateral, the money repayable in installments below market interest rates. These mortgages increased the circulating medium and greased the wheels of the domestic market while financing capital improvements. But colonial land banks did not lead to a specialization in cash crops or to a decline in "safety first" subsistence production.[16]

Beginning in the early nineteenth century, mortgages played an increasingly large role in the northern economy. On the western frontier, government land offices offered cheap credit to homesteaders and speculators until as late as 1820.[17] But consider the town of Concord, Massachusetts. In the late 1840s townsman Henry David Thoreau observed that no Concord tax assessor could name him a dozen farmers "who own their farms free and clear." To know the history of Concord "homesteads" was to inquire "as to the bank where they are mortgaged." To Thoreau, the consequences of mortgage debt were clear: the felling of forests; the intensification of labor ("work, work, work," he taunted his neighbors); the reduction of time into money values; the existential dependency of farmers upon markets. Farmers labored "under a mistake," driven "by a seeming fate, commonly called necessity." It was a "fool's life." Thoreau bragged at Walden that he "was more independent than any farmer in Concord" as he was "not anchored" to a commercializing farm.[18]

In 1850, while Thoreau was busily revising *Walden*, the politician George S. Boutwell addressed the same farmers of Concord. Boutwell was then a Van Burenite Democrat with free soil sympathies. In 1851 he would become governor of Massachusetts and in 1854 he helped found the Republican Party. In 1869, after a short stint in Congress, he became President Grant's Secretary of the Treasury. George Boutwell was also a local Concord dairy farmer. The agrarian vision he espoused in 1850 crystallized into the Homestead Act of 1862, which provided millions of western acres for men like Henry Ise to farm, and ultimately to mortgage.

Boutwell proclaimed that the farmer was still more "independent" than any other man. He had less "anxiety than men in other pursuits," as farming offered the "certainty of a competence." Farmers were not like merchants, a class of men perpetually "tempest-tossed" by forces outside their "control." There were, Boutwell argued, "great and necessary risks of business from which the farmer is exempt." "Agriculture" and "commerce" were not the same thing: the latter form of life was "dependent" (regardless of the riches it might hold out) while the former was "independent." A mercantile proprietorship was inherently more risky than a landed one. And yet, Boutwell also noted that farming in Concord had become "a very different pursuit from what it was twenty years ago." Commerce was encroaching. "All of you," Boutwell informed the farmers of Concord, have recently become "equally dependent upon the great laws of production, exchange, and consumption." Farmers were now being "taught to feel the force" of "competition." "Men may fear it," and "they may seek to avoid it," and "it may produce cases of individual ruin," but it was no longer escapable.[19]

But still, the land was a special form of property, a bulwark of security, certainty, and independence set apart from the vicissitudes of commerce. The source of Thoreau's independence was transcendental—"What a man thinks of himself, that is which determines, or rather indicates, his fate." The concrete source of Boutwell's independence, by definition, could only be the land. Freehold farming was "more certain" than any other employment, proclaimed a Middlesex County farmer in 1848. Let the "fluctuations of trade" worry the merchant.[20] No question, antebellum farmers sought to maximize their "marketable surplus." They demanded from politicians such as George Boutwell the roads, turnpikes, canals, and ultimately railroads to get their surpluses to the market. But with direct access to subsistence, with built-in hedges against the fates dispensed by markets, land ownership in antebellum America still offered a uniquely autonomous form of commercial life.

To be sure, this vision was already under economic threat. Not only Boutwell's message suggested that. His dairy farm did as well. By the 1850s a band of highly specialized wheat and corn farms stretched from the mid-Atlantic seaboard to the western prairies, driving many northeastern farmers out of the production of grains and into truck farming. Nevertheless, as the economists Jeremy Atack and Fred Bateman write in their study of late-antebellum Northern farming, "despite the growing emphasis on the market . . . the farmer who was able to provide virtually everything for his farm and family from the farm was regarded a success . . . even in a relatively well-developed area such as New York State." In 1860, Atack and Bateman write, farmers "were successfully straddling the fence between agriculture as a way of life and as a business enterprise." Echoing contemporary accounts, these authors end their econometric study by confirming that farmers preferred to give up more profitable opportunities in other economic sectors in favor of the "security" offered by the agrarian "way of life."[21] Indeed, the ideal of landed independence still gripped the American imagination. Lacy K. Ford sums up a generation of agrarian social history:

> [F]or many antebellum Americans, economic well being was not measured in terms of income levels (which were generally improving) . . . but of personal or household independence. The foundation of independence was ownership or control of productive property, and thus land ownership was a . . . better measure of economic status than income.[22]

Land ownership, put another way, was then considered the securest route to acquiring the wealth necessary for economic independence.

The old-age security provided to farmers by their accumulation of landed wealth filled out the ideal of landed independence. On average, late-antebellum farmers ceased to accumulate wealth at the age of fifty-five. That was when the process of distributing wealth to the farmer's household dependents began. Farmers followed careful, even delicate, strategies in ensuring the transmission of their property and, not unrelated, their children's care for them in old age. Again, cracks were evident in the system by mid-century. Eastern soils were suffering from declining marginal productivity. In some instances there were outright land shortages. Flourishing urban labor markets enticed many children away from the farm, a common agrarian lament. Eastern farm fertility declined. Meanwhile, fresh western lands held out the promise of sustaining and reconstituting the old logic.[23]

Landed independence had various other foundations. There was political ideology, expressed in Boutwell's brand of free-soil Republicanism which echoed the famous words of Thomas Jefferson, who had argued that landed independence was the very basis of popular sovereignty. Perhaps equally important as a political ideology was the religious view by which the certainty and security of farming were providentially determined. Edwin Freedley's popular 1853 *Practical Treatise on Business* posed the question: "How can independence be attained with the greatest certainty?" Land ownership was the answer. That was because the farmer "receives a real increase of the seed thrown into the ground in a kind of continued miracle wrought by the hand of God." Antebellum Americans often cited the biblical promise to Noah after the flood: "As long as the earth endures, seedtime and harvest, cold and heat, sum-mer and winter, day and night will never cease" (Gen. 8:22). Boutwell agreed: "The cultivation and the cultivators of the land have been eminently blessed by Divine Providence. God had spoken to the husbandman, and said, *Seed-time and harvest shall never fail*." The harvest was the bounty of God's "common providence," confirmed the 1819 *Farmer's Manual*. It insured a life of "indepen-dence" so long as farmers steered clear of debt.[24]

This was the logic of the "commercial agrarian republic" or "yeoman soci-ety."[25] It only sharpened with the rise of urban wage dependence, as well as with the failures of so many commercial proprietors following the panics of 1819, 1837, and 1857.[26] The farmer's vaunted "independence" was typically celebrated most loudly in the wake of commercial crises. Let the merchant, said one up-state New York farmer in 1838, suffer the "disastrous reverses of the commer-cial world" while the farmer secured his own independent livelihood from the soil.[27] Farmers, too, were subject to bankruptcy and financial ruin, although a series of post–panic of 1837 state homestead and stay laws protected enough acreage from foreclosure to provide farmers direct access to subsistence.[28] This vision of landed independence was what hung in the balance in the decades following the American Civil War, when the market in western farm mort-gages emerged.

Although these years are usually associated with large-scale industrialization and urbanization, the late nineteenth century witnessed a dramatic expansion of American farm acreage on the western prairies and plains. American farm acreage increased by 44 percent during the 1870s and there were 54 percent more farms. The result was a wave of farm staples washing onto the world market. Between 1866 and 1886 the corn produced in Kansas rose from 30 million bushels to 750 million. In 1880 the wheat crop of Dakota was not quite 3 million bushels. In 1887 it passed 60 million. These figures had no historical precedent. It took the states of Illinois and Indiana *together* fifty years to reach the level of wheat production that Dakota had achieved in seven. Within ten years, bragged the western farm mortgage broker James Willis Gleed in 1890, "the growth which occupied a hundred years in the older States" had been ac-complished in the lands north of Chicago and west of the Mississippi River. According to the US Department of Agriculture, half of all Kansas farmers owed mortgages to "Eastern capital" in 1886. In turn, western farms quite literally fed eastern industrialization—a process that entered its most inten-sive phase in the 1880s. Triumphantly, Gleed concluded, "The mortgage did this."[29] The mortgage was an external agent, capable of doing the work itself.

That agent—a network of abstract interdependence—chipped away at the foundations of landed independence.

Western farmers turned to the mortgage market both by choice and from necessity. If from necessity, it was partly because the western farmer encountered difficulties with the very nature of the lands west of the Mississippi. A vast expanse of grasslands turning to plains was organized into rectangular quarters of 160 acres, settlement being encouraged by the Homestead Act of 1862.[30] Settlers removed, killed, or starved a native population that was also susceptible to their diseases. But the ecological mix that was necessary for traditional American agricultural practice was absent in the West.[31] There was a reason, in other words, why the Native Americans of the plains were nomadic. East of the Mississippi, more plentiful forests and waterways, and more diverse soils and vegetations, provided a better basis for a mixed farming that combined production for subsistence with production for markets, both local and global. Forestal areas were more difficult to clear, but they were blessed with a more diverse resource base—timber for fuel and construction, cover for wild game. Waterways provided fishing streams, another energy source, and access to markets. The few western lands that offered this ecology that was so familiar to eastern farmers were the first to be settled. After 1870 this forestal frontier closed. The plains offered fertile soil ripe for commercial grains but, apart from buffalo chips, that was all.[32] Plains farming proved impractical without product markets of great geographical scale, together with the railroads to connect them. The railroads carried timber westward and grains eastward.[33] Windmills raised water. In 1888 Henry Ise borrowed $100 against his land to purchase a windmill. Free soil could make a farm by itself on the plains.

The amount of cash required was varied, but it was far more than most had.[34] The 1880 guidebook *Where to Go to Become Rich* recommended arriving to the Kansas plains with at least $1,000, but better yet $3,000. A thousand dollars allowed a man to purchase 160 acres on a six-year mortgage, paying $150 down. The "other necessary expenses will run, house building, $250; team and harness, $180; breaking plow, $22; harrow $10; cow, $30; interest payments on land one year from purchase, $35; total, $677. This will leave . . . $323 for seed and to carry him through till the crop can be raised." This $1,000 figure is not far from the later estimates of historians.[35]

Nevertheless, the hopeful farmer had several options. Henry Ise saved his wages in Iowa and delayed marriage. Tenancy was another avenue. An agricultural ladder was at work, ascending along the life cycle from wage work to tenancy to proprietorship.[36] The first rung was often decisive. In route to western Kansas, a woman stole $300 from Henry's misplaced wallet. He grumbled about the theft for the rest of his life, especially in periods of debt. Only when possessed of more capital could western farmers climb the ladder and, under competitive pressures, stay there. This was the principal reason to mortgage. An 1890 census sample determined that 83 percent of mortgage debt was for land "purchase money" or "farm improvements." The category of "business" was assigned another 9 percent and "family expenses" 2 percent.[37] The western farm mortgage market, in other words, was a capital market.

But the desire for cash for any reason might lead to a mortgage. Henry Ise, for instance, first mortgaged his homestead to pay a quack doctor to tend to his polio-stricken youngest son. The consumer baubles of the cities, brought to the countryside on the same trains that brought back the farm staples, were fast becoming emblems of a rural gentility. The Ises never mortgaged to purchase consumer items, but they were conscious of their expanding consumer desires. They noticed when for this reason their neighbors did mortgage their farms.[38]

Between 1860 and 1890 total factor productivity—a broad measure of the productivity of all business inputs—soared in the agricultural sector like never before.[39] But the same period that witnessed such a dramatic extension and intensification of American agriculture also witnessed a decline in the use of wage labor. The incidence of wage labor in American farming rose from 27 percent to 35 percent of all those engaged in agriculture between 1860 and 1870 but it fell back to 27 percent by 1890.[40] It was a rise in mortgaging, not wage labor, that pushed American agriculture into the age of capital.

In the 1870s and 1880s the mortgaged western farmer entered a complex series of market transactions that together constituted a systematic market structure. The farmer's dependence on this complex system now became an objective fact of his life. Take, for instance, the mortgage of Willis and Mary Olmsted's farm in eastern Nebraska. In 1876 the couple read an advertisement in their local newspaper placed by A. W. Ocobock, a Chicago banker. Ocobock was offering mortgage loans in their county through an agent named C. C. Cook. The Olmsteds contacted Cook and Cook contacted Ocobock, who sent yet another man from the nearby railroad town of David City to inspect the farm. Satisfied with the inspection results, Ocobock offered the Olmsteds a $400 loan for a term of five years, at 10 percent interest. Ocobock instructed the Olmsteds to make their payments by mail to the "Corbin Banking Company," a banking and real estate broker partnership of New York City. In addition, the Olmsteds agreed to pay Ocobock an $80 commission. Meanwhile, the Corbin Banking Company did not own their mortgage. The bank was the transactional agent for a corporation, the New England Mortgage Security Company of Boston, which then stapled the Olmsted mortgage together with other western farm mortgages, securitizing them into bonds for public sale. The man pulling strings behind all of these transactions was the managing partner and president of the Corbin Banking Company, Austin Corbin.[41]

Austin Corbin was a native of New Hampshire and an 1849 Harvard graduate. He established a law practice in Davenport, Iowa, in 1851 but quickly began to broker Iowa farm mortgages for eastern investors.[42] In 1865 he moved to New York City. The new Corbin Banking Company operated under the 1864 National Banking Act, which was initially interpreted as prohibiting commercial banks from owning mortgages.[43] The Corbin Banking Company, created in 1874, became a conduit for institutions that were allowed to own mortgages on their own balance sheets. Corbin was a director, and the largest stockowner, of the New England Mortgage Security Company of Boston — but also the New England Loan Company of Manchester, New Hampshire. He was one of the largest stockholders of the American Mortgage Company of Scotland, a company chartered in Edinburgh for which the Corbin Banking Company acted as American agent. He had the same relationship with the American Freehold Land-Mortgage Company of London.[44] Corbin would become a prominent New York financier and philanthropist, once causing a public splash when he imported western buffalo for a preserve on his New Hampshire estate. He would eventually take his mortgage-derived riches into the railroad industry. But in 1876 Austin Corbin himself signed a circular forwarded to Ocobock that instructed the Olmsteds that "interest payable at this office on a day certain" meant money was due "*on that day*." And when not paid "*promptly* we shall return to the owners, and they will send to an attorney for foreclosure."[45] This is how the Olmsteds mortgaged their farm.

Their experience was revealing of the dynamics of the western mortgage market after 1870. Thoreau had observed that the history of Concord homesteads was to be discovered at the local bank. That is to say, it was still possible in the 1850s to connect the dots.[46] In the decades that followed that would no longer be the case. This is what gave the increasingly systematized western farm mortgage market a novel appearance, distinguishing it from centuries of farm mortgaging. The Olmsteds had to haul Ocobock to court before they even learned of the existence of the New England Mortgage Security Company. When Henry Ise brought a mortgage broker named Armstrong, papers in hand, to inspect the farm, Rosie greeted him "with scarcely concealed hostility." Homestead laws demanded that wives sign mortgages. To Rosie, Armstrong "the capitalist" embodied the mortgage. But what she actually greeted at her door was a network of eastern capital. (Armstrong passed the mortgage through to the Pennsylvania Mortgage Company.) Capital wanted wheat. Brokers and their agents such as Armstrong accordingly inspected homesteads for their value as capital assets. The western brokerage giant Edward R. Darrow required his agents to take photographs of inspected farms, opening a new chapter in the aesthetic commodification of nature that Thoreau had so detested. Photographic representations of homesteads that had entered the swirl of financial intermediation were filed away in the offices of innumerable brokers.[47]

Other aspects of the Olmsteds' mortgage were likewise emblematic of the system. On average, farmers mortgaged half the value of their farms. Corbin never mortgaged more than a third.[48] Most mortgages were for five years and occasionally as low as three. They never extended beyond seven years. The mortgages were not fully amortized and they featured balloon payments in the final year of repayment. As for the interest rate, there were usury laws on the books of every state, many of them a legacy of rates as high as 40 percent that had been charged by local agents in the 1840s and 1850s.[49] In 1890 the census-recorded interest rate in Kansas was 8.68 percent, below the usury ceiling of 10 percent.[50] There were voices in these years calling for the abolition of usury. The loudest was that of Richard H. Dana Jr., author of the famous sailing memoir *Two Years Before the Mast* and a noted former abolitionist. In 1867 he called upon the Massachusetts legislature to abolish the practice of usury. In the new era of "competition," the "the borrower is no longer the trembling suppliant at the threshold of the patrician lender." Interest rates, rather, should be set by "the market of the world," which moved with the "irresistible power of ocean tides." Indeed, many judges enforced usury statutes also while characterizing them as barbaric relics. In any event, the western farm mortgage market brought western interest rates down, as it fueled the national convergence of eastern and western rates.[51]

In those terms the West had become a more efficient capital market. True, exploitation was still evident in the commission charges of brokers. Henry Ise was offered a loan at the usurious rate of 15 percent, but that included Armstrong's commission. The Olmsteds brought Austin Corbin to trial in Nebraska on usury charges after they failed to make their payment and Corbin foreclosed on them. The Olmsteds paid 10 percent, the legal limit, but they also gave $80 to Ocobock in addition. They claimed that since Ocobock was the agent of the New England Mortgage Security Company, that extra $80 was usury. Corbin countered by describing Ocobock as the agent of the Olmsteds, which meant that the $80 was a fee for the service he rendered them. The Nebraska Supreme Court sided with the Olmsteds but no judicial standard emerged in Nebraska or anywhere else.[52] Struggles over usury were local in character and eluded generalization. For this reason, statistical totals regarding late nineteenth-century interest rates cannot be trusted. The Olmsteds' mortgage was not unique but their effort to trace Ocobock back to Austin Corbin was. When Rosie Ise asked Henry if he could do better than 15 percent, he replied that no one in town would lend for less. The Ises needed the money and the mortgage was signed, as were hundreds of thousands of others in that same decade.[53]

Mortgages passed from brokers to investors. Many mortgages—more than half of all national mortgages although a lesser percentage in the West—moved into the hands of individual private investors. Some of these were speculators. Some still subscribed to the notion that land was relatively the most secure form of investment. In the 1870s the country's savings rate soared above 20 percent, and savers and investors searched for new outlets.[54] A daily Boston newspaper in 1877 noted the "anxiety" experienced by many of the city's purchasers of western mortgages.[55] Ten years later, between her sojourns to the Old World, twenty-seven-year-old Jane Addams caught the "western farm craze." She later wrote of visiting a "western state" where she had "invested a sum of money in mortgages," her recently deceased father having left her $50,000. Addams was "horrified by the wretched conditions among the farmers," a result of drought. The scene provoked a moral anxiety. "It seemed quite impossible to receive interest from mortgages placed upon farms which might at any season be reduced to such conditions." Addams withdrew the investment. She bought a sheep farm near her Illinois home instead, a purchase sound "both economically and morally." But she was no farmer, and the enterprise "ended in a spectacle scarcely less harrowing than the memory it was designed to obliterate." Addams departed for Europe "sadder for the experience."[56]

Jane Addams's effort to personalize her investment was no ordinary act. Equally extraordinary farmers would occasionally seek out even one of the many owners of their mortgages. The broker Edward Darrow warned potential investors of this possibility. Farmers might discover "the name and address of the investor" and "write directly." Any investor, Darrow instructed, "who attempts to deal with the borrower directly under such circumstances is acting against his own interests." A western mortgage was a commodity, like any other "regulated by the price of supply and demand."[57] The market, through brokers, brought borrowers and investors together. Direct interaction of any sort was counterproductive.

Sometimes, no matter how hard they tried, farmers and investors might not be able to find one another. In the 1880s another financial innovation introduced an extra level of mediation. These were companies such as Austin Corbin's New England Mortgage Security Company. They purchased mortgages, which they guaranteed, repackaged together, and then securitized for public sale. Mortgage terms in the 1870s and 1880s prohibited a farmer from the early repayment of his loan's principal, thus stabilizing mortgage companies' cash flows and allowing the process of securitization to proceed. The Olmsteds' mortgage, which was securitized by the New England Mortgage Security Company, was destined in bits and pieces for eastern holders of such "debenture bonds." Here, the western broker James Gleed bragged, the farmer "cannot treat directly with the eastern owner of the mortgage, for he cannot ascertain who that owner is; the assignment from the company to the investor is not recorded." The Olmsteds read the advertisement of Ocobock in their local Nebraska paper. Their mortgage's future owners—perhaps with bread made of western wheat on their dinner tables—read in their own local newspapers of investment opportunities in western mortgages. The New England Mortgage Security Company commonly advertised ten-year bonds at 5 percent that were backed by western mortgages. Or investors might see circulars such as Austin Corbin's "Ten Per Cent First Mortgages on Improved Farms in Iowa and Kansas" in 1872. Mortgage companies flooded the advertising back pages of the eastern press, especially during the latter half of the 1880s, the height of the "western farm craze." In a single sheet in 1889, *The Independent* featured forty consecutive such ads, interrupted by a sole advertisement for safe deposit vaults: "7% Kansas Farm Loans," "All loans made on Corn Growing lands of the west," "A solid 9 per cent," and so on. The aggressive marketing worked. By 1893 private eastern investors had purchased at least $93 million of mortgage debentures.[58]

The rationale of the debentures was to spread investors' risk—to reduce their anxiety. According to Gleed, "the investor is not compelled to stand or fall with one mortgage or one piece of real estate. Each debenture bond is, in a sense, insured by all the rest of the series."[59] Furthermore, companies could engineer bonds whose value was below that of than any single mortgage. A Boston newspaper announced in 1887 that a new company was offering debentures as low as $50, enabling "small investors" to get into the game. A 3 to 4 percent spread between western interest rates and eastern bond rates was not uncommon. An Iowa outfit was the first to sell debentures in 1881. Ten years later, according to New York bank regulators, there were 167 such companies selling bonds in the state. Anecdotal sources testified to hundreds more operating both in the East and West.[60]

The new system suddenly grew in the 1880s and then collapsed in the panic of 1893. The broker Edward Darrow had always detested the new financial engineering. The aim was to hedge against market uncertainty. But securitization, he thought, created a false sense of security. The multiple layers of interweaving mediation made it too easy for financiers and investors to disregard the underlying assets—the farms themselves. Western farms had become so fractured and abstracted that the actual assets were difficult to see. If she had been a debenture bondholder, Jane Addams would have had to spend years searching the western plains; in this market structure, the very notion of locating individual moral responsibility was an absurdity. The investor in "mortgage securities," Darrow surmised, was like a man who bought a horse "without the least examination as to whether the animal was blind, halt or lame." Making a bad situation worse, mortgage originators were often paid upon closing. That is, they had no stake in the loan's future repayment. A few years of drought and then financial panic caused many western farmers to default on their loans. Farmers feared foreclosure but so, in fact, did their creditors. Mortgage companies attempted to turn foreclosed farmers into their tenants, but the Supreme Court had already blocked them and state legislatures were equally unfriendly to that aim.[61] After 1893, then, almost all of the mortgage companies went into receivership. Wall Street observers remarked that most of them had been too highly leveraged and too poorly managed. One Wall Street bond rater claimed that western farm appraisements had been "absurd." Many agents "did not know a sand-hill pasture from a bottom-land garden."[62] But this would not be the last time that financial securitization would—quite literally—lose sight of the underlying assets.[63]

After 1893, institutional investors—savings banks, building and loan associations, and, most significantly, life insurance companies—stepped further into the breach. These institutions were large investors prior to the panic as well. In 1890, for instance, life insurance firms owned approximately 41 percent of all western intermediated mortgage debt, compared to 18 percent for savings banks, 17 percent for building and loan associations, and 34 percent for the mortgage companies.[64] These institutions brought another layer of mediation and interdependence; now, for instance, life insurance policyholders acquired a stake in western mortgages. A few East Coast savings banks, heavily invested in western farm mortgages, failed during the panic of 1893. "[M]any a hardworking New Englander poured his savings of years into the gold West," the same Wall Street bond rater recalled, "only to get him a bit of buffalo-grassed sod in the middle of the township of Nowhere."[65] Life insurance firms, with larger capital reserves, withstood the panic.[66] They would come to dominate the national mortgage market.

Life insurance shifts our analysis from the institutional dynamics of the western mortgage market to the actual fate of landed independence. The life insurance industry was born in the 1840s and first targeted the rising commercial classes in the cities. It sold policies as newly necessary bulwarks of "independence." In a world of booms and busts—1837, 1857, 1873—firms explicitly marketed insurance as the only secure form of wealth for families no longer living on the land. Contractual and market-driven, life insurance became a necessary hedge against the uncertainty of urban commercial life. It commodified one's "life risk." What's more, economic security was no longer acquired on the basis of land ownership but on self-ownership. In 1840 the value of the industry's policies stood at $15 million. In 1870 it reached $2.3 billion. Firms began to accumulate flexible forms of financial capital that required investment. Life insurance was also actuarial. In lieu of the providential certainty of God's bountiful harvest, there was the new epistemological certainty of the statistical law of large numbers.[67]

Only in the 1870s did firms begin to aggressively target wage earners as well as farmers—and especially mortgaged farmers in the West—as potential customers. In 1874 the largest firm advertised that "a mortgage on real estate ought always to be offset by a policy of insurance on the life of the mortgager."[68] Farmers took note. An 1895 survey of Wisconsin farmers found that 30 percent carried life policies—coincidentally or not, about the same percentage that had a mortgage.[69] Western agrarian periodicals repeatedly published editorials extolling the necessity of insurance. The circularity and symbiosis is striking. If one was mortgaged, as the reasoning went, the life policy became the bulwark of economic security rather than the land. Agrarian policyholders were saving (there was a dearth of depository savings banks in western states that might have competed with the life insurance firms) while they were also, though indirectly, investing in the "western farm mortgages" market themselves, the market that might be the very reason why they bought life insurance to begin with. One firm, the Northwestern Mutual Life of Milwaukee, set up branch offices throughout the West from where agents solicited both mortgages and life policies. The same man who inspected a farm might then inspect the farmer's life as a viable capital asset.[70] Other firms purchased mortgages directly from originators, or from the new intermediaries. These developments generated even more abstract interdependence since the security of many policies now depended on the farmer's future mortgage payments. Even the potential eastern investor who avoided the temptation of speculating in western mortgages and bought a life policy instead thus ended up with an interest in the fate of western homesteads.

A farmer's insurance policy—a turn away from his land in favor of yet another financial market—was itself a measure of the loss of landed independence. The mortgaged farmer did not own land outright, to do with what he
would. What he did own outright was the "risk" on his life, which he could insure. If a mortgaged farmer experienced a single bad harvest or a plummet in a
product market, he might lose his land. A policy now remained the family's sole
source of secure wealth. (Life policies could be redeemed for a cash "surrender
value.") In the event of the farmer's untimely death, the cash might allow the
family to hire enough hands to run the farm that year and avoid foreclosure. Of
course, a life policy could also replace the generational succession of the family
farm. In this respect both Henry Ise's life insurance and his son John's career as
an Iowa State agricultural economist were representative. The Ises had twelve
children, nine of whom went to college. One son kept the farm. The others
found their way to cities and towns. Rosie Ise spent her final years living in her
daughter's home in Lawrence. Tellingly, Henry Ise gave each of his children
$100 in cash when they turned eighteen to invest as they saw fit. This was not
just true of the Ise family. Old patterns of generational succession were generally
disrupted in the countryside as fewer and fewer farms stayed within the family.
More often, they were put on the market for sale to the highest bidder.[71]

The lesson was clear: a mortgaged farmer's human capital was his most valuable asset. Western farmers were not slaves or servants. They could mortgage
their land, not themselves or their dependents.[72] In 1890 a Kansas agrarian
periodical carried the shocking title of a Yale professor's recent lecture on agriculture—"Man is worth more than land"—a pithy summary of the passage of
a landed, commercial republic to a capitalist economy in which liberal notions
of self-ownership, or financialized "life risks," constituted the bulwark of economic security.[73] This transformation was visible even on the land itself.

New forms of security achieved through new financial markets arose to
accommodate the transition. In the 1870s insurance firms developed a new
"accident policy" that was specifically targeted at industrial wage earners and
mortgaged farmers. If a farmer was injured or fell ill for at least a week (but no
more than twenty-six weeks), the policy compensated him for the value of his
"productive labor." The Travelers Insurance Company of Hartford, chartered
in 1864 to insure railroad passengers against accidents, dominated this new
field in the 1870s and 1880s. In contrast to the mutual firms of the 1840s,
the Travelers was a joint-stock company. Its shares were sold on the New York
stock exchange. The Travelers opened for business in Kansas in 1875. That
year it paid a claim to William Potter, a farmer who "fell from a bridge" and
was then "kicked by a horse."[74] The firm was also a heavy investor in western

farm mortgages. In 1887 the company reported assets of almost $11 million to the Kansas Superintendent of Insurance. Nearly $4 million of that was held in "loans on bond and mortgage on real estate," a modest sum on its own, but part of over $200 million then invested in mortgages throughout the country by insurance firms. The Travelers' public financial disclosures once listed 496 shares in the "Kansas Farm Mortgage Company" of Abilene. In 1898, with its assets listed at $17 million, the Kansas Superintendent of Insurance grew suspicious of Travelers' valuations of its real estate and mortgage holdings in Kansas and asked to see the company's books. The firm consequently sued for a blocking injunction and ceased to do business in the state for a short period.[75]

Meanwhile, anxious to meet their mortgage payments, many western farmers began to feel they were working for an outside agent, "the mortgage," which was, in truth, a vast and intricate system of debt and investment. "The mortgage" was a systematized network of financial interdependence that connected farmers with A. W. Ocobock, Austin Corbin, Jane Addams, the New England Mortgage Security Company, and the holders of mortgage company debenture bonds—along with the stockowners of the Travelers Insurance Company, and, finally, that firm's policyholders, who were now often western farmers themselves.

That external agent commodified the farm household's labor power. The mortgage could do the kind of work a wage-labor market more commonly performed. As a "business man," as Rosie Ise had put it, the farmer learned to treat his household's labor power as replaceable units of capitalist account. The labor bureaus of Nebraska and Wisconsin—in 1887 and 1895, respectively—surveyed hundreds of farmers in investigating the sources of agricultural success and failure. Many farmers voiced typical agrarian discontents: the nefarious railroads, the eastern moneylenders, the deflationary gold standard. Many celebrated the virtues of western farming, chiding their peers for wasting time in political agitation that would be better spent running their farms. But both sides, often in the same breath, announced that farming had now become a "business." "Farming is very much like any other business," one Wisconsin farmer bluntly stated. "The farmer needs to understand his business as well as any other man who goes into business and makes a success of it," said another. Farmers must "adopt a system that will in the end secure the greatest amount of products at the lowest minimum cost of production." This meant that they had to employ a "thorough business instinct" and to be "economical" in keeping down costs.[76]

Households squeezed their own labor. And as nonmortgaged households competed with those striving to pay their debts, they too might do the same or mortgage their own farms to finance improvements or increase acreage. "To successfully compete with the world nowadays," one Wisconsin farmer stated, with no sense of complaint, "one must be awake early and late." For another, "from four o'clock in the morning until eight o'clock in the evening is not an unusually long day's work for a farmer."[77] "Waste of time," a Nebraska farmer claimed, had become the greatest nemesis. Successful Nebraska farmers repeatedly cited the threats of "loafing," "laziness," and "shiftlessness." Time must be diverted from competing diversions, whether these were "amusements," "going to town," "drinking whiskey," or "telling fish stories."[78] In Kansas the Ise farm suffered because Henry spent too much time reading instead of attending to the business of the farm.[79] Some considered this an appropriate work ethic. There had always been high land-to-labor ratios on American farms and squeezing labor was nothing new. But the western mortgage market led farmers to voice a novel sense of time-work discipline.

No less significant than the absolute amount of time spent working was the work's productivity. The Ises' experience is once again instructive. Since the Civil War Henry suffered chronic shoulder and stomach problems. Once he began paying back a mortgage the question of replacing his flagging labor power with that of a youthful hired hand became a constant issue. Prudent calculation was called for. What's more, Rosie often complained that Henry got "less work out of hired hands than anyone else in the neighborhood." She often insisted on doing the work herself. The Ises were busy measuring the relative value of their labor power against the general wage force. Rosie was better at this than Henry, as was revealed in their decision to borrow $100 against their land to purchase a windmill. At first, the Ises drew their own water from a well whenever they "wouldn't be doing anything else that counts."[80] But Rosie realized that it would be cheaper to hire extra hands to do that, allowing them to divert the household's labor elsewhere. Finally, she wondered whether a windmill would not be the best solution since it would reduce the cost of boarding hands. She made the appropriate calculations on the back of an envelope. The Ise household's labor was a fungible input weighed and considered against others.

Rosie Ise's labor was of critical significance. When mortgaged, to remove a wife from the fields, much less from household chores, was economic suicide. This constraint was a common source of male lament. An author wrote about the "young girl who married a poor farmer" in the 1882 *Michigan Farmer*. She settled down to the "task of paying off a mortgage on their home." The young wife "likes music, books, pictures and all sorts of nice things" but instead "plods along year after year, doing lots of hard, drudging work." It was as if the mortgage had also been placed "upon her own health and strength." Once more, labor power rather than the land was the foundation of the farmer's independence. With the mortgage ultimately paid off, "her face is thin and faded, her form bent, and her hands brown and calloused." Her "fingers have lost their affinity for the keys," and she was too coarse to "go out into society." John Ise's narrative is also no tale of bourgeois domesticity. Indeed, children were also busily at work in the fields. The Ises had neighbors who were Swiss immigrants, "a large family of children" that "worked like beavers" to pay a mortgage, which seemingly had the entire household working longer and harder.[81]

Whether farmers were working longer and harder than they had in the past is impossible to determine. It is also not the critical question. What we do know is that farmers now began to feel that they no longer controlled their own labor. Henry had escaped the wage labor of his youthful twenties, which was no small feat. No human boss directed his work. But he sensed that he had acquired another kind of boss. A popular poem from the 1880s captured this sentiment. Its author was the equally popular Midwestern author Will Carleton, a Michigan native who grew up watching his father struggle with mortgage debt. In the "Tramp's Story," published in a book of verse entitled *Farm Festivals*, a father gives his son a bequest on the latter's wedding day of an eighty-acre farm, one fit for an "independent start." "Land-hungry," the son mortgages the homestead to purchase an adjacent eighty acres. Although skeptical, his wife agrees to work "hard from day to day." For "we knew that life was business, now we had that debt to pay." There followed a section from the poem that was widely excerpted in agrarian periodicals:

> We worked through spring and winter—through summer and through fall—
>   But that mortgage worked the hardest and the steadiest of us all;
> It worked on nights and Sundays—it worked each holiday—
> It settled down among us, and it never went away.
> Whatever we kept from it seemed a'most as bad as theft;
> It watched us every minute, and it ruled us right and left.
> The rust and blight were with us sometimes, and sometimes not;
> The dark-browed, scowling mortgage was forever on the spot.
> The weevil and the cut-worm, they went as well as came;
> The mortgage staid forever, eating hearty all the same.
> It nailed up every window—stood guard at every door—
> And happiness and sunshine made their home with us no more.

"Failing crops," "sickness" (this farmer had no insurance), and "foreclosure" brought about the wife's death: "She died of *mortgage*." The widower subsequently falls into alcoholism and becomes a wandering tramp dependent for subsistence upon alms.[82]

Carleton anthropomorphized the western farm mortgage market. Indeed, it exerted supervisory control over the household—"it settled down among us" and "watched us every minute." It "ruled us." The verses echoed others then capturing the experience of industrial wage work in the East.[83] The Ise mortgage "hung like a pall over the spirits of all, even the children." At the supper table, "the family conversation, no matter where it started, usually led finally back to that engrossing and disturbing theme." The mortgage had settled down among them—the "relentless master of the family destinies."[84] Who was that master? Carleton's farmer willfully chose to mortgage his farm. The owners of the Ise mortgage resided at the end of a winding path of financial intermediation. Still, unlike the factory boss, the mortgage followed the farmer out of the workplace, out of the fields, into his home.

What's more, if the farmer had purchased a life or accident policy, he had to exercise a legally enforced standard of caution while at the "workplace" in order to maintain his policy. A precedent was set in a case adjudicated in New Jersey in 1871. An insured farmer had built a barn. To view the results of his labor he climbed up onto the top joint. The joint broke and he fell to his death. "At the time of the accident," his insurers explained to the court, attempting to void the policy, "he had on two overcoats, and was said to be an awkward man." The court did not accept this argument. But as the Travelers explained to its policyholders in 1871, it was not liable for losses due to "unnecessary exposure to danger or peril." The US Supreme Court accepted that reasoning in 1873 when it announced the standard of "limitation of risk."[85] In the industrial workplace, this was manifest in the legal principles of "fellow-servant rule," "assumption of risk," and "contributory negligence," all of which shifted the burden of responsibility for industrial accidents onto the backs of wage earners, inducing many to insure their lives. Both they and the insured farmer were now bound by the rule of "limitation of risk." To engage in "unnecessary exposure to danger or peril" might be to risk the entire farm. Thus, in all of these ways, the nebulous nature of "the mortgage," its subtle and abstract power, as much as the time and effort that households spent in the fields, contributed to the widespread sense that the farmer's legendary independence was under threat.

A similar dynamic was playing out in the relationship between market chance and security. After 1870 mortgage debt pressured farmers into growing the product that brought in the most cash. The great western staple was, as always, wheat. Despite incipient soil exhaustion and an onslaught of insects and crop diseases, western farmers were tempted by wheat monoculture in the 1880s—much to the dismay of a rising class of scientific agricultural reformers who urged them to move toward market diversification.[86]

According to contemporary accounts, mortgaged farmers in the 1880s were more likely to practice monoculture, the "single-crop" system, and sacrifice mixed farming. On the nineteenth-century frontier the normal sequence had been for households to move from initial wheat monoculture to a more diversified basket of goods intended for both local market exchange and home consumption. That practice continued along the edge of the wheat belt. In 1888 a mortgage broker of Lake Preston, Dakota, observed new farmers specializing in wheat, the crop that "always brings cash as soon as possible." If they survived the first years, their attention then turned to "other things" such as "livestocks, fruits, vegetables, poultry, etc."[87] In the 1880s, however, this logic was losing its grip, at least according to the labor commissioners of Minnesota, South Dakota, and Nebraska, and observers in Iowa and Kansas.[88] The balloon payments due on the final years of mortgages applied the most pressure. The harvest in the year before the note came due was a make-or-break moment. Oftentimes, all possible acreage was devoted to wheat. The crop rotations of mixed farming were also sacrificed. In Wisconsin, a farmer wearily observed that there was "plowing and seeding every year."[89] What was the point of minding future soil fertility if the foreclosed farmer no longer owned the farm?

The result was heightened regional specialization: the "corn belt" of Iowa and Illinois, continuing wheat production on the Great Plains, and dairy farming in Minnesota and Wisconsin. Scholars dispute the postbellum western farmer's degree of "specialization." It does seem that the logic of diversification, where it continued to be practiced, changed. Instead of mixing a variety of subsistence with singular market goods, farmers were now more likely to diversify within a batch of goods produced for the market. After the bust in the western mortgage market in 1893 the move to this new style of diversification intensified.[90]

As such, western farmers fueled a regional, national, and even global feedback loop of competitive pressure in the 1880s. In George Boutwell's state of Massachusetts price convergence in farm products was first evident in the early years of the republic.[91] By the 1890s the price of "#2 wheat" in Chicago, New York, and Liverpool had nearly converged.[92] Western grains pushed all of American agriculture towards regional specialization. Noting a continuation of antebellum trends, the Connecticut Labor Bureau's 1889 report on mortgaged farming—a striking complement to the Connecticut Insurance Department's 1889 report on its financial institution's investments in western farm mortgages—noted the inability of the "rocky hillsides of Connecticut" to compete with the "fertile prairies of the West" in grains. The "contagious spirit of manufacturing" consequently came to dominate Connecticut's economy. Landowners now functioned as "real estate dealers" rather than "farmers." Those farms that continued to produce specialized in fruits, vegetables, and dairy goods. The report added that abandoned farms were being sold in small lots to industrial wage laborers who "desire a little land for cultivation."[93] It was now proletarians, in other words, not farmers, who engaged in subsistence production as a hedge against their market lives. George Boutwell, now an aging retired politician, described the dynamic in an 1878 essay he wrote for the *Massachusetts Ploughman*. Boutwell announced that the farmer's chief problem was "to produce a given quantity at the least cost." In light of western competition, dairy farming was the only "certain . . . source of revenue" for the Massachusetts farmer.[94] That was the fate of the "certainty of a competence," which Boutwell had juxtaposed to the "anxiety" of "commerce" in 1850.

The American South was similarly transformed. The number of Southern acres given over to cotton production surged after the Civil War. The freed slaves sought landed independence. But whereas the Union soldier Henry Ise received his western claim, freed people failed to get their southern claims. The freed slaves had hoped to grow subsistence crops and a bundle of market goods but ended up cropping cotton on a share basis. The flood of western grains made this possible. Chattel mortgages—mortgages on personal, not real property—dominated the South and the comparison to the western market is revealing. Filtered through race, the Southern credit market was more local, personal, violent, and nakedly exploitative. The western market was more abstract and impersonal, which raised fundamentally different problems for landed independence. Henry Ise's Southern counterparts—the white upcountry yeoman—shifted their acreage into cotton in these years.[95] There was a national psychological dynamic at work. As a Georgia newspaper editorialized:

> We can tell a man who has corn enough a mile off. The corn man cocks his hat one side and swings along at an easy stride. The "no corn" man has his hat pulled over his eyes and shambles along with a slouching gait and a side-long look as if he expected every minute for someone to sing out, "I know what ails you, you haven't corn enough to last until May."[96]

After the Civil War, the western mortgage market helped strip an existential sense of security and certainty from American agriculture. Here was another depiction of a loss of personal autonomy and control, but manifest in the slouching gait of the Southern farmer with all of his acres in the cultivation of cotton.

Farmers had to look beyond their lands for security, again, to new financial markets. For their human capital they had recourse to the new insurance policies. For their products they turned to the new commodities futures markets and bucket shops centered in the pits of the Chicago Board of Trade, which offered hedges against their physical products but also outlets for speculative manias far more wild than any that ever gripped the Yankee wheat farmer. Farmers stayed more aloof of futures markets than insurance policies.[97] But in both instances they tinkered at the margins of those institutions, ranging from local, cooperative insurance and storage schemes to ultimately successful demands that the federal government provide such services.[98] These were all results of the loss of landed independence.

A future of agricultural cooperation, possibly fostered by the federal government, looked bright to some farmers.[99] For others this was a poor substitute that could never capture the old sense of autonomy once sought through land ownership. Independence, a young Henry Ise proclaimed, was as much a *feeling* as an objective economic fact, a feeling that one was responsible for one's own future, that the Ise family rather than its mortgage, or anyone or anything else, was the master of the family's destiny. Instead, according to John Ise, western farming constituted "years of anxiety." The Ises' dependence upon markets had become existential. The problem with plains farming, to repeat Rosie's mantra once again, was that "Nobody's responsible."[100] The Ises felt they worked hard year after year. Regardless, the world market fluctuated, and in these decades prices tended downward. The Ises' fate had become interdependent with the wheat crops of Canada, Argentina, India, and Poland. To pin down the mortgage as an external agent was also to put a name, if not a face, on the world market.

There were forces outside the farmer's control long before 1870 as well. But the older perils of drought, flood, and insect now took on a different meaning. The subsequent losses—grasshoppers assaulted western farmers in the late 1870s, followed by cinch bugs and hessian flies—were not the same on a mortgaged farm, as the world market connected the Argentine drought with the Kansas beetle. "All the uncertainties of the weather, crops and prices had been borne with heavier weight," John Ise recalled of the family mortgage. An 1896 article on farm mortgaging in *The Independent* noted how the "farmer's life" was considered to be "the most independent in the world." Yet with a mortgage it was "full of uncertainties and anxieties." "A single untimely frost may empty his pockets and blast his hopes." Carleton's "Tramp Story" began: "Worm or

Beetle—drought or tempest—on a farmer's land may fall; But for first-class
ruination, trust a mortgage 'gainst them all."[101] It was as if the risks of the market constituted a new element in a world of uncontrollable natural factors.

Was religious thinking still capable of making sense of the contingencies
that afflicted farming? What if markets—with no ground for the farmer to
stand upon outside of them—dispensed ill fates, tumbling prices downward?
George K. Holmes, the chief statistician of the 1890 census mortgage survey,
queried the responsibility of the failed Kansas farmer:

> Did the mortgage cause his misfortune, or was it a miscalculation of the "bounty
> of Providence"? Again, by way of question, is a mortgage ever a cause of misfor-
> tune, except secondarily through the borrower's want of prescience or through his
> inability properly to manage the borrowed wealth?[102]

A notion of Providence was still present, however weakened. In the hands of
this statistician—a profession born a half century earlier—even the "bounty of
Providence" was subject to calculation. But where was the line to be drawn between the farmer's autonomy and those forces outside of his control? Holmes
had no answer. But in contrast to the antebellum years, there were presently
few celebrations of the farmer's divinely secured "independence."

Rosie Ise also had difficulty squaring religion with the western farmer's predicament. One evening a prominent evangelical minister and his wife visited
the Ise household. Over supper, Rosie blurted out a question. Why would God
ever bring drought? The minister stammered a nonanswer and Rosie pressed.
Surely, the Ises had done their part, working hard and living right. The minister said something about minding one's responsibilities and having faith in
God. Greatly embarrassing her husband, Rosie blurted out again that God was
failing them. Rosie was especially anxious for the starving farm animals and
her worried children, anxieties resembling those of the investor Jane Addams.
The minister's wife reminded Rosie that God had sent drought to smite the
farmer's pride. One must not rebel against His will. Whether it was the will
of God setting the tune of western farming, to Rosie the ruling source was no
rational, let alone ethical, agent. As she looked around her, the business of
western farming simply made no sense.[103] Certainly, confidence and faith in
the ways of Providence rang empty.

Others did not experience the new uncertainty as a source of anxiety but as
a font for energy, even liberation. When Henry Ise contemplated the reality
of a mortgage, he regretfully looked upon it as a game of chance. For many
Yankee wheat farmers, the chanciness of western farming was precisely the

point. An 1889 editorial in the *Michigan Farmer* recommended that young farmers take out mortgages. They could thereby unleash "the enterprise and energy of youth." The young farmer would be "compelled" to "develop his abilities as a business man" and become more "industrious" and "economical." He would necessarily produce more cash crops. And he would not be able "to let his talents lie hid in a napkin," for "he must keep them actively employed." A mortgage was a "blessing," the "secret of success." Forget the "certainty of a competence." What about striking it rich? This was the audience B. C. Keeler had in mind in 1880 when he published *Where to Go to Become Rich*. "Men are becoming rich there in all branches of farming," Keeler boasted of Kansas.[104] Even Henry Ise once speculated in town lots, although he later regretted doing so. Taking her $100 bequest, one of his eighteen-year-old daughters did the same. In addition to the riches, there was an existential thrill—not angst— that could be found on the western plains. Many farmers coped better with the chance-world of markets than did Henry Ise, even if they were not in search of it. In the 1895 survey of Wisconsin agriculture, many farmers, without il-lusions regarding the inherent perils and possibilities of their trade, reported that they were satisfied with their lot and spoke of feelings of "independence." Such talk of independence circles back to the fundamental question of how to define a style of farming that had no precedent in the country's history.

The issue came into sharp focus in 1890, at the height of the "western farm mortgage" craze, when the Census Bureau sought to quantify the mortgage debt of American farmers. The terms of the debate alone revealed the loss of *landed* independence. That is, if the farmer was to be called independent, that now meant something entirely different.

The 1890 census project was initiated by B. C. Keeler, the same author of *Where to Go to Become Rich*. By 1890 he saw things differently. President of the "Western Economic Association of St. Louis," Keeler wrote a circular en-titled "Farm Mortgages" and distributed 2,000 copies. Because of mortgage debt, he argued, "farmers and other producers of the country do not obtain an equitable share of the wealth which they create." Keeler called upon his readers to demand a census count of what percentage of citizens actually owned their farms, and how much of them they owned. The Census Bureau later reported a flood of petitions from "Single Tax Clubs, Knights of Labor assemblies, and farmer's and workingmen's associations" having adopted Keeler's language word for word. Even a petition from the Chicago Board of Trade was received, equally curious, although with a different formulation.[105] Senator Eugene Hale of Maine, chairman of the Committee on the Census, commissioned a special taskforce. Findings were already trickling out by late 1890. In 1895 the Census Bureau issued a 921-page report of its findings.

The *Report of Real Estate Mortgages in the United States* counted 3,142,718 farms and found that 28.9 percent of all taxable farm acreage was encumbered with mortgage debt. Mortgage debt had increased by 41.54 percent since 1880, mostly due to an increase in the numbers west of the Mississippi. Kansas and Nebraska were the heaviest mortgaged states, the only to surpass the 50 percent mark of mortgaged acreage. The average interest rate on mortgages was 7.36 percent, ranging from 10.9 percent in Arizona to 5.44 percent in Massachusetts. The average life of a mortgage was 4.54 years and the average loan $1,032. Of all debt, 89.92 percent was for land purchases or farm improvements.[106]

That was the quantitative picture of American farm mortgage debt. Its interpretation was another matter. George K. Holmes, who was charged with managing the census count, read a paper before the American Statistical Association in early 1890 that set out the task before him. He was already skeptical about whether numbers alone could address the real question at hand: "What if the county containing the most prosperous people in a state has also the largest per capita mortgage debt, or the largest ration of debt valuation?"[107] The more exact the collection of numbers the better, but the figures alone could not get to the root of the question, as even Holmes admitted. Indeed, his ultimate findings were cited as compelling evidence on all sides of the debate over what conclusions to draw from the census count.

This debate revealed two things. First, "independence" and "dependence"— along with a series of other cognates evoking a sharp binary—were still the standards for evaluating the western farmer's commercial life. The spectrum of possibilities to be found between these two poles, together with the subtle network of abstract financial interdependence that underlay the system, was missing. Furthermore, the farmer's purported independence, if it did indeed exist, was no different in kind than the independence of any other successful proprietary capitalist. That is, the farmer's independence was now based on his successful pursuit of a money income.

Indeed, the debate was carried on by two ships passing in the night. The Kansas Republican paper, the *Atchison Daily Champion*, for instance, examined Holmes's preliminary numbers and concluded that the mortgage debt was neither "burdensome" nor "oppressive." Chicago's *Daily Inter Ocean* likewise concluded that western farmers were "comparatively free from debt." The *Milwaukee Journal* headlined its story on the subject as "Farmers are prosperous. More than half their lands without encumbrance of any kind." Meanwhile, the Democratic-leaning *St. Louis Republic* claimed that the census found that eastern moneylenders had "a force of nearly two and a half million men" in the west working under a system worse than African slavery.[108]

The census count resolved nothing. There was no more clarity now than during the 1870s and 1880s, when disgruntled mortgaged farmers called themselves "slaves," "serfs," "tenants," and "hirelings"—anything but "mortgaged farmers"—while champions of the western mortgage market referred to farmers as wonderfully "independent."[109] In addressing farmers' descriptions of their dependent status, W. F. Mappin responded in the 1889 *Political Science Quarterly* by arguing that claims that "the independent small farmer in the United States is in danger of extinction" because of mortgage debt were erroneous. Look only at "how much of the capital invested in manufacturing was borrowed." The sum was even greater than in agriculture. Debt, in other words, was a necessary reality of any successful proprietary capitalist enterprise. Yes, western farming required an "energetic" people willing to take on "risk." But in the end western farmers were "their own employers." To compare them to "factory wage-workers" was a categorical mistake.[110] There was difficulty reaching any common conclusions regarding western mortgages precisely because of the overriding desire to determine if farmers were "independent" or "dependent," once stable concepts which now only generated confusion and obfuscation.

Tellingly, the most widely circulated analysis of the census figures was a piece that appeared in the 1894 *Forum* written by the Massachusetts industrialist Edward Atkinson and entitled "The True Meaning of Farm Mortgage Statistics." Atkinson concluded that "the burden of farm mortgages is a very light one." He argued that there was no "class in this country" who were "so free of debt" and "so absolutely independent as the Western farmers of the grain-growing states." Despite the recent bust of eastern mortgage companies, American homesteads were actually underutilized as collateral. Atkinson, a successful proprietor of New England cotton mills, was evaluating western farming as if it were a business like his own. He knew what it was like to be in debt. What was the problem with that?[111]

Atkinson had good reason to take a hard look at western farming. He had been a founding member of the Free Soil Party. A prominent abolitionist, Atkinson even raised funds for John Brown's raid on Harpers Ferry. During the Civil War Atkinson found himself in the Union-occupied Sea Islands of South Carolina. Thwarting the freed slaves' desire for land and abhorring their preference for raising subsistence crops, Atkinson had insisted that they work for wages, grow cotton exclusively (for export to the Northern mills), and subsist on western grains.[112] Now, in 1894, Atkinson, a Republican gold bug, looked west and, in spite of the agrarian protest, saw the fulfillment of freedom's promise.

Atkinson's essay was written as a rejoinder to another geriatric abolitionist, Daniel Goodloe. Also writing in the *Forum*, Goodloe had previously invoked emancipation by calling mortgaged farming a new form of slavery.[113] What kind of freedom was Atkinson now championing? Free soil was an ideology in which land had not only economic but profound social and political significance: the Jeffersonian-inspired dream of a landed, commercial, republic. In Atkinson's hands, by 1894 the land was just another capital asset.

The polemic between Goodloe and Atkinson guaranteed that such heated binaries as freedom and slavery obscured any adequate view of the complex, ambiguous structure of financial interdependence. Subsequent histories of the postbellum western farmer have often replicated this simplified dichotomy. One set of scholars has emphasized the burdens of mortgage debt and its coercive aspects, lumping mortgaged farmers together with agricultural wage-laborers and tenants.[114] Another group of historians, subscribing to the same conceptualization as Edward Atkinson, argues that the market position of mortgaged western farmers improved over the 1870s and 1880s.[115] The missing context for both sides is a discussion of the fate of landed independence itself, one decided by a process of financial systematization. This was a process that generated a whole new material and psychological reality that many observers at the time could not quite find the right conceptual vocabulary with which to describe, an enduring reality whose characterization remains elusive to this day.

Of course, this was not considered to be a conceptual problem at the time but, rather, a momentous political dispute that culminated in the failure of the populist revolt in the presidential election of 1896. Mortgage debt was at the center of that revolt, warranting the expansion of the money supply, which was supposed to reduce the farmer's debt burden. And so, on one hand, populism looked back to the ideal of landed independence while, on the other hand, it anticipated the federal government's twentieth-century role as a guarantor of the citizenry's economic security. Regardless, landed independence had given way to subjection to the world's market. A successful populism might have changed the terms of that subjection, but it did not have the tools to end it, assuming that it would have wanted to.[116] After 1870 a bridge in American agriculture was burned.

After 1896, with the agrarian revolt going up in smoke, the world market turned. The prices offered for American farm staples soared. By 1908, as the USDA noted, "the farmers of the mortgage-ridden state of Kansas of former days have stuffed the banks of that state full of money."[117] The irony was that in Edward Atkinson's industrial East, the depression of the 1890s pulled the rug out from under individual proprietorship, clearing the way for the corporate dominance of the industrial sector. Meanwhile, western farm proprietors entered their so-called Golden Age of American agriculture in the second decade of the twentieth century. Soon, however, the wheel of the world market would turn yet again, and the Golden Age begat the Dust Bowl.

Acknowledgments

I would like to thank the contributors to and editors of this volume for their helpful comments on this chapter, and in particular Michael Zakim. Participants at the Economic History Forum at the University of Pennsylvania and the Economic Sociology Workshop at Princeton University, along with the readings of Hendrik Hartog, Gautham Rao, and Daniel T. Rodgers, also greatly improved the chapter.

3

Toxic Debt, Liar Loans, Collateralized and Securitized Human Beings, and the Panic of 1837

Edward E. Baptist

In 2004 an Ayn Rand disciple named Alan Greenspan, who as chairman of the Federal Reserve Board had been trusted with the US government's considerable powers for steering the financial economy, stated his faith in the ability of that economy to autoregulate its own stability:

> Recent regulatory reform coupled with innovative technologies has spawned rapidly growing markets for, among other products, asset-backed securities, collateral loan obligations, and credit derivative default swaps. These increasingly complex financial instruments have contributed, especially over the recent stressful period, to the development of a far more flexible, efficient, and hence resilient financial system than existed just a quarter-century ago.[1]

A mere six years later, after Greenspan's faith failed to prevent the devastating crash of the global financial system, a prominent economist reflected on Greenspan's credo. Criticizing the dogmatic belief in the self-regulating market—a belief that had existed since at least the early nineteenth century—Robert Solow offered an updated version of another old belief. He responded to Greenspan's claims by voicing his suspicion that the financialization of the US economy over the previous quarter century had created not "real" but fictitious wealth:

> Flexible maybe, resilient apparently not, but how about efficient? How much do all those exotic securities, and the institutions that create them, buy them, and sell them, actually contribute to the "real" economy that provides us with goods and services, now and for the future?[2]

Solow is not the only observer to distinguish between the "real" economy, on the one hand, and the "exotic" realm of securitized debts such as mortgage bonds, credit default swaps, toxic debt, and zombie banks, on the other. In fact, this dichotomy is almost reflexively made. As a widespread assumption—a persistent distinction in our thought between "real" and "fictive" money, wealth, or productivity—it may be one factor that accounts for the reluctance of many scholars to delve into the material history of financial dynamics in accounting for the vicissitudes of capitalism in nineteenth-century America. Recently, the historical profession has found it comforting to analyze events such as booms, busts, and their aftermaths with the tools of the linguistic turn. It is enough, it sometimes seems, to demonstrate that the fictions on which economic actors build their ideas of their own economic worlds are indeed fictions. (Also relevant is the reluctance of most US historians to engage with quantitative modes of analysis.) And yet, when collective euphoria, financial innovation, and astonishing disproportions of power mix together, what bubbles into being is not merely vapor. We can minimize its weight by calling it fiction, but we do so only at grave risk to our understanding of what happened in the economy and why. For in such financial exchanges we see not only the generation and transfer of real wealth and real effects in the social and political world, but also that such transfers can incorporate great violence and disruption for some as the causes of great profit for others.

If one reads casually through the pieces of paper that document Jacob Bieller's life and enterprises, this planter of Concordia Parish, Louisiana, might look like someone who lived not just thousands, but millions of miles away from the center of international financial markets in the 1830s. His business might seem even more distant in kind from the markets that worry us in our own day. Browse the letters between Bieller and his son Joseph, the latter writing from the bank of Bayou Macon, thirty miles or so from Jacob's own place on the Mississippi River. Joseph wrote his father in an untutored orthography, recounting the events of life in a cotton labor camp: "I shall be short of corn." Or: someone had found the body of Enos, the overseer's father, "drownded in Deer Drink."³ The cyclical rhythm of forced agricultural labor thrummed onward—"I send you by Enos fifteen cotton pickers they are all I can spare. We have twelve thousand weight of cotton to pick yet from the appearance of the boals [*sic*] yet to open." The urge to extract more product constantly clashed with the objection of the enslaved to their exploitation: "I have had a verry sevear time among my negros at home. they have bin swinging my hogs and pigs. Harry & Roberson I caught. I stake Harry and gave him 175 lashes and Roberson 150. since that I found two hogs badly crippled."⁴ The reader can almost see the Spanish moss on the low branches, parting as the whining hog lurches out, can picture Enos as he poles his pirogue. His booted foot slips on the wet edge; he splashes frantically, the dark water gurgles.

For good and for ill, though, Jacob Bieller was much closer to the core of the global financial system of his day than we might initially suspect. The panic of 1837 launched America's biggest and most consequential economic depression before the Civil War. And it was the decisions and behavior of thousands of actors like Bieller that created a perfect financial storm: bringing an end to one kind of capitalist boom, destroying the confidence of the slaveholding class, impoverishing millions, and demolishing the already disrupted lives of hundreds of people like Harry and Roberson. Historians have usually described the panic of 1837 differently, fitting it into their own boxes: Arthur M. Schlesinger Jr., the court historian of New Deal Democrats, identified "the business community," with their "dizzy pyramiding of paper credits," as the problem. Historians of American banking, usually a specialized breed interested in—what else—banking, often blame the panic on Andrew Jackson, who has often appeared in this telling as an ignorant lout obsessed with the idol of precious metal. For some of them, the cause of the panic was the Specie Circular of 1836, which forced US government agencies to stop accepting the paper banknotes pumped out by state-chartered banks and to accept nothing but specie (metal coins made of gold or silver) in payment for federal land and other obligations.⁵

These stories about the panic are capsules that carry other stories about American capitalism into the bloodstream of the broader historical narrative. The panic was the result of a struggle between factory owners and factory workers, with a dash of hardy Jeffersonian farmers suspicious of the new way of making money! No, it was created by a struggle for greater efficiencies, a process of sweeping away old institutions and prejudices so that the market could be all in all! Yet through the history of the modern economy, Americans have received repeated education in booms and busts, bubbles and panics. The first lesson is that a financial crisis is a mighty and powerful thing. The actors will respond to its dynamics in all sorts of ways that can be investigated with the tools of cultural history. It is surely significant that businessmen in the 1830s were "embarrassed" when their "friends" would not "sustain" their "credit" (note how the scare quotes "problematize" each word, demanding that we unpack its contextual meaning). Certainly, we can't leave the mechanics of financial crises to the court historians of the great banking dynasties, or to economists. In fact, when we look closely at the transformations and innovations that led to the panic of 1837, we find new evidence about the role of slavery and slave labor in the creation of our modern, industrialized—and postmodernly financialized—world. Neither economists nor even historians of slavery have given this evidence its due.

Generally speaking, historians, economic or otherwise, need to focus more on the history of financial markets, and how they interact with other markets, and with other aspects of society and culture. For the evidence strongly suggests that—left to their own devices—neither economists nor the banking dynasts they often serve have learned the lessons of the past. The events of 2007–8, for instance, only temporarily chastened many of the economists criticized by financial journalist John Cassidy in *How Markets Fail,* his comprehensive history of the profession. Cassidy charged the scholars with blind faith in what he calls the "utopian" idea that financial markets will always deliver the most efficient, wealth-generating, and utility-maximizing outcomes, like the markets drawn up on the chalkboard in the simple graphs of Intro to Microeconomics (Assume an island with two castaways and five coconuts . . .). Such arguments claim that the more unregulated the market, including financial ones like those for stocks, bonds, and various forms of credit, the more productive—and stable—it will be. So also Greenspan had proclaimed, insisting on the effectiveness of so-called counterparty regulation: that carried out by trading partners—by the market itself. For who would be so foolish as to buy a bad stock? Or lend money to a company incapable of paying it back?[6]

In the years bracketing the dawn of the twenty-first century, Congress had responded to the political power amassed by those who found utopian-economic dogma convincing (or merely convenient) by slashing regulations in the financial industry. This allowed investment banks to create a myriad of new securities. They were bewildering, and perhaps intentionally so, but their proliferations and permutations actually help illuminate the nature of 1830s developments in markets similarly shaped by the collusion of state and financial elites. For instance, take a look at bonds backed by home mortgages. Firms like Merrill Lynch, Bear Stearns, and Lehman Brothers sold billions of dollars worth of them in the quarter-century leading up to 2008, especially to each other. To fund their purchases, firms increased what financial writers call "leverage"—the ability to wield much more capital than they own, because they are able to borrow—to giant proportions, to the point where they owed 30, 40, or more times their equity—again, often to each other. Another popular innovation was the "credit default swap" in which one investor bought insurance from another on the securities a third party had issued. It works like this: I pay you an annual percentage of the total value of a bond someone else has sold, and that will be the premium for an insurance policy in which you promise to pay off the bond if the original borrowers are unable do so.[7]

The mutual obligations that connected major financial players in thick networks of mutual indebtedness actually grew out of a strategy called "hedging." Hedging means creating safeguards against the possibility that a trading partner's failure to pay could also bring oneself down as well. Such safeguards usually take the form of either insurance or the spreading of risk into multiple investments. While credit swaps were a kind of insurance, mortgage-backed bonds rested on the idea of diversification. Each bond was composed of minute percentages of thousands of individual home loans that had (in effect) been chopped up and "securitized." Thus, no single homeowner who stopped paying and entered foreclosure was going to destroy the bond's value. This was allegedly the case even though some bonds were created from only the riskiest kinds of mortgages. Moreover, if worst came to worst, the bank could always find someone to buy the home again, right? After all, house prices had been rising for as long as anyone could remember. These securities seemed foolproof and only a fool would fail to keep up with his or her rivals by failing to invest in a sure thing. More and more entities—investment banks like Lehman Brothers, commercial banks, institutional investment pools, hedge funds, and insurance giants like AIG—jumped into the game.[8] There was no need to fear their abandonment of caution. According to many experts, the new rules on Wall Street were so brilliantly conceived that systemic financial crashes were rendered impossible by the spreading of risk and the careful hedging strategies of firms. Since explaining such disasters has been one of the great unfulfilled challenges of professional economists over the century, it was a relief to take their inconvenient possibility off the table.

But it had all happened before. Look a little more closely at Jacob Bieller, who can tell us things worth our due diligence. In 1837 Bieller was sixty-seven years old. He had grown up in South Carolina, where in the early years of the

nineteenth century he and his father took advantage of that state's reopening of
the African slave trade, speculating in survivors of the Middle Passage. In 1809,
a little more than a year after Congress closed the legal Atlantic slave trade,
Bieller moved west. Driven in part by divorce from his first wife, but drawn
by the opportunities for an entrepreneurial enslaver in the new cotton lands
opening to the west, Bieller took his son Joseph and twenty-seven enslaved
African Americans and settled just up the Mississippi River from Natchez, on
the Louisiana side.[9]

The enslaved people that Bieller brought to Concordia Parish became
the root of his fortune—as they and a million others like them would be the
root of the prosperity of not just the antebellum southwestern states but of
the United States as a whole. And perhaps one could go beyond the United
States. By the 1830s, the cotton that enslaved people grew in the new states
and territories taken from Native Americans in the early nineteenth century
was the most widely traded commodity in the world. It was also the raw material of the Industrial Revolution. The creation of textile factories in the British
Midlands launched a process of continuous technological innovation, urbanization, and creation of markets that broke the Malthusian traps of traditional
agricultural society. First Britain, then the United States, and then the rest of
western Europe achieved sustained rates of economic growth never before seen
in human history.[10]

This growth is often credited to the increasing division of labor and
rapid pace of technological innovation—the spinning jenny, the mechanical
loom—that emerged in the eighteenth-century British manufacturing sector.
But world historian Kenneth Pomeranz insists that we also have to look at the
capacity of environments to produce resources if we want to understand what
really allowed the West to open such a lead on the rest of the world. The cotton
fields of the slave South were particularly crucial because they allowed Britain
to break out of its own "cul-de-sac" of resources: limits imposed by the delicate
balances between labor, land, fuel, food, and fiber; limits that in other societies had ensured that such a revolution would not happen. Even if every acre
in Britain could have been converted into fiber production, the island would
have been incapable of matching the capacity of the slave South to produce
the raw materials for a textile-based economic transformation, to say nothing
of the labor that would have to be taken out of the pool of potential factory
workers to produce fiber.[11]

The capacity of the slave South to produce cotton expanded at an astonishing rate. In the lifetime between the ratification of the Constitution and the
secession of the Confederacy, enslavers moved more than a million enslaved

African Americans to cotton-growing areas taken by the new nation from their original inhabitants. The disrupted lives, forced migrations, and stolen labor yielded an astonishing increase in cotton production: from 1.2 million pounds in 1790 to 2.1 *billion* in 1859, and an incredible dominance over the international market. By the 1830s, 80 percent of the cotton used by the British textile industry came from the southern United States. Enslaved people and the land where they were forced to sow, weed, and pick cotton augmented the capacity of the western world's new industrial sector, with very little direct cost in terms of wages, foregone agricultural production, or environmental pressure in the commercial core. Collectively, Pomeranz calls this phenomenon the development of "ghost acres," and they explain for him why industrialization happened first in the West and not in China. (By 1860 these enslaved people were picking cotton — and picking was the bottleneck in the production process — four to six times faster per individual, per day, than their grandparents had been doing in 1800.)[12]

Therefore, when Jacob Bieller put his two dozen slaves to work growing and picking cotton on the acres he had forced them to chop out of the bayou woods, his whip was also driving the creation of a new, more complex, more dynamic world economy. We live today in the product of their labor. We also live in a world distantly shaped by the financial decisions of cotton entrepreneurs on both sides of the Atlantic — as well as by the forgetfulness of those who have not learned from their lessons. Specifically, we are shaped by their decisions about how to obtain and use credit, and how to manage risk. And there was risk aplenty. Up and down the chain of (mostly white) people who sold, traded, shipped, and speculated on the cotton that enslaved people made, credit and risk were present at each stage and for each of the actors. Their experience of moving the world's most important commodity through a chain of buyers and sellers that stretched from the Louisiana cotton field to the Liverpool cotton exchange was almost bipolar, an incessant counterpoint of mania and fear. Prices dropped suddenly when rumors raced through New Orleans, New York, or Liverpool: "optimism prevailed" — till the market learned that the US crop is too big for the demand this year. Cloth wasn't selling, reports had it, because of "overproduction." The mill workers in Manchester have been "turned out," that is, laid off, said the rumors, leading in turn to a "suspension of consumption of cotton" that "in many lessened the speculation ardour." And so on, and so on, in almost every crop year.[13]

Dreams, futures, debts — all were denominated in the fluttering price of cotton, and all soared and rose with it. When rumors of bad news for that price overwhelmed the desire for speculative gain — when the "animal spirits" of the marketplace, to use a term coined by John Maynard Keynes, turned negative—a massive, systemic crash could be the result. This is what almost happened in 1824–26. At first, in the winter of 1824–25, cotton buyers were convinced that the 1824 crop had been small. After buying all the bales that they could at rising prices, middlemen discovered that, in fact, the crop was very large.[14]

Beginning with Adam Smith, utopian economists have argued that the logical outcome of profit-maximizing behavior by all market actors will result in the maximum possible collective benefits. In this case, when the price of a pound of cotton plummeted, merchant firms were unable to pay back the short-term commercial loans they had taken, and so they demanded repayment from their fellow firms to whom they had made loans. But individual rational behavior—shoring up liquidity as pressure for payment increased—led to collectively irrational outcomes. Every firm was suddenly moving in the same direction, every firm faced the same crisis, each one responded in the same way. The result was crash and paralysis in the British cotton and credit markets.[15]

The financial panic of 1824–26 underlined the problem of systemic risk. The fact that the mid-decade's outbreak of animal spirits did not end in full-scale economic disaster in the United States was a result, some believed, of the expanded ability of the Second Bank of the United States (BUS) to regulate the level of systemic risk in the American economy. The Bank's able director was Pennsylvania's Nicholas Biddle. Biddle was a true Renaissance man: a poet, a legislator, a financial genius. In a later century he would have been more than arrogant enough to run a financial empire like Goldman Sachs if the "giant vampire squid attached to the face of humanity" happened to have an open position and access to a time machine.[16] Under Biddle, the BUS fulfilled many of the functions of a modern central bank. By forcing smaller, state-chartered banks to redeem their own credit in highly convertible currency, like gold dollars, British pounds, or banknotes of the BUS itself, Biddle's Bank kept a tight rein on those institutions. They could not issue too much credit. By making and by calling in its own loans, the BUS also "curtailed" speculation on the part of private individuals.[17]

In practice, the Bank defined its mission through two tasks: (1) preventing the speculation that helped create a forest choked with fuel for financial panics to burn; and (2) promoting and driving steady growth. The single biggest creditor in the US economy, it lent directly to individual entrepreneurs, including enslavers like Jacob Bieller, who were always eager to buy more human capital whom they could put to work in the cotton fields of the Southwest. "The US Bank and the Planters Bank at this place has thrown a large am[oun]t of cash into circulation," wrote slave trader Isaac Franklin from Natchez in 1832. Franklin was the Sam Walton of the internal slave trade in the United States, selling hundreds or even thousands of men and women in New Orleans and Natchez in a given year. In fact, by the early 1830s, the Natchez and New Orleans branches had lent out a full third of the capital of the BUS, much of which was used to buy thousands of enslaved people from the Chesapeake, Kentucky, and North Carolina. Some of the lending was in the form of renewable "accommodation loans" to large-scale planters who were members of, or connected to, the clique of insiders who ran the BUS branch and the series of state banks chartered by the Mississippi government. Even more of the lending was in the form of commercial credit to cotton buyers. This kept the price of cotton steady, finding its way to the planters themselves, inspiring Natchez-area enslavers to buy more of the people that Franklin and others purchased in the Chesapeake states and shipped to the Mississippi Valley.[18]

Control over lending in the Mississippi Valley helped the BUS accomplish its most significant annually recurring task: ensuring the reliable financing, growth, harvest, and movement of a massive pile of cotton. This was indeed important business. That pile represented half of the value of all exports produced by the export-led, anxious-for-foreign-earnings US economy. First, there was the need to carry planters while their slaves grew and harvested a mountain of cotton. Second, that mountain of cotton had to be moved from New Orleans and other Southern ports to Liverpool. Third, payment had to be distributed through the paths and channels of banking/mercantile networks back to everyone who had shared the process of making and financing and marketing and transporting a piece of the mountain—except, of course, for the "hands" who picked cotton faster every year. The systemic stability that the BUS ensured allowed individual participants in the markets that it regulated to come up with workable strategies for hedging against individual counterparties, whether they were cotton buyers in New Orleans, New York, and Liverpool, textile manufacturers in Manchester and Fall River, or banks in London, Philadelphia, New York, and New Orleans—who also all hedged their bets in all kinds of individual ways. To avoid the possibility that they might be left holding the hot potato if cotton prices dropped suddenly, middlemen began insisting on shipping cotton bales on consignment. This meant that each planter still owned his or her crop and bore most of the risk of a drop in price, until a Manchester textile company purchased its bales in the Liverpool cotton exchange.[19]

While planters like Jacob Bieller waited for payment, merchants lent them operating funds that in turn helped tie up the crops of cotton growers in the hands of that same merchant, sometimes over the span of several harvests to come. In the 1820s Bieller regularly sent his cotton (more bales every year, as he bought more slaves and they cleared more acres) to the Natchez broker Alvarez Fisk, a Massachusetts-born man who funneled bank money to planters and cotton to Liverpool.[20] Ultimately, the entire structure was founded on, funded by, the bodies of enslaved people: both on the ability of enslavers to extract cotton from them and on the ability of enslavers (or bankruptcy courts) to sell them to someone else who wanted to extract cotton. The fact that cotton fields were the place where the margins of growth were created presented lenders with both needs and opportunities to hedge against the risk that individual counterparties would default.

Many things could cause individual counterparties, especially planters, to fail on an individual basis. They depended on the bodies and the lives of the same people whom they forced to migrate to a deadly environment, and disease could destroy economic schemes. The cotton country of the Mississippi Valley was hot and wet, and the people transported there died of fevers in great number. One of the chatty letters written by Daniel Draffin, an Englishman Jacob Bieller hired to tutor his grandchildren, described mosquitoes that flew in phalanx formation: "I have been out gunning when I could not take sight they were so numerous." Mosquitoes loved all of the new blood, and there was plenty of it: 155,000 transported from the old slave states to the new ones in the 1820s, for instance, according to the best existing estimate. In 1824–25 J. J. Coiron brought dozens of people from Georgia to his Louisiana slave-labor camp, "Ste. Sophie." This brought the total slave force there to 134, but over the next three years, at least 74 of them died in two separate epidemics. Coiron and his creditors fought in court for the next decade over the bones of the disaster.[21]

Malaria was probably what killed the Georgia migrants, but other diseases could also run wild in the radically new environment of the ghost acres, just as the settlers unwittingly carried weeds adapted to thrive in the disrupted soils of new fields. In 1832–33 cholera raged through the slave-labor camps of Mississippi and Louisiana, carried on the same steamboats that brought new slaves in and took cotton out. At the "Forks in the Road," the huge slave market located just outside of Natchez, Isaac Franklin desperately hid the evidence of epidemic among his "fancy stock of wool and ivory," as his cousin coarsely put it. "The way we send out dead negroes at night and keep dark is a sin," wrote Isaac about dark-lantern burials in the woods behind his barracoon. He kept the secret hidden, and with it the price of men at $700 per, until "I sold Old Man Alsop's two scald headed boys for $800 one of them Took the Cholera the day afterwards and died and the other was very near kicking the Bucket."

During boom times in particular, death rates for the enslaved in the new south-western states and territories were comparable to those in the Caribbean or in the lowcountry of South Carolina.[22]

Then there was simple failure, sometimes for reasons endemic to slavery's new frontiers, sometimes not. Even as cotton markets boomed in the 1830s, for instance, Jacob Bieller plunged into his own personal crash. His fifteen-year-old daughter by his second marriage eloped with an ambitious young local lawyer named Felix Bosworth. It seems likely that Bieller's wife Nancy encouraged the elopement since she too left home in short order, joining her daughter and beginning divorce proceedings. Nancy, who was claiming half of Bieller's property, claimed that not only had Jacob threatened to shoot her in 1827 but for years "he kept a concubine in their common dwelling & elsewhere, publicly and openly." (The courts of Louisiana declined to rule on either charge when they eventually granted the couple a divorce. Jacob's last will gave tacit freedom "to my slaves Mary Clarkson and her son Coulson, a boy something more than five years old, both bright mulattoes.")[23]

In a moment of despair, Jacob wrote inside the cover of a family Bible that his daughter's elopement had "destroyed my welfare, family, and prospects."[24] But it was clear that for him, for Nancy, for Alvarez Fisk and Isaac Franklin, the ultimate hedge against the destruction of prospects and welfare was the relative liquidity of enslaved people. Bieller, for instance, had recently purchased dozens of additional slaves on credit from Isaac Franklin, paying more than $1,000 each and bringing his total number of captives to over eighty.[25] The slaves were usually saleable for highly liquid funds on local markets. All he and Nancy had to debate about was the method: he wanted to sell all those determined to be community rather than separate property and then divide the cash. She wanted to divide the men, women, and children up, "scattering them" intentionally, she wrote. Enslaved people, Nancy said, were "susceptible to a division in kind without injury to us." Or to a sale, so long as the system was not in crisis and there was a steady market, Jacob could have retorted. Either way, the families of the almost one hundred people listed in Bieller's documents would be melted like ice in his summer drink.[26]

For everyone drawing profit from the system, enslaved human beings embodied the ultimate hedge. Cotton merchants, bankers, slave traders—everybody whose money the planter borrowed and could not pay until the cotton was sold at a high enough price to pay off his or her debts—all expected that enslaved people would eventually either (1) make enough cotton to enable the planter to get clear, or (2) be sold in order to generate the liquidity to pay off the debt. In 1824 Vincent Nolte, a freewheeling entrepreneur who almost

cornered the New Orleans cotton market more than once in the 1810s, lent
$48,000 to Louisiana-based enslaver Antonio Walsh. The terms? Walsh had to
pay the money back in four years at an annual rate of about 8 percent. To secure
payment he committed to consigning his entire crop each year to Nolte to be
sold in Liverpool. And, just in case, he also provided collateral: "from 90 to a
100 head of first rate slaves will be mortgaged." In 1824 those nearly five-score
people meant up to $80,000 on the New Orleans auction block.[27]

In 1827 one Louisiana enslaver, drowning in debt thanks to overambitious
leveraging of his sugar labor camp outside of New Orleans, created another
way to turn enslaved people's bodies into money. His financial scheme would
help to revolutionize—and destabilize—the Atlantic economy over the next
ten years. It would also help exile a quarter-million enslaved people from their
homes. So it is perhaps no surprise that J. B. Moussier seems to have thought
up this scheme while he was embroiled in a suit for nonpayment of $21,000
to the firm of Rogers and Harrison, Virginia-based slave traders who had sold
him seventy men, women, and children a few years earlier. What if, Moussier
reasoned, we planters and local merchants create a bank that raises its capital
overseas, from people who need our cotton and sugar—but lends its money
under local control? He went to Hugues Lavergne, a New Orleans local who
was simultaneously a politician, merchant, and a commodity-selling enslaver.
The two men engineered Moussier's idea into the charter of the Consolidated
Association of the Planters of Louisiana, which they rammed through the
Louisiana state legislature in 1827.[28]

The CAPL (despite being called an "association" it was a bank) still used
human beings as collateral so that planters could borrow money from investors in the rest of the industrializing world. But it rearranged the structure of
the existing system of lending and hedging in order to create more leverage for
enslavers at less cost, and on longer terms. It shifted the location of the debt
holder—sometimes right into the family of the borrowing planter—giving a
greater sense of control to the borrower. But it also securitized slaves in such a
way as to hedge even more effectively against losses by the individual investor,
so long as the financial system itself did not fail. Here is how it worked: potential borrowers began by signing up to buy stock in the CAPL. They mortgaged slaves and cultivated land, and received stock certificates in exchange.
The stock certificates enabled them to borrow up to half the face value of the
stock from the CAPL in banknotes.[29]

Yet no one would take these banknotes at face value unless something else
backed them, and the BUS was also going to insist on redeeming those notes
for its own bills, or for precious metal. So how was the CAPL to get liquid

capital? Working in consultation with Thomas Baring, who was visiting as the representative of the great London merchant bank Baring Brothers, Lavergne came up with a solution.[30] The CAPL would mobilize the power of the state—the state of Louisiana—to create an essentially new kind of debt instrument that would allow enslavers to derive multiple streams of income from every slave. Lavergne and the rest of the CAPL board of directors convinced the state government to back the issue of $2.5 million in bonds. These would be due in ten to fifteen years and would pay purchasers an interest rate of 5 percent. Baring Brothers would take the responsibility for selling them on the European securities market. In practice, the Barings and the CAPL told potential investors, the profits of the bank from loan repayments by planters would make the redemption of the bonds absolutely painless. Just in case, the commitment of the "faith and credit" of the state put the taxpayers of Louisiana on the hook should the CAPL somehow default.[31]

In 1828 Lavergne traveled to Britain to finalize the agreement and to hand over the state-backed bonds. Baring gave him in exchange the first payment of what would ultimately be $2.5 million in "sterling bills"—redeemable for silver at the Bank of England in London, if necessary. The Barings set to selling the bonds, which they advertised, while Lavergne packed up his suitcase with the $3.5 million in CAPL banknotes he had had printed up by a London engraver and headed back to New Orleans. The sterling notes would serve as a cash reserve. The CAPL immediately began to leverage that reserve: not only by putting their own hot-off-the-presses banknotes out to planter-stockholders, from which they entered the bloodstream of the US economy, but by issuing commercial credit to local merchants.[32]

The bonds of the CAPL were a true financial innovation, one that dramatically increased enslavers' options. The bonds allowed planters to hedge their risk and maximize their return, redistributing the risk undertaken by stockholders in the bank to all the citizens of Louisiana. (In retrospect, of course, we can see that the risk undertaken by investors in mortgage-backed securities in the last quarter of the twentieth century was ultimately loaded on the US taxpayer, through the agency of bailouts.) The CAPL bonds also converted the biggest investment of the enslaver—human beings, "hands" from Maryland and Virginia and North Carolina and Kentucky—into multiple streams of income. The first stream, of course, was the annual product that enslavers anticipated from the bales of cotton and barrels of sugar that said slaves would be forced to make. The sale of the bonds created a pool of high-quality credit to be lent back to the planters at a rate significantly lower than the rate of return that they could expect that money to produce. That pool could be used for all sorts of income-generating purposes: buying more slaves (to produce more income, to serve as the collateral for still more borrowing) or lending to other enslavers. Clever borrowers could also add to their leverage in additional ways—by borrowing on the same collateral from multiple lenders, by also getting unsecured short-term commercial loans from the CAPL, by purchasing new slaves with the money they borrowed and borrowing on them too. In contrast to what Walsh had to promise Nolte in 1824, this type of mortgage gave the enslaver tremendous margins, control, and flexibility. This was especially true since many of those who borrowed the most from this and similar banks were often officers or relatives of officers of those banks. It was hard to imagine that such borrowers would be foreclosed, even if they fell behind on their payments. After all, they owned the bank themselves.

In effect, slaveowners were now able to monetize their slaves by securitizing them and then leveraging them multiple times on the international financial market. But they also allowed a much wider group of people to profit from the opportunities of slavery's expansion. Perhaps it was no accident that the typical bond issued by the CAPL and the series of copycat institutions that followed was denominated at roughly the price of a field hand—first $500, and a few years later $1000. For the investor who bought it from the House of Baring Brothers or some other seller, a bond was really the purchase of a completely commodified slave: not a particular individual, but a tiny percentage of the income flows derived from each one of thousands of slaves. The investor, of course, escaped the risk inherent in owning an individual slave, who might die, run away, or become rebellious.[33]

In the wake of the CAPL bonds, other banks emerged and created similar securities, which they also sold on European financial markets. In 1831 Edmund Forstall, a merchant and officer of the CAPL, cooked up the idea for the Union Bank of Louisiana while meeting in London with the board of Baring Brothers. This bank was chartered by the legislature in 1832, which allowed it to issue $7 million in state-backed bonds. Baring took on the task of funding the bond issue, giving the bank advances on the sales while dealing them through major London bond brokers like the firm of Gowan and Marx. The massive Citizens' Bank of Louisiana issued its bonds through W. Willinick and Co., merchant bankers of Amsterdam, and most of the $9 million initial issue of securities was purchased by the famous house of Hope and Company, both for speculative resale and for its own investment. Other securities issued between 1828 and 1837 by banks created in Louisiana, Mississippi, Florida, Tennessee, and Alabama were shepherded onto the market by still other major merchant banking houses like the Rothschilds of Paris or de Lizardi and Company of London.[34]

British political economists who criticized slavery during the 1830s objected both to the way that institution denied free choice to sovereign individuals, and to what some of them believed was the inevitable inefficiency of forced labor. Therefore, one might think that British and other European investors, making choices during a decade that saw the emancipation of all slaves in the empire by act of Parliament, would object to purchasing securities that clearly funded the expansion of an immoral and allegedly inefficient institution. But that would be wrong. The objections raised to the southwestern bond issues in the British financial press actually focused on other issues. They wondered if the securitization of slaves really eliminated risk. Were the banks based on a sound footing? Would they repay their debts? And was it safe to invest in a slave economy? An enthusiastic bondholder who wrote to the *Times* of London to defend his investment was parried by the paper's editor, who commented that "he may find himself mistaken in his estimate of the security of the Louisiana planters, or of any estates wholly dependent upon slave labour for their cultivation." Within recent historical memory, the enslaved people of St. Domingue had led a rebellion that destroyed the most profitable colony on earth in the course of the Haitian Revolution. Even more recently, 60,000 Jamaican slaves had risen in revolt during the Christmas holidays at the end of 1831, helping to push Parliament toward centrally mandated emancipation.[35]

These were not questions about the morality of investing in slavery. These were questions about the profitability and security of those investments. And boosters of the southwestern banks responded in the British press on precisely those grounds. They insisted that Louisiana loans, and the other ones modeled on them, were sound because the bank would pay the bonds back out of the profits generated by "this channel of our commerce," one of the most profitable economic sectors on the planet: the slave-labor camps of the lower Mississippi Valley. The bank itself loaned money only on the basis of legally mortgaged property (slaves and land) that (at least in the case of the slaves) had a ready market. In addition, Louisiana planters were not only good at making money, they were also virtuous and steady in their economic dealings. "The whole body of planters are remarkable for their good faith in money transactions . . . it would be difficult to cite an instance of pecuniary loss arising out of default of payment by a Louisiana planter." Beyond that, of course, there was the state guarantee of the bonds, so the investor was hedged in multiple ways against loss.[36]

As for the supposedly incendiary nature of an economy based on a poten-
tially rebellious slave population, Edmund Forstall, president of the Citizens'
Bank of Louisiana, sent talking points for rebutting that idea to his counterparties in the House of Baring. The black population of Louisiana, he claimed,
was no larger than the white. This was more or less accurate, and certainly
the Louisiana slave population was much smaller in a relative sense than that
of St. Domingue. Hence "London and Paris have much more to dread from
their rabble than Louisiana will ever have from her blacks." Since quotations
of Louisiana bond prices appeared opposite stories like the one about a revolutionary's 1835 attempt to assassinate the French king with an "Infernal Machine," and the southwestern banks kept declaring dividends, it is no surprise
that the British press came around. "The profits of banking business in the
South are so striking" that the demand in the market for securities was ready to
soak up more supply, should US federal and state governments permit further
issues of bonds.[37]

Between 1831 and 1834, for reasons about which historians have argued long
and hard without reaching consensus, President Andrew Jackson fought a brutal battle against the Second Bank of the United States. The Bank had pumped
millions of dollars of loans into Mississippi and Louisiana in Jackson's first
term—almost half of the Bank's total balance sheet was there by 1832. But in
large sections of the Southwest the BUS was hated. Creditors are not always
loved by those to whom they lend. Jackson vetoed the recharter of the BUS in
1832 and won reelection that fall against a pro-Bank opponent. The next year,
he ordered the transfer of the government's deposits out of the Bank. Jackson
claimed that by giving the BUS effective control over the financial market, the
federal government had made "the rich richer and the potent more powerful."[38] No doubt it had done so. But he distributed the deposits to a horde of
so-called pet banks—state-chartered institutions that, at least initially, were
run by his political allies, who in turn were often not members of the old
cliques that had run the banks that the BUS treated as favorites. In reaction,
Biddle called in millions of dollars of loans, provoking a recession that began
in late 1833. But by early 1834 he had to concede. The BUS moved on to doing business as a still large, but significantly shrunken, ordinary bank. It was
no longer the regulator of the financial economy in the United States. In fact,
there was now no regulator.[39]

Utopian economists, who took control of the academic profession and
policymaking during the late twentieth century, usually took as their core axiomatic belief about policy the dogma that a self-regulating market will unleash

innovation, leading to the best possible outcome. Unfortunately, the history of the 1830s suggests that unregulated financial markets permit financial innovation that then actually leads to speculative bubbles. Bubbles explode. This hardly seems like the best possible outcome. The innovations that were already straining against BUS control before its disestablishment, and which ran wild after its defeat, had massive, complex consequences for all involved. Not least affected were the enslaved people whose productivity and (as it turned out) futures had been chopped up and sold on distant markets.

Economists of financial crisis, like Hyman Minsky and Charles Kindleberger (both names were highly unfashionable in their profession before 2008), argued that three elements are present in historical bubbles: policymakers who believed markets were stable and did not need regulation; financial innovations that made it easier to create and expand the leverage of borrowers; and what John Cassidy helpfully shorthands as "New Era thinking typified by overconfidence and disaster myopia."[40] By "New Era" thinking he means those who believe that, to quote the title of another recent work on financial panics, "This Time is Different"—that the rules have changed and prices will continue to climb. Hence one can buy into the speculation, even if one must take on large debts to do so, because prices will keep rising and one can sell to some other buyer further down the road. In this way, every boom takes on aspects of a Ponzi scheme. "Disaster myopia," meanwhile, refers to the common propensity of economic actors then and now to underestimate both the likelihood and the likely magnitude of financial panic. The magnitude is exacerbated by the extent of indebtedness and the degree to which individual hedging and leveraging make it likely that pulling at one card will bring down the whole structure.

The destruction of the BUS as the regulator of the financial economy opened the way for all three developments. For several years the anti-BUS elements in Jackson's administration did not make even the slightest gesture toward replacing Biddle's institution with any other check on or within the financial system. In fact, state politicians, to whom the ball was in effect handed, apparently assumed that nothing could go wrong. The pattern of the CAPL proliferated. So did the securities emanating from the Southwest. There were the Union Bank and Citizens' Bank of Louisiana in addition to those created by other states by 1834. After 1834 and the final defeat of the BUS by Jackson, state legislatures only stepped up their creation of bank charters, proceeding as if there was no tomorrow. Louisiana was at the forefront: the New Orleans and Carrollton Railroad and Banking Company—$3 million. The New Orleans Gas Light and Banking Company—$6 million. By 1836 New Orleans was, per resident, probably the US city with the greatest density of bank capital—$64 million in all. "I think we have not yet reached the neighborhood of a sufficiency of Banking Capital," wrote one of Jacob Bieller's correspondents, "but taking this as true I would prefer to approach the point gradually, and not with such rapid strides."[41] And other states and territories in the area, self-consciously copying Louisiana, began to create new banks of their own, each one exploiting the loopholes of the now-unregulated system with innovative financial devices. Mississippi issued $15.5 million in state bonds to capitalize its own Union Bank. By the end of the 1830s, the state-chartered banks of the cotton-growing states had issued bonds denominated at well over $50 million.[42]

Armed with repeated infusions of new cash lent by banks who handed it out with little concern for whether or not the mortgaged property actually existed, southwestern enslavers brought tens of thousands of additional slaves into the cotton states. Some were purchasers, long-time residents in states like Louisiana, Alabama, and Mississippi. Some were new migrants fired by the "spirit of emigration," the belief that "there is scarcely any other portion of the globe" that could permit "the slave holder or merchant of moderate capital" to convert said capital into a fortune. They calculated the money that they would earn from the cotton a "hand" would make: "between three and four hundred dollars" a year, said one man who thought his expectations modest, "though some claim to make six or seven hundred dollars." These were incredible returns on an "asset" purchased for only two or three times the more conservative amount, which could also be mortgaged to produce additional streams of income.[43] So migrants and long-term residents alike trooped to the banks, mortgaged property—some of which they owned, some of which was already mortgaged—and spent the credit they received. Huge amounts of money shifted around: to slave traders, to the sellers of goods like food and cheap clothing, to slave owners in the Chesapeake who sold people to the Southwest, to the banks in Virginia and elsewhere that took their slice of profit as the financiers of the domestic slave traders. By the time the decade was out, at least 250,000 enslaved men, women, and children had also been shifted from the old terrain of slavery to the new. There they were set to work: clearing forests from which Native Americans had recently been evicted by Andrew Jackson's policies; planting cotton seed; tilling it while the harvest neared.[44]

By late 1835 at the latest, the third development of the 1830s' radically new financial world should have been abundantly clear. That was the boom psychology that promoted still more of all the above: more and more opportunities to leverage borrowing and spending, more people caught up in the swirl of euphoria, assuming the speculative bubble would never burst. "Everybody is in debt neck over ears," was the word from Alabama, but slave "traders are not discouraged"; many believed that cotton prices would rise and rise.[45] After 1835 or so the fever of speculation raced up the rivers to the cotton states' trading partners, who were profiting mightily from sales of corn and pork and people. States and territories without slaves or cash crops that were traded on the world market began to issue their own bonds: Illinois, Michigan, Indiana. Purchases of land soared in both the slave and the free states. Waves of speculation rushed through all sorts of markets. Thomas Harrison, after finding that price of land in Kentucky was rising rapidly, wrote to his son, who was trying to invest the family's capital in an Alabama slave-labor camp: "People say that it will never fall again, but this I do not believe. That the whole real property of a state so long settled should increase permanently in value 500 per cent in five years is impossible."[46]

A quarter of a million human beings were moved by force, sold, mortgaged, collateralized, securitized, and sold again 3,000 miles from where they actually toiled. As winters passed, they cleared fields. They planted the newly turned dirt. And in late summer they learned how to pick cotton at the end of a whip. From 1831 to 1837 cotton production almost doubled, rising from 300 million pounds to over 600 million. The bubble had encouraged overproduction. Too much was reaching Liverpool for Manchester to spin and weave, much less to sell to consumers in the form of cloth. Prices per pound at New Orleans, which had begun the boom in 1834 at eighteen cents, slipped to less than ten cents by late 1836. Even as the slowing prices began to pinch in the late summer of 1836, the Bank of England—alarmed at the outflow of capital to the United States in the form of securities purchases—cut its lending. At about the same time, Andrew Jackson issued his Specie Circular, which slowed the purchases of public land but appears to have had little effect on what transpired next in the cotton market. Merchant banks and companies began to call in their loans to each other.[47]

In early 1837 a visitor to Florida, which was already—as it has been ever since—one of the most bubble-prone and speculative parts of the United States, wrote that "there is great risk to the money lender and paper shaver—for the whole land, with very few exceptions, are all in debt for property and a fall in cotton must bring a crash with most tremendous consequences to all trades and pursuits."[48] In fact, the fall had already begun. Back in Britain, low cotton prices failed to cover commercial debts. Three massive Liverpool and London firms, whose finances were completely entangled with each other in a mass of mutual debt that in sunnier days served as hedges, collapsed at the end of 1836. The tsunami rushed across the ocean to their trading partners in New Orleans. By late March each of the top ten cotton-buying firms there had collapsed.

Almost all market actors—planters, cotton merchants, dry-goods merchants, Southern bankers, Northern bankers—now realized that they were both creditors and debtors. But as they scrambled to collect debts from others so that they could pay off their own, two things blocked them from preventing their own individual collapse, blocked their own attempts to use their contingency plans and take advantage of hedging. The first was that their individually rational pursuit of liquidity created a collectively irrational outcome: systemic failure, in fact. As each debtor tried to raise cash by calling in his credits, they all moved ever closer to a full-scale systemic lockup. Suddenly no one was able to pay debts. Buying and selling ground to a halt. An attempt to restart the system on the basis of "post notes"—credit ultimately grounded on future receipts from the 1838 cotton crop—seemed to get things going again. But the 1838 cotton crop was far too large, collapsing prices, and a second, bigger crash in 1839 finished off many of the survivors of the 1837 crash. Meanwhile, a second consequence of the system had emerged: the discovery that most of the debt owed by planters and those who dealt with them was "toxic," to use a recent term. That is, it was unpayable. The planters of Mississippi owed New Orleans banks alone $33 million, one expert estimated, while they could not hope to net more than $10 million from their 1837 crop to pay off that debt. Future crops, which would have to be financed with short-term credit (as would interest payments and/or court fees related to the old debts), would only sink them further into the hole unless cotton prices rose dramatically. Local sources of credit, meanwhile, were collapsing. Nor could they sell off capital to raise cash, because prices for slaves and land, the ultimate collateral in the system, had plummeted in the wake of the first wave of bankruptcy-driven sales, which tapped what little cash there was in the system. This meant that not only was the financial system frozen but that many creditors' balance sheets were overwhelmed.[49]

Massive numbers of cotton-brokerage and plantation-supply firms collapsed. By 1839 the next rank of dominoes began to fall: the southwestern banks, whose currency and credit were now worthless. They were unable to continue to make coupon payments—interest installments on the bonds they had sold on far-off securities markets. Some might have been able to collect tradable currency from their debtors by foreclosing mortgages on slaves and land, but, of course, the markets for those two assets had also fallen dramatically and, in many places, closed up completely. Many enslavers were in still worse shape. They had layered multiple mortgages on each slave. Eventually banks would get them all. So, in state after state, some enslavers allied with nonplanter whites (who didn't want the states to have to tax them in order to pay off the banks' bonds if the banks failed) used political leverage to protect themselves from the consequences of financial overleverage. By the 1840s political pressure for repudiation of the government-backed bonds by the legislatures of several southwestern states and territories grew too intense to resist. Mississippi and Florida were the most notable repudiators in the Southwest. In effect, these polities toxified the bonds themselves, emancipating slave-owning debtors from the holders of slave-backed securities. The power of the state had created the securitized slave, and now the power of the state destroyed it.[50]

The long-term consequences of the panic of 1837 and the succeeding economic disruptions of the next decade remain underexplored and underthought, in no small part because historians have too often segregated financial from social and political histories, considering cultural and economic effects of the panic separately, or not at all.[51] Repudiation and the persistence of toxic debt created multiple problems for southwestern planters. But the enslaved people whom they manipulated as assets faced outcomes more devastating and more immediate. Planters, merchants, and others who had lived off the cotton economy on slavery's frontier struggled through constant legal troubles in the shape of suits for debt collection. The result was often the seizure of property, forced sales of slaves at rock-bottom prices, or the surreptitious removal of slaves.

Beginning in 1837 newspapers like the *New Orleans Picayune* were filled with announcements of court-ordered auction sales of debt-encumbered property. These lasted for half a decade or more. The records of the federal courts of Louisiana, currently housed in Fort Worth, confirm that thousands of enslaved people had changed hands in the lower Mississippi Valley by 1841–42 as a result of the legal processes of the cotton boom's death spiral. After that the federal bankruptcy law offered new options to debtors. Consider John Richardson, a New Orleans merchant and a planter who owned a slave-labor camp in Jefferson Parish outside the city before the panic. He had been both creditor and debtor to dozens of other parties; in the wake of the crash, credit froze and he could pay nothing. Some debts he could delay, but by 1838 he was being sued repeatedly—he owed the Union Bank of Louisiana a large sum of money—a situation that would drag out for years. Richardson tried to transfer his property to his brother-in-law, but creditors found him out and pressed their demands. He was forced to give up some of his slaves to creditors who held mortgages on them. These people would probably be sold at auction, or to slave traders for what they could bring. To raise cash to satisfy other debts, Richardson also had to auction off the few slaves who were not already mortgaged: the men Tom and Jacob (bought by two different purchasers), the woman Caroline and her three children (luckily bought by a single individual), and Squire, sold for $430 to another man, one H. Lockett. Such debacles, which demolished communities, friendships, relationships, and families created out of the wreckage inflicted on enslaved people by the massive forced migration of the 1830s, were a continuous legacy of the panic.[52]

If the domestic slave trade that moved the majority of the quarter-million forced migrants to the Southwest during the 1830s was one major cause of the disruption and atomization of family relationships for African Americans in the nineteenth century, another was the implosion of the financial house of paper constructed to finance the expansion of that trade. Indeed, from 1837 to the late 1840s, when economic hard times finally eased in the Southwest, enslaved migrants to the southwestern states were dragged through what survivors recalled as a second period of disruptive, forced internal migration. Enslavers decamped with mortgaged human property, scampering across state lines or even national ones, into Texas. When he was interviewed in the 1930s about his experience in slavery, centenarian Dave Harper told an employee of the WPA that his mother and he were sold from Virginia to Missouri one hundred years earlier. The crash came and his mother was swept up in an "attachment"—a legal process that forced a debtor to sell specific property. Her owner still owed money to "Nigger traders from Virginia," and so she was sold at auction to raise money. A neighbor intervened and bought her, so her son got to see her from time to time as he grew up. Less lucky was John Bates, whose enslavers moved him and his mother from Arkansas across the border to Texas around the same time. John never saw his father (owned by another enslaver) again, and got to keep nothing from him but his last name.[53]

Financial innovation in the 1820s and 1830s had massive, unforeseen, and often ironic consequences. These were consequences in the "real" world, the "real" economy, and the "real" social world. True, there is something magical, fictitious, and strange about commodifying houses, land, and, most of all, human beings. Each of those things has its own claim to being treated as something unique, with moral rights. The house is constructed more by the lives that are lived in it—and the ideology-ridden hopes that are assigned to it—than by the wood and skills of the carpenter. The land is still more immovable than the house, and teems with claims, both human and nonhuman, historical and ecological. And the securitization of a human is far more foreign to the moral sensibilities of most. The financialization of American slavery that took off in the late 1820s was even more devastating since it incorporated and then amplified the internal slave trade's disruptions. It turned people into numbers, the values of their bodies and labor into paper, chopped them, recombined them by legislative fiat, carried them in suitcases across the ocean, and sold them to people on other continents—some of whom undoubtedly believed that they believed in emancipation.

On one level, if the abstractions and thefts of human value that allowed the financialization of human beings are not fiction, then nothing is. And yet, these things were done, and the chopping and the moving and the commodifying of people became social reality—reality with significant consequences. For enslaved people, the reality was grim and devastating. Meanwhile, the disruptions that limited enslavers' credit, curtailed their entrepreneurial schemes, and made them feel less-than-equal in the national economy affected how they thought about the Union, and how they thought about their role within the global project of modernity. They could not escape from these questions, which galled them every time they heard from their creditors. Many of their debts ended up in the hands of Northern firms. Entire plantations were foreclosed. Brown Brothers, the New York merchant bank that would become Brown Brothers Harriman, collected multiple Louisiana sugar and cotton plantations in the 1840s, while the receivers of Nicholas Biddle's old Bank—in bankruptcy by the 1840s—took possession of hundreds of Mississippi slaves and thousands of acres of land in the same decade. Other creditors left nominal ownership of the property in the hands of their debtors but attached their tentacles to the streams of income that issued from the plantation, claiming interest first and principal second. These attempts to collect increasingly brought Southern planters to recalculate the value of the Union. Nor could Southern entrepreneurs easily recapitalize their own institutions. After repudiation, outside investors were cautious about lending money to Southern institutions.[54]

In the 1830s it was an open question as to where the center of gravity of the national financial economy would be located. Philadelphia, home of the BUS, and New Orleans were both in contention. But by the early 1840s Wall Street and New York had emerged as the definitive victor. Enslavers continued to supply virtually all of the industrial world's most important commodity, but the inability of Southern planters to pay debts, control their own financing for future expansion projects, or get the capital that would enable them to diversify led them to lose massive skimmings of their profits to financial intermediaries and creditors. So they sought greater revenues in the only ways that they could. The first was by making more and more cotton. They forced on enslaved people an incredible intensity of labor, developed new kinds of seed, and expanded their acreage, but the increase in cotton production (which rose from 600 million pounds in 1837 to 2 billion in 1859) was more than the market could absorb. The price remained low in most years, compared to historic levels, only exacerbating the problems of cotton growers.

The second route Southern planters took was to seek new slave territory, not just to add to the land that they could cultivate, but to acquire land with the hope of provoking a new boom. Unleashing the animal spirits of speculation on new territories had almost worked before, so why not try it again by acquiring California, Cuba, Mexico, or Kansas for slavery? The result of the commitment of political capital to that end was, of course, the Civil War, in which the consequences of the long-term financial difficulties of the cotton economy played a major role in the South's defeat. In the end, the reverberations set off by the leveraging of slavery's inequities into further equity for those who exploited them were, ironically, what brought the structure of real-life slavery crashing down.

Acknowledgments

For careful readings and thoughtful suggestions, I would like to thank the following individuals: Michael Zakim, Donnette Chambers, Thomas Humphrey, Gregg Lightfoot, Barry Strauss, Robert Wright, and an anonymous reviewer for the University of Chicago Press. For suggestions and assistance during the research and writing that led to this essay, I thank Germain Bienvenu and the staff of the Lower Louisiana and Mississippi Valley Collections at the Hill Special Collections Library of Louisiana State University, Richard H. Kilbourne, and Sophia Robinson. An earlier version of this essay was the text for a meeting of the Cornell University Department of History Faculty Colloquium: I thank Thomas Balcerski, Cynthia Brock, Judith Byfield, Derek Chang, Duane Corpis, Ray Craib, Paul Hyams, Mary Beth Norton, Eric Tagliacozzo, Robert Travers, Robert Vanderlan, Claudia Verhoeven, and Rachel Weil for their invaluable questions and suggestions during and after that discussion. Finally I gratefully acknowledge the support of a short-term Fellowship for the Study of the Global South from Tulane University.

4

Inheriting Property and Debt
From Family Security to Corporate Accumulation

Elizabeth Blackmar

In the early years of the American republic, death rivaled and shadowed the market as the occasion for reckoning value and transferring property. When someone died, property changed hands. In an economy organized through personal proprietorship and household enterprise, the transactions that followed the death of free adults touched creditors, kin, and neighbors alike. "The whole property of the community, both real and personal, passes through" the probate courts, Lemuel Shaw observed in 1821.[1] The administration of estates exposed the inner workings of the institutions of property—and especially the changing status of land—in the transition from family capitalism to corporate capitalism.

In an agrarian world, property meant first and foremost land—"real property." Through the early modern era, European landed societies countered the catalytic effect of death through customs and law that insulated real property from creditors and privileged its descent to male heirs. So powerful was the En-

93

glish regulation of the transfer of land through inheritance that as late as 1874 7,000 people (0.007 of all landowners) owned 80 percent of the land in Great Britain.[2] By contrast, colonial settlers gained early access to land, and by the time of the American Revolution, real property constituted the prime asset of three-quarters of free households.[3]

Widespread land ownership went hand in hand with fundamental shifts in laws governing its devise at death, none more important than colonial statutes permitting the creditors of the deceased to lay claim to the value of real property when personal property—livestock, crops, furnishings—proved insufficient to satisfy a debt. Such protection of creditors anchored the extended exchanges of communities that lacked for cash.[4] In the aftermath of the Revolution, state lawmakers declared the unencumbered circulation of land to be a fundamental precept of a republican society and abolished primogeniture and entail, alongside all manner of "feudal tenures." Most states adopted the system of partible inheritance, all children receiving equal shares from an estate in the absence of a will. Legislatures also reconfirmed probate laws that tied the new republic's greatest resource to the demands of creditors, whether or not land had been specifically offered as collateral for loans. These policies did more than free land to market exchange, however. They also recognized local social orders constituted through proprietorship and personal obligation that underlay family capitalism.

Real property remained the economic as well as imaginative foundation of the republican and largely agrarian social order through the first half of the nineteenth century. Yet, by 1875, despite the persistence of comparatively widespread ownership and the great expanse of unoccupied land, the United States had ceased to be a landed society. Most Americans could no longer confidently identify land with security, opportunity, or personal wealth. Social critics blamed land monopolies and eastern creditors, as well as waged labor, for closing down access to proprietorship, whether across the Great Plains or in growing cities. Many Americans, however, encountered the changing value of land ownership within a volatile industrializing economy most immediately in the changing conditions of its transfer over generations, that is, in the displacement of land as patrimony.

Where estates had once rested on the security of land as both a resource for livelihood and a means of storing wealth, probate became a primary site for settling debts and liquidating real property, contributing to its transformation into new forms of capital beyond the governance of families. Land remained a means of agricultural production, a "factor" of industrial production, and an outlet for savings, of course. But the gradual assimilation of real property to instruments of debt and finance laid the foundation for the new property regime of American corporate capitalism in which security—and implicitly wealth—derived from claims to income generated by intangible assets rather than from real property that sustained direct productive activity.

The uncertainties and conflicts that accompanied the settling and administration of estates reveal the uneven process through which the institution of real property as a foundation of family capitalism eroded in the nineteenth century. In arbitrating disputes probate courts oversaw, domesticated, and disciplined new practices of investment. Yet by the end of the century probate itself—like families—had ceased to represent a primary channel for the flow or accumulation of property. The corporate organization of finance borrowed heavily on family practices for two generations before achieving autonomous institutional power, a power most viscerally symbolized in the corporation's juridical immunity from death.

Heirs and Creditors under Family Capitalism

During the era of "family capitalism" that extended through the 1840s, most productive property was owned by individuals who relied on household labor— their own and that of family members, servants or apprentices who received their keep as well as training, and, in the South, slaves—to produce both subsistence and surplus for exchange.[5] Free children understood their inheritance as a deferred payment for their contribution to the household economy as well as an entitlement of birth. Even as Northern proprietors turned to wage labor in crafts and manufacturing, family firms formed the model for partnerships among unrelated owners. Merchants especially relied on family connections to place trusted agents on ships and in ports around the world. Marriage served as an occasion both to transfer property through daughters to sons-in-law, many of whom entered the family enterprise, and to forge new kinship alliances.

In a world in which loans provided the glue that held communities together through the miseries of "scarce money" and "poor markets," family and commercial obligations often intersected. Family members called on one another not only for loans but also to serve as sureties, guarantors who were answerable for the loan should the debtor default on its payment. The book debt of most farmers, planters, shopkeepers, and artisans kept track of exchanges with kin, neighbors, and tradesmen across several towns; some proprietors periodically settled up their book debts, others kept them open ended for years.[6] Death, however, always brought a settlement and, indeed, provided the ultimate security for loans alongside a reckoning of family obligations.

Americans relied on local custom as well as law for disposing of the property of the deceased, but the general procedures recurred throughout the new nation. Within days of a death wills had to be proved before magistrates or justices of the peace who authorized executors named in the will. When property owners died intestate, that is, without a will, courts appointed administrators, most often a widow or son, but also creditors. Considered the "personal representatives" of the deceased, executors and administrators posted bonds with sureties to guarantee that they did not misuse the property in their hands. Courts also appointed appraisers to draw up detailed inventories of estates. Newspapers announced probate appointments, which placed creditors on notice to submit their claims within a year. Administrators found debts listed in account books, often without interest, or they sifted through personal bonds and scraps of promissory notes. By the early nineteenth century statutes against fraud required all contracts to be written, but administrators and judges continued to wrestle for decades with the claims of parole—spoken—loans and bequests and especially with the question of whether proprietors intended gifts to children to be reckoned as advances on the estate. For most households, for good or for ill, estates were settled, creditors paid, and any remaining property distributed to heirs within a year.

Proprietors who wrote wills conventionally directed that their "just debts" be paid, but most of their energy went into providing for family members. Before the Revolution, farmers and planters devised land with the expectation that their heirs would continue to look to agriculture for their livelihood. Colonial farmers had lovingly and precisely detailed in their wills the physical features of land bestowed on sons, with the eldest frequently receiving double shares in the North or the largest plantation in the South and younger sons inheriting outlying properties, often acquired with their interests in mind. Well into the nineteenth century, many a farmer's or planter's will balanced specific fields, pastures, woodlots, and mill streams to arrive at a sustainable farmstead or plantation for each son. Both law and custom secured widows' dower right to a life interest in one-third of the value of land. Before the Revolution and even after, daughters most often received their inheritance in personal property made as marriage settlements or bequeathed as legacies to be paid by their brothers or by administrators settling the estate. In the ports, merchants and successful artisans regularly devised town lots, purchased with the profits of trade, with the expectation of rental income providing annuities for widows as well as a patrimony for heirs.

Partible inheritance changed probate practices at the end of the eighteenth century.[7] Whether out of more egalitarian sentiments or in recognition of the exhaustion of family farmsteads, Northern farmers not only ceased to favor oldest sons but increasingly directed that their land be sold in order to insure that each son and daughter receive an equal share of the family property. Southern planters continued to favor eldest sons, yet they too authorized in their wills the selling of land—often in preference to the selling of slaves—in order to facilitate the distribution of legacies as well as to settle debt. As statutes institutionalized partible inheritance for proprietors who died without a will, administrators also moved from partitioning land directly among heirs to arranging for equal distribution of the returns from its sale. Historians have argued that partible inheritance recognized the claims of daughters and younger sons at the same time that lawmakers and judges were contracting the dower rights of widows. When land was sold rather than partitioned, the widow's claim on her husband's realty converted to the interest on one-third of the proceeds from sale, often of less value for support than the use of land.[8]

Whatever the sentiments expressed in wills toward family members, probate laws first and foremost governed the settlement of debts. Americans followed English precedent in providing that debts of the deceased should be paid from the personal property—stock in trade, perishable crops, livestock, household furnishings, banknotes—but also expected land to be sold if personal property did not suffice. The distinctions between personal and real property especially troubled heavily indebted Southern planters, who both cast themselves in the image of England's landed gentry and knew that the value of their lands—and hence their estates—rested entirely on slave labor.[9] Throughout the eighteenth century, lawmakers in Virginia and South Carolina had experimented with defining slaves as real property in order to insulate them from sale for an estate's debts. In the end, the best Southerners could do was to place slaves in a category between moveable goods and land in the legal priority for attachment for debt.[10]

Credit flowed in two directions and until an administrator added up what the deceased was owed and received all the claims against an estate, it was impossible to know what remained to the heirs and legatees. Many an heir expressed shock as probate dashed their great expectations. "Though I was prepared from previous accounts to receive tidings of a considerable depreciation in the value of the property, I confess my gloomiest apprehensions embraced nothing so truly sad and appalling as the vast & astounding reduction announced in your letter; and I am sure my disinterested and excellent father himself conceived of nothing so perfectly disastrous," the Reverend David Parker wrote to lawyer William Minot in Boston concerning his father Nathan's estate in 1831.[11]

Based on his successful trade with Newfoundland and London, the children of Deacon Nathan Parker had every reason to expect a handsome patrimony. But at the merchant's death in 1831, it was discovered that his determination to use his wealth to serve his God left his heirs an unusual form of real property: some 105 pews in the Union Meeting House on Essex Street.[12] In 1818 Deacon Parker had given a bond and mortgage to purchase land for the new church, but he had failed in his effort to auction the pews—estimated by one son "at a valuation of $22,000"—in order to pay off the mortgage and cover construction costs. After the deacon's death, Minot urged the heirs not to sell the pews in a depressed market, noting that the congregation was trying to recruit a "popular clergyman . . . who will build up the church and give value to their property."[13]

Other forces ate away at the deacon's stored wealth. In addition to a one-fourth share of land inherited from his own father (and subject to his step-mother's dower), Parker had placed his savings in mortgages, shares in a mill dam and two bridges, and US bonds. Not only had the pews depreciated, Parker's administrator reported, a judgment against one debtor for $2,773 "is not probably worth more than one-half its nominal value, as he is poor and unable to pay his debts in full" and his wife held the house in her own name; moreover, the bridge stocks sold for "less than the appraisement, owing to the depression of the value of bridge shares, by reason of a steam boat ferry."[14] In the end, Parker's three surviving children each received $3,800, from which the administrator deducted advances made to them during their father's lifetime.[15] It was a substantial sum, however much Parker's heirs felt their expectations blasted by their father's piety.

The settlement of more modest estates reveals an essential vulnerability of family capitalism, for proprietary independence was often jerrybuilt on credit. Nathan Brooks, a lawyer in Concord, Massachusetts, administered many of his neighbors' estates as well as those as of his own extended family. In 1821, when the hatter Joseph Brown died, he owned a farmstead, meadow, orchard, and several wood lots, together valued at $3,400, and a personal estate appraised at $2,595 that included household furnishings, notes due from customers and neighbors, and his stock in trade of hats, furs, felt, and lamb's wool. But when Brooks submitted his final account as administrator, the estate still owed $4,300 to 139 creditors, more than half of them for sums of less than ten dollars. The court ordered sixty cents on the dollar "of their respective debts, which is all that they can receive until some further discovery of said deceased's estate or till his widow's death."[16]

Samuel Burr, a Concord storekeeper, one-time state representative, and a director of the Middlesex Fire Insurance Company (organized in 1826), also appeared to be a substantial proprietor when he died in 1829. Burr owned real property valued at $4,480 and a personal estate worth $6,800, including notes due from thirty-two different debtors valued at $5,400. As it turned out, Burr had raised funds by mortgaging his land, and his own total debts came to $12,763. Brooks was a tenacious administrator who kept the estate open for years as he tried to collect and pay debts. By 1849 the estate's creditors had still received only forty-one cents on the dollar for their remaining claims, which, with interest, had risen to $20,127.95 over the course of twenty years.[17] The estates of many Concord farmers fared no better when death stopped the flow of exchange only to reveal insolvency.

On the face of things, it seems something of a paradox that a country so abundantly endowed with land (once taken from Indians) could not directly sustain proprietorship over generations. Yet the failure of republican patrimony emerged from the very institutions that supported household enterprise. With free farm families averaging six or seven children, estates propelled the dispersal of property over each generation, and even where land remained relatively cheap, indebtedness itself steadily increased with the costs of taxes, tools, machinery, and the addition of livestock, fields, or barns. If creditors' claims diminished the size of estates, the pressure of competition from more fertile lands to the west further devalued the property of heirs along the eastern seaboard. In the South, the heirs of planters had the peculiar advantage of being able to transport their most valuable property—slaves—with them to new, more fertile territories.[18] The majority of Southern farmers, however, did not own slaves. Merchants, artisans, and small manufacturers faced the same conditions of partible inheritance and debt when it came to passing on the fruits of their trade. Partnerships dissolved upon the death of one of the proprietors, and repeated bankruptcies, before and after death, punctuated American enterprises in the early nineteenth century, leaving firms—like farms—to be repeatedly reorganized or started anew.[19]

The weight attached to "opportunity" in republican discourse acknowledged the simple fact that the division of estates left the majority of heirs with limited resources, at best, for starting up a farm or a shop. Whether or not they could make a go of it depended on the composition of their own households and their own ability to secure loans. The anger of workingmen in the 1830s rested in part on the recognition that in the absence of patrimony wages did not suffice to save the means to independence. But the failure of patrimony loomed largest in the public imagination in the figure of widows and orphans left destitute by a proprietor's death.

Between 1829 and 1831 Massachusetts appraisers valued just under two-fifths of the 3,698 estates in that state at less than $500.[20] Such an estate might at best generate $25 a year for a widow or leave a meager inheritance for children. The poorest households had little reason to go through probate, though widows continued to look to the courts to shield them from voracious creditors.[21]

But as uneven economic expansion generated new mercantile fortunes in the early republic, estates also appeared as repositories of new wealth. The top one-fifth of Massachusetts estates exceeded $5,000, with eleven estates valued at more than $100,000. The wills of merchant princes of Boston and Salem—like those of New York and Philadelphia—displayed their confidence in their own prosperity by endowing widows handsomely and making outright bequests of $10,000 to sons and daughters (for the latter often in the form of a mansion upon their marriage) in addition to a share of the estate's remaining property worth upwards of $50,000.[22]

Against the backdrop of the failure of patrimony to endow most American farmers and artisans with the means of independence, then, stood a second family plot, the turning of the property of the most successful families into investment capital. Indeed, family property laid the foundation for accumulation that derived not from labor but from the placement of savings to generate first interest and then dividends, a corporate claim to the surplus produced by labor. By the early nineteenth century, the logic of investment—the deployment of property to generate income—was well established in mercantile circles. Yet the administration of estates, under the close supervision of probate courts, provided the occasion to organize investment widely and channel family property into domestic institutions of capital accumulation.

Probate Courts and the Discipline of Investment

In the wake of the American Revolution state legislatures spent fifty years revising probate laws, both expanding the number of probate courts—variously named orphans' court, courts of chancery, surrogate courts, and, in the South, the ordinary courts—and extending the powers of equity, which in England governed personal estates, mortgages, guardianships, and trusts.[23] In addition, courts appointed numerous adjuncts—clerks and registers, commissioners, masters in chancery—who were charged with auditing the accounts of estates and trusts and insuring their conformity to the courts' standards of faithful administration. So central did local courts and their officers become in governing the administration of property that in South Carolina, as Thomas Russell has shown, court-ordered sales operated as the largest slave market in the state.[24]

Courts aimed first and foremost to enforce contracts and to quiet title, confirming the instruments of exclusive ownership. Much of the business of probate continued to revolve around determining the relation and divided interests of real property and personal property, for land retained legal privileges that added both to its security and its value. Title to land descended directly to heirs, whereas the personal representative of the deceased held the personal property (whether tangible personal property like livestock and furnishings or intangible property like financial notes) until the estate was settled and legacies distributed. Land thus insulated could not be sold for debt until all personal property had been exhausted, and even then heirs—like owners who mortgaged their land—retained a right of redemption, that is, the right to purchase back land from creditors within a year. Yet with privileges came obligations.[25] Whereas contracts dispatched the transfer of titles to moveable goods or money, transfers of real property frequently carried conditions that set limits on the rights of ownership. Judges' opinions devoted pages to determining what heirs could or could not do with inherited land and how far to extend the definition of real property. With a lengthy historical exposition, Judge Lemuel Shaw explained in 1855 why a share in an incorporated Boston wharf company was real rather than personal property and thus could not be used to satisfy the debts of an heir who died before the widow, who held a life interest as her dower right.[26]

Courts also enforced statutes that ranked the priority of an estate's creditors and in doing so established the value and security of different kinds of claims. After taxes, court judgments, the widow's dower right, and the sums owed doctors at a final illness, undertakers, and landlords came debts "under seal," that is, bonds secured by mortgage and recorded with the county clerk. Given the costs and nuisance of recording mortgages, eighteenth-century proprietors frequently had relied on personal bonds backed up by sureties to secure large loans. If the debtor could not pay, creditors could take the sureties to court for satisfaction. Such bonds and other contractual debts (including bills of exchange on goods) still ranked ahead of mere promissory notes, which covering lesser amounts, had served as the effective currency before 1820. Personal bonds, however, required knowledge of the guarantors' own assets and reliability, knowledge harder to come by as Americans began migrating to western lands and to cities. Mortgages, by contrast, secured loans with a known and durable asset.

The legal priority assigned to mortgages reinforced perceptions that land represented security in a dual sense, as a usable resource and as indestructible backing for credit. By the 1790s merchants and farmers regularly turned to mortgages to place surplus funds out at interest for a term of years, on the one side, or to obtain funds for their enterprise, on the other. With access to European creditors frequently blocked by imperial politics, merchants especially used real property as leverage to raise money for their commercial adventures. At the same time, they continued to invest the profits of trade in the purchase of land, which stored family wealth but could also be used to mobilize it. The mercantile boom that accompanied American commerce with India and China, as well as the wheat trade to war-ravaged Europe, spurred the purchase of land that in turn secured new mortgages. Credit and land markets thus expanded together, creating a primary circuit of investment for family property, a circuit that probate courts extended by encouraging administrators and guardians to put the undistributed funds from estates into mortgages as a secure investment. Mortgages generated much of the domestic capital of the early republic.

Probate courts oversaw another legal instrument of family property, the trust.[27] The practice of conveying property to a trustee who managed it on behalf of beneficiaries dated from the seventeenth century and was most commonly used to provide for dependents, especially orphaned children. By the late eighteenth century, more and more wealthy proprietors created trusts in their wills as a way of controlling their property from beyond the grave. The increase in trusts for adult beneficiaries as well as minors went hand in hand with the spread of partible inheritance, for it was daughters' property that most often went into the hands of trustees in order to protect it from the debts of their husbands. Trusts—like the laws of dower—distinguished between life estates, that is, the right to the benefits or income from property during the lifetime of the beneficiary, and residual estates, the right to all the remaining property (or as it was increasingly called, the capital) after those holding a life estate themselves died. Full inheritance was thus often contingent on subsequent death; in the interim, property had to be managed as an investment, its use organized to deliver a steady stream of revenue.

Where administering estates meant managing property over time, courts acted not just to establish the rules for settling debts or distributing legacies but also to determine precepts of sound investment. From the 1790s through the 1840s, the judiciary took charge of disciplining customary practices of probate. In the process courts brought commercial reasoning and accounting into the affairs of households and communities accustomed to informal arrangements and personal prerogatives in managing family property.

At the most basic level, courts enforced an imperative to invest rather than let family property "lie idle."[28] Judges found trustees, executors, or guardians who simply held on to property without generating revenues liable for waste ("devastit," in the language of the law). Following a legislative directive in 1817,

New York's Court of Chancery introduced new procedures for masters in chancery, appointed by judges, to review annually the records of estates and report "whether the accounts have been correctly kept, whether there has been any waste or misapplication of the funds, and whether the same are properly or safely invested or secured."[29] The masters held hearings and took evidence when they had doubts about an account, and their reports often determined whether guardians or trustees could sell, mortgage, or improve real property on behalf of their beneficiaries. Surviving reports from Albany County in the 1830s and 1840s show the difficulties of disciplining farmers and merchants used to keeping their own accounts and their own counsel.

James King, a master in chancery in the 1830s, found widespread ignorance or indifference to the court's rules for keeping accounts. Again and again he complained of "the very unsettled condition" of estates with inventories "very inartfully stated" and "personal property not valued."[30] King repeatedly urged the "expediency of having printed forms of inventories and accounting to be appended to every order appointing a trustee, committee or guardian." Such forms would overcome "the extreme ignorance of some trustees etc. in stating their accounts" and "abridge the vexation and trouble to which officers or the court are subjected in examining such accounts."[31]

Most vexing to the chancery masters were administrators who failed to state "in what manner" they managed balances that ranged from several hundred dollars to nearly $3,000. Money from the sale of real estate "does not appear to be invested or secured except by the personal responsibility of said guardian and his sureties," one master complained. "The infants money should be loaned and security taken on real estate by mortgage or paid into this court or deposited in a savings bank under the direction of the court," King echoed in another case. Particularly incensed by a guardian who managed the "pecuniary interests" of his four wards' estate with "an unprecedented degree of looseness, most egregiously, providing no record of how he had used their funds," King demanded the court intervene. The guardian in turn filed "a formal protest against the manner in which this court requires him to account."[32]

Still, the masters found some accounts exemplary. In 1824 Margaret Jones, wife of a prominent Manhattan landowner and the court-appointed guardian of her two orphaned nieces, submitted an exhaustive final account with four attached schedules specifying every dollar received and expended. When she took charge of her wards' inheritance in 1815, she continued to hold the bulk of her brother-in-law's previous investments—nine mortgages totaling $29,000. Jones used the income from interest to meet her nieces' expenses, including paying for clothing, schoolbooks, laundry, music lessons, ribbons, and the services of a governess, hairdresser, and dentist. She reinvested the remainder. At the end of her guardianship, each niece received just over $28,000, a tidy return that positioned the wards in the marriage market for which they had been so assiduously prepared. In approving the report the master in chancery effusively commended the guardian's "prudence and judgment" in managing the property for the children's advantage while taking no compensation for her services.[33]

Jones stood out not only when compared to inexperienced guardians or trustees whom courts sought to train in the proper arts of accounting and investment; her administration also contrasted to that of gentlemen who saw little difference between their own business affairs and their fiduciary responsibilities to heirs. In 1823 the orphaned wards of the patrician merchant and rentier Frederic De Peyster—their maternal uncle—challenged his final account as their guardian since 1802. Taking control of an estate valued at more than $60,000—most of it in Brooklyn farmlands—De Peyster had held "large balances no less than $8,000, sometimes exceeding $13,000" from rent, his wards charged, but kept no accounts of his investments, even as he paid himself commissions on both collections and expenses for the wards' maintenance. De Peyster answered that he found it "more convenient and at least equally safe to suffer the moneys to remain in his own hands." He had not invested the property because the War of 1812 had rendered stocks "precarious" and "investments on bond and mortgage were, generally, attended with difficulty."[34] De Peyster had not only used the estate's income for his own purposes but also paid for his wards' maintenance out of the capital. His wards demanded their uncle pay $38,000—the legal interest of 7 percent computed on the value of the estate semiannually since 1802—because properly invested, the estate would have yielded interest every six months and any funds not required for the children's maintenance would have been added to the principal. After a five-year battle, New York's highest court ruled in favor of the wards: "If the trustee neglects to make investments he ought to be made chargeable with the interest of the unemployed funds."[35]

As probate judges enforced the "duty to invest," they also tried to uphold the benevolence of administering family property. Shocked by trustees who followed mercantile customs and paid themselves 5 percent commissions for their collections and dispersals, Chancellor James Kent invoked English precedent in 1815, ruling that "a trust is regarded in chancery as a matter of honor and conscience and undertaken with humane or friendly or charitable, and not with mercenary, views."[36] But if charging commissions "debased the sanctity" and "honorable duty" of administering family property, other judges more readily conceded that "it is not to be expected that executors should sacrifice their time and subject themselves to hazard without some remuneration."[37] In response to growing disputes lawmakers gradually instituted new guidelines. Some states fixed commissions at 2 percent; others gave probate judges discretion to set trustees' payments. Still, across the country judges faced ever more complex challenges as they sought to secure the investment of family property while at the same time preserving the distinctively disinterested character of family obligation, that is, as they tried to reconcile the duty to invest with the fiduciary duty to withstand the temptations as well as the logic of capitalist enterprise.

Executors and Shifting Terrain of Landed Wealth

With probate courts aggressively supervising executors and trustees, lawyers began to supplant kin in the administration of many large estates by the 1820s. In major cities probate became a specialized legal practice. Much of the lawyers' work revolved around the management of both land and mortgages—the core of most large estates. Yet as new venues of investment opened, most especially government bonds and bank stocks, the requirement that administrators securely place property "at interest" begged the questions of what constituted security and what level of interest satisfied the requirements of prudence. If land represented the epitome of security, administrators nonetheless discovered that its management presented constant headaches and unexpected costs. By the 1830s, after a generation of struggling to make land pay, administrators in the Northeast reinforced a movement of family wealth away from land, both in the form of direct ownership and as collateral for credit.

Northern merchants had long stored wealth in town lots, and executors and trustees in Boston, New York, and Philadelphia found themselves serving as landlords to deliver income to heirs. Conventional wisdom held that land should yield 5 percent of its value in annual ground rents. For all that rent established the standard for a secure return, however, its collection intimately tied wealthy families to the disquietudes of labor markets and cycles of commerce. When shipping dried up following the 1807 embargo and then war with Britain, rents fell. Estates that owned houses erected during the boom years of the 1790s faced increasing maintenance costs twenty-five years later, as well as competition from new buildings after commerce recovered. Common law allowed executors little power to improve real property unless explicitly authorized by the deceased's will or by a court order, and few executors or trustees welcomed the burden and risks of new construction. But feeling pressure to capture the gains of a revived real estate market, some administrators turned to the courts for permission to mortgage or improve land. New York masters in chancery generally supported petitions to raise funds to replace "dilapidated houses" with new stores that would bring three times the rent to heirs.[38] Yet, many a trustee simply deferred to common law restraints and secured the return in rents by subdividing old houses for multiple working-class tenants. As the estates of some of the nation's most prominent citizens became slumlords, their administrators hired agents to collect rents, willingly paying 5 percent commissions to be freed of the difficulties of personally managing the property.[39]

Collecting rents to realize the value of land as an investment was even harder in the countryside, where many an estate consisted of scattered tracts of meadows, woodlots, and fields, each leased to a different farmer. The maintenance of leased property took on a different meaning in the South, where executors were more likely—and indeed were often required by judges—to rent out slaves. Though the lessees of slaves remained liable for the year's rent even if the slave became ill or ran away, executors knew that at any moment the property could be entirely lost to death. In preference to either leasing or selling slaves, laws in Georgia and Alabama permitted administrators to continue to operate plantations in order to generate income for heirs prior to an estate's final settlement.[40]

The solidity of family wealth invested in *unsettled* land proved especially illusionary. In the early republic, enterprising land agents organized syndicates to take advantage of generous federal policies and acquire thousands of acres in Maine, Ohio, Georgia, Tennessee, and points extending ever west. Seldom did the original investor live to see any return from these speculations, however, for their very value lay in prospective settlement. In the absence of a known market, appraisers often did not assign value to "wild lands" that were listed in inventories. Collecting the unearned increment of land purchased during speculative bubbles plagued heirs and executors for generations to come.

In 1792 Benjamin Comstock and his brother Joseph, merchants of Providence, Rhode Island, jointly purchased one share in the Ohio Company—organized in 1784 and controlling millions of acres in the Northwest Territory—for five shillings, roughly 62 cents.[41] When Benjamin died in 1828 at age eighty-one, his will devised three-fourths of his five-sixth stake to three surviving children and one-fourth to the five children of a deceased son.[42] When the Comstock share was converted into titles to specific land, it included one entire section of 640 acres, a 262-acre tract of "rough land" in Meigs County, and scattered other parcels. Benjamin's son and executor, William Comstock, relied on the Ohio land agent David Putnam to seek purchasers and pay taxes, which increased as local governments started building schools and courthouses.[43] In 1839 Putnam warned Comstock that unknown persons "have been cutting and taking off timber" from the Meigs County land and that invoking the law of trespass "would be only a threat, about which these desperados would as little regard as the whistling wind."[44]

The depression that followed the panic of 1837 hit the land market hard, and though he arranged to have the land surveyed, Putnam reported that "since 1840 our land sales have been almost totally suspended in consequence of the scarcity of money among our people. They have no money to buy or to pay for what they have heretofore bought."[45] Sixty-two years after the organization of the Ohio Company, the Comstock family had received some $2,500 for the land encompassed by their one share.[46] It was an impressive return on 62 cents, but the expenses of managing the investment nonetheless consumed at least half that sum. William Comstock divided the payments among his father's eight beneficiaries and the cousins who still held a one-sixth stake.

In 1849 William Minot advised heirs of an interest in a 6,000-acre tract of Virginia land acquired by their grandfather to accept a local land agent's offer of three-fourths of the paper value of deeds and mortgages from scattered purchasers. Most of the land had long since been lost to squatters' assertion of preemption rights, but Virginia courts had protected the portion held by heirs who had not come of age. Minot regretted that one heir expressed dissatisfaction with the terms of the deal:

> I have had a good deal of experience of the value of wild lands in Maine and know the great difficulty of obtaining payment after sales are made. The purchasers are of course settlers of little or no property, whose only hope of paying anything is generally out of the timber they may cut or the crops they may raise and these hopes are in a majority of cases frustrated and the land taken back and sold again. I have known as many as three sales of the same lot before anything was paid. I apprehend things are still worse in Virginia, which is a poor state in which few new settlements are made.[47]

Such stories appear in the correspondence of virtually every executor or trustee who managed multiple large estates. Again and again, heirs along the eastern seaboard found that they paid taxes on lands in Maine or Alabama or Illinois but could neither sell nor lease the property. Again and again, distant agents reported that money was scarce, they had no way to establish the value of the land, squatters had cut down timber, and that new taxes or assessments were due.

The nuisance of managing tenants and the abysmal failure of absentee
ownership of "wild land" in the 1830s and 1840s underscored the advantages
of placing family wealth in personal rather than real property. Mortgages, of
course, had long straddled that distinction. In contrast to the labor of collecting rents, which registered the immediate financial condition of tenants, or
of finding purchasers for land, collecting semiannual interest on mortgages
appeared a straightforward business transaction, especially where the debtor's
reputation offered additional assurances of regular payment. When probate
judges authorized administrators to sell land, many advocated investing the
proceeds in mortgages. In contrast to the standard calculation of 5 percent
from rents, interest on mortgages ran from 6 to 7 percent—and considerably
higher in the lower South—for a period of five to ten years. Despite the provision of a specific term, such mortgages were often open-ended, continuing
beyond the stipulated term of years so long as the borrower continued to pay
regular interest on the principal. Whereas the mobility and economic vulnerability of tenants undercut the reliability of rental income, mortgagees generally remained attached to the land that they had offered as security.

With migration and turnover decreasing the intimacy of credit of all kinds,
and with more and more merchant capital seeking an investment outlet, mortgage brokers joined executors and trustees in both arranging initial loans and
assigning mortgages to new creditors when trustees needed to liquidate the
investment.[48] Even as the credit market expanded, the reliance on brokers as
well as agents marked the specialization of financial services as well as a growing demand for liquidity. After 1819, the proliferation of new financial institutions further drew family property into the mainstream of capitalist enterprise.
Banks and marine and fire insurance companies all relied on kinship networks
to marshal the capital of stockholders and counted on the patterns of investment worked out in family estates. In 1831 two-thirds of the funds raised by
mortgages in New York City still came from individuals or estates, but the one-
third extended by incorporated companies pointed to the future.[49]

Estate Administration and the Rise of Corporate Investments

As lawmakers chartered more and more fire insurance companies and savings
banks in the 1820s and 1830s, they drew on the model of family investment
and required these institutions to place their capital in mortgages or government bonds, drawing a distinction between those tried-and-true securities
and investments in commercial enterprises that implied greater risk for larger
returns. Yet once that family model had been institutionalized, it became an

engine of accumulation. Probate courts directly participated in this process. Looking for alternatives to the untutored or high-handed personal administration of estates, judges and will-writers directed that legacies or trust funds be placed in savings banks as well as in mortgages, or, particularly for larger amounts, in new institutions that advertised their willingness to administer the property of estates.

In 1823 wealthy Bostonians secured a charter amendment for the Massachusetts Hospital Life Insurance Company (first organized in 1818) that authorized it to manage family trusts. Within five years, the company had attracted 783 trust accounts worth more than $3 million, three-fourths held for the benefit of women and minors.[50] The legislature restricted the company's investments to mortgages within Massachusetts, federal or Massachusetts bonds, and stock in Massachusetts-chartered banks, whose number had jumped from 28 to 63 between 1820 and 1830.[51] The 1830 charter of the New York Life Insurance and Trust Company restricted the investment of capital funds only to government bonds or mortgages in the state. By 1836 New York Life held $5.1 million in trust deposits, more than one-fifth by order of the Court of Chancery; deposits directed by the court, moreover, made up nearly half of long-term "trusts of accumulation."[52] The company placed 75 percent of its capital in farm mortgages at 7 percent interest. Paying out from 4 to 5 percent interest on trust accounts to beneficiaries, New York Life—like the Massachusetts Hospital Life—delivered dividends that reached as high as 10 percent to stockholders. Such institutions in effect siphoned off a share of family property to corporate investors.

Although receiving corporate charters in exchange for their fiduciary service, the new institutions understood their trust to be the management of family *capital* and advertised both the security and the efficiency that came from holding multiple accounts. The trustees of the Massachusetts Hospital Life Insurance especially prided themselves on their shrewd assessment of outlets for investment, including new enterprises organized by their peers and kin from elite mercantile families.[53] With private and institutional trustees in other cities observing their strategies, Bostonians placed themselves at the forefront of an emerging debate over how far family property could be integrated into a corporate order of banks, manufacturing, and railroads. Although the Massachusetts legislature and courts granted administrators wide discretion, by the 1850s judges in other states began to rein in trustees and administrators who invested in corporate stocks.

The Massachusetts Supreme Court acknowledged the changing landscape of investment in 1830 when it authorized a bold departure from conventional wisdom and sacrosanct English precedent that privileged the security of land or government bonds for family property. John M'Lean had died in 1823 with nearly half of his personal estate of $228,120 in textile manufacturing stocks. His trustees (the Massachusetts Hospital Life Insurance Company) continued the investment on behalf of his widow, who held a life estate. When the residuary heirs (Harvard College and Massachusetts General Hospital) protested that investments in textile industries endangered their own future interests, Chief Justice Samuel Putnam answered by cataloging the risks of all forms of investment. "Do what you will, the capital is at hazard," he wrote. "If the public funds are resorted to, what becomes of capital when the credit of the government shall be so much impaired as it was at the close of the last war? Investments on mortgage of real estate are not always safe. Its value fluctuates more, perhaps than the value of insurance stock. Again, title to real estate, after the most careful investigation, may be involved and ultimately fail, and so the capital, which was originally supposed to be as firm as earth itself, will be dissolved."[54] The most that could be asked of a trustee, Putnam famously concluded, is that he "observe how men of prudence, discretion, and intelligence manage their own affairs, not in regard to speculation but in regard to the permanent disposition of their funds, considering the probable income as well as the probable safety of the capital to be invested."[55]

As professional trustees in Massachusetts embraced the court's mandate "to observe how men of prudence . . . manage their own affairs," they turned from real property as the bedrock of investment to corporate securities. In the 1820s, the lawyer Waldo Flint had invested the capital of estates in mortgages. In the 1830s, following the lead of his entrepreneurial clients, he added Massachusetts bank stocks, in effect diversifying the portfolio by holding shares from multiple banks, and by the early 1840s, he added stocks in the Boston and Worcester Railroad.[56] In 1857 Flint administered the estate of John Simpson, descendant of a wealthy shipping family, who owned no real estate other than a lot in Mt. Auburn Cemetery but held personal property appraised at close to $75,000, with $38,500 in four mortgages and the rest of his wealth in the stocks of nine banks.[57] Simpson left his estate to his five sisters, including Henrietta Welles, widow of a bank president. When Welles died in 1871, she held $90,000 entirely in stocks of banks and the Boston and Albany Railroad. Aside from her house, she held no real estate and no bonds secured by mortgages.[58]

Rents and interest from mortgages had constituted the income that turned family property into capital, but when the 1837 panic devastated both real estate and banks, few New England trustees could resist the security of railroad bonds, backed by assets, and especially the returns from railroad stocks. Like bank stocks and in contrast to the fixed interest that came from mortgages and bonds, railroad dividends delivered a share of increasing profits. But despite this trend and Justice Putnam's sanguine assessment of risks associated with all forms of investments, judges in some states sought to uphold the special protections required of family property. Indeed, in contrast to the Massachusetts court, in 1854 the Pennsylvania Supreme Court announced as "settled law" — though the point had only been settled within the decade — that "investment by a guardian or other trustee, unless authorized by the deed of trust, in the stock of an incorporated company, whether a bank railroad, canal, manufacturing or mining company, cannot be made at the risk of a ward" or other beneficiaries.[59] And although most executors and trustees steered clear of manufacturing stocks, in 1859 the Pennsylvania court excoriated what it judged to be the increased speculation with the property of widows and orphans in upstart industries.[60] While probate judges and masters in chancery continued to endorse trustees' investments in bank and railroad stocks on a case-by-case basis, repeated bank failures and the panic of 1857 prompted courts of appeals to sharpen the lines between suitable outlets for family property and the "adventures" or "experiments" that judges associated with incorporated enterprise.

The appellate judges in effect disciplined probate courts as well as trustees who had ventured too far into the emerging capitalist regime. In 1869 the New York Court of Appeals declared that trustees who had invested in railroad, canal, or bank stocks had violated their fiduciary duty because the property "has left the control of the trustee; its safety and the hazard, or risk of loss, is no longer dependent upon their skill care or discretion" but rather depended on corporate managers.[61] The court made an exception for corporate bonds secured by mortgages, but only if the trustees determined the "nature, location and the sufficiency of the security." Whereas in 1859 South Carolina's chancellor observed that "trust funds were commonly invested in stocks of the Charleston banks and bonds of the South Carolina Railway," in 1870 that state's Supreme Court also banned such investments by trustees or administrators.[62]

Massachusetts judges continued to defer to the prudence of inbred Boston trustees, but elsewhere judges cited the reservations of the New York and Pennsylvania courts and reaffirmed the imperative to invest family property in the "real securities" of mortgages and government bonds as opposed to "personal securities" of corporate stocks. In 1872 Jairus Ware Perry in effect codified this caution in his treatise on trusts, which provided the legal profession with guidelines for the rest of the century. Perry strongly advocated the wisdom of conservative English precedents. Dutifully noting the Massachusetts exceptions, Perry nonetheless insisted that for private trustees "it would seem the wiser course to withdraw the funds, settled for the support of women, children and other parties who cannot exercise an active discretion in the protection of their interests as much as possible from the chances of business." He urged judges to "establish the safest rule" in overseeing the duty to invest and stick to mortgages and government bonds.[63]

As the turbulence of the industrializing economy pushed judges to weigh the security of capital investments, some Southern judges continued to invoke the special status of land itself. In the aftermath of emancipation, planter families discovered that their wealth had evaporated. Confederate legislatures had contributed to the loss by requiring that the undistributed assets of estates be placed in Confederate bonds or risk confiscation. In the late 1860s hundreds of desperate heirs turned to the courts to hold administrators accountable for wasting family property. Judges throughout the former Confederacy absolved administrators from responsibility for the devastation that had "been the result, not of misconduct, but of misfortune, against which human foresight could not guard."[64] Yet, as late as 1877, Virginia judges argued among themselves over whether executors should have known by 1863 that the Southern cause was lost and refused to accept rapidly depreciating Confederate currency as interest payments on mortgages instead of holding on to their claim to the collateral. "What better investment or safer security could possibility been made or desired" than land, asked a dissenting judge in a case that was appealed three times, took two weeks of oral arguments, and produced a 500-page record before the court's majority ruled that the executors were not guilty of "palpable recklessness and gross negligence" in losing nonslave property that had been appraised at $215,000 in 1862.[65]

As emancipation and Confederate bonds destroyed the wealth of Southern planter families, mortgages brought down the landed elite of the far West. Yankee émigré Abel Stearns had made a vast fortune in southern California in the 1840s and 1850s from cattle ranching, which he steadily expanded by extending loans and then foreclosing on fellow rancheros, including his own father-in-law, Juan Bandini. But in the late 1850s drought and competition from Texas ranchers gutted his wealth. In 1868, at age seventy, Stearns placed nearly 180,000 acres of land in the hands of trustees who organized the Los Angeles and San Bernardino Land Company to pay off his debts and secure his estate. Stearns appears to have had little confidence in the future value of his lands without cattle, however, for he also started purchasing a life insurance policy for his wife, Arcadia, in 1870.[66] As it turns out, Arcadia did well enough after Stearns's death by marrying another landholder who had moved into sheep ranching as well as silver mines. When she died childless in 1913 she left an estate valued at $6.6 million, including nearly $5 million in real estate, to some forty descendants of her father, Juan Bandini. Sixteen of the heirs organized the Bandini Estate Company to subdivide extensive land in Santa Monica and east-central Los Angeles.[67] Arcadia Stearns Baker's longevity made her estate an exception in California, but it also illustrated a new rule: the growth of cities and the intensification of real estate development in the late nineteenth century restored the value of landed family property through its corporate organization.

Real Estate Trusts and Corporate Forms of Family Property

By the Civil War new institutions had formed to capitalize on the wealth accumulated in family estates, often working in alliance with the courts that directed administrators to place funds in them. The Massachusetts Hospital Life Insurance Company provided the model for trust companies that claimed the probity of the Boston trustee while placing millions of dollars of aggregated family property at the disposal of finance capital. Yet, unlike savings banks or insurance companies, the number of trust companies did not grow rapidly before the 1880s.[68] Moreover, it is telling that estates constituted only part of their business, as trust companies managed the certification and transfer of stocks and bonds and specialized in corporate receiverships. Still, whether within private firms or companies, managing trusts had become a full-time profession.

If trust companies did not entirely supplant the personal administration of wealthy estates, corporate practices dramatically transformed the personal relations of probate in other ways. Throughout the country, the war and its aftermath had exposed the difficulties of relying on personal sureties for bonds posted by administrators. In place of a system that called on family and friends to answer for their honesty, administrators turned to "fidelity" insurance companies that pooled the risks of hundreds of thousands of executors and trustees. Then, too, by the late nineteenth century, as real property declined to less than one-fourth of probated wealth, both salaried and wage-earning families turned to life insurance policies to secure their dependents.[69] More significantly, with the rise of corporate enterprise on a national scale, probate courts oversaw a diminishing portion of the nation's wealth and steadily receded in importance.

As was true of all aspects of American capitalism, the state—courts and legislatures at all levels—helped transform the status of family property within a corporate economy. By forbidding commercial banks to "hold the possession of any real estate under mortgage," the 1864 National Banking Act endorsed classical economic theories of commercial banking and underscored the requirements of liquidity to sustain industrial enterprise.[70] Such provisions gave new institutional form to the distinction between entrepreneurial investment and older "real securities." At the same time, state legislatures, chastened by repeated panics, depressions, and corporate scandals, began to follow the path marked out by appellate judges overseeing estates and to restrict more aggressively the investments of trust and insurance companies—as well as savings banks—to the classic outlets of government bonds and mortgages.[71] By nationalizing and centralizing the commercial banking system, the National Banking Act reinforced the agrarian economy's dependency on eastern banks for the marketing of crops and on specialized financial intermediaries—as Jon Levy shows—for mortgages.[72] At the same time, state regulation of the investments of fiduciary corporations spurred the movement of concentrated pools of capital into mortgages that underwrote the construction of American cities.

In effect, Congress, the courts, and state legislatures helped structure corporate capital into sectors that distinguished between "passive" investments long associated with family security and "active" investments identified with capitalist risk-taking. If such policies constructed a double standard in expectations for returns from capital—interest versus dividends—they also laid the foundation for a circuit of accumulation through real estate and finance that might absorb the gains and buffer the risks of industrial capital for propertied Americans as a class. The state in effect codified the principles of risks and hedges while introducing new dynamism into capital circulation within each sector. With the agricultural economy in a sustained depression, trustees of wealthy estates, who had long underwritten farm mortgages, could continue to invoke the security of land as they turned their attention to capitalizing on expanding opportunities for real estate development in cities. One of their tools was the institution of the real estate trust.

Lawyers and executors organized real estate trusts to solve the difficulties of holding land for numerous heirs. With multiple descendants of elite northeastern families still tied together in joint ownership of wharves, town lots, or suburban land, the partition of estates threatened to leave descendants with only a fraction of the prospective wealth arising from intensified land use after 1865. This was especially true as property that had been tied up in life estates for a generation vested in the grandchildren of the merchant princes who had so assiduously provided for family security. In seeking a way around partition, Boston families in particular took their cues from mill companies that moved into real estate following the advent of steam power. Having bought up large tracts to control water rights, the mill companies began paying dividends to their shareholders derived from the profits of subdividing and selling land. By issuing shares to land trusts—a new form of securities—trustees, too, could pay out dividends to heirs from ongoing joint investments in large-scale real estate projects.

Long mistrustful of institutional land monopolies as vestiges of feudal society, the Massachusetts legislature repeatedly excluded real estate companies from its general incorporation acts. Some trustees, claiming a particular hardship in partitioning land among multiple heirs, secured special state charters for improvement companies. At the same time, wealthy Bostonians who wrote wills granting their trustees broad powers had laid the groundwork for the specialization of real estate trusts as an alternative to incorporated land companies. Authorized by the deceased to sell, buy, or improve property, trustees could consolidate land parcels, raise funds through mortgages, build commercial blockfronts and office buildings, and distribute rents and profits in the form of dividends to the heirs.[73] Moving beyond managing family lands on behalf of heirs, moreover, by the late 1880s, Boston's genteel scions had become entrepreneurs as well as trustees, organizing real estate trusts as investment syndicates to erect hotels and office buildings or to oversee the subdivision of large tracts of land such as Back Bay in Boston.[74] Still relying on the close kinship networks that governed "State Street," their city's financial and fiduciary core, Bostonians also formed real estate trusts to build the first generation of ten- to fifteen-story "skyscrapers" in Chicago (including the signature Monadnock and Marquette buildings), as well as retail blocks and office buildings in Minneapolis, Duluth, Denver, Seattle, and Kansas City—western railroad cities starved for construction capital.[75] A final assimilation of family and corporate capital came with the selling of shares to these trusts on the public real estate exchange. By 1912 the state tax commissioner valued Boston's 103 real estate trusts at $250,000,000.[76]

Not all real estate trusts went public, however. When Charles Francis Adams died in 1887, his four sons and daughter placed real estate—scattered lots in Quincy as well as in Boston—in a trust valued at close to $1 million, managed by Charles Francis Jr. and John Quincy Adams II. In a remarkable departure from their ancestors' caution and the hard-earned lessons of prudent trustees before them, the Adams brothers mortgaged the Massachusetts real estate and joined other New Englanders in a speculative frenzy in western lands and railroad towns in the late 1880s, only to lose $500,000 in the panic of 1893. After 1914 another generation of Adamses took over the family real estate trust and oversaw the remaining investments in Kansas City, Salt Lake City, Helena, and Spokane, but as obsolescence, recession, and then the Great Depression took their toll, a predictable chain of correspondence from local agents reported that money for purchase was scarce, tenants in arrears, the market uncertain, and taxes and assessments due—until the cousins finally closed the trust in 1945.[77]

Commercial real estate developers in other cities often formed syndicates or partnerships rather than real estate trusts as they built American downtowns, but they joined the Bostonians in tapping the deep and restricted pockets of fiduciary corporations to underwrite their adventures through mortgages. (And after the 1906 Armstrong investigation of New York life insurance companies subjected those juggernauts of capital accumulation to the same investment constraints that governed fire insurance, trust companies, and savings banks, the amount of capital available for real estate development increased exponentially.[78]) Still, in the end it was the early Massachusetts real estate trusts that provided the institutional template for today's real estate investment trusts (REITs). Following a congressional act in 1960 conferring special tax benefits and declaring as its goal the democratization of real estate investment, REITs emerged in the late twentieth century as a dominant corporate form for holding and managing commercial real estate in the United States. REITs especially attracted investments from pension funds, the new institutional repositories of family savings after World War II. In 2009, after a decade of remarkable consolidation and a real estate bubble sponsored by the Federal Reserve, Americans once again discovered that landed wealth is no more secure than any other sector of a capitalist economy. Indeed, the nation's second-largest retail REIT, General Growth Property—itself started as a family firm—declared bankruptcy that year, with assets of $29.56 billion and $27.29 billion in debt.[79]

The rise of the REITs marks out a vast transformation in both the organization of land and family enterprise in the United States. In the early agrarian republic, families had constituted the nation's primary economic institutions, the sites of property ownership, labor, and the credit relations that allowed households to bring property into productive use. Yet, even as the abundance of land allowed American lawmakers to depart from British precedents and privilege the claims of creditors in the settlement of estates, the priority assigned creditors also exposed the essential vulnerability of families to expanding market relations. Family farming persisted through the nineteenth century and into the twentieth, but even before the Civil War the transmission of specific family farms over generations was becoming the exception rather than the rule within the industrializing nation.

By the end of the nineteenth century, however much they continued to regard land as a bedrock of security, few American families could expect to devise land as the means of independence to their children or grandchildren.

Yet if in dispatching the claims of creditors, probate courts left many an heir bereft, judges also insured that executors, guardians, or trustees not waste family property by letting it stand "idle." Thus, judges worked out the terms for the use of family property as capital, insisting that it be invested while simultaneously demanding that it not be risked. Such a golden mean could hardly be achieved in the volatile nineteenth-century economy, but by proselytizing the necessity and possibility of secure investments, courts encouraged wealthy families to adopt legal instruments—most especially trusts—to forge dependable institutions of accumulation. By the late nineteenth century, even as probate declined in importance for the majority of American households, elite family trusts did secure the transmission of wealth over generations and thus helped entrench a new class hierarchy. Family trusts became another institution of capitalist enterprise alongside partnerships and corporations, even as professional trust managers insisted that the unique status of family property as a passive investment required that it be sheltered from federal as well as state taxes.[80] When real estate trusts turned to intensified land development that drew much of its capital from institutions governed by the rules for family investment, their management both capitalized on and effectively dissolved the distinctions between passive and active capital, between security and risk, between family property and corporate property.

The administration of estates helped organize the transition from family capitalism by tying land to credit, providing pools of investment capital for the first generation of corporations, and ultimately by structuring new sectors of accumulation. As American judges drew the line between secure investments in land, mortgages, or government bonds to support widows and orphans and the untethered adventures of industrial capitalism, they both oversaw the demise of republican patrimony and bequeathed a way of conceiving of land as still the nation's own unique inheritance, the permanent guarantor of the prosperity of future generations.

5

Slave Breeding and Free Love

An Antebellum Argument over Slavery, Capitalism, and Personhood

Amy Dru Stanley

A most intimate human relationship lay at the heart of the connection between American slavery and worldwide capitalist transformation in the nineteenth century—the propagation of chattel slaves. Frederick Douglass spoke of that connection to abolitionists in London in 1846. "I will give you an invariable rule," he said. "When cotton gets up in the market in England, the price of human flesh gets up in the United States." Masters thus harvested slaves: "they grow them for the market." A decade later, no less a spokesman for slavery than Howell Cobb, the Georgia cotton planter who presided over the US Treasury, figured that a master's prosperity lay first "in the Negroes he raises." And in the midst of the Civil War, when the conflict between slavery and capitalism finally split apart the Union, Karl Marx, writing in London for the *New York Tribune*, also dwelled on slave-growing. According to Marx, the American crisis had forced English industry to "emancipate cotton from slave-breeding and slave-consuming oligarchies." Across the Atlantic world, as across the Mason-Dixon line, slave procreation was reckoned to underwrite the cotton revolution creating capital throughout the world. What the slave ship afforded in the era of sugar, slave breeding supposedly supplied in the era of cotton: a link between human bondage and capitalist revolution.[1]

For almost a century, however, historians have argued over the truth of slave breeding in the Old South. Did masters raise slaves like they raised livestock? Did they systematically seek to turn a profit on the love life of slave property? Were the older slave states in the East a nursery for the cotton kingdom in the West?[2]

Some points are well settled. In mainland North America, alone of New World slave societies, the slave population reproduced itself, with the fertility rate surpassing the death rate. Notably, too, the stakes of slave reproduction rose over time, heightened by the abolition of the African slave trade in 1808, the reign of cotton, and the spread of slavery into frontier lands acquired through purchase, treaty, annexation, and war, as an American middle passage forcibly carried nearly a million slaves into the deep South. Finally, by the eve of the Civil War, the value of slave property exceeded that of all other wealth but land, including the total capital invested in manufactures, railroads, and banks, with cotton produced by slaves accounting for half of all American exports.[3]

But did masters purposely grow slaves to reap profits? Did planters in Virginia or Kentucky compel breeding with an eye to selling the offspring one day in New Orleans? And sometimes did masters themselves deliberately and forcibly beget their slaves' increase?

Here nothing is settled. Again and again, the infamous questions have been famously argued. Consider the classic statements, nearly a century ago, of Ulrich Phillips, Frederic Bancroft, and W. E. B. Du Bois. According to Phillips, all masters were certainly interested in the "multiplication" of slaves, and some might even have been attuned to "commercial eugenics" and "stimulated breeding" and "exerted a control," but most chose to leave slaves to their "own inclinations." Conversely, according to Bancroft, though masters rarely bred slaves directly for sale, some "virtually compelled" their mating, especially where depleted soil made field labor less profitable, and overall "slave-rearing was the surest, most remunerative and most approved means of increasing agricultural capital." According to Du Bois, cash value flowed from rape, with "commercial breeding" producing the "intermingling of black and white blood." The dispute endures, as some historians discount slave breeding as a myth, while others highlight the obsession of masters with slave increase and their efforts to coax and coerce breeding.[4]

The point here is not to join the empirical debate about slave breeding. The query is not whether such a business existed, not whether masters' interest lay in more than the natural multiplication of slaves, not whether historians are right or wrong.

Rather, the point is to return to the moral argument between abolitionists and slaveowners over the potent question of slave breeding. And the query is why sensual love mattered so much in the conflict between slavery and freedom. Turning aside from the debate among historians opens the way to asking why slave breeding became so vexing to critics and defenders of slavery as sectional crisis deepened, even as profits soared from the traffic in cotton across the world.

At stake in the antebellum argument over slave breeding are themes central to understanding the counterpoint between slavery and capitalism—the antagonisms as well as the interconnections between the personal relations of chattel slavery and the abstractions of impersonal market exchange, between domestic bonds and the commodity form. If once American slavery appeared in, but not of, the world of capitalism, a newer scholarly wisdom holds that a market revolution sprawled indiscriminately across the Mason-Dixon line. Those very boundaries interested abolitionists and slave masters as well. In arguing over slave breeding—over wealth, love, power, and personhood— they were quite explicit about appreciating the forms of commerce peculiar to freedom and slavery. Neither the slave auction in all its publicity nor forcible labor out in the fields aroused greater outcry than did the ambiguity of what occurred in the private space of the plantation to create the increase of slaves.[5]

Likewise, it has been well established that the rise of industrial capitalism was yoked to an ethos of asceticism. With roots in Protestantism, that ethos flowered in abolitionism, it is said, and was made still more sacrosanct by contrast with the sins of slavery's licentiousness, sins ascribed to the master's unbounded dominion over his chattel.[6]

But the antebellum argument over slave breeding offers a different vantage, illuminating the meaning of sensual love in the moral opposition between Yankee capitalism and Southern bondage, and belying the sway of a strictly ascetic antislavery impulse. In congressional debates over slavery's westward expansion, in the tracts of abolitionists and slaveowners, in the legal pleadings of slave masters, and in the narratives of ex-slaves—in all those precincts there was excruciating talk of slave propagation as the lifeblood of the wealth accumulation and commodity exchange that carried cotton to factories across the world. And where that talk counted unfree love as the essence of slavery, freedom came to mean not only the duty of wage labor and marriage bonds, not only self-discipline and self-denial, but the emancipation of desire rooted in self-mastery and moral agency. The antebellum argument over the truth of slave breeding spawned an antislavery vindication of loving freely as a condition of being human.

In the US Congress *slave breeding* became a fighting word, a dirty word, a forbidden word. It conjured up plantation habits that turned love profane by accumulating value in human property. Especially it entered the strife over slavery extension, from the annexation of Texas through the settlement of Kansas. For in the spread of the cotton empire across the country a most basic market rule was manifest—a supply of slaves must fill the demand for unfree labor. Without slave accumulation, there could not be either a worldwide cotton trade or a domestic slave trade. Even in his memoirs, John Quincy Adams, the president turned congressional abolitionist, decried the evil of the "slave-breeding South."[7] It was an epithet abhorred by slaveholders. And the argument reached from the halls of Congress to the houses of Parliament.

Consider the Senate in 1850, as Henry Clay defended his plan of compromise concerning slavery's entry into territory acquired during the Mexican War. While speaking of saving the Union, Clay, a Kentucky slaveowner, paused to deny that Southerners grew slaves for sale. "This charge upon the slave-holding States of breeding slaves for market is utterly false and groundless. No such purpose enters, I believe, into the mind of any slaveholder," he declared. "This talk, sir, about, the cotton power, the lords of the loom, and the breeding of slaves, will do for the bar room of cross road taverns; but I never hoped or expected to hear upon the floor of the Senate such epithets." Instead, paying tribute to the master's paternalism—"He takes care of his slaves; he fosters, and treats them often with the tenderness of his own children"—Clay claimed that even the most beneficent master might end up with an unintended oversupply of slaves, who were unprofitable except if sold. "They multiply on his hands; he cannot find employment for them," Clay said regretfully of the need to market the surplus through the slave trade.

> And he is ultimately, but most reluctantly and painfully, compelled to part
> with some of them. . . . But to say that it is the purpose, design, or object of the
> slaveholder to breed slaves as he would domestic animals for a foreign market, is
> untrue in fact, and unkind to be imputed, or even intimated, by any one.

In particular, Clay rebuked a Massachusetts senator, John Davis, for using the taboo word, for claiming that the Mexican territory, though unsuitable for cotton, could be "adapted to the *breeding* of slaves."[8]

But Senator Davis interrupted, saying that he had never accused the South of slave breeding, only of aiming to expand the traffic in slaves.

> Mr. Davis. One cannot always remember precisely the language he uses in the hurry of debate. I can only say that I have no recollection of using the word "breeding.". . . According to the best of my recollection, I spoke of the capacity of the country for "traffic" in slaves.
>
> Mr. Clay. . . . The word "breeding" was used by the gentleman, or I never heard a word of the speech. Several Senators took a note of it, and we expressed how much we were shocked and surprised at it. It was one of the principal topics of the Senator's speech to talk about the cotton power, the cotton interest, and the *breeding* of slaves.

Thus the senators argued over slave breeding. While justifying the slave trade as an unfortunate product of overly fertile slaves, a surplus reflecting the good master's bounty, Clay denied that cotton inspired a union between slave breeding and industrial capitalism. In turn, Davis denied using the epithet, while condemning both the slave trade and all compromise over slavery extension.[9]

Sparring over words, the slaveholder and the Yankee could agree only about a fundamental distinction. It was one thing to deplore the slave trade, another to talk of raising slaves for sale. Where *traffic* might be uttered, *breeding* was forbidden. If what was said was in dispute, what was meant was not. The unspeakable business was not marketing slaves, but slave breeding.

Others spoke more plainly. Consider the debate over the Compromise of 1850 in the House of Representatives, where the implacable Pennsylvania congressman Thaddeus Stevens equated slavery extension with the spread of leprosy and damned the state of Virginia as "the *breeder*" of slaves. According to Stevens, wealth creation on Virginia farms was not a matter of land and labor, as on Pennsylvania farms, but of sex and slave growing, with the slave surplus a product of the master's intent.

> Instead of attempting to renovate the soil, and by their own honest labor compelling the earth to yield her abundance; instead of seeking for the best breed of cattle and horses, to feed on her hills and valleys, and fertalize the land, the sons of that great State must devote their time to selecting and grooming the most lusty sires and the most fruitful wenches, to supply the slave barracoons of the South!

Stevens drew on the words of a Virginia congressman, Richard Meade, who had endorsed slavery extension by affirming that supply and demand regulated the value of slaves: "Virginia has a slave population of near half a million, whose value is chiefly dependent on southern demand." Stevens's claim was not that Southerners adhered to universal rules of the market but just the opposite—that those rules operated differently under slavery and capitalism, and that as long as the market for slaves kept expanding into new lands masters in the older states would see more profit in cultivating fruitful human chattel than in tending the fertile earth. "In plain English, what does it mean?" asked Stevens. "That Virginia is now only fit to be the *breeder*, not the employer, of slaves."[10]

As Stevens spoke, Congressman Meade rose on the floor, crying out, "Indelicate scurrility!" His aim was not to deny that the value of Virginia slaves rested on the market in the black belt, for he reaffirmed that the necessity of slavery extension owed to the correlation of slave prices with "the price of cotton and the southern demand." But the wanton talk of slave breeding revolted him. "I believe there is not a kennel . . . that would not expel a member who would disgrace the brotherhood by such low vulgarity." The Virginian warned of secession—"not a man from the South . . . does not at times feel his attachment to this Union giving away under a disgust of their associations here"—while extolling the Southern benevolence that made slaves "the happiest and most cheerful people on earth."[11]

It was the furor leading to the annexation of Texas in 1845 that had made slave breeding such a potent political epithet. By 1838 John Quincy Adams was already orating in Congress about the perils of Texas—that the problem was not simply "the more slaves the better" but "who shall breed these human chattels"—and soon he would address his constituents in Braintree about the "slave-breeding passion for annexation." An open letter had been sent to Henry Clay, written by the antislavery minister William Ellery Channing, protesting that annexation would give new license to "slave breeding and slave selling." And crediting the propensity of American slaves to multiply to nothing more than the food and clothing bestowed by masters, "how well they have been taken care of," Southern statesmen proclaimed a sectional interest in opening up a market for the surplus. "Why, sir, the annual increase of these people by procreation is one hundred thousand," coolly calculated the South Carolina senator George McDuffie, himself a cotton planter. "Now, if we shall annex Texas, it will operate as a safety-valve to let off the superabundant slave population from among us." Yet less coolly, McDuffie remarked that Southern masters inherited, in perpetuity, the offspring of the "original sin of slavery" committed by Northern merchants in pursuing the African trade. Meanwhile, the antislavery argument quickened. Relentlessly, for instance, the Ohio congressman Joshua Giddings spoke of the "slave-breeding power" and the "business of slave-breeding" and of "truckling to the slave-breeding interests." Scathingly, he quoted McDuffie's safety-value theory in claiming that the goal of the South was "most obviously to enhance the price of human flesh in our slave-breeding States." On both sides of the Mason-Dixon line, it was no secret that territorial expansion swelled the value of slave procreation.[12]

The argument resonated across the Atlantic as well, then echoed back to amplify the outcry over slave breeding at home. Consider the House of Lords in 1843, as it deliberated about the progress of emancipation worldwide and the fate of Texas. A plan had been proposed, to be brokered by England, providing that the Texas republic would abolish slavery and in exchange Mexico would recognize its independence. As Lord Henry Brougham asked the British foreign minister, Lord Aberdeen, about its prospects, he turned the lords' attention to American slave breeding. "Georgia, the Carolines, and Virginia," Brougham began, "constantly sent their surplus slave population, which would otherwise be a burthen to them, to the Texian market." Destroying that market, he went on, would eventually lead to the downfall of slavery by curbing "the habit of breeding slaves." Thus he claimed that British influence "must put an end to one of the most execrable crimes—for I would not designate it by the honourable name of traffic—that could disgrace a people—namely, the rearing and breeding of slaves." Brougham's words were relayed to the Capitol by ambassadors, designated "highly significant by the Government of the United States" in diplomatic correspondence, and broadcast across the country by newspapers. "Aberdeen, and Brougham, and their aiders and abettors on this continent, may rant about humanity . . . but *slavery must continue to exist in Texas*," vowed an Alabama congressman. "Like the law of merchandise, the slaves of the South will find their way to the best market." Everywhere in the South, railed Joshua Giddings, stump speeches clamored about the "maintenance of slavery and slave breeding" against the designs of British abolitionism.[13]

Up through the Civil War the agitation over slave breeding continued, pervading arguments over the moral differences between wealth creation in the South and the North. It was said, for example, that enforcement of the fugitive slave law increased the profits of "negro-breeding," while a "crop of human flesh" figured among slavery's barbarisms so famously enumerated by Senator Charles Sumner in declaring that Kansas must be admitted to the Union as a free state. In the House of Commons, when debate turned to imposing punitive duties on the produce of slave labor, it was the Whig leader Thomas Macauley who charged that the American master did not simply raise, but

sired, slaves for sale: "that a civilised man, a baptized man . . . should breed
slaves for exportation, and, if the whole horrible truth must be told, should
even beget slaves for exportation . . . for four or five hundred dollars a head."
And as the war raged, Union Army men gloried in obliterating the "gains that
might accrue from slave breeding."[14]

Always, however, slaveowning congressmen disowned the business of slave
breeding, though defending the market in slaves that made a virtue of slavery
extension. Always they denied that the demand for slaves on the cotton frontier led to depravity, attributing to humanity alone the unintended oversupply
in the older states. Some refused, as an Alabama congressman said, to "descend
to the argument of negro-breeding," only asking why antislavery men knew so
much about that branch of agriculture. Others took up the gauntlet, protesting
that there was "no fouler calumny against the South" than accusing masters of
selling their own increase. A North Carolina congressman shuddered at the
shamefulness of slave breeding: "I say it is horrible to think of. I have spent
most of my life among slaveholders—religious men of all denominations are
slaveholders—but I do not know one man in my district, or my State, who
raises negroes for 'southern demand'—to sell. I should be ashamed to own
such a constituent."[15]

According to the Southern argument, masters would no more breed slaves
for sale than put beloved heirlooms in the market or auction off kinfolk. The
values that made a master unhappy about selling home-grown slaves—even
for a high price—were those that the Virginian Richard Meade pondered in
reconciling instincts of paternalism with the Southern marketplace. "Every
southern man well knows that the last piece of property which a southerner
will part from is the slave which he raised, or which descended to him from
his father," he averred.

> When he is forced to sell his property, every other kind goes first, while the sharer
> of his childhood's sports, or the being whom he has raised from infancy, is clung
> to with the regard almost of a brother or a parent. . . . [A] slave is scarcely ever sold
> in Virginia, except from necessity or misconduct.

However expansive the slave system, however high commodity values soared,
there were limits to the profits that could legitimately be made on the price of
human flesh. Yet meditating further on those moral limits, even while arguing
that slavery must extend to the Pacific or the price of slaves would plummet,
Meade inquired why his Southern brethren should speak of feeling "ashamed
of a constituent who would breed a slave to sell." Wonderingly, he asked about

such qualms, "Does not the gentleman from North Carolina overrate his sensibilities . . . . I presume the gentleman has constituents who buy to sell; can he draw a sensible distinction in their favor?" Thus the Virginian posed the fundamental question: what was the difference between trafficking in slaves and slave breeding? Beyond remonstrating about antislavery vulgarity and masters hating to sell slaves raised at home, the only answer he offered hewed to the rule of supply and demand—that the trader, unlike the breeder, was "useful" in dispersing slaves across the South, thereby "keeping in bounds the black population" in any one state.[16]

A different answer came from Horace Mann during the debate over the Compromise of 1850. Occupying the congressional seat left vacant by the death of John Quincy Adams two years earlier, Mann spoke more explicitly than any other antislavery statesman about the nature of the commerce that made slave breeding so inexpressibly wrong. Attacking slavery extension, he exposed the connection between slavery's sensual bonds and the ways of the market. He likened the upper South to the African interior as an axis of the slave trade, echoing arguments that linked Virginia slave prices to cotton prices worldwide. Then, more bluntly, he deplored the value of slave women "young and sprightly and voluptuous"—the coining of "celestial qualities" into money. It was a mainstay of congressional abolitionism to condemn slavery's annihilation of home life, and some spoke more boldly about slavery as prostitution, as well as about masters selling their own children. But Mann took up matters circumvented, despite all the arguing over slave breeding. Slavery was a "bedside institution," he said: a system designed to corrupt the "holiest affections." Picturing the bondsman whose wife was "violated before his eyes," he cried out, "Instead of saying, with the Apostle, that wives shall submit themselves to their husbands, command them to submit themselves to anybody, and to the master as husband over all." He implored Congress to envision the outcome of allowing slavery to spread west: "the self-styled freemen, the self-styled Christians, of fifteen great states in this American Union, shall engage in the work of procreating, rearing, and selling . . . often from their own loins." Rather than safeguarding the Union, sectional compromise would simply "increase the profits of negro-breeding."[17]

On one thing, therefore, free soilers and slaveowners agreed, despite irreconcilably different perspectives on surplus slaves, slavery extension, the domestic slave trade, and the right to human property: the unspeakable evil was not buying and selling human beings, but debasing their creation to the level of brutes by tying it to the market. No endorsement of growing slaves for sale rang out in Congress. All who talked about it, or said that it could not be talked

about, deemed it a filthy business. And all who said that it existed, or said that
it did not, set it apart from the traffic in slaves. Whether slavery appeared as a
curse or a blessing, slave breeding figured as peculiarly wrong.

Outside of Congress, the argument about slave breeding went to the heart of
the matter—love, unfree and free. It moved from the ground of slavery extension into realms spiritual and philosophical, as antislavery reformers and
proslavery theorists strove to unravel what cotton joined together: slavery's
intimate bonds and capitalism's abstractions as an interwoven system of commodity production and exchange. Interested in wealth creation, they also examined the nature of personhood. Arguing over slave breeding, always they
returned to the idea that love marked a fundamental distinction between slavery and freedom.

   In the view of the enslaved, the establishment of breeding states began with
the closing of the African trade. As the ex-slave Thomas Smallwood put it,
recalling the transition in his native state of Maryland, the ban on slave importing gave "an impetus to the infamous traffic of slave breeding." Calculating the
value of the thousands exported from the older slave states into the deep South
during the 1830s, Smallwood arrived at a sum of nearly $2 million, based on a
reliable source—"Mr. Clays average estimate, $400 for each slave." But the suf-
fering was incalculable, he wrote. "Nothing but the day of judgment can bring
it to light, when all secrets will be revealed."[18]

   Some of the secrets of slave breeding came to light in the outcry of Frederick Douglass. He too spoke from his own experience of bondage in Maryland.
"Although it is harrowing to your feelings, it is necessary that the facts of the
case should be stated," he told the abolitionists gathered in London in 1846.
"We have in the United States slave-breeding states . . . where men, women,
and children are reared for the market, just as horses, sheep, and swine are
raised for the market. Slave-rearing is there looked upon as a legitimate trade;
the law sanctions it, public opinion upholds it, the church does not condemn
it. It goes on in all its bloody horrors, sustained by the auctioneer's block." In
My Bondage and My Freedom, Douglass recollected how wealth was created, in
private. He wrote of sex: the slave breeding practiced by the slave breaker, Edward Covey, who aimed to base his fortune on forcibly pairing his slave woman
with a hired man. "Covey himself had locked the two up together every night,"
boasting that he had "bought her simply 'as a breeder,'" wrote Douglass.

   This professedly christian slaveholder, amidst all his prayers and hymns, was
   shamelessly and boastfully encouraging, and actually compelling, in his own

house, undisguised and unmitigated fornication, as a means of increasing his human stock.

Summing up the opposing values of slavery and freedom, Douglass thus spoke without evasion of the slave quarter as an erotic prison where human stock was accumulated.[19]

Not always, however, had slave breeding been central in inventories of slavery's wrongs. That came after the ban on the African trade, along with the reign of cotton and the westward expansion of slavery. At the founding of the American Convention of Delegates from Abolition Societies in 1794, for example, none of the petitions listing the evils of treating human beings as property—"rapine and murder" in the African trade, "rebellion against the authority of a common Father" in domestic slavery—had included slave breeding. Yet by 1833 abolitionists belonging to the newly created New England Anti-Slavery Society assailed the business, claiming that Virginia and Maryland, "having for some time found the cultivation of the soil by slaves less profitable than it was formerly, now raise slaves for sale and exportation to the southern markets." A year later the Yankee abolitionists led by William Lloyd Garrison developed a fuller protest. Home-grown slaves had replaced the supply brought by slave ships, according to an *Address to the People of the United States* issued by the New England Anti-Slavery Convention. A new "middle passage" was being traveled, as the "produce of the slave-breeding is conveyed to the slave-consuming states." The protest began by contrasting slave breeding to the story of creation told in Genesis, where man was made in the image of God.[20] It was then that the epithet of slave breeding became a staple of abolitionism.

Distilling the moral stakes of the argument, the *Address* of the Anti-Slavery Convention set forth why slave breeding was so singularly wrong. By definition, slavery denied free will, and the whip tore the body, and the auction split apart the family. But slave breeding made human creation a work of the market. "It licenses the profanation of all that is sacred and dear to the wretched victim of avarice and prejudice," the *Address* declared. The slave was reduced to the level of swine and cattle, a thing denied human divinity in its very origin; not a person stolen violently from Africa and transformed into chattel, but rather a thing born directly of unfree sensual life in Southern households under a system of domestic slavery. "He himself is the product of slave-breeding industry, a marketable and heritable commodity," stated the *Address*.

The voice of nature and of reason has sanctioned the privacy of domestic life, and has placed the law of the land like a cherub with a flaming sword before the garden of life. But the law of the land which declares the house of the white man his castle . . . the same law, like a faithless sentinel, admits to the unguarded dwelling, of the colored man, every selfish and brutal passion. . . . Though conjugal fidelity, parental and filial affection and brotherly love be all placed in one scale, yet the market price in the other, seldom, if ever, fails to kick the beam.

A creature born to be bought and sold, without a birthright, the slave was denied the condition of "God in man."[21] Sacred desires descended into acquisitive passions; for the very law that shielded intimate bonds in a free man's home from the ways of the market diabolically fused them in the slave's. The price of flesh, the rule of profit, reigned supreme. And love itself was profaned.

Thereafter, from every antislavery pulpit—at conventions and public lectures, in tracts, treatises, newspapers, and literary works—spokespersons for all strains of abolitionism advanced the argument against slave breeding. There was the sensation created by William Lloyd Garrison at a meeting of the American Anti-Slavery Society in declaring that slaves did not worship "a slave-breeding Jesus," and the treatises written by a founder of the Liberty Party, William Goodell, denouncing the enrichment of the "negro-breeding states." There were the stories told by Harriet Beecher Stowe in *Uncle Tom's Cabin* of slaves made to "breed chil'en for market," and the verses composed by Frances Ellen Watkins Harper, a free-born black poet, imagining the state of Virginia boasting: "one of my chief staples has been the sons and daughters I send to the human market."[22]

The effort of empirically documenting slave breeding began with Theodore Dwight Weld's 1839 classic, *American Slavery as It Is: Testimony of a Thousand Witnesses*, which aimed to expose both the value of slave increase and the brutality of masters in securing it. A year later, the charges were amplified in *Slavery and the Internal Slave Trade in the United States*, a report prepared by Weld for the world antislavery convention in London. Protests filled antislavery newspapers, warning of "slave-breeding sinners" with designs on Mexican territory and reporting that slave stud farms existed in the upper South, plantations where supposedly female slaves greatly outnumbered men. "Mount Vernon a Human Stock Farm," announced *Frederick Douglass' Paper* in 1852. "What a burning shame, what a violation of all our republican professions, to permit the home of Washington to be *a slave-breeding pen*! Shame! Shame! everlasting shame!"[23]

Meanwhile exponents of perfectionism in the American Anti-Slavery Society censured churches for tolerating slave breeding among their congregants, and the Liberty Party called on Congress to end the business by using the com-

merce power to prohibit the domestic slave trade. From afar, British abolitionists joined in protest, decrying, as John Stuart Mill put it, the fusion of
"gain" and "force" in the ill-begotten profits of slave breeding. The arithmetic
was simple, declared the British and Foreign Anti-Slavery Society: "the larger
the slave increase the greater the masters' gains." Above all, it was the relation
between cotton weaving in Manchester and slave breeding in Virginia that
interested the editors of *The Economist*, who stressed the complicity of British industry. "Our interests as a manufacturing country are bound up, with
somewhat painful closeness, with the prosperity of the South," *The Economist*
declared. "Exactly in proportion as the slave population increases . . . the cotton crop becomes larger." The answer was to find a cotton supply elsewhere—
in India.[24]

The idea that Yankee industrial capitalism depended on Southern slave
breeding—the painful closeness of freedom and slavery—was never a mainstay of the American argument against slave breeding. To the contrary, the
point of all the agitating about love's violation was to establish stark moral
boundaries, even where material realities blurred them. The argument was that
the free labor of the North and the slave breeding of the South belonged to
separate worlds.

Seldom, then, was slave breeding on Virginia plantations said to be linked
with manufacturing in Massachusetts mills; nor were such claims ever more than
glancing. Perfunctorily, for instance, in an 1841 essay on *Emancipation*, William
Ellery Channing noted that importing cotton from India might counter the
"stimulus to slave-breeding." A decade later, speaking at a free soil convention,
Horace Mann prophesied that the fugitive slave bill would "raise the price of
manufacturing stocks," as well as "increase the profits of negro-breeding." But
he never raised the linkage in his diatribes against slavery extension. More
pointedly, after the outbreak of the Civil War, already foreseeing the downfall
of slavery, the cotton manufacturer Edward Atkinson, in an antislavery tract
titled *Cheap Cotton by Free Labor*, mourned that the multiplication of spindles
in Northern mills had formerly meant a "constant drain upon the slave-breeding
states for good field hands at $1200 each" to produce enough bales of cotton.
Yet such claims were the exception. For the notion that Northern enterprise
and Southern slave breeding were connected by transcendent rules of the market ran contrary to antislavery claims about sectional difference. Where pointing explicitly to a link between bondage and free commerce—as in abstaining
from buying the products of slave labor—abolitionists tended to speak of un-
paid work rather than unfree procreation. The wrong at stake, as the Requited
Labor Convention of 1838 explained its vow to furnish the market with "free

goods," was that slaves were denied the "fruits of their toil," not the fruits of their loins.[25]

Almost always, the antislavery argument was not that cotton created an unholy union between slave breeding and Yankee capitalism, but that ways of accumulating wealth were categorically different in the South and in the North; and that slave growing, by profaning love, was slavery's worst sin and its peculiar sin—a wrong without parallel in free society. That was the antagonism described by Channing in his 1835 treatise on *Slavery*, as he contrasted the "unfeeling cupidity" in slave society with the "influence of love" in free society. "What! Grow men like cattle!" he wrote of the South. "Rear human families, like herds of swine, and then scatter them to the four winds for gain!" But of the North he wrote that a husband, roaming far in search of work, carried his family with him "in his heart," and that even the sailor, "in his lonely night-watch, looks homeward." Slavery blighted the heart, sullying the "deep fountains of its love," disfiguring "natural affections." It was not unrequited, involuntary labor that so troubled Channing but rather the master who raised slaves for sale, treating human beings as the "passive instrument of his gratification and gain," even planting the seed himself, and reaping profit from the fruit of his loins: "But the worst is not told. . . . Many a master has children born into slavery. . . . Still more; it is to be feared that there are cases, in which the master . . . sells them to undergo the miseries of bondage among strangers."[26] In explaining why slave breeding was so wrong, the Reverend Channing revealed why love mattered so much in the opposition between freedom and slavery.

At the worst, then, under slavery, alone of commodity relations, a master of a household penetrated his own commodities to multiply them. And under slavery, alone of domestic relations, the master violated his own dependents to sire commodities. That was the innermost secret of slave breeding, taught abolitionists—a business of bondage more awful than any other because in turning a profit on human creation, it made commerce out of sensual relations that ought to have been sanctified by love. It was why slave breeding was worse than the slave trade, as Theodore Dwight Weld explained in his 1840 report to the world antislavery convention. "While the slave trader only buys and sells, retaining possession no longer than till he can reach the market, the breeder is engaged in the protracted process of *raising human stock*." Although both split apart families, the slave breeder's "transcendent vileness towers alone, for while the trader deals with *strangers*, the master is perpetrating these outrages upon those whom he has reared from their birth, in some case upon the companions of his own boyhood . . . and often, worst of all, on his *own offspring*." Transposing the commodity form onto "a system softly called a 'domestic institution,'" the slave breeder "rewards amalgamation, he punishes sterility, he coolly calculates upon the profits of fecundity, takes vengeance for miscarriages. . . . Does the trader buy? the master sells; does the trader *drive* men and women like cattle? the master *breeds* them like cattle."[27] Thus slave breeding was uniquely evil, embodying the most extreme affinity between avarice and violence, the most inhuman abuse of intimate power. Unlike the slave trader who trafficked in strangers, the slave breeder sinned at home. Nothing insulated love from the accumulation of wealth.

As the secrets of slave breeding came to light, so too did the revelations of masters. Allegedly, through their own words slave owners betrayed conditions in the breeding states, words that abolitionists quoted again and again. A wealth of evidence came from the 1832 debate over slave emancipation in the Virginia legislature, where Jefferson's grandson, Thomas Jefferson Randolph, argued on behalf of emancipation that Virginia had been "converted into *one grand menagerie, where men are to be reared for market, like oxen for the shambles!*" Other famous expressions of Southern opinion also filled antislavery tracts: the distress of James Madison about "licentiousness" on Virginia plantations; the observations of Henry Clay about planters "tempted to RAISE SLAVES BY THE HIGH PRICE OF THE SOUTHERN MARKET"; and the findings of Professor Thomas R. Dew, at William and Mary College, about the slave trade representing "an advantage" that led masters to raise slaves in "the greatest number possible." Sometimes notices reprinted from Southern newspapers, advertising "prolific" slaves, skilled at "propagation," appeared beside Dew's conclusion, advanced in an 1832 treatise, that "Virginia is in fact a *Negro*-raising state for other states; she produces enough for her own supply and six thousand for sale." It was the Virginian Dew whom William Bowditch quoted in his study of *Slavery and the Constitution* (1849) as proof for the proposition that human beings counted in the South as "stallions and brood mares."[28]

Yet as the coming of civil war seemed ever more likely, another Virginian, George Fitzhugh, answered the outcry over slave breeding in his consummate defense of chattel bondage, *Cannibals All!* (1857). This business was merely one of the "imaginary abuses" invented by abolitionism, for masters went west with "their negroes," wrote Fitzhugh. "No man in the South, we are sure, ever bred slaves for sale. They are always sold reluctantly, and generally from necessity, or as a punishment for misconduct." He asked, "Will some Yankee or Englishman, ere the charge is repeated that slaves are bred to be sold like horses, when they are old enough for market, point out a single instance in the present, or the past, of a Southerner's pursuing such a business?"[29]

In so arguing, Fitzhugh elaborated on disavowals collected in *The Pro-*

Slavery Argument (1852), a set of illustrious Southern essays on the benevolence of American slavery. According to that collection, the system of domestic slavery did not yoke cotton growing and slave breeding in the creation of Southern wealth, but rather love and dominion in the bond of master and slave. Without a word about his own intimate pleasures with bondswomen on his South Carolina plantation, James Henry Hammond contrasted the "patriarchal scheme of domestic servitude" with the "dominion of *capital*—a monster without a heart"—and reviled abolitionists for claiming that masters "breed up slaves, nay beget children for slaves, and sell them at so much a-head," while ranting about the bestial morality of slaves, and warning about the cotton crop that "no calamity could befall the world at all comparable to the loss of two millions of bales," and about emancipation that the outcome would be racial amalgamation. Chancellor William Harper of South Carolina extolled slavery's "kindly relations," and Hammond denied that masters were "hard-hearted" in exercising power. There was no echo of Dew's matter-of-fact appraisal of slave raising, which had been issued before abolitionists drew up their bill of indictment. Rather, Harper asked, "Is it not natural that a man should be attached to that which is *his own*? . . . Do not men everywhere contract kind feelings toward their dependants? Is it not natural that men should be more attached to those whom they have long known—whom, perhaps, they have reared?" Under slavery, the "tenderest and purest sentiments of the human heart" arose from a foundation of force.[30]

To the proslavery way of thinking, therefore, dominion was love's source, not its ruin. It was antislavery, as Hammond wrote, which meant to "turn love into hatred."[31] For abolitionists, the absolute power based on owning human beings was irreconcilable with human love; but for slaveowners, the reconciliation of love and power was as natural as property ownership itself. For both, however, the argument over slave breeding was ultimately about the ways of the heart, as much as about the ways of the market.

What Fitzhugh devoted his work to arguing was that freedom's commodity relations, not slavery's bonds, desecrated the love intrinsic to being human. In other words, the idea that domestic slavery turned love profane—the wrong embodied by the slave breeder—was as false as the existence of breeding states. In slave society, Fitzhugh wrote in *Cannibals All!*, it was "natural for men to love one another." For there, the family, "including slaves," was the elemental institution. Conversely, the world of freedom was one of "universal selfishness, discord, competition." As for Yankee enterprise, inanimate wealth, "capital or other property did not 'breed'" without taking a pound of flesh from free persons as "profits." Earlier, in his *Sociology for the South* (1854), a study of the ills of free society, Fitzhugh had begun to reflect about the problem of love and the nature of personhood and power. "Love for others is the organic law of our society," he explained, whereas "self-love" alone prevailed in free society. Fitzhugh's premise was that a man naturally loved his property—that Providence transformed the "selfishness of man's nature" into domestic affection that embraced "wife and children, slaves and even dumb animals"—and therefore affection suffused the entire system of domestic slavery. But love could not exist where freedom was a universal right. "There is no love between equals," Fitzhugh wrote. "A state of dependence is the only condition in which reciprocal affection can exist among human beings. . . . A state of independence always begets more or less of jealous rivalry and hostility."[32] Inherently, then, love constituted a relation of sovereignty and subjection, precisely because it emanated from innate instincts of proprietorship.

Indeed, *free love* was Fitzhugh's epithet for the Yankee world of capital—just as *slave breeding* was the abolitionist epithet for his own state of Virginia. Supposedly, the ethos of free society would culminate in love based purely on consent, a disordered, immoral situation where no human ties were sacred or eternal. "A plunge into the soft and sensual waters of the lake of Free Love," he wrote in *Cannibals All!*, was the necessary outcome of antislavery, the corollary of free market relations, the endpoint of the "despotism of capital, which has taken the place of domestic slavery." Where freedom was universal—where individual volition dissolved all domestic bonds, where hard bargaining supplanted affection, and where human exchange was founded on "equality, the social contract, the let-alone and selfish doctrines of political economy"—free love was inevitable. "Cut every human relation . . . reduce whatsoever was compulsory to voluntary. . . . Loosen by Assiduous Wedges, in every joint, the whole fabrice of social existence." Thus antislavery would usher in a new age of "Free Love and Free Lands . . . Free Women and Free Negroes . . . No-Marriage, No-Religion . . . No-Law and No-Government." The world, Fitzhugh prophesied, would "have to choose between Free Love and Slavery."[33]

In choosing slavery, Southerners defended it in the name of domestic affection. But in choosing free love, abolitionists defended it by any other name. Across the sectional divide free love was as taboo as slave breeding—each signifying the negation of marriage as the bond that sanctified sexual exchange, free love meaning unbounded liberty, slave breeding meaning unbounded dominion. Both evoked lust and license, a "system of whoredom," explained a writer in *The Liberator*, who marveled, "What hypocrisy!" that any apostle of slavery should denounce free-love doctrine as annihilating marriage and promoting "promiscuous intercourse like brutes." For as the argument over slave breeding deepened, so too did a sensationalized protest against projects of political and social transformation said to inaugurate the reign of free love, projects ranging from women's rights to the founding of utopian communities. It was simpler to speak of products—to contrast, as did the Boston minister Theodore Parker, the "flour, oxen, and swine" and "cottons and woollens, hardware and shoes" of the Northern states with the "men-servants and maidens" of Virginia, the "produce of her own loins" that was "bred and begotten for the Southern market."[34] Abolitionists did not claim to be free lovers, any more than masters admitted to being slave breeders, pointedly choosing other words than free love to contrast with slave breeding. But the meaning was plain. And it was not prudish.

The argument against slave breeding presupposed volition—in love as in labor—as a birthright of freedom. It was that attribute of free personhood that Gerrit Smith, who would one day underwrite the raid on Harpers Ferry, vindicated in an open letter of 1839 to Henry Clay: "The laborers of the North are freemen and not slaves ... they marry whom they please, and are neither paired nor unpaired to suit the interests of the breeder, or seller, or buyer, of human stock."[35] No wrong lay in a free man's rightful desire, only in the master's absolute power. With the abolition of domestic slavery would come love's emancipation within the bonds of marriage, alongside the triumph of free market relations and wage labor.

On both sides of the Mason-Dixon line, therefore, love became a potent measure of the opposition between slavery and freedom. On some propositions there was accord—that love lay at the core of being human and transcended the calculus of dollars and cents. But not on the choice between free love and slavery. While proslavery doctrine exalted bondage as love, abolitionism validated the right of self-owning persons to love freely. If nothing else, all the arguing over slave breeding made explicit how much the legitimacy of creating wealth and exchanging commodities owed to the ways of love.

Just a week after the first Battle of Bull Run in July 1861, a planter in Alamance County, North Carolina, wrote a letter to Justice Thomas Ruffin about ordinary, neighborly property matters. As the dead were buried in Virginia, the letter proposed a slave marriage. Dated July 28, 1861, it stated:

> I am informed by my Boy Thomas that he wants your Negro girl Emily for a wife if it is agreeable with you and wants a recommendation. I can say that Thomas is a boy of good character sober and honest as far as I no of and is permitted to pass and repass to your house and home monday morning on good behaviour.

The letter spoke of the desire of slaves and the sovereignty of masters, noting that the planter's bondsman wanted a certain slave for his wife, asking whether Ruffin would agree, arranging a time for allowing the lovers to meet. It was a humdrum letter to a state court judge famed across the country for once ruling that a slave was a creature "who has no will of his own."[36] Written as war was overturning its premises, the planter's letter revealed how masters clung to their dominion over the love of slaves, still claiming it as a prerogative of ownership. By then, however, ex-slaves were recalling that in bondage they had dreamed of possessing human will as the emancipation of desire—and the end of slave breeding. Of all abolitionists, those who knew slavery best most keenly valued free love in claims of personhood.

Whether or not masters purposely bred slaves for sale, they surely appreciated the fortune to be reaped from slave increase, valuing it as a right of proprietorship. They pleaded so in court, resting not only their own wealth, but that of their children, and their children's children, on slave procreation. Especially in disputes over inheritance, contract, and debt, masters and would-be masters told of aspiring to grow slaves, not just crops. With ownership went deep interest in slaves' breeding.

The pleadings to the county courts told of future hopes and past promises—life stories, not simply livelihoods, that were bound up with the breeding of slaves. For instance, a Kentucky man pleaded in 1829 of "being anxious to obtain a negro woman about twenty four or five years of age of good qualities that would breed" and of being greatly damaged on discovering that he had bought an unhealthy woman. Two men in South Carolina, joined by their wives, asked permission of the court in 1820 to sell bank stock that the women had inherited from their father in order to buy slaves, figuring on better profits from investing in slave propagation—that "the increase of the Females would bring in a much greater Interest to them than the said Stock now produces." Planning on the prosperity that slave procreation would bring his own offspring, another South Carolina man specified in his will written sometime before his death in 1819 that his estate should be sold and the money for his heirs used in the "purchase of a negro woman that would breed."[37] Where no breeding followed from expectant buying, it fell to the courts to judge complaints of fraudulent contracts.

Ordinarily, masters simply bequeathed slave "Increases" to their own descendants, the wishes of the dead at once endowing and binding the living—as owners and owned—along with the progeny of both. Thus a North Carolina man at some point had willed to his granddaughter, and "her heirs & assignees forever," a slave woman "and her increase," property the mistress implored the court in 1836 to forbid other claimants from selling to "a slave speculator." There was a "very valuable" girl left by a Virginian, whose grandchildren declared "her value . . . enhanced from the fact that she is in a pregnant condition" in petitioning in 1832 against her being seized to pay their father's debts. Anxious about their inheritance, the grandchildren of a South Carolina testator asked the court in 1846 to order his widow, who held his slaves in a life estate, to treat them well, with "wholesome food and sufficient clothing," especially the women who "were in the habit of breeding very fast in the life time of the Testator."[38]

But when slaves did not breed, the pleadings record how masters strove to put them up for sale. A Virginia mistress had inherited "a negro girl . . . and her future increase," but her trustee asked the court in 1858 to be allowed to sell the girl, complaining that she "has had several miscarages and on that account not likely to bear children" and was "of very little or no value." Likewise, the guardian of four young boys in South Carolina asked in 1859 to sell a slave who had "stopped breeding," calling her "entirely valueless." That same year, the children of a planter who had left them about a thousand acres of South Carolina land and thirty-two slaves, pleading that "the females are barren and unproductive," also begged leave from the court to put them up for sale, contrary to the will's provision that families "not be separated." Some masters hedged against misfortune, such as a Kentucky man who in 1823 willed his daughter a slave while instructing that if "the said negro woman should not breed or increase . . . she should be sold."[39]

The pleadings reveal a world where masters banked on the increase of slaves, apparently foreseeing small risk in investing in the unborn, despite the deepening crisis over slavery. They afford no insight into how owners went about promoting slave increase or what occurred in the slave quarters. But the records do reveal how enterprising men dreamed of transforming a few "breeding negro women" with a handful of children into "fifty valuable slaves" in just a few years' time. As late as 1859, a South Carolina guardian still saw a "benefit" for his ward in paying $1,750 to purchase just one "breeding woman" and her two children. Sometimes masters complained of the costs involved in turning a profit on breeding women and raising their young. But it was only when the war came, and the Confederacy's fate grew uncertain, that a breeding slave came to appear worthless—a present burden, not an asset for the future. By 1864 the trustee of a bequest of Virginia slaves pleaded to the court that the "exigencies of the times and the great scarcity of provisions" made the cost of their upkeep greater than the revenue from "the said slaves, Martha, Patsey, &

Beckey and their increase." A slave who "breeds very fast" had simply become a "heavy expense," explained a South Carolina man who held in trust and sought to sell some slaves unreached by the Emancipation Proclamation.[40]

Thus slave masters gave new meaning to biblical injunctions about being fruitful and multiplying—the meaning deemed profane by abolitionists. None who petitioned the courts about slave breeding spoke of siring the increase. Yet contrasted with buying bonds, investing in stocks, or even buying the time of free laborers, or otherwise accumulating capital, there was nothing abstract about profiting from the love life of slaves. Agricultural journals detailed the husbandry at stake, the intimate power: from controlling slave marriage to lightening the fieldwork of breeders to allowing time for suckling.[41] The wealth of a plantation plainly lay in a measure of solicitude for the breeding body, if not for the heart or soul.

Of course, the desires of slaves did not govern their masters' narratives about the value of their increase. In perpetuity, masters bequeathed, deciding when the wants of their chattel suited their own interests, while slaves, without a will of their own recognized by law, were bought and sold on account of their procreative properties. It was only an ex-slave who had the standing to plead to lawmakers about the anguish of unfree love. Thus John Winston, a man emancipated by the will of his Virginia master but compelled by statute to leave the state or forfeit his liberty, petitioned to return home to his enslaved wife and children in Henrico County, Virginia. It was recorded in 1820 that he "laments that 'he was induced from the love of Liberty (the predominant passion of man) to make a sacrifice of his domestic happiness by quiting his Wife & two children whom he most ardently and tenderly loves—without whose society, he finds it impossible for him to be happy.'"[42] Two passions warred in the freedman's heart: the love of liberty and the love of his wife and children. No master knew that conflict; nor did any man coming of age in free society, no matter how far necessity might compel him to wander to make a living, or how much more alluring personal liberty might seem than marriage bonds. Free love was a right not readily won for persons bred as slaves.

Meanwhile, as masters planned for posterity, ex-slaves who rose from obscurity by depicting their lives in bondage poured into memoirs their longing for both love and freedom.[43] In those narratives, loving freely represented the antithesis of slave breeding. And the slave's rightful desires stood opposed to the master's appetites; before even the yearning for marriage bonds came the stirring of sensual love.

"When I was about seventeen, I was deeply smitten in love," recalled Jacob Green, a runaway from Kentucky, in his 1864 autobiography. But his beloved

belonged to another master. Still, her smiles were "like the May morning sun-
beams," her voice was "sweet as the dulcimer," and her eyes broke his "heart in
pieces, with a stroke like that of an earthquake." He described his passion—"O,
I thought, this girl would make me a paradice, and to enjoy her love I thought
would be heaven"—and how he stole away to her quarters at night, despite
"either patroles or dogs, who stood in my way." He remembered the "crazy love
and courtship." But it ended when his master whipped Green, "having learnt
all the particulars," forcing him to marry a slave who soon bore their master's
child: "At the age of 20, my master told me I must marry. . . . We had been
about five months married when she gave birth to a child, I then asked who was
the father . . . and she said the master, and I had every reason to believe her, as
the child was nearly white."[44]

Forcible mating went hand in hand with slave breeding, wrote another Kentucky fugitive, Andrew Jackson, in his 1847 narrative. Down from the master
came "the order for us to 'get married,' according to Slavery—or, in other words,
to enrich his plantation by a family of young slaves. The alternative of this was,
to be sold to a slave trader."[45] With an iron collar around his neck, chained in
a coffle of slaves bound from his native Maryland to Georgia, Charles Ball had
dreamed of home at night, while seeing by day the wealth accruing from growing slaves—all the while plotting his own liberation. Sleep brought "pleasant
dreams . . . I thought I had, by some means . . . made my way back to Maryland;
and was again in the cabin of my wife," Ball remembered in his 1837 account
of his life. But the living nightmare of the coffle's Southern march returned
at sunrise. A stranger rode up, asking if the slaves were for sale, breeders in
particular:

> He wanted a couple of breeding-wenches, and would give as much for them
> as they would bring in Georgia. . . . He then walked along our line, as we
> stood chained together . . . then turning to the women, asked the prices of
> the two pregnant ones. Our master replied, that these were two of the best
> breeding-wenches in all Maryland . . . and that such wenches would be cheap at
> a thousand dollars each.[46]

So ex-slaves counterposed the desire to love freely with the wrong of slave
breeding.

Visions of free love haunted slave narratives of emancipation as powerfully
as the pursuit of wealth guided masters' narratives of proprietorship. For some
ex-slaves, the vision was so powerful that it meant avoiding all unfree love. In
an 1847 narrative of his bondage in Missouri, William Wells Brown described

feeling promptings of the heart and the flesh, and evading the wife that his mistress chose for him, for his "love had already gone in another quarter." But he vowed never to have a slave wife, refusing all but the bonds of free love. "I determined never to marry any woman on earth until I should get my liberty," Brown wrote. "I knew that if I should have a wife, I should not be willing to leave her behind; and if I should attempt to bring her with me, the chances would be difficult for success." He recalled slaves whose masters forced them together, pointing out that Missouri was a breeding state, "very much engaged in raising slaves to supply the southern market."[47]

Others recounted falling in love and asking for their masters' consent—and knowingly collaborating in the accumulation of wealth. As a Kentucky slave, wrote Henry Bibb in an 1849 memoir, he lost his heart to "a mulatto slave girl . . . of an extraordinary make," though having resolved to seek only freedom. He spoke of the "smooth texture" of her skin, her "red cheeks, with dark penetrating eyes," and her "benevolence, talent and industry." He described sensuous desire as potent as the dream of emancipation, marveling how the "fascinating charms of a female" had distracted him from aspiring to "be free or die."

> In spite of myself, before I was aware of it, I was deeply in love; and what made this passion so effectual and almost irresistable, I became satisfied that it was reciprocal. . . . These strong temptations gradually diverted my attention from my actual condition and from liberty.

The siren song of unfree love led to a slave marriage, his master agreeing, on "one condition . . . too vulgar to be written." And so Bibb bred a slave—"propagating victims"—yet then escaped alone, only to return as a fugitive several times, in vain, to carry away his family, risking his own liberty for the sake of an elusive free love.[48]

No ex-slave meditated more deeply than Harriet Jacobs on love as defining the difference between slavery and freedom. It was not simply that her 1861 account of life as a slave in North Carolina told of being the object of her master's desires, but that it brought to light a conflict of wills about sensual experience. She testified that slave breeding always interested masters, with slave women being obliged to "increase their owner's stock," and her own children, fathered by a white lover, claimed by her master as property that would one day bring "a handsome sum of money." But Jacobs was interested in loving freely. She wrote of feeling the "ardor of a young girl's first love"—how once she had created a "love-dream" destroyed by slavery of marrying a free-born black man—and of defying her master who claimed dominion "in *every* thing." She recalled her master as "restless, craving," and decreeing her "made for his use" and "subject to his will." She remembered one exchange, especially.

> "So you want to be married, do you. . . . If you *must* have a husband, you may take up with one of my slaves."
>
> What a situation I should be in, as the wife of one of his slaves, even if my heart had been interested!
>
> I replied, "Don't you suppose, sir, that a slave can have some preference about marrying? Do you suppose that all men are alike to her?" . . .
>
> "Do you know that I have a right to do as I like with you . . . ?"

Laying bare the conflict between love and slavery, Jacobs pondered her own desires as she asked, "Why does the slave ever love?" She dreamed of the "freedom in having a lover who has no control over you," as she pitted her own moral will against her master's power.[49]

And no ex-slave wrote more searingly than Frederick Douglass of unfree love as a condition of being chattel and of the emancipation of desire as a condition of being human. In *My Bondage and My Freedom* he described the love between two slaves owned by different masters, a union that his own master violently forbade from motives "brutal and selfish." Yet the slaves "loved and courted," for their passion was too powerful. "Meet they would, and meet they did," remembered Douglass. "A woman's love is not to be annihilated by the peremptory command of anyone." But then came the whip. It fell again and again on the slave woman who stood half naked on a bench in his master's kitchen, her wrists tied with a rope attached to a joist above. "Each blow, vigorously laid on, brought screams as well as blood. '*Have mercy; Oh! Have mercy*' she cried; '*I won't do so no more.*'"[50]

If only, Frederick Douglass despaired, the lovers could have joined "in the high sense," bound not by slavery, but only by "such hearts as are purer and higher than the standard morality around them."[51] Thus he claimed free love—obeying the heart's desire—as intrinsic to the personhood negated by slavery, an institution whose essence arguably lay in making a profit from human procreation through slave breeding.

When the Yankee minister Charles Grandison Finney, whose antebellum revivals inspired the conversion of multitudes of sinners, sought to reveal the meaning of freedom and slavery, he turned to the condition of a woman bound to a man she did not love. "If she preferred another man to him, and lived with her own husband, from other considerations than love, she would be a slave and not free." The lesson came in Finney's *True and False Religion*, an 1839 lecture that linked sensuous life to abstract doctrine in teaching that slavery was treating a human being endowed with "moral agency" as a thing. Of course, true freedom did not amount to "unrestrained indulgence of lust and selfishness." But the very essence of slavery was being "obliged to choose against our feelings and inclinations."[52] Preaching an ethos not of self-abnegation but of desire, in keeping with a new gospel of Protestantism that glorified free will rather than predestination, Finney revealed the place of love in distinguishing between freedom and slavery.

By the time Finney spoke of loving freely, the argument over slave breeding had been joined, with a vengeance. Virginia slave masters had spoken of the business in their statehouse, and Yankee abolitionists were decrying the rise of slave-breeding states, protesting the Southern interest in annexing Texas as a new market for slaves. Soon, in disputing slavery's westward extension, legislators in Congress would agitate about the unspeakable wrong of breeding slaves for sale—a debate that would resonate across the Atlantic. Meanwhile, testators and their heirs counted on an abundant slave increase, even as proslavery theorists disowned the enterprise, and abolitionists contrasted it to the fruits of free labor on free soil. And ex-slaves counterposed the ideal of loving freely to the evil of slave breeding, understanding moral agency to mean not simply self-mastery—and with it self-discipline and self-denial—but the emancipation of feelings and inclinations, of the heart and flesh. All the while spindles wound with American cotton multiplied across the world.

The past does not readily yield up the secrets of Southern plantations, where the master's dominion was said to touch *every* thing. The truth of slave breeding is hard to know—if it was a myth invented by abolitionists to contrast the wrongs of bondage to the rights of freedom, or if it was a fact rooted in the commerce in cotton and slaves that joined the agony of unfree love to the burgeoning of industrial capitalism as well as to the spread of chattel slavery. By no means is it clear what transpired between master and slave to produce an increase of slaves.

But what was said—how abolitionists and slaveowners argued about slave breeding—is not inscrutable. How they disagreed irrevocably about the nature of slavery's intimate bonds, about the virtues of free market relations, about the legitimacy of raising human stock as a source of wealth along with land and labor, about the reasons slaves were in oversupply in the upper South and ended up in the cotton kingdom, and about the fortunes of love under the interlocking but opposing systems of capitalism and slavery. And how they agreed only that growing slaves for sale was worse than trafficking in slaves, because it implanted the values of the market within the most private recesses of life and profaned the divinity of human procreation. Establishing love's potency in the conflict between slavery and freedom, their argument was as much about eros and civilization as about profit, power, and personhood. Morally it severed what cotton joined—the sway of capitalism and the unfree propagation of persons as commodities. Not only deepening the strife that led to the Civil War, the argument over slave breeding gave rise to an antislavery vision of free love as a birthright of human beings.

Acknowledgments

I am grateful for the insights and criticisms of Craig Becker, David Brion Davis, Leslie Harris, Dirk Hartog, Michael Johnson, Walter Johnson, Gary Kornblith, Jane Lyle, Jon Levy, Mary Ryan, Emily Remus, Kristin Warbasse, Ron Walters, and Michael Zakim, as well as for the opportunity to present versions of this essay at the Gilder Lehrman Center for the Study of Slavery, Resistance, and Abolition at Yale University, the Nineteenth Century Seminar at Johns Hopkins University, and a conference on Slavery's Capitalism jointly sponsored by Brown University and Harvard University.

6

Capitalism and the Rise of the Corporation Nation

Robert E. Wright

When did America become capitalist? The answer depends on whom one asks. It was always capitalist and yet is still not to this day. In fact, dating the rise of American capitalism depends on how *capital* is defined. Physical capital encompasses the material implements of production and distribution, including farms, factories, and ships.[1] Human capital refers to people's ability to use physical capital to produce economic goods, physical products, and services that consumers value. Financial capital refers to contracts—bills of (foreign) exchange, bonds, book or trade credit, equities (stocks), hybrid securities, loans, and mortgages—that individuals and businesses use to obtain cash they subsequently exchange for physical and human capital.[2] Today's capitalists, as well as early America's "moneyed men" or "men of capital," could be corporate stock- and bondholders, proprietors of their own businesses, partners in mercantile "houses" or other business firms, or, in many cases, all three simultaneously.[3] They owned or controlled some combination of physical, human, and financial capital, but the financial capital alone set them apart from other types of economic elites. Ancient despots, feudal lords, communist dictators, and criminal kingpins wanted not for land, laborers (free, slave, or in between),[4] or even money, but most observers do not consider them capitalists, or the systems in which they acted capitalism, because they lacked the more sophisticated forms of financial capital, those associated with for-profit business corporations (hereafter simply corporations). Capitalism does not rely solely on wage laborers but can use serfs, slaves, sole proprietors ("contractors" and "consultants"), and even other corporations as labor inputs. By contrast, capitalism does rely on stocks, bonds, hybrids, bank loans, and other sophisticated forms of financial capital, which serve as its hallmarks. The ebb and flow of financial markets and institutions therefore demarcate capitalism's emergence, development, and abeyance better than any other marker, including wage labor.

It is important to note here that financial capital did not *cause* capitalism. Rather, its appearance and proliferation was an effect of capitalism, of the supply of and demand for the financial resources needed to own or control the large amounts of physical and human capital necessary to produce goods at low cost (as opposed to price, as discussed below). Financial capital is the trail left behind as capitalism wended its way through the forests of economic history. The causes of capitalism are too complex, too contested, and too little understood to resolve here. It is necessary to know *what* happened before exploring reasons *why* it happened. Students of the early American economy are still a long way from agreeing on what, making a consensus on why impossible to achieve.

Encouragingly, financial capital can be measured, though imprecisely to be sure. All types have left some traces in the historical record. Some varieties, like mortgages, bonds, and equities, left a better trail than others, like book credit, bills of exchange, and personal loans, but the general outline is clear. Bills of exchange, book credit, personal loans, and mortgages came to America with the Pilgrims. Their quantity is unknown and unknowable (except for mortgages) but undoubtedly small. Later in the colonial period, more sophisticated forms of financial capital, such as negotiable bonds, equities, and bank loans, became available but only in extremely limited quantities. Not until the early 1790s did the newer forms begin to grow rapidly in importance, becoming a veritable flood in the early decades of the nineteenth century.[5]

Government bonds—interest-bearing IOUs issued by governments—were rarely issued or traded in colonial America and few colonists invested in British government bonds like Consols. After mid-century British authorities forbade the New England colonies from issuing bills of credit, which served as a medium of exchange and a means of government borrowing. After the ban, Massachusetts had to issue interest-bearing bonds to finance its budget deficits. Even in Boston, however, little trading occurred in government bonds. During the Revolution, the national and most state governments issued bonds to help finance the war. Bond trading expanded in the 1780s but remained a highly speculative activity due to the inability of the new governments to pay interest and principal as promised. After the formation of a new national government under the Constitution of 1787 and the reforms implemented at the behest of Treasury Secretary Alexander Hamilton, including tariffs, funding of the old national debt, assumption of the states' debts by the national government, and establishment of a central bank, government bond trading flourished. Beginning in 1790, thousands of trades encompassing millions of dollars of government bonds took place each year in the securities markets and exchanges of Boston, New York, Philadelphia, Baltimore, Richmond, and Charleston, South Carolina. Most bondholders, about three-quarters of the 20,000 or so economic entities (individuals, businesses, governments) who owned bonds at any given time, held bonds with a total face value of between $100 and $10,000, but fewer than 200 entities (state governments, business corporations, nonprofit corporations, large mercantile partnerships, and wealthy individuals) owned over half of the bonds by face value. Most of the bonds (by face value) were held by entities in more commercial states, but even in agricultural states like Virginia bondholders could be found in almost every county.[6]

Government bonds were so frequently traded that early national newspapers regularly published their prices, alongside the prices of the stocks (equities) of the largest and most important corporations.[7] Capitalists routinely invested in both public and private securities. Trading in corporate shares was not as active as today but was nevertheless often considerable. Early brokerages handled thousands of trades totaling hundreds of thousands and sometimes millions of dollars annually. Stockholding patterns were similar to the government bondholding patterns described above and, indeed, stockholding patterns today. In most cases, a large number of investors owned a few shares each while a handful owned large blocks of stock.[8] Most corporate shares were owned by residents of the nation's bigger towns and cities, but investors in some corporation or another could be found in almost every village and hamlet, even in remote areas like Maine and upstate New York. That was possible, nay necessary, because of the prodigious quantity of corporations and corporate financial capital formed in the United States between 1790 and 1860.[9]

Despite a clarion call issued by Thomas Cochran in 1974, scholars to date have explored corporation formation in only a few states and in every case concentrated solely on the number of corporations and not their total authorized capitalization, the aggregate number of dollars they were lawfully empowered to raise from equity investors, which is arguably the best metric of US financial capitalism available.[10] Presented here, for the first time, are the number and authorized capitalization of all corporations to receive a special charter or act of incorporation before the Civil War (see tables 6.1 and 6.2, respectively). Both figures are conservative estimates because corporations chartered under general acts of incorporation are not included and only the minimum authorized capital is reported. Many corporations were allowed to raise more than the minimum reported, and the many early charters that did not specify capital requirements are counted as zero.

Before 1861, state governments specially incorporated over 22,000 businesses representing a wide range of industries, including banking (commercial and savings), cemeteries, education (schools, circulating libraries), entertainment (hotels, theaters, parks), infrastructure (canals, railroads, turnpikes), insurance (marine, fire, life), manufacturing (of all stripes), mining (coal, precious metals, sundry ores), transportation (common carriers from stagecoaches to steamship lines), gas and water utilities, and others. Several thousand more corporations formed under general incorporation laws, most late in the antebellum period. Research is ongoing but slowed by the relatively poor record-keeping of state governments. It is clear, however, that nationwide many more antebellum corporations formed under special laws than under general ones. Whether chartered by a special law or a general act establishing a purely bureaucratic incorporation process, most early US corporations could extend de facto limited liability to stockholders. By protecting stockholders from their corporations' creditors, limited liability widened the pool of potential investors and hence made it easier to attract much needed capital.

Proliferation of the corporate form began in the 1790s and the first two decades of the nineteenth century. The movement began primarily in the North, where the number of corporations per 100,000 people jumped from less than 1 to almost 23 and corporate capitalization per person soared from $0.27 to over $12. The panic of 1819 slowed the rate of growth in the 1820s in both the North and South, but corporate capitalism accelerated in the 1830s and became a national rather than a largely Northern phenomenon. The best evidence of the former claim is at the bottom of table 6.2, which shows that the ratio of minimum authorized capital to Gross Domestic Product increased from the low double digits in the 1800s and 1810s to almost 70 in the 1830s. The latter is best seen by comparing the South's per capita (including slaves) minimum authorized capital, which at $60 was just shy of the North's $62 in the 1830s. In the 1850s, the South's $99 of corporate capital per capita greatly exceeded the North's $59. The South that decade chartered more corporations per 100,000 people, around 33, than the North did at 28.5, and on average Southern corporations had much higher minimum authorized capitalizations than Northern ones did.

The growth of corporations and corporate capital slowed in the 1840s in both the North and South, largely due to the extended recession that followed the financial panics of 1837 and 1839. Per capita figures remained well above those of the 1820s in both sections, however, suggesting that the corporate form had already become a major structural feature of the economy. By the 1850s, it was clear that the West would join the corporation nation as well. Railroads were certainly an important part of nineteenth-century US economic development, but they thrived in America like no other place because the corporate form was already so well established there. Alfred Chandler and other scholars who place greater emphasis on the second half of the nineteenth century simply overlooked the process of becoming, the precise timing and path by which the US economy broke loose the shackles of traditional, precapitalist, and proto-capitalist forms of ownership like sole proprietorships and partnerships and evolved ever-larger and ever more efficient modes of production.

The United States was the world's first "corporation nation," the first country suffused with corporations. The rapid economic development of Canada, France, Germany, Japan, the Scandinavian countries, and others came only after America had become a nation of corporations, a land endowed with billions of dollars of the most sophisticated forms of financial capital. Although Holland and Britain started to become capitalist well before the United States did, neither country by the early nineteenth century had embraced the corporation as a major form of business organization. Until the middle of the century, financial capital in both countries mostly took the form of government and business bonds, bank loans, foreign exchange, and mortgages. Their late adoption of the corporate form may explain their relative decline.

Americans readily recognized the distinctiveness of their corporate version of capitalism. "The practice of carrying on business by corporations," one observer noted in 1829, "has been much more prevalent in the United States than in England."[11] "What is done in England by combination," authors Joseph Angell and Samuel Ames argued in 1832,

> is most generally done by a combination of individuals, established by mere articles of agreement. On the other hand, what is done here by the co-operation of several persons, is, in the greater number of instances, the result of a consolidation

Table 6.1. For-profit business corporations specially chartered in the United States through 1860, by decade

State	Through 1790	1791–1800	1801–1810	1811–1820	1821–1830	1831–1840	1841–1850	1851–1860	Total
NORTH									
Connecticut	3	41	53	25	16	23	68	174	403
Delaware	0	2	8	13	15	32	24	56	150
Illinois	0	0	0	9	7	173	76	420	685
Indiana	0	0	2	6	12	227	292	63	602
Maine	0	0	0	2	152	488	271	467	1,380
Massachusetts	6	75	219	273	330	539	499	581	2,522
Michigan	0	0	0	4	10	87	224	0	325
New Hampshire	0	29	54	71	117	184	183	180	818
New Jersey	0	12	39	66	74	180	174	431	976
New York	1	26	218	266	314	535	167	200	1,727
Ohio	0	0	8	60	58	432	575	172	1,305
Pennsylvania	4	19	67	208	151	425	436	1,029	2,339
Rhode Island	3	17	30	48	40	73	62	168	441
Vermont	0	18	56	52	66	134	117	221	664
Wisconsin	0	0	0	0	0	26	51	235	312
North no.	17	239	754	1,103	1,362	3,558	3,219	4,397	14,649
North pop.	2,027,136	2,388,996	3,291,264	4,528,799	6,157,536	8,426,494	11,502,742	15,437,506	
Per 100,000	0.84	10.00	22.91	24.36	22.12	42.22	27.98	28.48	

SOUTH

Alabama	0	0	9	22	88	98	182	399
Arkansas	0	0	0	0	27	9	60	96
District of Columbia	0	0	5	1	0	1	4	11
Florida	0	0	0	9	51	13	42	115
Georgia	1	9	11	20	112	75	278	506
Kentucky	1	7	72	24	184	238	625	1,151
Louisiana	0	2	13	18	81	6	45	165
Maryland	17	30	83	71	171	220	220	816
Mississippi	0	2	5	4	83	58	100	252
Missouri	0	0	2	1	69	72	508	652
North Carolina	8	16	29	25	101	75	351	606
South Carolina	6	14	12	22	56	51	108	273
Tennessee	0	2	15	6	110	98	92	323
Texas	0	0	0	1	8	36	136	181
Virginia	11	31	118	72	463	350	812	1,863
South no.	15	113	374	296	1,604	1,400	3,563	7,409
South pop.	2,229,853	2,982,918	3,910,639	5,092,132	6,513,771	8,414,735	10,888,141	
Per 100,000	1.97	3.79	9.56	5.81	24.62	16.64	32.72	

Source: Richard Sylla and Robert E. Wright, "U.S. Corporate Development, 1801–1860," National Science Foundation Grant.

Table 6.2. Minimum authorized capitalization (MINAC) of for-profit business corporations specially chartered in the United States through 1860, by decade (millions of dollars)

State	Through 1790	1791–1800	1801–1810	1811–1820	1821–1830	1831–1840	1841–1850	1851–1860	Total
NORTH									
Connecticut	0	0.62	1.63	2.16	3.55	4.01	15.713	30.048	57.731
Delaware	0	0.6	1.085	0.592	2.506	5.728	2.925	6.826	20.262
Illinois	0	0	0	0.55	1.501	31.283	9.261	83.81	126.405
Indiana	0	0	0.1	2.2	0.447	8.995	8.943	2.431	23.116
Maine	0	0	0	0.15	15.227	47.08	26.788	140.063	229.308
Massachusetts	0	2.006	9.842	35.956	58.73	88.265	90.307	102.159	387.265
Michigan	0	0	0	0.1	0.57	17.15	36.483	0	54.303
New Hampshire	0	0.4	0.002	0	2.05	24.238	41.512	18.347	86.549
New Jersey	0	0.528	1.022	6.469	8.578	21.291	11.924	32.318	82.13
New York	0.15	4.747	13.098	33.511	38.806	88.948	22.716	127.571	329.547
Ohio	0	0	0.82	6.485	5.751	89.728	102.864	30.037	235.685
Pennsylvania	0.4	2.74	10.814	27.579	24.801	62.942	70.615	171.072	370.963
Rhode Island	0	0.961	2.07	3.943	2.065	12.842	8.679	32.37	62.93
Vermont	0	0	0.025	0.155	2.966	16.506	5.475	16.62	41.747
Wisconsin	0	0	0	0	0	3.37	1.961	111.474	116.805
North MINAC	0.55	12.602	40.508	119.850	167.548	522.376	456.166	905.146	2224.750
North pop.	2,027,136	2,388,996	3,291,264	4,528,799	6,157,536	8,426,494	11,502,742	15,437,506	
Per capita	$0.27	$5.28	$12.31	$26.46	$27.21	$61.99	$39.66	$58.63	

SOUTH

									Total
Alabama		0	0	1.262	2.681	22.845	11.313	19.525	57.626
Arkansas			0	0	0	2.879	0.945	5.515	9.339
District of Columbia		0	0	0.852	0.25	0	0.05	0.95	2.102
Florida		0	0	0	0.174	14.518	2.725	7.103	24.52
Kentucky		0.016	1.242	13.995	4.431	39.176	37.148	167.532	263.54
Louisiana		0	0.2	4.175	6.706	63.545	1.81	148.874	225.31
Georgia		0.004	2.33	4.01	6.97	43.161	20.528	65.808	142.811
Maryland	0.251	2.862	9.601	16.809	26.82	40.852	41.501	66.688	205.384
Mississippi		0	0.052	0.635	1.125	14.064	8.794	6.418	31.088
Missouri		0	0	0.4	0.001	24.001	24.624	241.755	290.781
North Carolina		0.145	2.635	0.832	0.526	21.333	3.831	59.945	89.247
South Carolina		0.35	2.15	3.1	1.356	25.503	12.08	31.88	76.419
Tennessee		0	0.212	1.92	0.545	26.34	6.489	8.304	43.81
Texas		0	0	0	1	7.608	3.615	91.54	103.763
Virginia	0.436	1.116	3.39	11.88	14.166	47.432	37.078	155.217	270.715
South MINAC	0.687	4.493	21.812	59.87	66.751	393.257	212.531	1,077.054	1,836.455
South pop.	1,902,078	2,229,853	2,982,918	3,910,638.5	5,092,132	6,513,770.5	8,414,735	10,888,140.5	
Per capita	$0.36	$2.01	$7.31	$15.31	$13.11	$60.37	$25.26	$98.92	

Table 6.2. (continued)

State	Through 1790	1791–1800	1801–1810	1811–1820	1821–1830	1831–1840	1841–1850	1851–1860	Total
WEST									
California	0	0	0	0	0	0	0	0	0
Colorado	0	0	0	0	0	0	0	0.147	0.147
Iowa	0	0	0	0	0	1.383	0.864	0	2.247
Kansas	0	0	0	0	0	0	0	249.053	249.053
Minnesota	0	0	0	0	0	0	0.025	172.011	172.036
Nebraska	0	0	0	0	0	0	0	53.781	53.781
New Mexico	0	0	0	0	0	0	0	14.3	14.3
Oregon	0	0	0	0	0	0	0.005	13.874	13.879
Utah	0	0	0	0	0	0	0	1.015	1.015
Washington	0	0	0	0	0	0	0	16.86	16.86
West no.	0	0	0	0	0	1.383	0.894	521.041	523.318
West pop.	0	0	0	0	0	21,556	204,771	943,491	12,242
Per capita	$0.00	$0.00	$0.00	$0.00	$0.00	$64.16	$4.37	$552.25	
Total MINAC	1.237	17.095	62.320	179.720	234.299	917.016	669.591	2,503.241	
GDP	190.000	380.000	560.000	920.000	810.000	1,330.000	1,840.000	3,940.000	
MINAC/GDP	0.65%	4.50%	11.13%	19.53%	28.93%	68.95%	36.39%	63.53%	

Source: Richard Sylla and Robert E. Wright, "U.S. Corporate Development, 1801–1860," National Science Foundation Grant.

effected by an express act or charter of incorporation. We cannot but be impressed
with a deep sense of the importance of this law in our own country [because]
in no country have corporations been multiplied to so great an extent, as in
our own.[12]

Even more than individual capitalists, partnerships, or other forms of business organization, corporations lay at the nexus of all three types of capital—
physical, human, and financial. Almost invariably, they issued equities, bonds,
and hybrid securities and took out bank loans to command the cash needed
to purchase plant, equipment, and raw materials and to obtain the services of
managers and laborers. As investors, corporations held bank deposits, owned
government bonds as remunerative secondary reserves, bought insurance policies, extended trade credit to suppliers and customers, and even purchased the
stocks and bonds of other corporations. The variety of financial instruments
available to investors was staggering.[13] Before the Civil War, U.S. newspapers
listed the prices of at least 365 different state, 177 municipal, 125 U.S. government, and 318 corporate bonds, and the share prices of 356 different manufacturing, mining, and utility companies, 301 transportation concerns, 300
banks, and 217 insurers.[14]

The importance of early US corporations lay in their ubiquity and their
great size relative to most proprietorships and partnerships. "Manufactures
cannot be carried on to any great extent in this country," textile magnate Nathan Appleton claimed, "in any other manner than by joint stock companies. A
large capital is necessary to success." Corporations were necessary, an observer
noted in 1835, "to accomplish those vast and important enterprises that individual effort and skill are inadequate to perform." "With regard to establish-
ments where considerable capital is requisite, other things being equal," another observer noted, "persons acting under a charter of incorporation would
have great advantages over persons doing the same business under articles of
copartnership."[15]

The corporate form made large-scale operations possible in several ways.
Foremost, the vast majority of early American corporate charters automatically provided limited liability, the shielding of stockholders' assets from the
corporation's debts, which made it relatively easy to attract investors.[16] They
also provided entity shielding, which protected the corporation's assets from
its stockholders' debts and eased the development of secondary markets in
stock. Other boons to investors in corporate securities were perpetual succession, or the power to change owners without having to dissolve and re-form
the company, and the right to sue and be sued in the name of the company,

legal privileges not available to traditional partnerships or most other business forms. The ability to buy and sell shares quickly and cheaply of course further added to investor demand, enabling corporations to grow much larger than unchartered competitors.

The large scale, however, imposed costs, known by economists as agency costs, which threatened profitability at the hands of lazy, incompetent, or rapacious managers. Adam Smith was a staunch critic of most types of corporations, arguing persuasively that agency costs made them inefficient and unjust. "Being the managers rather of other people's money than of their own," Smith argued, managers did not watch over the business "with the same anxious vigilance with which the partners in a private copartnery frequently watch over their own."[17] Indeed, some early US manufacturing endeavors, including iron production and tanning, did not benefit from being big, at least not at first. Unsurprisingly, the corporate form was relatively unimportant in those sectors until the mid-1800s.[18]

Many early US capitalists discovered that agency costs could be ameliorated by forming a corporation. A wide variety of corporate governance strictures, including prudent mean voting rules (between the extremes of one vote per stockholder and one vote per share) and explicit charter provisions that constrained managerial decision making regarding the scope and location of corporate activities, made it difficult for corporate officers to steal, self-deal, or otherwise promote their own interests ahead of those of stockholders.[19] Incorporation certainly did not eliminate agency costs, but it usually lowered them enough to underline the benefits of bigness, which were fourfold. First, large size sometimes allowed corporations to decrease the unit cost of production by increasing the volume of output or, in other words, to exploit economies of scale. Second, large size could enable vertical integration, the acquisition of suppliers or distributors.[20] For example, Francis Cabot Lowell's Boston Manufacturing Company, which was initially capitalized at $400,000, was the first to arrange "all the processes for the conversion of cotton into cloth, within the walls of the same building." Similarly, integration of pig iron producers with rolling mills beginning in the 1850s led to greater administrative and production efficiency.[21] In the 1840s gas works began to establish fitting shops to help their customers enjoy better-quality light than that provided by the fixtures installed by many third-party vendors. Third, bigness allowed for greater research and development efforts, like those that went into the power loom, dressing machine, and double speeder at the Boston Manufacturing Company. New corporate manufacturing processes, like printing textiles with automated cylinders rather than by hand with blocks, created great fortunes but also sometimes benefited consumers by enabling companies to cut production costs and, ultimately, prices.[22]

Due to corporate market power, however, lower production costs per unit did not necessarily equate into lower prices for consumers. The fourth benefit of large size, in other words, was the ability of some corporations to influence prices and hence to earn large profits by passing taxes and other costs onto consumers.[23] Early consumers readily recognized market power, which became the source of considerable anticorporation sentiment. For instance, a consumer complained in 1827 that an incorporated oil company created vitriol that was "neither better or cheaper than before."[24] A few years later, Pennsylvania corporate critic George Taylor claimed that a few coal companies deliberately glutted Philadelphia with coal in order to depress prices and run independent miners out of business. Other customers of corporations with market power clearly realized that they were paying more, or getting less, than they would have in a more competitive market.[25] "It may be safely asserted, as a general rule," a New Yorker wrote in 1835, "that when any set of men, acting in private business under a grant of privilege, make more than the usual rate of interest, the excess above that usual rate is so much deducted from the earnings of the great unprivileged masses." "Monopolies, throughout the world, and at all periods," a peeved New Jerseyite wrote in 1848, "have been marked by certain distinguishing characteristics. Their *object* has always been the same, that of imposing heavy taxes by selling bad commodities at high prices, and thus picking the pockets of those who were compelled to trade with them."[26]

It is important to note that early Americans did not possess the vocabulary to express market power with precision, so they labeled as "monopoly" every business that did not function in the perfectly competitive markets (characterized by numerous small firms with no control over prices) described by Adam Smith. As William Alexander Duer put it, "monopolies are sole grants of any trade or occupation, or of exclusive privileges, which ought to be common."[27] Such a broad definition allowed Taylor to claim, without contradiction, that the Pennsylvania coal trade had been "surrendered to *three* incorporated Companies, to speculate on the property; to *monopolize* the trade; to buy and sell at their will and pleasure."[28] Thus early anti-*monopoly* laws tried to serve the same purposes as today's anti-*trust* or *competition* laws, that is, to prevent sellers from "compelling the necessitous to pay an exorbitant price."[29] Very few early US corporations fit today's definition of monopoly (a single company that controls an entire market and can mandate prices and quantities) or even duopoly, but almost all sought to garner some market power (ranging from monopolistic competition to oligopoly).[30]

American producers who competed against corporations, especially those who did so unsuccessfully, understandably complained bitterly about the proliferation of the corporate form.[31] Marine insurance underwriters failed to compete successfully against the new joint-stock insurers and screamed bloody murder about it. The corporate "dry dock and steam sawmill throw hundreds of useful mechanics out of work," a critic complained in 1827. Similarly, Taylor argued that Pennsylvania coal-mining corporations were much less efficient than proprietorships and partnerships but nevertheless still threatened to "ruin . . . the individual operators engaged in the Coal Trade."[32] Journeymen cordwainers at an 1835 meeting in Newark, New Jersey, said that they "entirely disapprove of the incorporation of Companies, for carrying on manual mechanical business, inasmuch as we believe their tendency is to eventuate and produce monopolies, thereby crippling the energies of individual enterprise, and invading the rights of smaller capitalists."[33] A related fear was that corporations, especially large manufacturing ones, would degrade American artisans to the level of European laborers, who "were notoriously of the lowest character, for intelligence and morals." In response, many mill owners, North and South, engaged in paternalistic practices, including employing mostly unmarried female operatives.[34]

"Corporations, like individuals," Appleton argued, "will succeed or fail, as they are directed by skill and intelligence, or without them." Critics, however, continued to argue that corporations were often crippled by agency costs, specifically by managers who enriched themselves at the expense of shareholders. Managers of the Camden and Amboy Railroad, for example, allegedly charged high freights on New Jersey farmers' peaches so that their own peaches, transported at reduced rates, could win the lucrative New York market. Similarly, Taylor argued that chartered coal companies were "overwhelmed with debts created by their incapacity, profusion and mismanagement."[35] Managers of the incorporated companies, he claimed, regularly defrauded shareholders by hiring inept engineers and indifferent traders, by manipulating stock prices, and even by directly expropriating corporate assets.

Other critics bemoaned the bankruptcy of corporations, usually because they believed, sometimes but not usually correctly, that the failed businesses had been founded merely to expropriate wealth from the community.[36] According to one observer, many state legislatures had granted charters "in many cases no doubt injudiciously, and without making a suitable provision for the protection of their creditors."[37] "The company goes into operation," one critic explained, "the stock is puffed up like an empty bladder—divers beggars get on horseback—divers men swell out to the dimensions of a *plum*." Then, as suddenly "as the bubble swelled it bursts . . . and no traces of the 'company' remain, but the disgrace of the community and the ruin of thousands." "We need not wonder at the immense exertions," Taylor wrote, "and the cunning devices used to get hold of a charter."[38] Corporate monopolies helped the rich to grow richer, critics contended, but did little or nothing for the common person. Such sentiments were particularly strong after the corporate governance scandals that rocked New York in the mid-1820s.[39]

Unsurprisingly, many early Americans also feared that corporations would destroy republican political institutions with bribery and graft. To obtain a charter "every species of artifice and circumvention were resorted to," complained Taylor. "What cannot be obtained by intrigue," he noted, "may be yielded to entreaty."[40] "A knot of needy or greedy speculators," began one common story, "get together, and engender some specious project, as a pretext for an act of incorporation." They then proceed to "select some dealer in political corruption, grown grey in the slimy vortex of shifts and expedients," who actively seeks out each legislator's most pressing need. If necessary, the lobbyist, as we would term him today, meets that need by promising anything necessary to obtain the legislator's vote, including a job in the new concern for a friend, debtor, or wayward cousin, other favors, stocks, or even cold cash. The lobbyist picks his victims with an expert eye, then "dogs him from his lodgings to the capitol, and from the capitol to his lodgings—he fetches and carries for him—gives dinners and suppers—sports Champagne and Burgundy and whiskey punch—tells excellent stories and sings good songs." If the vote fails on the floor, the lobbyist redoubles his efforts. "So potent have sometimes been these endeavours," one observer claimed, "that a single night has been known to bring about the conversion of at least a dozen members." Early Americans also saw in banks and other types of for-profit corporations the broader threat of "inequality and despotism" and a type of "special privilege" that smacked of a "permanent aristocracy of wealth" that would eventually enslave the common man. One critic called corporate monopoly "the natural child of Tyranny and Usurpation." Such sentiments were common enough that in 1830 New York attorney Henry Van Der Lyn predicted that corporations "ere long will control the government."[41]

Corporations also threatened to enslave Americans to European capitalists, some of whom owned large quantities of US stocks and bonds. While some Americans believed foreign investment was salubrious, others complained that it allowed "foreigners ... to draw from us every year large sums of money as Interest, in specie" and made America "dependent on them for every thing we need" while simultaneously allowing foreigners who were "enemies of our republican institutions" to promote "their own views and interests on American ground" and to "agitate our councils, divide our people, set law at defiance, and unnerve the arm of our general government."[42]

For all those reasons, by the late 1820s many Americans, especially those tied to the banner of Jackson, were fed up with special incorporation. "The inequality in the laws," one critic argued, "is a perversion of the laws of nature, and totally repugnant to the principles of equity, which nature ordained for the harmony of her works."[43] In 1827 a Manhattan-based author railed against corporations because they entailed the "granting of exclusive privileges" that "in the nature of things, the great mass of the people cannot exercise." He pressed further, claiming that corporations probably injured many Americans, which led him to question the very constitutionality of the corporate form. In 1833 Taylor castigated corporate organizers for "striving to get exclusive privileges." Two years later a New Yorker attacked the corporate form as an "exercise of privileges which the main body [of people] can never enjoy."[44] Clearly, special incorporation was not prohibitively expensive for some Americans, especially groups of wealthy and well-connected elites. Nevertheless, obtaining a special charter was beyond the means of many, who rightly resented being excluded from the special privileges and profitable opportunities, like limited liability and entity shielding, that corporate charters provided. "An individual operator is liable both in his person and in his property for the utmost farthing of debt he may contract," Taylor noted. "Is not this a glaring inequality, and the more so as it operates in favor of the capitalist, who merely contributes money to the prejudice of him who contributes both his time and his money?" he asked.[45]

Had they thought corporations incapable agents of economic improvement, Americans could have destroyed them, as they did privatized lotteries. In the 1810s lotteries "for the promotion of medical science, opening roads, &c." could be found "at every corner, in every street of city, town and village through the land." Sold off by the state to speculators, lottery schemes were sliced and diced "as to suit all ranks, characters, and conditions, from the chancellor to the chimney sweep; from ten dollars to five cents." Critics argued that due to the plethora of lotteries "millions are sported away, and thousands of the citizens from this source, contract a habit of gambling and all its concomitant vices."[46] By the 1820s, lottery brokers were widely deprecated as a "new race, luxuriating on the imaginative schemings of some, and the aversion to honest labour in others" and antilottery petitions flooded state legislatures.[47] By the early 1830s, lotteries were "very properly suppressed" in several states, including Pennsylvania, which in 1833 passed an act for the "entire abolition of Lotteries" and successfully urged other states and the national government to enact similar legislation.[48]

Several important Supreme Court decisions to the contrary notwithstanding, state governments could have pressed for the destruction of corporations on the grounds that they had not fulfilled one or more of the terms of their charters. States could shut down corporations by writ of quo warranto or buy them for fair compensation using the power of eminent domain. In 1842, for example, the state of Vermont bought the West River Bridge from its corporate owners for $4,000. Constructed between 1795 and 1797, the bridge subsequently fell into disrepair until it became "a sore grievance, both to the traveller and the inhabitants of the towns in the vicinity."[49]

It is tempting to imagine that elites forced common Americans to accept corporations that they did not want. Proponents of corporate monopoly, critics claimed, were adroit rhetoricians. "They shield their selfishness under dexterous pretexts," one critic argued, "and their demeanor is so bland and amiable; their love of the people so strong; their attachment to free institutions so powerful; and their desire to promote the welfare of society so invincible, that to question the purity of their intentions is wil[l]ful blindness and monstrous extravagance."[50] But the simple fact is that had they wanted to, the American people could have choked the life out of corporations simply by depriving them of equity capital. Instead, they clamored for shares and, if anything, complained that organizers, stock commissioners, and other insiders prevented them from subscribing as much as they would have liked.[51] As noted above, stock ownership was surprisingly widespread.[52] Ownership was unequal—the rich of course could afford to own more shares and bigger policies than the poor could—but it was open to all on equal terms.[53] Creating numerous large-scale business enterprises, after all, required accumulating the savings, directly or indirectly, of the numerous poor and middling sorts as well as of the wealthy few. The corporation nation, an observer in Connecticut noted circa 1835, was built with the investments of "widows and children, and persons in moderate circumstances as to property" as well as planters and wealthy urban merchants.[54] The mutual savings banks revolution (barely known in 1820, savings banks were among the largest and most respected financial institutions in the nation by 1860) made indirect corporate stock and bond ownership available to the poor, including domestics, laborers, mechanics, factory operatives, and even newly arrived immigrants.[55] The relatively affordable and reliable insurance provided by incorporated companies arguably helped "those of moderate property, and those who are just embarking in business with a small or borrowed capital" more than the rich, who could better afford to absorb losses out of their net worth.[56]

Americans did not hypocritically bash corporations with one hand and in-

vest in them with the other. Rather, they recognized that the corporate form
was merely a tool. Like other tools, corporations could be used for evil ends but
also for good, like conducting research and development that lowered prices
or providing infrastructure that other entities, including governments, could
not or would not provide. So reform, not eradication, was their aim. As one
observer noted in the 1830s, "almost every instance of valuable public improvement that meets the eye, is to be traced directly or indirectly to the agency of
the much decried *monster*—Corporation!" That same observer also claimed
that private projects were generally more efficient than public ones because
"an undertaking, prosecuted by those who are immediately interested in its
success, will be more speedily and better accomplished than it would be in the
hands of public agents, whose only motive for exertion would be the expectation of a salary from the public purse."[57]

Many Americans were therefore reticent to end or even restrict incorporation because they realized that corporations were engines of economic growth
and an arena where the upstart United States led the world. "It can scarcely be
questioned," an observer claimed in 1829, "that the readiness with which corporate powers have been granted have multiplied the resources and improvements of the country." "Manufactures, mines, and improvements of every sort,"
Achille Murat wrote in 1833, "roads, canals, bridges, railroads, all these societies are corporations . . . and become an immense source of prosperity." "The
great improvements of the age," a New Yorker noted in 1835, "are the result
of those laws which permit, and those systems of government which do not
trammel, the association of wealth." The hardy stone turnpikes of Pennsylvania, Samuel Breck claimed in 1818, had "changed the face of the country."[58]
Similarly, canals and especially railroads, which could only be constructed by
pooling large sums of capital, were thought to "impart instant motion to stag-
nant society;—give vigor to all the sinews of industry;—develop the hidden
stores of wealth, and furnish to an awakened and renovated people, the means
of enriching their localities and elevating their communities." Corporations
also allowed Americans to bridge major rivers like the Charles, Delaware,
Potomac, Schuylkill, and Susquehanna.[59] Banks were often credited with the
success of towns like Utica and Buffalo.[60] Last but not least, some state governments kept taxes low by investing in the stock of banks, turnpikes, and other
corporations. In 1817, for example, two-thirds of Pennsylvania's state budget
came from bank dividends.[61]

So instead of urging the destruction of existing corporations, critics increasingly called for their more stringent regulation and, seemingly paradoxically,
for their proliferation.[62] Corporations, particularly banks but other chartered

companies as well, were simultaneously adored and abhorred, even by the same people. Because of that love-hate relationship, the economically and ultimately the politically logical solution to both consumers' and producers' complaints about corporations was to charter more of them. More corporations meant more competitive markets and, *ceteris paribus*, lower prices. Making it easy to create new corporations meant that proprietors and partnerships could compete against existing corporations by forming corporations themselves. Depoliticizing incorporation also reduced the threat corporations posed to republican institutions. Such reasoning led to pressure for general incorporation laws that allowed anyone to establish a corporation for any legitimate business purpose simply by filing a few papers and paying a small fee.[63]

"Let us all be placed upon an equal footing. The door must either be thrown wide open or be entirely closed," Taylor argued in 1833. Two years later, another observer argued that there was "nothing vicious but their exclusive origin; and that if they could be freely assumed by all, without license, no reasonable ground would be left for hostility to them. They would then be perfectly compatible with equality of rights and freedom of trade." He therefore suggested that New York "enact a general law, providing for the creation of *Corporate Partnerships*, and declare that such corporate partnerships shall have all the powers now enjoyed by corporations."[64] That same year, a group of Democrats set forth a similar policy recommendation in the pamphlet *The Doctrine of Anti-Monopoly in an Address to the Democracy of the City of New York*. Some "*spoiled children* in the republican family," the pamphleteer asserted, had "for a long series of years" subverted "all the cardinal interests of society" in favor of "a mere money-making mania" that culminated in "special grant after grant, and charters upon charters, [that] have come to constitute nearly the whole mass of legislative enactments." Most incorporators, it was further charged, sought "exorbitant profits" at the expense of the "*unchartered* multitude." The solution was clear, the extermination not of corporations but of specially chartered ones by means of a "general law of partnerships." The argument was difficult to refute:

> A general law, by which any two or more individuals may declare themselves in business partnership, as well for wood-sawing, if they choose, as for manufacturing or banking; and regulated by such provisions as careful inquire and practical experience may point out, would possess nothing of an exclusive or monopoly character. Without some such law, the suspension of special charters would totally prevent the prosecution of every business which requires a heavy capital; inasmuch as ordinary partnerships are constantly liable to be suddenly dissolved by

the death or self-will of a member. A limited form of permanent succession, and a circumscribed right to transfer an interest in such partnerships, seem to us to be perfectly reasonable and requisite. We are confident that a wholesome system of general business on this scheme, would grow up gradually amongst us, infinitely more favorable than the present, to the small capitalist, on account of the plenitude of semi-incorporated partnerships to which it would give rise, and its evident tendency to divide, and not, as the present system, to concentrate patronage.[65]

The panic of 1837 prompted legislators to reconsider government's proper role in the economy, and induced several states, including New York, to introduce general incorporation for banks.[66] The system of special chartering, however, eroded slowly, coexisting with general incorporation statutes in many states until the early twentieth century.[67] Moreover, several literal monopolies persisted despite political pressure urging their elimination. By the late 1840s, for example, farmers in the hinterlands of New Jersey wished to break the monopoly of the Camden and Amboy Railroad (C&ARR). Although the company claimed the right to veto the establishment of other New Jersey railroads, its case was legally flimsy, especially for local railroads. Nevertheless, the C&ARR used its economic and political influence, including hiring "literary bullies," to limit the number of Jersey roads. The lack of an extensive system of local railroads increasingly pinched the profits of farmers from underserved counties like Burlington, Hunterdon, Middlesex, and Somerset who could not get their fertilizer, fruits, and timber to market cheaply enough to be competitive. "Free Legislation should therefore be accorded to them [local railroads] with general concurrence," the farmers concluded, arguing that "Free Legislation accorded to country railroads . . . will convert New Jersey from her contracted and straightened condition into a free, generous, and growing commonwealth." Only after the Civil War did New Jersey formally end the C&ARR's special status.[68]

In Illinois, a railroad company was accused of promoting the incorporation of a river improvement company that somehow finagled a charter that most citizens of the state found repulsive. "All classes," one observer claimed, "met on the common platform of antagonism to that act. Farmers, merchants, and mechanics — ministers, doctors, lawyers — impetuous youth, and over-cautious age, all made common cause against this obnoxious charter," which apparently granted the corporation the right to seize private property without compensation and to tax river traffic and even those taking water from the river for personal or business use. According to its critics, the goal of the corporation was to impede navigation along the river rather than improve it, thereby forcing farmers into the clutches of the railroad.[69]

The negative reaction to the river improvement company's charter suggests that Americans were keen to limit monopolies if they could so without hindering legal business activities. So too do calls for the cleansing effects of competition on ocean steamship travel, which long enjoyed a federal subsidy under the guise of international postal delivery. William C. Barney argued in 1856,

> By creating a monopoly and paying to one line of steamships [the Collins line], a compensation sufficient to liquidate nearly its entire running expense, the government has adopted the very best method to prevent the construction of Ocean Steamships, and to deter capitalists from continuing lines already established, or from creating new ones. If the governments of the United States and Great Britain, would put down the monopolies of transatlantic Steam navigation, and throw open to free competition the mail service between the two countries, [it] would beget an emulation and wholesome rivalry between our lines of Ocean Steamships, the effect of which would be to ensure the regularity in the days of sailing, the greatest speed compatible with safety, a due attention to the comfort of the passengers, and reduction of rates for passage and freights to a minimum.[70]

After the Collins line and other federal mail subsidies expired in 1858, Cornelius Vanderbilt and others were able to dramatically slice prices and improve service. What had worked on the Hudson River, in short, also worked on the high seas.[71]

In the 1840s and 1850s, the general incorporation movement gained momentum. Louisiana (1845), Iowa (1846), New York (1847), Illinois (1848), Wisconsin (1848), California (1849), Michigan (1850), Massachusetts (1851), Maryland (1851), Ohio (1851), Indiana (1851), Minnesota (1858), and Oregon (1859) all placed provisions for general incorporation into their constitutions. New York and others, however, left the door open to some special chartering: "Corporations may be formed under general laws; but shall not be created by special act," article 8, section 1 of New York's 1846 Constitution read, "except for municipal purposes, and in cases where in the judgment of the legislature, the objects of the corporations cannot be attained under general laws."[72] By about 1875, most other states had joined them and many banned special acts of incorporation altogether. In some states special chartering still occurred— the advantage of special charters was their flexibility—but it was no longer the norm and gradually faded into insignificance.[73]

As charters became less expensive to obtain, the number of businesses opting to obtain one blossomed.[74] Replacing the original system of special incorporation laws with general incorporation laws reduced both the perception of special privilege and the ability of corporations to maintain their market power. More banks, insurers, manufacturing, and similar types of corporations tended to increase competition. General incorporation, however, was no panacea. For starters, it did not end the monopoly or quasi-monopoly status enjoyed by some transportation, telecommunication, and utility corporations, which were expensive to construct and maintain and required eminent domain powers over private property, always a contentious issue.[75] Building several competing roads or water or telegraph lines so competition could weed out the inefficient producers would have been a costly system indeed. So reformers tried to avoid the "enormous mistake" New Jersey made with the C&ARR by keeping internal improvement corporations and utilities on a short leash, with the right of pre-emption and caps on profitability to "an equitable (not a monopoly) per centage."[76] Reformers did not always succeed. Telegraph companies spread the benefits of rapid communication to new areas but seldom directly competed against established companies. Instead, they merged or forged long-term exclusive arrangements with each other, jostled for government largesse, and sought to control international connections and other crucial junctures. As a result, the US telegraph network was relatively expensive and inefficient.[77]

General incorporation also weakened traditional corporate governance and in so doing exposed the US economy and investors to malfeasance and other agency costs on an unprecedented scale. New corporations, and many older ones, fell under the sway of large stockholders who wielded one-vote-per-share voting rules to control the membership of the board of directors. Protecting "minority stockholders" from the depredations of majority stockholders became a major public policy concern. The heyday of the large stockholder was short-lived, however, because already by the 1860s observers noted the increasing power of managers, particularly in railroads, where managerial dominance led to governance difficulties. "The average railway management," Henry Wood, a retired businessman and popular author, complained in 1889, "is autocratic, irresponsible, and often definitely dishonest in its relations towards its shareholders."[78] In the Erie Railroad, "a large part of the owners" had "for many years" been "entirely excluded from the management" and "kept in ignorance of the company operations." The disease spread quickly. "What has been done in Erie," a concerned group complained in 1874, "has, to a lesser extent been done in thousands of other corporations, and is possible in all." The group's call for increased minority stockholder representation in stock companies went largely unheeded, as did similar proposals. Instead, the government combated rising agency costs by moving toward the direct regulation advocated by Wood: accounting and auditing rules, tighter bribery laws, proscriptions against insider trading, and executive affidavits.[79]

Wood's call for shareholders' associations, by contrast, was generally ignored.[80] By the turn of the twentieth century, stockholders, even relatively large ones, had lost most of their ability to constrain entrenched managers, who faced none of the restraints traditionally found in special charters and who controlled boards through proxy votes and other mechanisms. (By the Great Depression, the separation of ownership from control was fully complete at many large, publicly traded companies.[81] The trend continued after World War II. By 1963 almost 85 percent of major US corporations were fully under management control.[82]) Another postbellum development, the creation of "trusts" unconstrained in terms of size and purpose and empowered to conduct any type of business they saw fit any place they saw fit, including across state lines and national boundaries, endowed managers with unprecedented power. Aided by newly liquid markets for industrial securities and largely unchecked by stockholders, managers went on a buying spree called the Great Merger Movement of 1895–1904.[83]

Like their predecessors a century before, the large, modern corporations that emerged circa 1900 proved to be double-edged swords. They spurred economic growth but often at the expense of their customers, who did not gain the cost or quality improvements a more competitive market would have brought; their employees, who increasingly lost their traditional autonomy to Taylorism and other managerial control mechanisms; and, ironically enough, even their owners, who suffered lowered dividends and stock prices due to managerial empire-building, compensation padding, and other forms of self-dealing. Contrary to common belief, however, megacorporations of the twentieth century did not spring forth fully formed but rather grew out of an earlier, but not less significant, wave of corporate development in the early nineteenth century—a wave for the first time specified and quantified in this chapter. The economic changes wrought by the Civil War, the Gilded Age, and beyond are important in their own right but too easily exaggerated if not properly situated in the context of longer-term historical trends.

Acknowledgments

Grants from New York University, the Department of Economics at the Stern School of Business, the Berkeley Center for Entrepreneurial Studies, the Ewing

Marion Kauffman Foundation, and the National Science Foundation are gratefully acknowledged as are the sage comments proffered by Richard Sylla and Michael Zakim, Gary Kornblith, and the other contributors to this volume. Any errors of fact or interpretation discovered herein, however, remain the author's alone.

7

Capitalist Aesthetics

Americans Look at the London and Liverpool Docks

Tamara Plakins Thornton

From 1803 to 1806, John Lowell, a Boston lawyer from a family of wealthy merchants, traveled through England, France, Switzerland, and Italy. Lowell did what gentlemen were supposed to do on the Grand Tour. He took in the Old World's art and antiquities, evaluated the scenery, noted unusual customs, and shipped Italian paintings and statuary back home. For the "pleasure and benefit" of his fellow Bostonians, Lowell contributed a series of twenty-eight travel letters to the *Monthly Anthology*. In these, his judgments were those of a gentleman of refinement, evaluating landscapes as they met or fell short of the stylized aesthetic criteria for what was beautiful, picturesque, and sublime. He disparaged French roads, for example, because their "straightness and uniformity" made for "dull, tiresome" views. And he praised "the charming roads" of England, which, "meandering through vallies, or winding over the hills," enhance "the beauty of the scenery," so that "art seems only to have come to the aid of nature." He was scarcely less formulaic in his private writings. "A

ship in a storm is a most sublime spectacle," he recorded in his shipboard diary during a gale. "The views in, and around this enchanting city, are the most
picturesque that human fancy could imagine," he wrote from Naples. All was
not reportage. From Bordeaux he sent a letter asking a Boston friend to order
furniture on his behalf, including a sideboard, card tables, and twenty-four
chairs "all alike, so that we can use them for dining parties," and "of a colour &
form from the most fashionable *at this time.*" It is not hard to see the gentleman partaking of the aristocratic culture of refinement here—the Grand Tour,
the elegant consumption and the elegant style of life it made possible, and of
course, the off-the-shelf aesthetic responses.[1]

In London, though, Lowell broke away from the pattern of responses.
While in his published letters he had derided the English capital—"she can
no where display that magnificence, and that splendour, which meet you at
every point of view in the city of Rome"—his private writings reveal a different response. It was the city's commerce that inspired him. Until you have seen
it, Lowell wrote his brother of the Thames, you can "have no conception of
the beauty & grandeur of this Commercial River." But above all, Lowell was
overwhelmed by the city's West India Docks. The "scenery of the Ships," the
"immense" range of warehouses, and the "inconceivable quantity of valuable
goods," he wrote of the commercial facility that had opened just three years
earlier, "all conspire to fill the mind with astonishment."[2]

The West India Docks were just one of a series of similar docks constructed
in both London and Liverpool. These were not the usual wooden wharves
found in other ports on both sides of the Atlantic, but immense engineering
projects.[3] Their stone walls enclosed numerous warehouses and anywhere from
tens to hundreds of acres of water at a permanent high tide in the manner of a
canal lock. The West India Docks, for example, contained ten six-story warehouses, covered 295 acres, and accommodated 600 vessels. In the first decades
of the nineteenth century, many Americans of the privileged classes—men of
affairs, lawyers, physicians, clergymen, scientists, naval officers, writers, and
their accompanying ladies—found themselves amazed by these commercial
complexes.

It would be hard to overestimate the attention the docks received. Urban guidebooks identified them as must-see sights. Commercial dictionaries
praised them. American periodicals and newspapers carried descriptions of
the docks and covered the ceremonies accompanying their opening. Travel
narratives almost invariably included visits to the docks. The private diaries
of American travelers indicate that a trip to the docks was almost de rigueur;
consider the London itinerary of Mary Thompson, who fit in a visit to "the

Docks and Tobacco warehouses" before going carpet shopping, or Philadelphia merchant Charles Cathrall, who on only his second day in the capital
visited both the East and West India docks. As early as 1788, an English travel
guide described the Liverpool docks as the city's "principal objects of curios-
ity." By 1803 a correspondent to the *Port-Folio*, reporting on his recent journey
to England, admitted that the Liverpool docks are "so frequently mentioned
by the traveller" that to describe them "would only tire your mind with the
trite and the flat." In 1817 *A Visit to London*, a children's book published in
Philadelphia, included a chapter detailing young George Sandby's visit to the
docks with his father, and, a generation later, Peter Parley entertained his juve-
nile audience with descriptions of the docks in both cities. The New England
clergyman Heman Humphrey identified "the docks themselves" as "above all"
what was "most worthy of the stranger's attention" in Liverpool; the Reverend
Orville Dewey, a Massachusetts Unitarian, referred to them as "the glory of
Liverpool"; and Charles Cathrall noted in his diary that "it is really worth a
trip across the Atlantic to have a sight at the splendid docks and wharves of this
city." "Oh the docks, those glorious docks," raved a London correspondent in
New York's *Commercial Advertiser*.[4]

Such responses indicate that aesthetic taste among America's privileged
classes did not begin and end with emulation of aristocratic refinement. Never
mind the picturesque roads and the magnificent antiquities; it was the West
India Docks that stimulated John Lowell's deepest sensibilities. Capitalism
spawned its own aesthetic responses. But capitalism is far too general a term,
for it was itself a moving target. When John Lowell was born in 1769, capitalists engaged primarily in international maritime commerce. By the time he died
in 1840, they were engaged in banking, insurance, land speculation, domestic
trade, manufacturing, and railroads. That shift, from mercantile capitalism to
industrial capitalism and the early stages of corporate capitalism, entailed the
displacement of older practices and values in favor of new ones. Rather than
the individual pursuit of profit, the new capitalist enterprise would entail the
methodical workings of an impersonal mechanism. Profit would not be derived from risk but from the neutralization of risk through rationalized economic activity. The modus operandi and the watchwords of this novel form of
enterprise would be security, predictability, precision, and order.

The very sorts of people who thrilled to the docks would transform American capitalism in the early decades of the nineteenth century and foster new
capitalist values of rational order in American culture. John Lowell addressed
his descriptions of the West India Docks to his brother, Francis Cabot Lowell, who would soon establish the prototype for America's textile mills. Like

the docks, the mills were massive engineering complexes without precedent that controlled natural forces and human laborers alike on the basis of a new economic and cultural system. But the primary significance of the docks for Americans does not lie in direct imitation. More critical is the ideological content of aesthetic experience as conceptualized and practiced in this era. Their novel response to the docks contained an equally novel message: in embodying capitalist practices and values, the docks aestheticized modern capitalism itself. In so doing, they endowed the new forms of business behavior and thought with transcendent value. Far removed from Old World set pieces which measured an individual's aesthetic acuity, these spectacles of rationalized economic activity entranced American visitors and readers with a vision of the emergent capitalist order as inevitable, desirable, and, indeed, sublime.

The City of Liverpool was the first to erect docks, with the municipal corporation itself taking the initiative in 1709. As the commerce of the port expanded, the public authorities added new docks, most in the late eighteenth and nineteenth centuries. Spurring their construction was the problematic nature of the Mersey River location. The wide fluctuations of tides and the vagaries of wind and weather made the loading and unloading of vessels at riverside quays and wharves difficult and dangerous. In 1797 an American *Naval Gazetteer* explained that as "ships at anchor in the river of Mersey are exposed to sudden squalls of wind . . . few ships anchor in the road, but get into some of the docks as soon as they possibly can." Once in these docks, explained the *Liverpool Guide* of the same year, vessels lie "afloat, in the most perfect security from every assailment of wind and sea." By 1838 more than a dozen docks stretched over two miles along the Mersey; twenty years later, they extended over nine miles.[5]

London did not erect its docks until the beginning of the nineteenth century, and the circumstances surrounding their construction differed from those of Liverpool. For one, these were never public undertakings but instead the endeavors of joint-stock companies first authorized by Parliament in 1799. Thereafter these corporations built one dock after the other: the West India Docks on the Isle of Dogs (1802), the London Docks at Wapping (1805), the new East India Docks at Blackwall (1806), the Commercial Docks at Rotherhithe (1807), and then, in 1828, the St. Katharine's Docks in the heart of the city. These were huge projects, drawing forth millions of pounds of private capital and often entailing the wholesale destruction of city neighborhoods. In Wapping, 1,300 houses were razed. Over a thousand more were demolished to build the St. Katharine's Docks. Until the 1820s most of these corporations enjoyed monopolies in their particular branches of trade, sugar at the West India Docks, tobacco and wine at the London Docks, and so on, with the concomitant right to levy tonnage rates on incoming vessels. Most profitable of all was the privilege of erecting bonded warehouses—and charging storage fees accordingly—so that the docks maintained an effective monopoly on all dutiable goods, in effect, on all foreign trade. Riverside wharfs and quays continued to dominate domestic commerce, but the docks were where the big profits lay and the economic power was concentrated. Once their monopoly privileges expired, the dock corporations faced competition and declining profits, a challenge they met in large part by reducing their permanent labor force in favor of a pool of desperately poor day laborers. After about 1850, the building of new docks, the government's policy of free trade, and such technological developments as the steamship, telegraph, and railroad favored other Thames facilities and reduced the demand for warehousing to the point that the dock corporations lost their economic dominance of the port. But in the first quarter of the nineteenth century, and well into the second, there was no more visible symbol of imperial wealth, economic power, and corporate privilege than London's docks.[6]

Besides their corporate structure, these docks differed from those in Liverpool in another critical way. Crowding and theft, not tides and weather, spurred their construction. The "Legal Quays" and overflow "Sufferance Wharfs" could no longer accommodate the traffic along the Thames. Vessels were obliged to wait for days or weeks to unload. Because of their deeper draft, the larger vessels characteristic of transoceanic trade could not tie up along the river's banks at low tide and instead moored in the middle of the Thames, sometimes seven or eight deep. There they unloaded their cargoes into smaller craft, called lighters, which then transported the merchandise to dry land. Costly delays were almost inevitable, but exciting even greater alarm was the pilferage that occurred as commodities passed from hand to hand or sat unprotected along the quays and wharves for want of warehouse space. In his highly influential *Treatise on the Commerce and Police of the River Thames*, Patrick Colquhoun, a Scottish textile factor turned London magistrate, identified the principal problem as depredation, committed by a motley crew of "nautical Vagabonds." What was criminal activity to Colquhoun was to the dock laborers a customary right; they had long considered themselves entitled to "sweepings," "samplings," and "scrapings" from holds, hogsheads, and warehouse floors. In the 1790s Colquhoun led a crackdown on such activities, culminating in the creation of the Marine Police Office in 1798 and, in the first years of the next century, the erection of the docks.[7]

London's docks thus came into being primarily because of the desire to control the port's labor force, and they were designed and administered accordingly. The West India Docks, for example, were surrounded by a thirty-foot wall and, beyond that, a ditch twenty-four feet wide and seven feet deep. Outside the wall was a lockup for those caught stealing. Police patrolled the perimeter. Separate facilities existed for imports and exports, as stipulated by the customs service, but also the better to monitor theft from the especially valuable inbound cargoes. The cast-iron window frames in the bottom four stories of the six-story warehouses were spiked. Regulations prescribed that the gates of the dock premises would be opened in the morning and locked in the evening according to a set schedule. As workers departed for the day, their names were checked off that day's employment rolls to make certain no one remained surreptitiously, and the dock's security personnel frisked them and checked their clothing for pilfered goods.[8]

While many Americans experienced the Liverpool docks firsthand as their countrymen's principal port of entry into England, in London only individuals with express business or permission were allowed to enter the premises. The capital's docks, though no less celebrated, thus required special efforts to visit, or even, given the height of the walls, to see. The fictional Mr. Sandby could visit the West India Docks because he had business to conduct there; Benjamin Silliman gained access to the docks at Wapping "by the politeness of Mr. W___"; and a party of Americans took pains to obtain tickets "from the proper authorities." But "to get tickets is worth while," added one of that party, "for nothing in London is better worth seeing."[9]

What exactly was there to be seen? Little evidence suggests that those who lived near or worked in the docks experienced them as an object of aesthetic appreciation. In sea chanteys, the docks are places of leave taking or homecoming, plain and simple ("Now to Blackwall Docks we bid adieu, / To Suke and Sal and Kitty too").[10] It is possible that London's poor may have recognized the visual novelty of the docks. When in September 1800 James Robins was tried for stealing seven geese, for example, he defended himself by testifying that "I was going to see the new docks, and going through the field, a man asked me if I would have a goose." But it is likely that dock workers perceived the docks primarily as spaces of labor, opportunity, surveillance, and danger. Masses of casual laborers pressed at the gates to get work for the day; for them the dock entrance loomed as the boundary between hunger and subsistence. For workers, the docks offered valuable goods that could be pilfered, but they also contained spaces of detection. "I am the Excise gate-keeper at the East India Docks," testified Walter Salter in July of 1821. "It is my duty to rub the labourers down as they leave." Informing eyes might lurk anywhere. James Darrett was caught when a suspicious employee flattened himself atop a pile of coffee bags to observe him. And the docks themselves might be the space of punishment for such thefts. For stealing three and a half pounds of sugar, the court sentenced William Rawey to be "publicly whipped, at the Wet Docks, in the Isle Dogs" in 1802. For stealing a gallon of rum, William Williams was to be "publicly whipped at the Wet Docks" that same year. And for stealing a pound of tea in 1809, Thomas Carter and Joseph Wood were sentenced to be "Whipped one hundred yards near the East India docks."[11]

Genteel visitors experienced the docks altogether differently. For them, the docks were aesthetically compelling. There was nothing natural or objective in this response, not because theirs was a positive evaluation, but simply because it was aesthetic in nature. Recent scholars have explored the ways in which the project of aesthetics—even the very word—was a creation of the eighteenth century. It is not just that notions of what is aesthetically pleasing or repellent change over time, but that the whole endeavor of apprehending the exterior world as a source of aesthetic stimuli, rather than of moral lessons, dates from this period. This project is most often linked with the social and political transformations of the era, especially the rise of a social order dominated by the rising middle classes. For Terry Eagleton, aesthetic experience, because it was theorized to be a universal attribute of humankind based in human physiology, served as a "binding force of the bourgeois social order," replacing "the coercive apparatus of absolutism" with "unthinking habit" and "the human subject's own pleasurable well-being." Other scholars focus on a particular contradiction in aesthetic thought: while theoretically all human beings experience the world aesthetically, most writers on the subject, and certainly most members of the privileged classes, believed that only the cultivated exhibit true aesthetic acumen. Aesthetics might therefore buttress the cultural prestige of those classes by using "taste" as a marker of superiority to those below them. Yet other scholars focus on aesthetics as a series of visual practices—the seeking of appropriate vantage points, the evaluation of natural landscapes, the parsing and composing of their visual elements, and the creation of such new visual forms as the 360-degree panorama exhibition. In these practices, the Foucauldian equation of vision and power took concrete form. Viewing the English landscape meant viewing land, for example, and as land was the source of power, wealth, and prestige, whether one "commanded" a view or allowed the eye "liberty" to roam had real ideological content. So too did the panorama visitor's simultaneous experience of physical enclosure and visual dominance. If visitors to the docks responded to the docks aesthetically, then, we must recognize both the novelty and the significance of this response. If we are to understand what this response means, we must first examine what they saw.[12]

Visitors admired the docks above all for their scale. They described the extent of the basins, the height of the warehouses, the volume of business, the cost of the undertakings, and the grandeur of the enterprise as a whole, and they used a set of adjectives—"vast," "immense," "magnificent," "stupendous," "gigantic," "prodigious," "massive"—that constituted a veritable lexicon of the traits associated with the Sublime.[13] Others reported the "wonder" and "astonishment" they felt upon viewing the docks, other catchwords for the Sublime.[14] Some commentators were direct in their aesthetic references. Swedish naval engineer A. G. Carlsund, for example, marveled at London's "spacious docks" and warehouses—"these colossal buildings," these "enormous masses"—as "sublime and imposing." In Liverpool, Calvin Colton, an Episcopal minister and Whig journalist, admired "the stupendous works of solid masonry" as "sublime objects of artificial structure."[15]

Over the course of the eighteenth century, Anthony Ashley Cooper, the third Earl of Shaftesbury, Joseph Addison, and most influentially, Edmund Burke had developed the concept of the Sublime in Britain. Educated people on both sides of the Atlantic assimilated the concept, along with such other contemporaneous aesthetic categories as the Beautiful and the Picturesque, through their exposure to the ideas of such thinkers and their growing familiarity with contemporary landscape prints and paintings, garden design, and travel literature.[16] Versions of the Sublime differed, and even within their own systems of thought, individual philosophers recognized different strains of the Sublime. There was the Sublime of Nature's dynamic forces, its thunderous volcanoes and waterfalls. And there was the Sublime of the seemingly infinite magnitude of natural phenomena—the vastness of the ocean, the cloud-piercing height of a mountain range. What these strains had in common, and what in fact defined the Sublime—or for that matter the Beautiful—was not a particular visual trait at all, but instead what Burke termed "the power of an object upon our passions," that is, the emotions stimulated in the viewer. The Beautiful stimulates pleasure, explained Burke. The Sublime stimulates awe, horror, and astonishment, all derived from the suggestion of pain and danger, and thus ultimately from terror, what Burke termed the "inseparable companion" of the Sublime. What made such stimuli a source of "delight" was the fact that "we have an idea of pain and danger, without being actually in such circumstances"; in other words, we actually have nothing to fear. "When danger or pain press too nearly," Burke elaborated, "they are incapable of giving any delight, and are simply terrible." The tourist in search of the Sublime thus sought out volcanoes and mountain peaks, then observed them from a safe distance.[17]

Burke listed a number of visual elements that stimulate the experience of the

Sublime because they induce feelings of terror. Sublime landscapes are "vast in their dimensions," but also "rugged," "dark and gloomy," "solid, and even massive." In works of architecture, "Succession and Uniformity" produce the artificial infinite by repeating a single element in a seemingly endless series. Burke gave the example of a colonnade, but we might think about what Benjamin Silliman described as the "immense ranges of ware-houses within the walls" of the docks. Burke also pointed to "Obscurity," and total "Vacuity, Darkness, Solitude and Silence," the latter generalized as "Privation." When observers stressed the Gothic qualities of the docks, then, the "vast extent and prison-like aspect of the ware houses" in Liverpool, or the "gloomy labyrinthine passages" and "interminable grim archways," of London's "tomblike" sherry vaults, the light "dimly gleaming over the long tiers of hogsheads," these were as much expressions of the Sublime as references to their scale.[18]

The response to a commercial landscape as sublime was novel. Harbors were not sought out as aesthetic destinations, and while visitors to British and American port cities might evaluate harbors with an aesthetic eye, the language of the Sublime was nowhere to be seen. Instead they invoked the Picturesque, a category Richard Payne Knight, Uvedale Price, and, most influentially, William Gilpin had introduced to educated audiences in the late eighteenth century. The defining features of the Picturesque were variety and irregularity, artfully disposed in visually and emotionally pleasing pictorial compositions.[19] Observers often made use of the Picturesque when describing the Mersey and the Thames—the rivers, that is, not the docks. A "number of vessels, of all descriptions, moving in all directions, so near at hand," wrote the *Liverpool Guide*, "forms a moving picture, highly engaging and interesting; and which, from the variety it always affords, is entertaining even to those who see it most frequently." New York lawyer and newspaperman Nathaniel Carter, describing the prospect from the top of Liverpool's Town Hall, noted that "the view is picturesque," with visual variety provided by the vessels "almost constantly arriving and departing." Later in his English travels, Carter described the visual variety along the Thames—"boats and vessels of all descriptions," which thereby "adds much to the picture." When crossing the Thames on the Waterloo Bridge, American naval officer C. S. Stewart stopped "to catch the varied living imagery, meeting the eye at every point, in the barge and the wherry, gliding swiftly across the mirrored water below."[20]

In descriptions of American ports, the dominant theme was that Nature had blessed the United States with an abundance of harbors ideally suited for commerce, a variation on the well-worn theme of America as Nature's nation, but commentators also drew on the Picturesque.[21] In some cases, the shores surrounding America's harbors drew praise, as when an early guidebook to New York noted that the blooming orchards of Brooklyn "renders the exhibition truly enchanting and Picturesque." In other instances, the harbor scene itself, with its characteristic juxtaposition of visual elements, was said to strike the eye. Thus one English visitor recommended the "picturesque scenery"—"the town, bay, shipping, neck, bridges, and the whole country round"—visible from the top of Boston's State House.[22] On both sides of the Atlantic, then, harbors called forth a different aesthetic response than that prompted by the great docks.

There was something else unusual about the aesthetic experience of the docks. Almost always, the Sublime was associated with Nature, specifically Nature at its most untamed and grand. From the late eighteenth until well into the nineteenth century, well-bred travelers in search of the Sublime commonly headed for Derbyshire's Peak District, the Alps, or Niagara Falls.[23] It was not entirely unknown for landscapes created by human hands to be regarded as sublime. Beginning in the later eighteenth century, many visitors to Shropshire responded to the region's industrial innovations as a sublime spectacle. The "noise of the forges, mills, &c. with all their vast machinery," wrote agricultural journalist Arthur Young of Coalbrookdale's iron works, "the flames bursting from the furnaces with the burning of the coal and the smoak of the lime kilns are altogether sublime." Visitors traveled to Coalbrookdale to experience the Sublime, many viewing the furnaces and kilns from the specially designed Rotunda at night to maximize the effect, and it became common to compare the works to either a volcano or to the Inferno.[24] By the middle of the next century, railroads and steam engines became associated with what historians have labeled the technological Sublime. Visitors to the 1876 Centennial Exposition in Philadelphia likened the Corliss steam engine to a great beast or giant, and they viewed it much as they did Niagara Falls, with astonishment, awe, and terror. In each case, we can see how the tropes of the natural Sublime—gloomy valleys, thunderous noises, explosions of fire—could be appropriated to characterize the ambivalence generated by the wondrous and frightening realities of industrialization.[25] Yet if the docks were not the Alps or Niagara Falls, neither were they iron furnaces or steam engines. They did not suggest volcanoes or Hell, or wild animals or monsters. There was nothing obviously dangerous or terrifying about them.

Furthermore, aesthetic responses to the docks diverged in critical ways from the stylized experiences of both the natural and the technological Sublime. Let us first reconsider the imagery of scale. As conceptualized by contemporaries, a good part of the power of the Sublime lay not just in vastness but vastness to

the point of infinity. Critically, while observers of the docks invariably commented on their immense scale, they did not suggest that the scale of the docks
was limitless. Quite the opposite; they set about defining those limits with
some exactitude. While one American visitor might claim to "despair of giving
any conception of the size and magnificence of these docks," he nonetheless
gave it a shot: twenty acres of water, a five-acre warehouse cellar, and 37,000
hogsheads of rum. Chemist John Griscom might insist that the facilities offered by the East and West India docks "must be incalculable," but he too tried
his hand at numbers: the largest of the East India Docks at 12¾ acres, the
largest of the West India at thirty, so that "the whole of the excavation must
exceed eighty acres."[26] Indeed, almost all accounts of the docks enumerated at
least some aspect of their magnitude. Many included long lists of figures and
measurements: the area, volume, and depth of water, the length and breadth
of the quays, the height of the warehouses, the cost of the projects, the duties
collected, the quantities of merchandise, the numbers of stories, vessels, cranes,
bales, and hogsheads, even the number of houses and people displaced to build
the docks. Mercantile reference works, such as commercial dictionaries, included this kind of information, but so too did publications for "belles lettres"
audiences. A typical account, a description of the Wapping Docks published
in a gentleman's magazine, ran in part:

> The great dock contains exactly 20 acres, and the little dock or basin about three
> acres, which together accommodate about 250 sail. A quay 100 feet wide sur
> rounds the great dock on all sides, excepting a small part subdivided and inclosed
> for tobacco, which is only about half that width, forming a length of wharfing
> nearly 5000 feet. . . . On the spacious quay at the north side of the dock, there
> are five distinct piles of building, each containing six divisions of warehouses. . . .
> Each body of warehouses has ten cranes on the inside. The cellars are ten
> feet high.[27]

And when Joshua White, a physician from Savannah, published his *Letters
on England*, he saw fit to include not only several paragraphs of numerical
information regarding London's docks but also a table detailing the breadth,
width, and depth of each of the Liverpool docks along with the width of their
gates.[28]

All this measuring and counting was contrary to the spirit of the Sublime.
It set exact boundaries to what might have been approached as Burke's "artificial infinite." More critically, the apprehension of the Sublime was understood
to so overwhelm the mind as to stifle any possibility of engaging in rational

mental processes. Typically, those experiencing the Sublime indicated their inability to comprehend, let alone describe, what it was they were seeing and to be rendered speechless by the scene. "THE PASSION caused by the great and sublime in nature," Burke explained, ". . . is astonishment; and astonishment is that state of the soul, in which all its motions are suspended, with some degree of horror. In this case the mind is so entirely filled with its object, that it cannot entertain any other, nor by consequence reason on that object which employs it."[29] But here were observers of sublimity, entertaining and reasoning away.

A second theme that ran contrary to notions of the Sublime was the safety the docks provided to shipping. Indeed, other than vastness, the primary characteristic of the docks noted by observers was "security." Such comments should come as no surprise. Safety, after all, was the raison d'être for these docks, and it had long existed as a desirable, perhaps the most desirable, trait recommending a port. American harbors, as we have seen, were celebrated as "natural havens." Eighteenth-century images of harbors emphasized the shelter they provided, enclosing the harbor basin within shores.[30] But if security was not a new theme, what is then out of place is any allusion to the Sublime. The experience of the Sublime, after all, was rooted in the apprehension of danger and consequent feelings of terror. On occasion, the fact of security was in fact expressed as one would expect it to be, in the language of the Beautiful, a feminized aesthetic associated with pleasure rather than fear.[31] When the West India Docks opened in August 1802, for example, one witness described a martial spectacle—sails billowing, flags flying, bands playing, a twenty-one gun salute, "huzzas" from the thousands of spectators—but reserved the greatest aesthetic praise for the security the docks provided. "Nothing can be conceived more beautiful than the Dock itself," he wrote. "The water of the necessary depth, about sixteen feet, and its surface, smooth as a mirror, presented to the eye an haven, secure from storms," then, continuing in increasingly feminized language, "and the mind anticipated those sensations of pleasure and delight with which all the nations of the world, after buffeting storms and tempests, must feel when lodged in its tranquil bosom."[32]

But far more often, references to security came cheek by jowl with those associated with the Sublime. From the top of St. Paul's, Alexander Mackenzie spied "those immense artificial basins, the docks of London, which the enterprise of her citizens has hollowed out to give security to commerce." Joshua White enumerated the vast expense of erecting the West India Docks, noted the "warehouses of immense size," then explained the source of the "incalculable benefits" the docks offered to the West India fleets. Once vessels enter, he wrote, "they are secure from the damage and confusion which commonly results from the immense crowd in the Thames." In Liverpool, wrote another American travel writer, the "vast excavations" render the Mersey's tidal shifts of no consequence, for when the tide ebbs, the dock gates are closed, and "ships of any tonnage ride within them in perfect safety."[33]

That distinctive juxtaposition of the language of sublimity with observations on security characterized commentary on natural and manmade dangers alike. Jacob Green, a professor of chemistry at Jefferson Medical College traveling in Liverpool, remarked that in these "stupendous works," these "immense basins . . . surrounded on all sides with high walls," the "foreign ships lie secure from the influence of the winds and waves, and from the depredations of thieves." But in discussions of security from theft, we find a particular strain of the Sublime, a vocabulary not so much of vastness as of gothic horror. At Wapping, reported one newspaper account, the dock walls are "as high as those around the 'King's Bench Prison.'" Another account detailed the "artificial fortifications" at the West India Docks, including "a fort or rampart surmounted by iron balustrades." A third journalist noted the "artificial fortifications" surrounding these docks, the "centinels [sic] . . . parading for the protection" of the goods within, the procedures for locking down a ship once it has entered the premises ("not even the Captain is permitted to go aboard"), and the instant clearance of the docks upon the ringing of the closing bell. "The clamour of business is succeeded by the stillness of a desert." In the image of the deserted docks, we hear Burke's enumeration of "terrible" "privations": "*Vacuity, Darkness, Solitude,* and *Silence.*"[34]

Descriptions of the docks, while loaded with such *visual* components of the Sublime as vastness, massiveness, and sensory privation, invoked a concept — security — that was the direct opposite of that associated with the Sublime. Here we have an apparent inconsistency as significant as the one between the infinite extent of the docks and the precise calculation of their dimensions. This is no simple transference of an aesthetic originally developed as a way of apprehending wild natural landscapes to manmade phenomena such as we see in the technological Sublime. The sublimity of the docks did not derive from their similarity to volcanoes or wild beasts but from the rational order they embodied. It was not danger that was being aestheticized, but the control of danger.

Thus the apparent juxtaposition between the language of infinity and danger on the one hand and the language of numeration and security on the other was no juxtaposition at all; both evoked the sublimity of the docks. Similarly, commentators often paired explicitly aesthetic terms with business terms. The Reverend William Sprague noted that the "Liverpool docks are celebrated for convenience and elegance," while the *Liverpool Guide* praised the docks' ware-houses as "handsome and convenient." In London an observer praised the Wap-ping Docks' "able and ingenious" architect for uniting "simplicity and gran-deur of appearance" with "the commodious stowage of goods." At the West India Docks, John Lowell rhapsodized over the "Immensity of this operation," but also the "scenery of the Ships lying so quietly & yet so conveniently afloat at the very door of the Stores."[35] The two sets of terms would appear to emerge from separate systems of assigning value. Convenience and commodiousness are mercantile priorities, while elegance, simplicity, and grandeur are aesthetic goals, but the pairing suggests that the two vocabularies were not just coinci-dent, but one and the same. Convenience *was* elegant. Commodiousness *was* grand. In short, capitalism was sublime.

But not just any form of capitalism. Mercantile capitalism had long func-tioned amid a risk-laden, unpredictable, and intensely personal world of indi-vidual merchants and small partnerships. Information was scarce and naviga-tional technology inadequate. Ships foundered, profits evaporated, merchants bickered, sailors jumped ship, dock workers pilfered. Already in the eighteenth century, Britain was pioneering enterprises characterized by a different type of conduct and mentality, ones that featured the order, regularity, and impartial-ity of a centralized, impersonal system. Among private ventures, Boulton and Watt's Soho Foundry, founded in 1795, led the way in establishing a rational-ized form of capitalism. But British historians have located the earliest forms of such systems in state institutions. John Brewer has characterized the Ex-cise Office as "more closely approximated to Max Weber's idea of bureaucracy than any other government agency in eighteenth-century Europe."[36] An even more compelling example of this kind of rationalized system is provided by the Royal Navy's shipbuilding facilities.

Between 1796 and 1807, almost the very years of London's corporate dock boom, Samuel Bentham headed the reform of the royal dockyards. His main goal was the same as that of Patrick Colquhoun in the latter's plans for Thames shipping, that is, solving the problem of worksite pilfering. William Ashcroft has argued that "the guiding mechanism" of Samuel Bentham's plans was one he shared with his brother Jeremy, the panopticon. There was nothing meta-phorical in the link between vision and power at the naval dockyards. The Ben-thamite reforms entailed "fierce rational regimentation," "systematic, formal, and visible" administration of operations, and an "abstract analytical organiza-tion characterized by precision, vigilance, accounts, and the division of labour." By such means, each of the navy's several dockyards would be able to function as the words of a naval commissioners' report stipulated it should, "as a part of one great machine." Bentham's approach, Ashworth argues, transformed Britain's largest industrial complex, replacing an old managerial culture with a new one inspired by the Enlightenment. "It is probably the case," he concludes, "that nowhere did the rational, calculating approach reach such extremes in Britain, perhaps throughout the nineteenth century, than it did at this moment in the history of the dockyards."[37]

In the first half of the nineteenth century, this same "rational, calculating approach" shaped London's corporate docks. Colquhoun, a central figure in both the creation of the Thames Police and the erection of the docks, had worked with Jeremy Bentham on the reform of the navy's shipbuilding facilities. Like the naval dockyards, London's corporate docks were walled, fortified, and policed. Workers at both were searched as they exited and prosecuted if caught pilfering. Like the Royal Navy, the dock corporations created a "great machine," at least in the eyes of their astonished beholders. While there were occasional references to the people managing dockside affairs, more often the docks were represented as functioning in the manner of an Enlightenment mechanism: automatically, precisely, impersonally, unchangingly, eternally. Descriptions of dock operations erased human beings, and commodities, vessels, and people alike proceeded passively through a frictionless system. The "carts are loaded exactly according to the rotation in which they are entered in the warehouse-books the preceding day," read one account of the West India Docks, and "the ships are disburthened of their cargoes with the same order and impartiality." Occasionally, the reference to a mechanism was explicit, as when one New York merchant compared the London docks to "a social engine, which rivals in utility, in vastness of operation, as well as wisdom of details, the phenomena of nature herself."[38]

It was this vision of economic activity as an impersonal mechanism that underlay the aestheticization of capitalism as sublime. In measuring the immeasurable and aestheticizing security and order, depictions of the docks seemed to contradict the tropes of the Sublime, yet the docks derived their aesthetic power from its deepest roots. Recall that Burke theorized that it was not the visual qualities of landscapes that accounted for the experience of the Sublime, but the emotions they stimulated. "Terror," Burke wrote, "is in all cases whatsoever, either more openly or latently the ruling principle of the sublime." Volcanoes and mountain peaks were terrifying in obvious ways—they "*directly* suggest the idea of danger"—and furnaces and steam engines produced "a similar effect from a mechanical cause." And what of terror present "latently"? "I know of nothing sublime, which is not some modification of power," Burke explained. "And this branch rises, as naturally as the other two branches, from

terror, the common stock of everything that is sublime."[39] The Sublime aestheticized the terrors of power.

The power of the docks was a terrifying fact. They were immense, massive
structures, like nothing else in the landscape. They employed vast numbers of
laborers. They represented the commercial might of an empire unequaled in
economic and military strength. To these forms of power, the London dock
corporations added others: the power of eminent domain and of monopoly,
the power to regulate movement and to control labor, the power to arrest, to
imprison, and to whip. By the middle of the nineteenth century, their labor
policies produced workers whose "struggle for life" was, in the words of Henry
Mayhew, "sublime."[40] If sublimity derived from power so great as to inspire terror, then the physical spectacle of rationalized capitalism was surely sublime.
More accurately, it was sublime to those not subjected to such power, indeed,
as members of the privileged classes, in control of it, at least imaginatively. If,
after all, the aesthetic pleasure of sublimity derived from the viewers' simultaneous proximity to and awareness of safety, then who could be safer from the
docks' power than the men and women who sought them out as aesthetic wonders of the modern world? The psychological state that defined the Sublime,
astonishment, could thus be, as one scholar has suggested, "a titillating flirta-
tion with surrender on the part of men who were (or at least felt themselves
to be) very much in control."[41] At the very least, we can say that those whose
power and identities derived from such economic activities were primed to
derive aesthetic pleasure from them.

The sublimity of rationalized capitalism emerges with striking clarity in the
pictorial views of the London docks that appeared in the early decades of their
operation. These images were not produced in an artistic vacuum. Painters and
engravers who depicted the docks could draw on any number of harbor-view
traditions. In the eighteenth century, the "over the water" prospect of port cities, emphasizing commercial prosperity, predominated in both Britain and the
American colonies. These horizontal views looked across harbors bustling with
shipping to the city beyond, while figures on the foreground shore watched the
maritime display. Harbor paintings of the first half of the nineteenth century,
many in the form of the newly popular genre of ship portraiture, continued
this theme of commercial activity, but now infused with greater energy (see
figs. 7.1 and 7.2). We see vessels of many kinds and sizes, angling across the
water, sails billowing and flags flying. In Thomas Thompson's view of New
York harbor (see fig. 7.3), the people on shore admire this gay maritime display. Such paintings stepped up visual claims of commercial prosperity into

Figure 7.1. Robert Salmon, "A Packet off Liverpool," 1809. Courtesy National Maritime Museum, Greenwich, London, England.

Figure 7.2. [Robert Dodd], "Shipping in the Pool of London," late eighteenth century. Courtesy National Maritime Museum, Greenwich, London, England.

Figure 7.3. Thomas Thompson, "New York Harbor from the Battery," 1829. Metropolitan Museum of Art/Art Resource, NY.

claims of commercial might, assuming nationalist overtones in an era of commercial rivalry. Finally, genre scenes depicted either a colorful bustle of goods and workers along the quays, or a physical chaos of commodities and a moral chaos of sailors, laborers, and prostitutes.[42]

Early nineteenth-century images of London's docks departed from these standard pictorial approaches in their depictions of rationalized order. They

Figure 7.4. Thomas Hosmer Shepherd, "West India Import Docks, Poplar," c. 1830. Courtesy National Maritime Museum, Greenwich, London, England.

emphasized not just the docks' massive dimensions, the standard trope of sublimity, but also the orderly procession of vessels through the docks, the centrally administered and policed loading and unloading of commodities, and the disciplined exit of loaded vessels. An 1811 engraving of the West India Docks depicts the view across one of the basins. Dominating the foreground ominously is a gallows-like gantry, but across the water in the middle ground is a line of immense, brightly illuminated warehouses. An 1815 engraving of the docks shows the same line of warehouses, receding apparently without end beyond the frame of the image. Thomas Hosmer Shepherd's "West India Import Dock, Poplar" (fig. 7.4) depicts the same elements, but with the sublimity of a thunderhead and rainstorm poised over the warehouses. Thomas Rowlandson's and Augustus Pugin's "West India Docks" (fig. 7.5) places the viewer at the head of this same basin. Although there is some human movement—a few rowboats in the foreground, a few small figures along the quay—the image is dominated by a line of identical dark ships, sails lowered, and moored alongside a line of identical warehouses. Commercial power is depicted not by a busy dock but by a regimented one. Instead of exuberance, there is discipline.[43]

Nowhere is this aesthetic more pronounced than in a remarkable series of aquatints executed by William Daniell between 1802 and 1813. The series includes renderings of the West India (fig. 7.6), London, East India, Brunswick

Figure 7.5. Thomas Rowlandson and Augustus Charles Pugin, "West India Docks," 1810. Courtesy National Maritime Museum, Greenwich, London, England.

Figure 7.6. William Daniell, "An Elevated View of the West India Docks," 1802. Courtesy National Maritime Museum, Greenwich, London, England.

(later East India), and Commercial docks. Despite the differences among the locations, the views are similar. Most important, they are bird's-eye views. Viewing cities from high above was a popular approach to urban tourism in the early nineteenth century. Travelers sought a panoramic view by inspecting the city from its highest points and by visiting panorama exhibitions that imitated such visual experiences. By the middle of the century, bird's-eye-view lithographs of cities displaced the previously standard ground-level images. But Daniell's depictions of the London docks did not replicate the welter of visual elements depicted in panorama paintings and they predated the bird's-eye lithographs by decades.[44] Instead of surrounding the viewer with the countless minutiae of the bustling city, Daniell offered a grand vista of mathematical order and preternatural quiet, devoid of disorder, noise, air, and people. From an immense height, higher than any actual vantage point could have provided, one observes vessels entering and exiting the docks in straight lines, like soldiers in a row. They moor along the quays in rows or in the center of the basins in gridded arrays.[45] Warehouses line the docks in parallel formation. What humans there are appear as tiny dots, and there is no sign of labor, other than the frictionless gliding of the vessels along the still rectangles of water. Beyond the docks the largely featureless landscape stretches far into the distance.

That Daniell was capable of portraying maritime activity differently is clear from his "View of the River Facing the Tower of London" (fig. 7.7) dating from the same period. Here we have the Thames, not its docks. Though the vantage point is elevated, it is from nowhere near as great a height as in the dock series, so that one can imagine that a real lookout exists, enabling a person to see what is portrayed. The vessels in the river are of many types and sizes, and they throng down the Thames, some bunched in fleets of sail, others rakishly akimbo to the river. Though the figures in the foreground are small, we can see what they are doing—rowing a boat, shaking hands, leading a horse and wagon. We are back to the commercial bustle.

Many verbal descriptions of the London docks followed the visual conventions of the bird's-eye view. "The scene, as you look down the vista of one of the landing sheds, is beautiful and wonderful," read one account of the West India Docks published in Massachusetts in 1844. "Hundreds of men are busy, like ants, in weighing and tumbling away the sugar, rice, tea, ginger, &c. &c.; and every thing proceeds with the order and discipline of a band of music."[46] Given the tensions between labor and capital, representations of dock laborers working under tight direction held obvious appeal, but we are encountering more than just a desire to control labor in these bird's-eye views. Even in 1844, there were not many enterprises that employed hundreds of men; the

Figure 7.7. William Daniell, "View of the River Facing the Tower of London" 1804, in Joseph G. Broodbank, *History of the Port of London*, 2 vols. (London, 1921), vol. 1, opp. p. 166. Courtesy University at Buffalo Library, Buffalo, NY.

sheer number was impressive. And the workers are not so much powerless as they are subsumed within a massive system that functions as a single, literally harmonious, unit.

Tellingly, observers applied the bird's-eye perspective to London's docks but not to Liverpool's. Instead, images of Liverpool drew on standard pictorial conventions. "Goree Warehouses, George's Dock, Liverpool, 1829" (fig. 7.8), for example, is not dominated by the warehouses, six stories high and massively built though they are. Nearby masts rise much higher, and the eye is drawn above all to the human activity in the foreground: the aproned laborer bearing goods on his head, the cluster of men and women gathered around barrels and bales, the sailors leaning over the stern of their vessel. One should not exaggerate the difference in the representations of the two cities. Other artists, especially those working after about 1830, depicted London's docks as a commercial bustle. At least one commentator suggested that the Liverpool docks functioned in some manner as an impersonal system. The *Liverpool Guide* praised the dockmaster of Queen's Dock for managing the movements of vessels in and out of the basin with "impartiality." "Without such a *regulator*," the guide continued, italicizing a term that also denoted a mechanical device designed to maintain even speed and pressure in machinery, there would soon

Figure 7.8. "Goree Warehouses, George's Dock, Liverpool, 1829," in Thomas Allen, *Lancashire Illustrated* (London, 1832). Courtesy Buffalo and Erie County Public Library, Buffalo, NY.

be "confusion."[47] Perhaps most significantly, observers in both Liverpool and London obsessively quantified the physical traits and economic activities of the docks, reflecting a calculating frame of mind characteristic of those engaged in the massive, rationalized enterprises of this era. That habit speaks to the values of rationalized capitalism, not the Burkean Sublime.[48] Nevertheless, while depictions of docks in both cities dwelt on their vastness and the security and convenience they provided, for the most part, the starkest images of rationalized order were restricted to London. Why that should be gives us a further clue into their meaning.

Recall that Liverpool's docks were publicly owned, while in London joint-stock companies controlled the people, vessels, and commodities within the dock walls. In Liverpool vessels were loaded and unloaded by outside contractors and the casual laborers they hired. In London corporate charters gave the dock companies the sole authority to employ dock workers. Liverpool's docks were in the midst of the city and publicly accessible. London's most important docks were constructed some distance down the Thames, walled, hidden, "a sort of third town, east of east," observed one traveler.[49] Within their precincts, the dock corporations exerted a sovereign force. If artists represented the London docks as an impersonal mechanism, then, it was not the mechanism of the rationalized state, as with Bentham's dockyards, nor even just of rationalized capitalism, but even more presciently, of the rationalized corporation.

From the 1830s, there arose a second strain of aesthetic responses to the docks. If the aesthetics of control depicted the docks as an abstract mechanism, this competing aesthetics took as its subject the very stuff of commerce, the commodities themselves in all their irrepressible exoticism, variety, excess, and sensuality. "In the warehouses," reported *Hunt's Merchant's Magazine*, "great masses of ivory tusks are encountered; wax, tea, cork; sugar, in quantity beyond our previously conceived ideas—the very drippings from the hogsheads would be a snug fortune." One Bostonian reported seeing

> spices, cinnamon, mace, nutmegs, cloves, &c. in vast quantities . . . astonishing quantities of raw unthrown silk . . . hides and leather, and dyewoods, and tallow, and beeswax, all nicely stowed away in ranges and poles, of which there seemed to be no end. Again, there were sugar warehouses, story above story, full of boxes, bales and hogsheads, enough to sweeten the sea.

Another American enumerated the contents of London's "immense warehouses": the "choicest of the vines of Portugal, Spain, France, and Germany; the cotton and tobacco of America, the ivory, gold, and spices of India and Africa, the silks and teas of China, and the coffee of Arabia and the Indies." One visitor, noting the "vast heaps of ivory," exclaimed: "Indeed the spectacle is one that carries you away at once to the African deserts, and shows you what is going on there while we are quietly and monotonously living at home." In William Daniell's dock landscapes, men and goods alike had been reduced to black dots, and the whole was devoid of life and movement. In these commercial landscapes, the commodities themselves animate and energize the scene.[50]

Representations of the docks as a bazaar reversed the aesthetic of the bird's-eye view, an aesthetic characterized by John Kasson as the displacement of "sensory experience" by "concrete abstraction."[51] The lists of exotic commodities read as a phantasmagoria of the senses: the shimmer of the gold, the feel of the raw silk, the aroma of the coffee, the taste of the spices, even the sound of the sugar dripping from a hogshead. Merchants were accustomed to using their senses in interacting with goods. When Malachy Postlethwayt instructed men of commerce in selecting good quality madder, a dyestuff, he told them to pay attention not just to color ("a strong but somewhat dusky red") and texture ("wrinkled," "not easily cut"), but also smell and taste, noting that stale madder would lack the characteristic "mixture of sweet and bitter" with "a very manifest astringency." Those consulting McCulloch's *Commercial Dictionary* for guidance on the proper choice of cloves found the following advice: "Good cloves have a strong, fragrant, aromatic odour; and a hot, acrid, aromatic taste, which is very permanent. They should be chosen large sized, perfect in all parts; the colour should be a dark brown, almost approaching to black; and, when handled, should leave oily moisture upon the fingers."[52]

The sensory qualities of these products translated into cold, hard currency, of course, but those who visited the docks did not experience commodities only as the objects of rational analysis. Visitors found themselves under the influence of commodities, whose subtle powers derived from their effect on the senses. The subversive potential of these powers is suggested by the focus on one sense in particular—smell. Henry Mayhew detailed the sights and sounds of the Wapping Docks in vivid detail ("men with their faces blue with indigo," "a goat bleats from some ship"), but his discussion of smell was limited entirely to commodities. "As you pass along this quay, the air is pungent with tobacco," he wrote, and "at that [quay] it overpowers you with the fumes of rum. Then you are nearly sickened with the stench of hides and huge bins of horns, and shortly afterwards the atmosphere is fragrant with coffee and spice." Visitors reported what they saw with their eyes, but it was the aromas of the warehouses that seemed to inspire the most vivid commentary. "The first sensation on entering," wrote one visitor, "is that of an intense acrid odor . . . for the atmosphere is loaded with tobacco effluvia." Making their way through 16,000 hogsheads of tobacco, Nathaniel Wheaton and his companion left only after "satiating our vision and regaling our nostrils with this abundance of the Indian weed." A visitor to the wine vaults recounted the "strange odor of wine, decayed wood, and oil-smoke from the numerous lamps" that "filled the atmosphere." The next stop on his tour was the tobacco warehouse, but "you need not inquire the way," explained this traveler, "for an atmosphere of the narcotic surrounds the building." So too the drug warehouse, where "the atmosphere was so laden with medicated vapors that I quickly turned away."[53]

Visitors might have dwelled on the pleasant aromas of spices or perfumes, but instead they focused on smells perceived as dangerous, especially alcohol and tobacco. There are several explanations for this selectivity. For the men and women who visited the docks, olfactory disgust may have spoken to their own gentility. Then, too, the temperance movement guaranteed that at least some who toured the wine vaults and tobacco warehouses would express moral disapproval. One such visitor termed sherry "the great brain-stealer" and reflected with horror on the many "bewitched for cigars and pipers [*sic*]." But the emphasis on bewitchment points to something else, namely, the imagined role of the senses in undermining the rational powers of the mind. Protestants had long regarded Roman Catholicism's appeal to the senses—the glitter of gold, the echoes through the nave, and, not least, the aroma of the incense—as an appeal to the irrational, designed to keep the laity in a state of ignorance and superstition. By the early nineteenth century, a reevaluation of the senses had taken place among the educated, whereby vision came to be associated with reason and civilization and smell with insanity and savagery. Indeed, writes historian Constance Classen, smell was marginalized because it was believed "to threaten the abstract and impersonal regime of modernity." If the aesthetics of commodities constituted an antitype to the aesthetics of rational control, it would make sense that the smell of goods, by definition stimulating the irrational, would be at the core of this counteraesthetic. And what better to symbolize the irrational than goods with narcotic properties?[54]

The aesthetics of the bazaar drew much of its power from an explicitly imperial vision. The "thousands of vessels from all quarters of the globe" bursting with "their ample cargoes," the "docks, swollen with the productions of every clime," and the warehouses, teeming with "piles of merchandize from every region and clime under heaven," spoke to Britain's commercial might. The British capital "is the centre of the world's commerce," wrote a Boston correspondent, "and it is here that one sees the greatest accumulations of the most valuable articles of trade." Here vessels arrived to "deliver up the freighted luxuries which they were bringing as a tribute from the remotest corners of the world." Although power is the ultimate reality in these representations of commerce, it is not the impersonal power of the mechanism, invisibly pervading a rationalized landscape, but more akin to the power of a potentate, loudly clapping for a command performance of his most colorful and entertaining subjects.[55]

Such imperial geographies were not new, but it is probably no accident that the aesthetics of the bazaar flourished in mid-century. By then, rationalized capitalism had secured its hold on the world of maritime trade. By the 1840s marine insurance, chronometers, and regularly scheduled packets had reduced the perils and uncertainties of ocean travel. Increasingly, shipyards turned out industrialized products—steam vessels, ironclads—and themselves followed an industrialized organization of labor. At sea, sailors worked under tight industrial discipline. Maritime trade was never without risk—the same holds true today—but by the mid-nineteenth century, it was a safer, more predictable, even routinized affair, when compared to ocean-borne commerce of even a few decades earlier. At the same time, it could appear rather staid when compared to its upstart cousin, manufacturing. Under such circumstances, a certain nostalgia for the old-time "merchant rover" entered the discourse of business. Where once merchants had scrambled to minimize risk, now such essays as "The Poetry of Trade" celebrated the merchant as risk-taker. Indeed, it was claimed, just this gusto for hazarding all gave commerce the edge over manufacturing. Both were critical to the economy, but "there is that in the spirit of commerce—in her activity, her daring, her enterprise and energy, which puts her, almost always, on the advance." And these "wild deeds of personal adventure" came in pursuit of exotic commodities: the spices from islands inhabited by "the swart savage," the gorgeous pearls retrieved by the "Ceylon diver," the "fragrant sandal-wood" snatched "from the pyre of the Hindoo widow."[56]

In reality, however, within the walls of the docks, the exuberant bazaar was transformed into rationally organized arrays of goods. An American visitor to St. Katharine's Docks reported that the warehouses were "marked A, B, C &c. in immense letters," mirroring the alphabetized organization of a merchant's bureau. "In the warehouse there is a place for every thing and every thing in its place." From this aesthetic perspective, the commodities themselves lost materiality, and it was the system itself that emerged as the fundamental reality of the docks, just as it did in the bird's-eye views. "A London merchant has no warehouse of his own," continued this American correspondent. "He takes the certificate of the dock company, and trades upon that. And the goods may be sold a dozen times without being moved at all." Another traveler reflected that "you never see the productions which the two Indies, Africa, and America, are pouring into the Thames, and which return to the four quarters of the world." Instead, "all this commerce with the universe is carried on by abstraction."[57] Much as the docks disciplined the chaos of river traffic into soldier-like formations of identical vessels, the warehouses subdued the sensory power of commodities.

Edmund Burke emphasized that landscapes are beautiful or sublime, not because of any inherent qualities, but only as they stimulate particular emotions in their viewers. As historians, we can take our lead from Burke and ask just what predisposed American viewers of the privileged classes to experience the Liverpool and London docks as sublime. These men and women considered themselves refined, and as refinement entailed aesthetic sensitivity and discrimination, it is no surprise that they applied what they had learned to commercial landscapes. Evaluating landscapes according to conventional visual criteria, they perceived commercial harbors as picturesque. But they did not seek out harbors, as they did other sites, as destinations for picturesque tourism, and it was not commerce itself they found picturesque. Instead, harbors provided them with a mix of visual elements suitable for composition into a pleasing picture, the characteristic mental labor of the Picturesque.

But the docks were something else altogether. Visitors did seek them out. They experienced them as sublime, even though the application of the Sublime to human-made landscapes was still a rarity, and even though many of their aesthetic responses—counting the incalculable, celebrating security, praising commodiousness—were out of place for the Sublime. What was in fact sublime were not the visual elements of the docks, immense as they were. Instead, it was the vision of rationalized capitalism itself that was sublime. We must not forget how novel this vision was in the early nineteenth century, how altogether different capitalism would look and how differently it would function within several decades. When the London docks opened in the first decade of the 1800s, nothing like them had been seen before. Britain's industrial enterprises, not to mention America's fledgling ones, existed on a much smaller scale. They could not match the physical presence of the docks, nor the heavy economic and social footprint they made. Moreover, the docks were experiments in a still-new form of rationalized organization, physically embodied in the landscape as never before. British observers may have had some inkling of such enterprises in their experiences with the Excise Office or the Naval Dockyards, but the former was not a physical structure, the latter were being reorganized along rationalist lines at the same time as the docks, and neither was a private corporation. As for American observers, what they saw in the docks went totally beyond their realm of experience.

And these spectators were transfixed by what they saw. The docks stood as an aesthetic marker of emerging capitalist values: security, regularity, precision, impersonality. The possibilities of a new, rationalized form of capitalism, a world that ran with the predictability and efficiency of a mechanism, appeared to them as sublime. But if rationalized capitalism was a novelty to early visitors, that would not remain true for long. Those who responded to the docks as sublime moved in the circle of Americans experimenting with new forms of capitalist enterprises and institutions. Recall that John Lowell described the West India Docks to his brother Francis, whose textile mills, much like the docks, featured labor discipline, rationalized economic activity, and a landscape at once imposing and utopian (fig. 7.9). When Frederick Law Olmsted toured Liverpool in 1850, he admired Birkenhead Park for its beauties, but he also marveled at the "spaciousness and grandeur" of the docks and praised the dock police force as "the most perfect imaginable." His subsequent conception for Central Park may well have been influenced by his visit to Birkenhead, but

Figure 7.9. David Claypoole Johnston, [City view featuring Lowell Mass], n.d. Courtesy American Antiquarian Society, Worcester, MA.

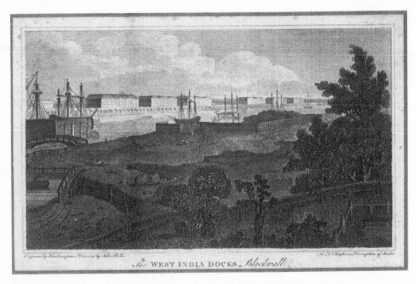

Figure 7.10. Robert Bremmel Schebbelie, "The West India Docks, Blackwall," 1805. Courtesy National Maritime Museum, Greenwich, London, England.

his work as park superintendent, which he considered to be an even more significant responsibility, may have been influenced by what he saw at the docks. He established the Central Park Police, whose task it was to protect the park from the disorderly behavior of visitors, as a paramilitary force. And in characterizing his management of the park's labor force, he claimed with pride that he had transformed "a mob of lazy, reckless, turbulent & violent loafers" into "a well organized, punctual, sober, industrious and disciplined body of 1000 men." The result, he stated, was "a perfect system, working like a machine."[58]

Whether or not the docks served as a prototype for American innovations, the responses they stimulated likely shaped the way spectators participated in the emergence of new capitalist values. Men and women of privilege sought out the docks expecting to be astonished, and so they were, at least in part because their social and economic positions allowed them to experience the power embodied in the docks as pleasurable. But this was no trivial titillation. To aestheticize a landscape is in some sense to legitimize the social facts and cultural values that landscape embodies, for it suggests a higher meaning that transcends the mean facts of quotidian reality. Sailors, laborers, pilferers, and smugglers, storms and tides, conflict and risk—all fade before the sublime vision of a perfect mechanism. It was, in fact, a utopian vision, but a utopia that Americans were determined to realize.

Perhaps nowhere is this utopian aesthetics more clear than in "The West India Docks, Blackwall," an engraving executed in 1805 (fig. 7.10).[59] Well over half the image is devoted to a dark foreground of natural and human disorder: a vast mudflat, marked here and there with untidy brush, rickety bridges that lead nowhere, and fences that fence in nothing. Over the water in the distance lie the docks, with their immense warehouses in a mathematically precise line. Although the warehouses were constructed of brick, in this engraving, they are shining white. In this capitalist version of *Pilgrim's Progress*, the Slough of "this world" is left behind and the Celestial City beckons, a foretaste of the rationalized world "to come."

8

William Leggett and the Melodrama of the Market

Jeffrey Sklansky

The Market

The market as we know it was the greatest invention of the eighteenth and nineteenth centuries. It was born of the union of classical economics and popular culture, of Adam Smith and Frankenstein. As a sovereign unto itself above any persons, places, or products, indeed any markets in particular, *the* market was a creature of industrial faith as much as works. Its authors were the scores of writers and reformers who made personal the impersonal, tangible the intangible, and visible the invisible hand of the market when it was still new to the throne.[1]

Few provided a more life-like portrayal of this powerful protagonist than the New York City newspaper editor and labor leader William Leggett (1801–39), who championed the beneficent force of the free market with surpassing influence, creativity, and zeal amid the riotous boom and bust of the 1830s. Yet, like many less ardent and articulate Jacksonians, Leggett found a nemesis for the market he revered in what was at once the most concrete and most abstract manifestation of its dominion, namely the rise of paper money and the marble-columned banks from whence it flowed. In the titanic conflict between the "natural economy" and the "money power," he and the many writers who followed his lead created a political melodrama that animated public debate for a century and still speaks to us today.[2]

The clash of what have come to be called Main Street and Wall Street arose in the political imagination as a means of making sense of the travails of men like Leggett himself, a blacksmith's son who struggled on the edge of failure and poverty throughout his career. Like many journalists in early industrial America, he shared the fortunes and fears of the besieged middling class of skilled artisans and small shop owners from which he came. What most urgently incited the self-styled "workingmen's movement" he came to lead was a devastating rise in the cost of food, fuel, and housing in the seaboard cities. Prices for basic commodities like bread and coal skyrocketed along with rents in the mid-1830s, while employment grew frightfully insecure amid a frenzy of speculative development of city lots and western lands fueled by an explosion of new banks and bank lending. When the bubble burst in the panic of 1837, hundreds of banks crashed across the country, bringing down thousands of businesses and tens of thousands of shopkeepers and workers, including Leggett. He died two years later as broke as the banks, at the onset of a depression that brought a violent end to the early republic of craft workshops and family farms.[3]

The nascent labor movement itself fell victim to the collapse of the household economy that had reared it. But it bequeathed to the class politics of the industrial age a set of lessons from the crash course in capitalism, which Leggett best expressed. In the rhetoric of the workingmen and their political progeny, the market ironically appeared as a bulwark of propertied independence against the onslaught of wage labor and finance capital.[4] An idealized vision of a simple market economy was twinborn with the fraudulent other against which it was defined: money as the ruler over industry and commerce instead of the subservient medium of exchange, forming the ends rather than the means of the market economy. Like gambling, counterfeiting, prostitution, and addiction, the "money power" constituted a haunting mirror image of industrial capitalism in its formative stage.[5] It reflexively provided both an enduring language for political opposition and a corresponding way of legitimating the always unrealized market ideal. The money power stood for what was oppressive, artificial, volatile, and corrupt in the new order; the market, by contrast, became exalted as inherently free, natural, stable, and true.

This chapter explores the melodrama of the market through the lens of Leggett's life and work. Though best known as an editor and labor leader, he began his career performing in plays and recitals, gained a reputation as an author of poetry, short stories, and literary criticism, and formed a close friendship with Edwin Forrest, the leading stage actor of the day.[6] He stood at the center of a revolution in literary as well as political and economic forms, marked by the advent of the star system in theater, the western and the detective story, and the penny press, along with modern political parties and industrial works. His previous writing and performing gave Leggett a repertoire of settings, characters, plots, themes, and standards that enabled him to find transcendent significance in the politics of corporations and currency. Yet his writing also exemplifies how the social and economic crisis of the 1830s stretched the literary logic of Jacksonian political economy to its breaking point.

Representation

At the crux of the contrast between the market and the money power lay a three-dimensional problem of political, financial, and literary representation.[7] The most basic lesson the workingmen drew from their experience was that economic misfortune reflected political misrule. Ruinous inflation and unemployment resulted from the kind of predatory government the American colonists had meant to overthrow at the time of the Revolution, a rapacious regulatory bureaucracy of licensers and inspectors who set up exclusive franchises charging extortionate prices. For the workingmen as for their forbears, misrule reflected in turn a grievous failure of political representation. As a committee of workingmen proclaimed in 1836, "Our greatest misfortune is that our interests have never been adequately represented in our publick councils."[8]

The financial turmoil thus signaled a crisis of democracy, a threat to workers' newly won political rights. It was not enough for them to vote if their elected leaders were corrupted by monied interests. As Jeremy Bentham put it in a passage that Leggett ran above the masthead in each issue of his weekly newspaper, "The immediate cause of all the mischief of misrule is, that the men acting as the representatives of the people have a private and sinister interest, producing a constant sacrifice of the interest of the people."[9] And the immediate cause of such corruption lay in the partnership of business and government embodied in the multitude of publicly chartered corporations charged with managing the machinery of market exchange, especially the means of transportation and the media of credit and currency.[10] "The people of this great state fondly imagine that they govern themselves; but they do not!" wrote Leggett in 1834. "They are led about by the unseen but strong bands of chartered companies."[11]

The proliferation of state-chartered commercial banks posed a special danger. Banks were ostensibly the representatives of the depositors and borrowers for whom they served as go-betweens. They were merchants of other people's money, occupying a central position in a burgeoning market economy dependent on the circulation of credit among strangers. But unlike other financial intermediaries, banks were legally authorized not only to convey funds from savers to spenders, but also to create currency, which had long been the exclusive prerogative of government. Amid a chronic shortage of coin and the absence of any government-issued paper money, the thousands of varieties of transferable notes issued by banks in the course of their lending served as Americans' main medium of exchange before the Civil War.[12] So, in addition to representing the political authority bestowed on banks, their notes represented the economic value of the widening panoply of commodities for sale, including labor and land. As the antebellum currency reformer Edward Kellogg observed, "Money is as much the representative of the property of the people, as the legislature are the representatives of their constituents."[13]

Seen in this light, the yawning gap between the money supplied by banks and the "real economy" of work and wealth it was supposed to serve manifested a distinctively modern betrayal of financial as well as political representation. It revealed the dual corruption of public servants by private interests and of markets by embezzling middlemen. "We are menaced by our old enemies, avarice and ambition, under a new name and form," Leggett warned, " . . . A CONCENTRATED MONEY POWER; a usurper in the disguise of a benefactor; an agent exercising privileges which his principal never possessed."[14] The flood of banknotes for which they blamed the soaring cost of living appeared to his followers as the ultimate servant turned master of the market economy. In what seemed an obscene paradox, the more bank money circulated, the higher the toll taken by the banking system in every transaction, and the less workers' paper earnings bought them. This understanding of hard times spawned what became the overarching demand of the workingmen's movement, which Leggett called the "separation of Bank and State." In concrete terms, it meant an immediate halt to the chartering of new banks and a ban on the issue of small-denomination notes of five, ten, or twenty dollars, the only banknotes workers generally saw. It also called for "free banking"—the banking equivalent of a "general incorporation law"—which would end the practice of special legislative charters and make banks simply businesses like any others without direct sponsorship by the state.[15]

At the same time, early Americans understood paper money as a form of *literary* representation, not unlike newspapers. This was the third dimension of the problem of representation in finance and government.[16] The increasing detachment of paper IOUs from the networks of borrowers and lenders in which they originated, allowing bills and notes to circulate like cash, mirrored the growing autonomy of banks and other financial institutions, raising related questions of misrepresentation.[17] More broadly, contemporary concerns about illusion and artifice in literature and oratory went hand in hand with apprehensions about political and economic corruption. What the philosopher Hanna Pitkin has described as "standing for," like a poem or play, and "acting for," like a lawyer or legislator, appeared closely linked in the new nation.[18] The many Jacksonian editors like Leggett who became partisan standard-bearers epitomized the widely presumed connection between literary and political representation.[19]

"Plaindealing" was Leggett's label for both his democratic philosophy and the polemic style in which he hammered it home, connoting a close conjunction of social and literary ideals that formed the key to his ability to articulate the lessons that many Americans took from the tumult of the 1830s. His rigorously republican approach to economic questions threw into stark relief the growing disjuncture between money and labor, or between market value and the people and things it was supposed to represent. Leggett's allegiance to faithful representation in business and government as in art and literature enabled him to pose the problem most vividly. Yet that core commitment could not bring forth a lasting means of rejoining literally as well as figuratively what had been torn apart.

Melodrama

Above all, Leggett's political commentary owed its expressive force to the theatrical conventions of melodrama. Broadly construed as a popular way of understanding and experiencing revolutionary change, melodrama provided the literary logic through which he, like many others, came to conceive the pervasive problem of representation.[20]

On both sides of the Atlantic, the early nineteenth century saw the rise of melodrama as the dominant form of commercial theater.[21] As a new genre in its own right as opposed to a longstanding element in other kinds of literature, melodrama emerged from the minor theaters in eighteenth-century Paris that specialized in pantomime, spectacle, and the stirring musical accompaniment for which it was named. Its hallmarks were everywhere recognizable: courageous heroes, chaste heroines, and dastardly villains; seduction and betrayal, wrongful accusations and family secrets; thrilling action and effusive oratory. But there was more to it than that. As the literary historian Peter Brooks argues in *The Melodramatic Imagination*, the mission of melodrama was to reveal the workings of elemental moral forces within the everyday lives of ordinary people.[22] It was predicated on an ideal of total and transparent representation, in which every character, setting, and scene disclosed an unambiguous message: the eternal conflict between freedom and oppression, virtue and corruption.[23] Reflecting its revolutionary origins, melodrama contributed to republican polemic such as the Declaration of Independence, with its paradigmatic narrative of cruelty, villainy, and tyranny, and it inspired a wide variety of public ceremonies, celebrations, and other political performances in Europe and America.[24]

It gave form, more particularly, to the revolutionary genre of political economy, which received its classic exposition in Adam Smith's *Wealth of Nations* (1776). Like melodrama, political economy brought to light the great public purposes operating through common private pursuits. It likewise uncovered the fixed principles at work beneath the flux of ordinary business, stripping away the "veil" of monetary transactions to reveal the underlying factors of production and laws of motion that governed the market economy. A fundamental materialism formed the bedrock of classical economics: market prices gravitated toward the "natural prices" of commodities determined by their real cost of production in labor and land; individual incomes were ultimately determined by the work and material wealth for which credit and currency stood.[25] Viewing market actors as representatives of immutable class interests driven inexorably into competition and conflict, political economy proved an ideal subject for the melodramatic imagination. And like the Shakespearean theater with which it was allied, economic theory made up a vital part of nineteenth-century popular culture before becoming the more or less exclusive province of an educated elite.[26]

Therein lies both a challenge and an opportunity for scholars of the period. The stereotyped characters, stilted speeches, and hackneyed plots of melodrama have long made it the stuff of parody, disparaged by twentieth-century writers for its transparent didacticism and apparent lack of irony or ambiguity.[27] For similar reasons, it is hard to read the vernacular economics of the nineteenth century without smiling at its histrionic language, its righteous certitude, its penchant for iron laws and rigid dichotomies: right versus wrong, truth versus fiction, supply versus demand, labor versus capital, population versus subsistence.[28] In recent years, however, film studies and feminist scholars have begun to rehabilitate melodrama as a more complex, protean, and inventively modern form than was previously appreciated, highlighting the ways in which the far-reaching moral conflicts it portrayed inevitably exceeded the narrow boundaries of its formulaic endings. Such work suggests that its inconclusive struggles between liberty and power, honor and treachery, made the genre uniquely revealing in periods of revolutionary upheaval. At such times, its stock stories cathartically dramatized the widely felt sense of an epochal social conflict underway and sharply delineated what was at stake, even as they failed in the end to resolve the contradictions between new social forces and inherited ideals.[29] The popular political economy that rose and fell with nineteenth-century melodrama merits similar reconsideration for what it revealed as well as concealed in the moments of crisis when it held greatest sway.[30]

Poetry and Performance

In a tribute to Leggett written shortly before he died, his friend and coeditor William Cullen Bryant traced the fervor of his political writings to his tour in the US Navy, ending in his court-martial in 1825. "The hatred which Mr. Leggett has shown to tyranny, in all its forms, was rendered the more intense by his having tasted its bitterness," Bryant wrote.[31] Indeed, Leggett's first battle was with his commanding officer, and the melodramatic transcript of his trial shows how poetry and politics came together in Leggett's life as they did in his death fourteen years later, apparently hastened by the lingering effects of an attack of yellow fever while in the Navy.[32]

Leggett served aboard the USS *Cyane* as a midshipman, or junior officer—a rank that rendered him immune to the corporal and capital punishment meted out to common sailors, but subject to the absolute authority of senior officers. Though he did not serve "before the mast" like his younger contemporaries Richard Henry Dana Jr. and Herman Melville, he learned from the quarter-deck how petty officers were torn between captain and crew in the shipboard struggles such writers chronicled. Leggett was evidently strong-willed and short-tempered, quick to sense an insult and repay it with interest, and given to reciting Romantic poetry and Shakespearean soliloquies for his shipmates, in addition to writing his own.[33]

Charged in January 1825 with having left his post to fight a duel, Leggett was confined for several weeks aboard ship, then imprisoned for much of the next five months. Meanwhile, he sent an indignant letter to the commander of

US naval forces in the Mediterranean, recited what his captain deemed "seditious poetry," and tried to stab himself with a dagger, all of which compounded his original offense. His ardor to express his inmost feelings—in highly stylized terms—formed the theme of his trial defense, replete with verses from *Hamlet* and *Richard III*. Deploring the captain's denial of his "constitutional priveledge of speech—one of the dearest priveledges of Nature," he derided the charges against him as "a superstructure of big words," "intended as a cloak . . . to hide the acts of tyranny which had preceded them." "But let the degrading treatment that I have experienced be tolerated," he told the court, "and there is a monster cherished among us that, in its brutal progress, will trample on every honorable impulse, poison every noble aspiration, and extinguish every manly and dignified sentiment."[34] The court apparently was unmoved, convicting Leggett on several counts and sentencing him to dismissal from the service. Reinstated in recognition of his long confinement, he quit the Navy in disgust.[35]

This was Leggett at twenty-four, already demonstrating a studied sensitivity to the power of language and the language of power. "I speak in the character of an insulted officer, I speak the language of an assured gentleman, I invoke your aid as an imprisoned freeman," as he put it to the naval commander.[36] The keynotes of his court-martial defense resounded throughout his career: the starkly drawn conflict of liberty versus tyranny, the defense of a middling class against a domestic despot, the struggle for free expression, the stylistic conventions of romance and melodrama. How had Leggett acquired these literary tools, and what can they tell us about the vision of political economy that he later fashioned with them?

His father's life had followed a largely downhill course of fleeting gains and major setbacks, fitting a pattern of downward mobility that formed a recurrent theme within Leggett's writing as in that of other antebellum authors to be found in the retreating ranks of urban mechanics and family farmers.[37] After serving with distinction in the Continental Army during the Revolution, Abraham Leggett had embarked on a series of failed business ventures, finally succeeding as a blacksmith in New York. There William was born in 1801, one of nine children of Abraham's second wife, Catherine Wylie. The elder Leggett did well enough for William to enter Georgetown College for a year, after which a serious downturn in the father's business forced the son to return home.[38] Four years later, the panic of 1819 left the Leggetts broke, their small property seized by creditors. Joining a floodtide of refugees, they headed for the new settlement of Edwardsville on the Illinois prairie. But the collapsing economy soon caught up with them, and Abraham's blacksmith business quickly sank under deepening debt.[39]

To help support his family, William acted in a few minor melodramas and offered public recitals of poetry and drama.[40] He also began writing poems for the weekly newspaper in Edwardsville, many of which appeared along with those written while in the Navy in a compilation entitled *Leisure Hours at Sea* (1825). These first published works of Leggett's exude an anxious sense of being at sea biographically as well as geographically, wandering adrift and apart from family, country, stable and sustaining roots. Smiles deceive, stars fade, lovers betray, living things decay and die. In their immature but serious style, these plaintive poems chronicle an endless search for secure footing—a prominent theme in much of his later writing on the falsity of appearances, ephemerality of fortunes, and fragility of households and communities that marked the Jacksonian economy.[41]

Though we have no eyewitness accounts of Leggett's performances in Edwardsville and in the Navy, we know he would have learned to recite from the cheap schoolbooks that appeared in virtually every home and school in the Northeast when he was growing up. These "readers and speakers" offered instruction in how to reproduce an author's thoughts and feelings through an elaborate system of facial expressions, vocal intonations, and bodily gestures, aiming to represent the meaning of each word fully and unambiguously. More than a means of literacy, such training in elocution was considered essential to citizenship in a modern republic.[42]

Leggett clearly understood patriotism to be a performance. His father had witnessed the emergence of popular politics in the street theater of the Revolutionary era, at a time when professional theater was banished as a symbol of monarchical culture. By the time Leggett was born, American theater was enjoying a revival as a forum for the kind of cultural politics earlier played out in liberty pole celebrations, tea parties, and tarring-and-featherings. The reborn playhouse became an arena of patriotic unity and raucous social strife among the servants, apprentices, and prostitutes in the gallery, the artisans and professionals in the pit, and the elites in the box seats, not to mention the English actors on stage.[43]

This was the republican theater to which Leggett was drawn as a young man, and to which he briefly returned after leaving the Navy. Unenthusiastic reviews put an early end to his acting career, but not to his abiding love of the theater.[44] That same year, Leggett formed a lifelong friendship with Edwin Forrest, then on the eve of becoming the first American star of the stage. Leggett soon became Forrest's staunchest champion in the press, and no wonder: the latter's sensational performances as the charismatic leader of a slave rebellion, a peasant revolt, and an American Indian uprising made him the embodiment of Leggett's vision of the theater as a school of righteous action, a model of freedom-fighting valor.[45] For Leggett, as for many of his contemporaries, the new role of the star actor exemplified the Jacksonian ideal of heroic individualism. Like Andrew Jackson, the statesman of the stage was to represent the popular will, much as Leggett would seek to do as a journalist.[46]

Fiction and Criticism

The dozens of short stories that Leggett began publishing in 1826 formed a bridge between his theatrical and his political vision. Unlike his poetry and acting, his fiction quickly gained a following. A long story called "The Rifle" was reprinted in newspapers across the country and adapted into a play. A shorter one entitled "The Main-Truck, or A Leap for Life" was widely published in British and American newspapers as well as in German, Spanish, and French translations, and was later turned into a popular poem and ballad.[47] More stories appeared in the next few years, and most were republished in two well-received collections, *Tales and Sketches. by a Country Schoolmaster* (1829) and *Naval Stories* (1834).[48]

As these titles suggest, Leggett's fiction fell into the subgenres of western stories and sea stories, closely based as it was on his time in Illinois and the Mediterranean. Yet the ships and towns in which his stories take place serve as microcosms of the metropolitan market society in which they were written. His are rootless places, less settled than unsettled by rootless people, marking less a geographical than a chronological frontier: a borderland not between East and West, but between a landed economy and a credit economy, or between a society in which money represents real property and one in which real property represents money. The stories feature orphans and widows, fugitives, migrants, and sailors adrift in a disorienting terrain of unclear title, mistaken identity, and ceaseless motion. Their fire-prone cabins and storm-tossed sloops reflect the precariousness of such humble characters' existence. The man who rises in the morning prosperous and respected goes to bed destitute and in jail. Leggett's naval adventures frequently culminate in a harrowing leap into the watery abyss, a nightmarish vision of survival in a world with no firm ground on which to stand. The scenario provided a versatile metaphor for antebellum concerns about paper money and speculative bubbles, and for the widespread prospect of downward mobility and "fear of falling" that prodded Leggett's later followers into political action.[49]

The common climax of Leggett's western stories comes in a different sort of trial. Here the general pattern involves a robbery or murder, an innocent man forced to stand trial, and an ultimate exoneration along with discovery of the true culprit. Unlike contemporaneous crime stories by James Fenimore Cooper and Sir Walter Scott, Leggett's stories inevitably hinge on the role of physical evidence.[50] Each case boils down to a question of property—what belongs to whom?—that poses a problem for two revealing reasons. First, the property in question is readily exchangeable and repeatedly exchanged. Second, certain kinds of property—such as clothing, newspapers, and especially money— prove consistently misleading. The kinds of evidence that do not deceive, by contrast, are those that supposedly can be neither changed nor exchanged: the gray hair of the robber's horse, the soft white hands of the defendant, the rifle-ball of the murder weapon. Leggett's style echoes the core concern of all his fiction with honesty and deceit. His narrators relate events as if from the perspective of the audience for a play in which motives and meanings are reliably signified through formulaic characters, transparent body language, and symbolic scenery. Even the most duplicitous characters betray their deepest sentiments in dialogue or soliloquy.

While he was establishing himself as an author of short stories, Leggett was also reviewing books and plays for the *New York Mirror* and the *Merchants' Telegraph*, and in the fall of 1828 he launched his own literary newspaper, *The Critic*. It lasted just eight months, enough to gain him considerable influence in New York literary circles.[51] Leggett shared with the other members of the so-called Knickerbocker school, whose leading lights were Cooper, Bryant, and Washington Irving, a fundamentally moralistic approach to literature.[52] "A novel," as he wrote, "should be a sort of practical commentary on the writings of the moral philosopher."[53] Seen in this way, the new forms of fiction and drama that drew his attention presented an unparalleled opportunity for popular education. But like the mass market on which they depended, these emerging genres also posed, in his view, a new kind of threat to the republican values they were meant to promote.

The danger lay in the tendency of literature, like money, to become an end in itself instead of representing higher ends. Just as "the desire for wealth is a feverish thirst, which rages with the more violence the more it is sought to gratify it," he wrote, so the desire for mere entertainment was liable to fuel a vicious cycle of self-indulgence rather than self-improvement. While he applauded the increasing availability of cheap books and periodicals, he lamented publishers' enthusiasm for "fashionable novels" that titillated more than they taught, resulting in "an increase of books without an increase of knowledge; the perusal of which, like inebriating draughts, does not quench, but inflames, the thirst of mind." Little wonder that he called intemperance "the besetting sin of the country." For Leggett as for many writers, addiction symbolized the self-sustaining spiral of desire associated with commercial culture. It connoted the corruption of representation that he soon found in paper money no less than in fashionable novels, the means become ends.[54]

The affinity between literary and monetary representation struck Leggett even before he began writing political editorials. "'Words are things;' they are the representatives of ideas, as money is the representative of value," he wrote, quoting Byron. "[W]ords are the coin made use of by the mind; and he who deals with the poor in understanding must use only such as the value of which cannot fail to be appreciated from their general currency."[55] In other words, much as the common man dealt in small change, so he naturally dealt in plain language, representing ideas as simply as coins did value. The value of money itself, however, was anything but clear when Leggett wrote these words, and this conventional analogy bore the seeds of his critique of the new banking system, through which methods of payment long reserved for merchants had become the common currency of workers, shopkeepers, and family farmers.

Free Speech and the Free Market

When William Cullen Bryant hired him as assistant editor of the *Evening Post* in 1829, Leggett took the job on the condition "that he should not be required to write upon political topics," explaining that he had neither "settled opinions" about nor "taste" for such issues. Yet "within a few months he found himself almost wholly devoted to them."[56] The ease with which he made that transition suggests how porous was the boundary between imaginative writing such as poetry and fiction and more ostensibly objective forms of literature such as journalism and economics.[57] His sudden penchant for politics also reflects how closely his ideas about market relations corresponded to his notions of honesty and sincerity in literary terms.

Leggett's editorials were forceful, innovative, and bracingly sharp, with a mixture of irreverence, invective, and indignation that exemplified the ascendant style of "middling rhetoric" in the popular press of the 1830s. In completing his move from poetry to prose to politics, he broke through the shell of his earlier efforts, allowing the literary logic he had long cultivated to show its creative agility. It was the logic of melodrama, or of what he called "plaindealing," dedicated to truthful representation in life as in literature.[58]

Leggett abstracted from Jeffersonian political economy the cardinal commitment to equal rights, presuming that economic inequity was rooted in a pernicious pattern of taxation without representation. By subscribing to banks, railroads, canals, and other economic ventures, he argued, state governments saddled middling taxpayers with an increasingly heavy load, while rich bondholders reaped the rewards. The states' reliance on tolls, tariffs, and taxes on transactions ensured that the bulk of the burden would be borne by the final consumers who paid in higher prices, according to Leggett.[59] He translated the longstanding popular resistance to public debt and indirect taxation into a sweeping indictment of virtually every form of public regulation, relief, or provision, from ferries to insane asylums to veterans' pensions.

Leggett's defense of the free market, however, stemmed from a more basic concern with the corruption of representative government through sponsorship of corporate monopolies. Instead of channeling private wealth to serve public needs, he argued, the system of special charters made public servants into the agents of the irresponsible private entities they created. By delegating exclusive authority to favored groups of investors, the legislatures were "bartering away the sovereignty of the People to little bodies politic, fattening on the great body." In demanding the separation of business and state, as the historian Marvin Meyers notes, Leggett sought to unhitch the market economy from speculative enterprise as much as to unfetter it from drags on its natural course. The "natural economy" he imagined was free-flowing, yet confined to its proper place: "an equal and uniform current, never stagnating, and never overflowing its boundaries," like the limpid streams that gurgled through the pastoral landscapes of his western tales.[60] Natural—as in "natural price," "natural right," "natural level," "natural equilibrium"—meant lawful, balanced, proportional, predictable, self-regulating. Freedom meant fixity, regularity, and stability, as opposed to addiction, inebriety, fanaticism, and frenzy.

Leggett's journalism career swiftly became bound up with the central demand of the New York workingmen's cause for proper representation in government, in the market, and in the press. Spurred into political action by the panic of 1819, local workers had successfully campaigned for the elimination of property restrictions on voting in the 1820s, then responded to the runaway inflation of the 1830s with an unprecedented surge of trade-union organizing. Employers enlisted the aid of the courts to declare the new unions in violation of a tailor-made conspiracy law against combinations "injurious to trade," prompting the formation of the Equal Rights Party in the fall and winter of

1835–36, devoted to workingmen's equal representation in economic as in political affairs.[61]

The other impetus for the new organization came largely from Leggett, who in August 1834 advised voters to support only those candidates pledged to oppose any further bank charters. That fall, the Democratic candidates took Leggett's pledge and won election with workers' support, but then promptly began chartering more banks. To Leggett's constituency of laborers, artisans, and shopkeepers, nicknamed the "Loco Focos," the betrayal of labor votes appeared of a piece with the suppression of labor unions, together amounting to a denial of due representation. Along with their core complaint went an enthusiastic identification of the defense of "equal rights" with that of the *Evening Post* and its embattled editor, whose literary representation of their interests the Loco Focos guarded as jealously as they demanded political and economic representation. In 1836 they nominated Leggett for mayor, but he declined to run owing to poor health and financial straits.[62]

Leggett viewed journalism as the ideal medium for both promoting and practicing plaindealing. "There is no species of literary composition so extensively read, or so eagerly sought after" as newspapers, he noted, and their close association with the emerging mass market dictated a distinctive literary style—or rather, a distinctive lack thereof. "He who relates the events of a battle, the effects of a whirlwind, or the political or commercial condition of his own, or of another country, is not looked to so much for an elegant flow of thought, or gracefulness of diction, as for accuracy of investigation and correctness of statement," he wrote, "and, provided he utters only the truth, the particular mode is a matter of but little importance." Such strict fidelity stemmed not only from newspapers' concern with business affairs, but also from their dependence on the market for subscribers and sales. Intensifying competition, according to Leggett, ensured that no paper could long afford to keep the truth from its readers. "Indeed, *in no branch of literature is implicit veracity more indispensably requisite* than in newspaper writing; for . . . no sooner is an error committed by one, than all the others are loud in censure or abuse," he wrote.[63]

Two months after he expressed such high hopes for the union of free speech and the free market, however, *The Critic* folded for lack of funds, like hundreds of other publications in these years. In a bitter notice in the final issue, Leggett complained that he had been unable to collect enough of what his subscribers owed—a common lament.[64] Each of his other three papers likewise capsized quickly under his command, as the aging partisan press of which he was part vied for working-class readers with a new breed of profit-driven "penny dailies."[65] After *The Critic* came the *Evening Post*, where Bryant soon made him his business partner and co-owner as well as coeditor. In June 1834 Bryant placed the thriving paper in Leggett's sole hands and departed for a sojourn in Europe. Under Leggett's direction, the *Evening Post* steadily lost the support of political patrons and commercial advertisers angered by his editorials. Bryant returned eighteen months later to find the paper close to insolvency, its revenues roughly a quarter of what they had been when he left. Leggett was forced to sell his share in order to pay off the debts he had incurred, and he left the paper shortly thereafter "without a shilling," as he confided in a letter to a friend.[66] He fared no better with the two papers that he founded after leaving the *Evening Post*, the daily *Examiner* and the weekly *Plaindealer*. Each survived for less than a year before falling victim to the panic, leaving him practically penniless and "overwhelmed with debts," as he wrote to his friend Edwin Forrest.[67]

His relentless financial troubles rattled Leggett's confidence that the market rewarded plaindealing. "He who strives to be a reformer, and to discharge his high trust with strict and single reference to the responsibilities of his vocation, will be sadly admonished by his dwindled receipts that he has not chosen the path of profit," he lamented to readers in February 1837. The remedy he proposed appears surprising at first glance, given his opposition to corporate privilege. Noting that editor-owners were peculiarly vulnerable to the vicissitudes of the market, he argued that newspapers should be operated instead by joint-stock companies, diffusing the risks of ownership among a large group of investors and insulating editors from the immediate pressures of running a business. Corporate control, he hoped, would afford newspapers the security they needed to survive without pursuing the short-term profits to be made in gossip and sensationalism. Plaindealing required protection against cutthroat competition, even as it depended on healthy competition to keep editors honest.[68]

Urban Riots and Abolitionism

For Leggett and his followers, any corporation established by legislative charter constituted an illegitimate monopoly. Any business without such exclusive state support did not. Indeed, his devotion to laissez-faire was rarely more adamant than in his defense of business combinations in the brutal winter of 1836–37, when the already inflated prices of food, fuel, and rental housing suddenly spiked. At a mass protest organized by the Loco Focos in February 1837, party leaders blamed the inflationary surge on the depreciation of the currency due to the proliferation of banks and banknotes. But outraged by reports that local merchants were hoarding flour in order to raise the price in a time of need, a large crowd left the rally to storm several flour warehouses, destroying property, hurling barrels of flour into the street, and resulting in dozens of arrests.[69] Leggett's denunciation of what he called the "causeless and disgraceful outrage" reflected his view that both the violent methods the rioters employed and the regulatory ends they pursued amounted to misrepresentation. "It was causeless," he wrote of the riot, "as the dealers in any commodity whatever have a perfect right to fix their own price; and it was disgraceful, as it sought to effect an unworthy object by unworthy means."[70]

Leggett's criticism was colored by his earlier response to the antiabolitionist riots of 1834 and 1835, which had made him the leading advocate of abolition within the Democratic Party. Much as he exalted melodramatic theater while decrying mere entertainment for its own sake, much as he embraced the free market but bemoaned the self-destructive cycle of limitless competition, so he defined his own vision of popular politics against the wave of urban riots that formed the underside of Jacksonian politics. Like the popularity of licentious literature and hard spirits, vigilante violence signified for him a failure of rightful representation. Indeed, the riots targeted the very forms of legitimate representation that the rioters lacked, in Leggett's view: merchants' associations, for example, and the newly organized abolitionist movement in New York City led by merchants Lewis and Arthur Tappan.[71]

The printing revolution in New York City made possible the national pamphlet campaign of 1835, in which the Tappan organization deluged the mails with abolitionist literature. In response, antiabolition committees and rallies arose everywhere that summer, turning the Jacksonian rhetoric of equal rights into a furious reaction against what was widely described as a monstrous conspiracy led by moneyed elites in New York and London.[72] Leggett initially shared the deep hostility toward abolitionism within the Democratic Party, viewing it as a "fanatical" and "aristocratic" movement to degrade Northern labor, and calling the pamphlet campaign "reprehensible to a degree for which language has no terms of adequate censure."[73]

Yet each time he took up the issue, he was provoked by violent efforts to suppress antislavery speech and association. When antiabolition crowds occupied the city in July 1834, he became the abolitionists' strongest defender in the press while still disavowing any agreement with their cause. The following year, his *Evening Post* became one of only three major papers in the country to condemn the US Postmaster General for allowing the confiscation of abolitionist literature by Southern postmasters—an action that Leggett called tantamount to "censorship of the press." His growing sympathy for antislavery stemmed less from the ideology of "free labor" than from that of free speech.[74]

Yet if Leggett's support was originally much narrower than that of leading abolitionists, it grew into something broader in important ways: a vision of the emancipation of labor that extended far beyond ending chattel slavery. When local and national Democratic organizations censured the *Evening Post* for its apostasy, Leggett broke decisively with the party and commenced espousing the cause of abolition with his customary zeal. When he founded the *Plaindealer* in December 1836, he proclaimed in its first editorial his intention to discuss the evils of slavery openly and relentlessly. Political journals that favored fealty to party over loyalty to principle, he noted in the language of representation, "substitute the means for the end."[75] Southerners who hoped to stifle antislavery agitation, he wrote in a similar vein a few weeks later, "never can induce the northern states to give up freedom for the sake of union; to give up the end for the sake of the means; to give up the substance for the sake of the shadow."[76] Leggett continued to believe that the Constitution did not allow the federal government to abolish slavery in the Southern states, though he supported congressional abolition in the District of Columbia. But as the historian Sean Wilentz has written, he articulated a distinctively Jacksonian brand of antislavery, which identified Southern planters with the "monied classes," Southern slaves with Northern workers, and democracy with equality under the law regardless of race.[77]

While Leggett's response to the flour riot flowed partly from its association with previous riots, his position also reflected broader convictions about economic representation in the form of labor unions and business corporations. Earlier in the decade, he had strenuously supported workers' right to organize amid the anticonspiracy trials of union leaders. "The rich perceive, acknowledge, and act upon a common interest, and why not the poor?" he wrote in December 1834.[78] But when laboring New Yorkers charged coal and flour dealers with collusion and price-gouging in the winter of 1836–37, Leggett applied the same principle to merchants' associations as to trade unions. Business combination posed nothing to fear, he argued, for as soon as merchants colluded to engross flour or any other necessity, they invited competition that would restore prices to their "natural value."

The immediate remedy for price-gouging was to be found not by opposing business combination, but by demanding that it be made equally accessible to working people through a general incorporation law, which would turn incorporation into a basic right of all qualified applicants. "The humblest citizens might associate together, and wield . . . a vast aggregate capital, composed of the little separate sums which they could afford to invest in such an enterprise, in competition with the purse-proud men who now almost monopolize certain branches of business," Leggett wrote.[79] But the root cause of exorbitant prices, he believed, lay beyond the market, in the banking system that sustained the inflationary spiral.

The Money Power

At the height of the panic of 1837, as more than a third of New York City workers were thrown out of work by an avalanche of falling prices and failing businesses triggered by banks' inability to redeem their notes, Leggett exulted that the crash had finally exposed Wall Street and Pearl Street for what they were. "[T]hese bankers now stand before the world, by their own confession, as a crew of swindling pirates, who have been preying on the property of the community," he wrote. "[T]heir promises now, instead of representing silver and gold, represent nothing but violated faith, and the folly of publick credulity in the honesty of soulless corporations which derive their very being from legislative corruption."[80] Much as contemporary religious crusaders sought divine deliverance from the torrential force of the financial crisis, Leggett and the workingmen turned for protection to the new gospel of the free market. Nothing inspires faith in a good god like bad times.[81]

The money question, as Jacksonian writers conceived it, appeared intrinsically melodramatic: dedicated to the truth of the free-market ideal as opposed to the fraudulence of current practice; convinced that the corruption they deplored stemmed from improper representation of the mutual interests of creditors and debtors, producers and consumers, by self-serving agents; confident that plaindealing truth would set the market free, restoring the balance of simple commodity exchange. By detaching the money supply from the "real economy" of goods and services, Leggett argued, banks sponsored overtrading, overbuilding, and reckless risk-taking at the expense of prudent investment in response to actually existing demand. They excited "a feverish and baneful thirst of gain—gain not by the regular and legitimate operations of trade, but by sudden and hazardous means."[82] Paper money, he wrote at the height of the panic,

is a curse to the poor, continually defrauding them of a portion of their hard earnings, without their knowing how or when they go. It is a curse to the rich, introducing among them an insane desire of boundless wealth, and leading them into the most demoralizing schemes of speculation. It is a curse to the whole country, unsettling the established modes of industry, creating false notions of the relative respectability of various callings, alluring men from the steady pursuits of agriculture and the mechanick arts, and setting them in full chase after those glittering stock-bubbles, which cheat the eye with the appearance of valuable substance, but turn to nothing in the grasp.[83]

Banknotes, in other words, were as volatile, seductive, and deceptive as the speculative machinery they fueled. They epitomized the tendency of money to become an overpowering end in itself instead of a mere means of exchange.

Leggett's foremost contribution to the money question concerned what he regarded as an especially insidious form of literary and financial fraud. He began with workers' common complaint that employers paid them in "uncurrent notes" issued by backwoods banks of little repute, bought from Wall Street brokers for this express purpose. In a variant of the well-known "Gresham's Law" that bad money drives out good, he argued that the most depreciated currency gravitated to those on the bottom rung, who had no choice but to accept it at face value, while their employers pocketed the difference between what they brought to Wall Street and what they paid their workers. But even if they were paid in hard money, he contended, workers were still robbed of their rightful wages by the circulation of depreciated banknotes. For the shopkeepers who sold them food and fuel had to pay off their loans in specie, not paper; and the wholesale merchants who sold to the shopkeepers paid for imported goods with gold and silver as well. The premium that shopkeepers and merchants paid to cash their banknotes, Leggett reasoned, they turned around and charged their customers in higher prices, each adding a margin of profit on top. The indirect tax on paper levied by banks and brokers trickled down "till it reache[d] the broad backs and hard hands of the mechanics and laborers," forced to bear the full burden in the end.[84]

So long as banks continued issuing small notes, Leggett urged workers to redeem their paper wages for gold and silver instead of passing along the bank money. Making the most of their undesirable position in the paper chain, he suggested a yet more direct remedy. "A cheap . . . method of disseminating the principles of those opposed to incorporated rag-money manufactories," he suggested, "would be for them to write upon the back of every bank-note which should come into their possession, some short sentence, expressive of their sentiments. For example—'No monopolies!' 'No Union of Banks and State!' 'Jackson and Hard Money!' 'Gold before Rags!' and the like." When called upon to endorse a bad bill, "it would be well to inscribe upon it in a clear and distinct hand, 'Wages of Iniquity!'"[85] By correcting the monetary misrepresentation in this way, wage earners could help to make the market the arena of plaindealing it was meant to be.

Behind Leggett's influential critique of the relationship between banknotes and wages lay an instinctive suspicion of "magnificent promises." A promise to pay, he held, was only fulfilled by being paid off in cash, not by becoming a means of payment itself. A contract between a borrower and lender remained sacred no matter how far the debt traveled or how many hands it passed through. Note-holders should be secure in their property, knowing that a bank was no less obliged to keep its promises than any individual. The object could be achieved, he wrote, by requiring bankers to maintain sufficient capital in "real, substantial, imperishable property, such as lots, farms, houses, ships, and the like" to redeem all their notes in hard cash, certified by a government comptroller or other authority, and periodically reappraised to ensure that the "unalienable property" remained equal in value to that of the note issue. Then, "each holder of a note would, in point of fact, hold a title-deed of property to the full value of its amount," never subject to change.[86]

Yet farms, houses, and ships, like gold and silver, were themselves increasingly liable to wide fluctuations. Even if bank paper were as good as gold, Leggett noted, prices might rise steadily if the supply of gold grew faster than the demand. Paradoxically, then, a fixed standard of value—one that would keep prices relatively stable, relieving those on fixed incomes of the persistent press of inflation and the recurrent crises that came in its wake—had to rest on the watery bed of the market itself. Like postbellum *opponents* of the gold standard, who faced the converse problem of prolonged deflation, he and like-minded Jacksonians sought to peg the money supply to the demand for its services, or to the volume of buying and selling for which currency was called into use.

This was the burden of Leggett's articulation of the so-called real bills doctrine, restricting banks to the business of discounting commercial paper or obligations directly tied to actual purchases and sales of goods. First elaborated by Adam Smith, the basic idea called for banks to limit their note-issue to essentially self-liquidating, short-term loans to merchants arising from wholesale transactions, as the early mercantile banks in American seaboard cities did after the Revolution. This conservative stricture ostensibly restrained banks from altering the supply of currency relative to the demands of commerce.[87] Leggett explained:

> When bank issues are limited within this circle, the notes of the bank in circu-
> lation are founded on the security of the notes of the merchants in possession
> of the bank, and the notes of the merchants rest on the basis of goods actually

purchased, which are finally to be paid for with the products of the soil or other articles of export. The maintaining of the currency at this point . . . would be supplying the channels of business to the degree requisite to facilitate the operations of commerce, without causing those operations to be unduly extended at one time, and unduly contracted at another.[88]

Beginning in the 1790s, however, American banking had spread from the city into the countryside and branched out into the riskier business of "accommodation loans." These were simply personal loans unconnected to any prior business transactions, typically to enable a borrower to invest in land or equipment, a new shop or a new venture. By the 1830s, accommodation lending greatly exceeded commercial lending, as banks took a leading role in sponsoring economic development.[89] The basic problem, as Leggett saw it, was that specially chartered banks channeled such accommodation lending away from petty proprietors and aspiring entrepreneurs, into the hands of politically connected speculators and stock-jobbers instead. The free competition for funds made possible by "free banking," he believed, would redirect loan capital to those truly deserving of credit.[90]

Implicit in the Jacksonian critique of banking was a vision of commerce as a sound and fair foundation for cash and credit, a level playing field from which the financial system had dangerously departed and to which it might safely return. This ideal market was best described in the most important economic treatise of the Jacksonian era, *A Short History of Paper Money and Banking in the United States* (1833), by the Philadelphia financial journalist William M. Gouge.[91] So impressed was Leggett by this work that he reprinted it at the *Evening Post*'s considerable expense while Bryant was in Europe—ironically going into debt in order to cover the costs.[92]

Without the corrupting influence of legislative favoritism, Gouge contended, the credit system would simply act as a neutral broker, uniting those who held idle funds with those who could put such funds to productive use. In the "natural order of things," credit would be based on moral character just as cash would be based on substantial property. Those with money to lend and those in need of it would negotiate with each other directly, without the illegitimate interference of government or banks. Freed from the tumult of a speculative economy, creditors would be able to judge the trustworthiness of debtors themselves, and aspiring farmers and mechanics could obtain the assistance they needed without becoming caught up in high-risk gambles. The trouble lay in the toll taken by parasitical middlemen standing between lenders and borrowers, preventing the harmonizing flow of market forces. "What would be the condition of the merchant who should trust every thing to his clerks, or of the farmer who should trust everything to his laborers," Gouge wrote, deploring bankers' irresponsibility with the funds of their owners and creditors. "Corporations are obliged to trust every thing to stipendiaries, who are oftentimes less trustworthy than the clerks of the merchant or the laborers of the farmer."[93] Leggett shared Gouge's faith that proper representation could reconcile older republican principles with new market practices, agrarian democracy with industrial capitalism.

As it turned out, the panic of 1837 paved the way for the passage of the New York Free Banking Act the following year, essentially enacting the main plank of Leggett's legislative platform. Fifteen other states followed suit over the next twenty years, and the state laws contributed significantly to the framing of the National Banking Act of 1863.[94] Along with the banning of small notes, the disestablishment of the Bank of the United States, and the creation of the Independent Treasury, free banking amounted to a major achievement for Leggett's cause.

Yet of course, these victories augured neither the demise of the "money power" nor the decline of speculation and the return to a simple market economy. The irony may be attributed, in part, to crucial aspects of the financial order that were not yet evident to Leggett or most of his contemporaries. Chief among these blind spots was the way in which banks altered the money supply through the creation of demand deposits and checks, which even then made up a large share of the means of payment with which commerce was conducted. Leggett's single-minded focus on banknotes typified the prevailing tendency to conceive the money question as a question of control over the physical means of exchange while neglecting the broader power of finance capital residing in the "credit system" that he only partially understood. Similarly, in adopting the orthodox monetary faith in "real bills"—the wishful belief that the supply of bank money could be safely constrained by tethering the issuance of banknotes to the "real needs of trade"—Leggett and the workingmen did not account for the role of banks' interest rates in determining the profitability of investment in industry and commerce to begin with. In other words, they overlooked banks' ability to manipulate the demand for credit and currency as well as the supply.[95] Selling and speculating were more tightly entwined than the stark polarities of the melodrama of the market allowed them to see.

Most important, Leggett could not conceive of the ways in which banks would continue to govern the main means of payment while being legally and politically treated as private enterprises rather than public servants. Like cutting the umbilical cord between government and business corporations more generally, the "separation of Bank and State" ultimately gave banks greater autonomy in exercising what had once been sovereign prerogatives. It made their power over the market economy increasingly taken for granted and off-limits to political debate.

Although we can no longer imagine our lives without the currency and credit that banks control, we might still learn from those who could. As the literary historian Raymond Williams has written, "Everywhere in the nineteenth century we see men running for cover from the consequences of their own beliefs. In our own century, they do not even have to run; the temporary covers have become solid settlements."[96] The value of uncovering such struggles over the rise of industrial capitalism lies in the complex questions they raised, such as the "labor question" and the "money question," not simply in the answers on offer in an earlier age. The popular political economy that emerged from the 1830s made it possible for Americans to consider the rising power of capital as an urgent constitutional question about how they were ruled, about the economic as well as political meaning of their fledgling democracy. At the same time, it inspired a widespread will to believe that financial panic and economic depression represented the corruption, not the completion, of the sovereignty of the market.

9

Producing Capitalism

The Clerk at Work

Michael Zakim

Industrial Revolution

The "merchant's clerk" became a fixture of American conversation after 1830, a common trope for talking about the capitalist transformation of life in the republic. This might seem surprising since the clerk generally kept aloof of those events most often associated with industrial revolution. He spent his workday far removed from any factory or shop floor. His skills were not debased by faster, more obedient machines, not even by a typewriter (whose appearance in the 1870s effeminized much of the scrivening, consequently enhancing the clerk's position within the office bureaucracy). He did, it is true, sell his labor power on the open market. But this did not lead him to join in any proletarian protests against capital's "bastardization" of the crafts or its general reorganization of property and privilege. Instead, when irked into collective action against the conditions of his employment—which happened not infrequently—the clerk focused his demands on "early closing," hoping to win the leisure time necessary for "self-improvement" and so secure a place for himself in the new bourgeois order of self-making men. Such personal ambition, in fact, was the truest expression of his class consciousness.[1]

The clerk thus proved to be a model citizen of market society. Variously engaged by brokerages, commission houses, jobbing firms, and "marble palaces" to administer the exploding volume of business, he manned the stations of a commercial system that otherwise transcended the tangible coordinates of time and place, tying far-flung buyers and sellers together in an opportunistic, and often anonymous, negotiation over the ever-shifting terms of exchange. What's more, his mass appearance on the historical stage—New York's census of 1855 reported clerking to be the third-largest (male) occupation in Manhattan, trailing only behind the city's petty laborers and servants—heralded the demise of once self-evident truths equating industry with productive effort. "The United States . . . is but one extended counter from Maine to Texas," as someone now drolly remarked. The quip was revealing of an important feature of commoditization, namely, its redefinition of industry to mean the making of profits rather than the making of things. Or, as the *Treasury of Knowledge* matter-of-factly explained to its readers in 1849, "if manufacturers and shopkeepers did not get profit on their articles, they could not sell them, for it is only the profit that they live upon." It was the clerk who oversaw the practical application of this "philosophy of money," increasingly detached, if not estranged, from plow and anvil, among other traditional tools for creating wealth. "Never has a value which an object possesses only through its convertibility into others of definitive value been so completely transferred into a value itself," as Georg Simmel observed of the unprecedented status of the cash nexus.[2]

Hunt's Merchant's Magazine consequently described a world in which "trade increases the wealth of a nation without the labor of producing or fabricating a single article." Such metaphysics were to be observed in the operations of a properly organized port warehouse, for instance, where tens of thousands of dollars worth of goods were moved each day between buyers and sellers, but in which "all the bustle perceivable, is one quiet clerk calling and taking away a bundle of warrants." This invisible hand of trade was exposed in all its prosaic detail when a young New York City entry clerk named Edward Tailer was sent on a January morning in 1850 to the Customs House to release merchandise. He encountered a phalanx of clerks collectively charged with moving all the sundry cargoes in and out of the harbor, that is, preparing them for general circulation in the American market. This required the assignment of standard money values and the determination of tariff categories, which would then make it possible to assess and pay duties, either in cash or in bonds posted as security. Permits, clearances, certificates, and debentures were also processed, countersigned, and certified at the Customs House. Inventories were measured and inspected, and then checked against manifests and permits, and occasionally reexamined if doubts arose regarding the accuracy of the initial inspection.[3]

Clearly, then, it was wrong to accuse the clerk of idleness simply because he did not make anything, which is what contemporaries were nevertheless still prone to do. *Putnam's Monthly* typically referred to a "dormant, sluggish ... narrow-minded class," while Virginia Penny blamed the clerk for female poverty in *Employments of Women*, explaining that "the reason there are so many young men performing the duties of clerks and salesmen, is, that they are lazy, and do not want to perform hard work." The *Vermont Watchman and State Journal* conjured a post-Jeffersonian dystopia of a whole generation abandoning family farms in favor of mercantile careers, and so becoming a "slave of the caprice of customers and the chicane of trade." The *American Phrenological Journal* proposed a time-worn antidote: "Be men, therefore, and with true courage and manliness dash into the wilderness with your axe and make an opening for the sunlight and for an independent home." Such slogans revealed just how much contemporaries—and not just modern labor historians—fetishized the redemptive virtues of producerism. Theodore Parker likewise savaged the clerk for violating a natural ethic that determined "if a man will not work neither shall he eat," and Henry David Thoreau observed in his contemptuously titled "Life Without Principle" that "God gave the righteous man a certificate entitling him to food and raiment, but the unrighteous man found a facsimile of the same." Both were appalled, and perplexed, by the dematerializing foundations of a world ironically filling up with more and more possessions. "Now the old is going down with a crash, and the new is appearing amidst revolutions, as if by magic," the *Phrenological Journal* concluded in an essay on the "demands of the age on young men" which was published in the same year that the "Communist Manifesto" more famously declared that "all that is solid, melts into air."[4]

It was, in fact, entirely appropriate to see the clerk as a central agent in the age's wholesale reorganization of the economy. Benjamin Foster, the sole clerk in a general store in Bangor, Maine, positioned at the end—or the beginning—of the commercial food chain, offered a practical sampling of what this meant. "My past season's labor has been ... almost incredible," Benjamin reported after reviewing the 400 or so pages of accounts he had filled up in just a few months. In fact, his work was far from done. All those entries still had to be examined and separately posted, and each posting needed to then be reviewed. Only after that did Benjamin actually draw up the store's final accounts for the season. Capitalism could not function without such a vigilant disposal of the books, files, and daily correspondence. That is why the clerk's desultory schedule of tasks—running "a day and night line, copying by sunlight and by candle-light . . . silently, palely, mechanically," as was remarked of Bartleby—became a defining act of the modern age. True, the job description was not yet accorded the general appellation of "paperwork," which would become twentieth-century shorthand for the routinized ubiquity of bureaucratic management. But the *New York Star* already sardonically remarked in 1870 that there were more bookkeepers than books in New York City, and it is certainly no anachronism to speak of an extensive "knowledge economy" in operation by the mid-nineteenth century.

The ubiquity of accountants was just one expression of the growing indispensability of knowledge for doing business, representative of a matrix of information industries specializing in credit, insurance, prices, schedules, communications, and professional training. Together, they effected a "business revolution" that lay the administrative foundations of the era's other, more spectacular, revolutions being wrought by steam and steel. In fact, the mercurial growth in the production and distribution of such knowledge was the foundation of a "new politico-business system," as Thomas Cochran once explained, in which trade and finance proved no less essential than manufacturing to the new industrial order. Without the former all the novel production technologies would have proven to be a far less practical—because a far less profitable—undertaking.[5]

Producing the Market

And so, *Hunt's Merchant's Magazine* proclaimed in 1839 that the "Basis of Prosperity" was to be found in "the vast modern increase of the facilities for diffusing and obtaining full and correct information on everything pertaining to trade." While railroads and telegraphs are the favorite historical examples of the era's new "information infrastructure," invoices, bills of lading, inventory counts, warehouse receipts, cheap postage, uniform accounting practices, trade journals, and regular travel schedules proved no less essential to prosperity. "The antebellum economy was structured as much around borrowed money and promises of payment as it was around the routes of rivers, roads, canals, and, by the 1840s, railroads," Edward Balleisen has observed of industry's practical needs. How could one navigate all the tributaries of "commercial paper"—the untold number of promissory notes, for instance, being handed from one businessman to another that, once endorsed by a third party, became negotiable currency—without having reliable digests in hand? The same was true for information regarding tariff categories, or the liabilities of shipping agents, or the intricacies of bankruptcy procedures. "Market Reviews" and "Prices Current" providing regular updates on the shifting values of stocks, staples, and a growing miscellany of other goods for sale were another foundation of the spreading market. They did not, in fact, contain a new kind of information, but their systematic publication and mass circulation were an entirely novel event. So was the fast growth of insurance, which reflected the rising costs of not having enough information.[6]

This led Warren Spencer to announce that "knowledge is power" in a lecture on business education which he delivered at the Buffalo Mercantile College in 1857. The metaphor was not lost on anyone: knowledge was a power source for industrial-age enterprise. Businessmen consequently devoted themselves to accumulating the "capital of mind," collecting and arranging information that would provide them with "a command of the subject, and a comparative fearlessness of surprise." Only with such knowledge in their possession—with answers to a rudimentary set of questions about "What has been done? What is the state of the case at present? What can be done next? What ought to be done?"—could maximizing agents rationally pursue their goals of profit. This entailed a system of continuous coordination between market agents transmitting orders, updates, requests, reports, specifications, and instructions to each other. Their multiple, cross-filed records of the minutiae of exchange removed communications from the idiosyncratic oral flows of personality, bestowing standard forms that functioned independently of this or that specific time and place and which proved to be at once highly stable and highly mobile. The "education of a man of business," *Hunt's* noted, began with digests and classifications, for only "competence at method" allowed one to "go farther, and build with his materials." Those most organized and prompt at such tasks would be the most successful in their trade.[7]

All this tasking was carried out at the office, where "a system of arranging your papers, as may insure their being readily referred to" could best be effected by "a staff of subaltern officials and scribes of all sorts" who consequently became an emblem of modern rationality, at least in the eyes of Max Weber. Clerks thus devoted whole days to making up banknote tables and inventory catalogues, or to filing bills and copying letters before carrying the originals to the post office by four o'clock. These might seem trivial measures, an expert acknowledged, "and so they are, unless you neglect them." The failure to keep extensive financial records, the *Philadelphia Merchant* announced in 1855, was the cause of "nine-tenths of the Insolvents in every Commercial City in the world."[8]

Business was reinvented as a taxonomic project whose ledgers, journals, invoices, orders, bills, receipts, and accounts current constituted a veritable assembly line of retrieval, duplication, comparison, aggregation, and transmission. This technology was universally applied to merchandising firms (which employed stock and partnership books, day-books and journals—or a day-book in journal form—cash-books, sales-books, invoice-books, bill-books, and ledgers, of course), commission businesses (that also required accounts current and sales accounts for calculating payment schedules, and an exact record of net proceeds for drawing up notes, drafts, bills of exchange, and orders), forwarding operations (that principally depended on keeping, receiving, and shipping accounts), not to mention brokerages, exchange houses, banks, railroads, steamboat companies (including lake steamboating), jobbers, and retailers (for whom the day-book, journal, sales-book, and invoice-book could usually be combined into a single record). All this accounting functioned like so many closely calibrated gears, which is why the books themselves required special bindings capable of enduring the physical wear and tear of constant referral by a range of hands.[9]

"Bookkeeping is a tool, just as tools for apprentices in the mechanical arts," Frederick Beck explained in the introduction to his *Young Accountant's Guide* in 1831. Double-entry itself was an old technology, a cultural legacy of the Renaissance. But it now proved powerfully adept at calculating the overwhelming detail and unprecedentedly large numbers generated by industrial capitalism, valuating fixed assets, measuring liquidity, overseeing personnel, accounting for costs, and regulating temporality, while doing so in a common denominator of dollars and cents. As new partnership and corporate structures provided unprecedented flexibility for organizing investment in the nineteenth century (as well as limiting one's liability for contracted obligations, thus making risk more tolerable), only the account books could ascertain each proprietor's relative earnings or the size of dividends due stockholders. Meanwhile, manufacturing projects organized outside the household, those that produced "solely with an eye to circulation"—and whose goods would only be sold sometime in the future—generated a new set of accounting problems. They needed to distinguish fixed capital from capital currently being "employed," as well as count overhead costs, rents, inventories, the stocks of raw materials, and the productive efficiency of hired laborers. It also became practical to calculate gross and net profits and to determine production prices, which would inform selling prices, a particularly important piece of information when the economy slumped and consumer demand fell.[10]

All this documentation turned the office into arguably the most important production site in the industrializing economy. This was where the capitalist incessantly labored to give the inchoate market a definitive, legible form, for only then would he be able to inscribe his own course of action on it. As one sympathetic observer spoke of the consequent success, account books effectively "display[ed] the mazes of a complicated business with a beautiful regularity." Facts-on-paper, as such, replaced facts-on-the-ground as the determinant operative reality in an increasingly commoditized economy.[11]

The country thus filled up with offices. At first, they occupied former residences. The New York branch of the first Bank of the United States, for instance, opened for business in 1797 in what had previously been someone's domicile. But by 1825 the Second Bank branch was built with banking needs specifically in mind, part of a general reconstruction of Wall Street for commercial purposes. Twenty years later the neighborhood was nearly filled with office buildings whose palazzo designs of Renaissance inspiration replaced the formerly dominant Greek temple as the preferred style for doing business. This was not just an aesthetic revolt against federalist neoclassicism. The new architecture proved far better suited to an economy that kept expanding its floor space, adding storeys, and rearranging interiors in accordance to the shifting requirements of insurers, lawyers, brokers, and private bankers, among other tenants now vying for commercial space in the city's business district. A rental market for office "suites" quickly developed, spaces that needed to be "fitted up with gas and every other convenience," sufficient lighting and ventilation, and even "acoustic tubes" that allowed the firm's partners to communicate with porters in the basement and clerks in the salesroom without ever having to leave the desk. Safes that protected financial records and banknotes from fire were also a basic requirement, as were self-acting locks, separate rooms for controlling access to conversations and records, an array of desks with pigeon holes and vertical recesses for filing documents, newly patented "office chairs," shelving, and a vast inventory of business accoutrements ranging from pen racks to paperweights.[12]

And yet these offices remained physically modest places. Their small scale might seem to belie the immense geographies of market-sponsored exchange, but, in fact, capital was a different kind of sovereign power, one not manifest in the physical conquest of territory. A New York commission house, for instance, did business in a space smaller than twenty-five square feet. This was enough room for the four partners—the three juniors respectively put in charge of the flour, grain, and cotton "departments"—to sell shipments of western and southern produce to metropolitan shippers and "home buyers."

They were assisted by a cashier, who was responsible for overseeing the office operations, and a chief bookkeeper who aspired to make partner. Two clerks kept the firm's running accounts while a third was put in charge of the "smaller books." Another exclusively attended to the senior partner's personal records, which included assets and debts left over from previous partnerships. A receiving and delivery clerk worked "from early in the morning until eight to ten o'clock at night" supervising freight and storage. The firm also employed a corps of salesmen who went to "change" every day where they engaged the trade, negotiating the practical exchange of goods. In addition, a collector processed the bills received from grain-elevator operators, city weighers, and inspectors of merchandise while he also issued the firm's own bills. He visited clients each day between ten and three o'clock, continued on to the bank, and then reported back to the cashier regarding the status of payments. Only when canal boat captains or various other personnel employed in actually moving the goods showed up at the office did the regular battery of desk and salesmen complain about distractions and overcrowded conditions.[13]

This division of commercial labor brought an end to the all-purpose trader who dominated eighteenth-century business, who had owned his own ships and served as agent for foreign houses, trading in both wholesale and retail markets while simultaneously importing and exporting, who financed and insured the transportation of his goods, and often loaned funds directly to artisans and farmers. He was replaced by an industrial system that separated out shipowners, bankers, jobbers, commission merchants, transporters, insurers, brokers, auctioneers, wholesalers, and retailers into respective specializations that were born of an attempt to narrow the scope of information necessary for doing business and so enhance one's practical mastery over what was now a market niche.[14]

This did not necessarily reduce the risks inherent in trade. In fact, the opposite was usually the case. The specialized merchant was more vulnerable to market commotions than his predecessor because he confined himself to a narrower segment of the economy. This effectively limited the scope of his response when encountering the invariable threats and pressures of doing business, whether these issued from changing fashions, rising duties, expensive credit, or failing crops that affected the customer's ability to pay at six, twelve, or eighteen months. Specialization, in other words, proved essential for rationalizing exchange and unifying markets, and thus allowing merchants to develop their business. At the same time, and for the same reason, it exacerbated competition, which would now be decided by ever-smaller comparative advantages. Edwin Freedley, a prolific writer on commercial subjects, consequently observed in his *Practical Treatise on Business* that in the new economy "the percentage of profits will gradually be less, but the aggregate of profits ... will be unprecedented and astounding." The difference between success and ruin, a Boston dry goods jobber remarked a few years later, was often a matter of "five to seven and a half or ten per cent." The knowledge economy, in other words, relentlessly narrowed profit margins which, in turn, redoubled merchant dependence on information.[15]

That was why "never, perhaps, was it so true as now, that 'the seller has need of a hundred eyes.'" The pedantic management practices that ensued marked a sharp divergence from a commercial past in which a few time-honored personal traits were considered enough to confidently close a deal. "But Young America has learned to make light" of the genteel parochialisms of a bygone age. The increasingly anonymous character of exchange made it impossible to infer the intentions of one's trading partner by studying his countenance. "Face value," as such, acquired a less tangible, and certainly a less reliable, meaning. The modern merchant had to depend instead on a disembodied collection of pertinent facts, which he then sought to "harmonize into a consistent and satisfactory whole." The hazards of trade could only be transformed into a set of calculable, and thereby controllable, coordinates by means of this proper organization of the data. Proponents of the new, and still controversial, system of credit reporting accordingly argued that the ability to purchase information about other businesses served everyone's interests, for "what is known to one is known to all." So effectively, in fact, did credit reports help to illuminate the opaque character of long-distance, long-term exchange that a businessman no longer needed to travel to make his purchases. "His order is as good as his presence" in a wholesale firm that kept an active file on him.[16]

This intensifying demand for commercial information is what gave birth to a giant clerking class, to the mass migration off the farm and workshop and into the office. Such demographics signaled a general need to retool, which led B. F. Foster, the country's leading mercantile pedagogue, to complain that while classical and mathematical studies were well developed in America, there was no comparable course for preparing young men for business. They were consequently left to "grope [their] way in comparative ignorance." *Hunt's*, too, bemoaned the "general and widely-felt want" of systematic business education that would train a reliable cadre of market bureaucrats. That shortage, and the business opportunities it presented, now spurred the founding of innumerable "commercial academies" throughout the country. Thomas Jones, Foster's former partner, opened his own school a few blocks further up New York's Broadway in 1839, announcing in a style typical of the genre that he "will receive on the 1st September next, a class of young gentlemen to whom, during a daily session of four hours, he will devote his exclusive attention." Most of that attention was given over to bookkeeping, commercial arithmetic ("embracing the most ready calculations of interest, Exchange, and Equation of Payments"), and business writing. Like scores of others in the field, Jones also began to produce textbooks in hopes of cashing in on the highly competitive publishing market for instruction manuals—"so as to qualify thoroughly for all the duties of the desk"—that vied for the endorsement of state and city boards of education now that business subjects were being incorporated into the common school curriculum.[17]

Desk and ledger thus rivaled the machine as both sign and praxis in the age of capital. Paperwork dedicated to precision, unambiguity, knowledge of the files, continuity, discretion, and subordination—a list borrowed, again, from Max Weber—amplified mental labor no less spectacularly than the steam engine had augmented humanity's physical efforts. The Price Current was worth far more than its weight in gold in an economy where, as we have seen, "trade increases the wealth of a nation without the labor of producing or fabricating a single article." Veteran New Yorkers still remembered Michael Boyle making his rounds of Pearl Street and Maiden Lane, "panting under the load of a bag of silver" in collecting on the various notes that had come due that month. Boyle's old-fashioned exertions were replaced by a system of discarnated records arranged, catalogued, and indexed in standard taxonomies of assets and debts that could then be reproduced, exchanged, and spread with infinitely greater facility. "All the instants of time and all the places in space can be gathered in another time and place," as Bruno Latour has described modern science's technical success in processing empirical knowledge, a technique that proved equally relevant to doing business.[18]

Indeed, capitalism was equally infused with civilization's general bias toward abstraction, that which allowed humanity to distill the confusing flux of nature into its constituent parts and then reconfigure them into more useful patterns. "By 'business' I mean habit," William Ross wrote in *The Accountant's Book and Business Man's Manual.* "Paradoxical as it may appear at first sight, business is nothing in the world but habit, the soul of which is regularity. Like the fly-wheel upon a steam-engine, regularity keeps the motion of life steady and unbroken—thereby enabling the machine to do its work unobstructively." The proverbial race after riches seemed, thus, to have been reduced to the organization of information, which promised to bring the mayhem of the free market under manageable control.[19]

In fact, however, the opposite was closer to the truth. That is to say, the market was not a living system that needed to be regulated and regularized by means of artificial information technologies. It was itself an artifice. Business, it could thus be said, administered the market by inventing it. Before anyone could produce for exchange it was necessary to produce a system of exchange: to form structures that would allow goods to "encounter" each other by famously suspending all their other attributes save what made them mutually replaceable. "The commodities are transformed into bars in the head and in speech before they are exchanged for one another," Marx wrote in 1857. "They are appraised before being exchanged, and in order to appraise them they must be brought into a given numerical relation to one another." This money economy was a cultural achievement, not a force of nature, which meant that the market was a quintessentially industrial event, a manmade reconstitution of the material world. That was the practical significance of the oft-discussed and much maligned category of "mental labor," which was identified with capitalism's abstract, even counterintuitive, practices. The temporal, physical, and political boundaries and constraints that were once considered essential for guaranteeing order and stability, as Karl Polanyi famously argued, were now relentlessly violated in turning apples into oranges, upstate butter into French silk shawls, and healthy plow-boys into lank and sallow clerks.[20]

Such transformations, and the profits they generated, were the foundations of a new social order. This is why Jacksonians celebrating hard money and the natural origins of the market identified the Bank of the United States as the source of "artificial distinctions [that] make the rich richer and the potent more powerful," as Jackson himself famously declared. They understood only too well that the new knowledge regime was creating a fungible, plastic world governed by organizations such as the Bank that were in the best position to collect and subsequently control information. The clerk was deeply implicated in these suspicions. Indeed, his paperwork proved to be an essential complement of paper money. Equally detached, and subversive, of the age-old certainties of land and landed hierarchies, both paper systems demonstrated a remarkable ability to transcend distance, reshape relations, and refocus power in the hands of men who had no obligations but to capital.[21]

Personal Ambition

Clerks themselves were generally uninterested in the structural implications of their employment. "The masses have no disposition to spend the best years of their lives in studying abstract theories," Warren Spencer explained to the Buffalo audience that came to hear his lecture on mercantile education. Rather, they desired knowledge that had a "direct bearing upon the practical things of life." Nothing was more practical than their own ambition. As members of the Massachusetts Charitable Mechanic Association were apprised in 1845, anticipating Horatio Alger by a generation, "every man . . . may become a capitalist" in America, a fact that acted as "a spur to exertion to the very news-boy in our streets." In fact, Alger's own mythological rise began by learning a fair writing hand and arithmetic, "as far as Interest," in hopes of landing a situation in some store or "countin'-room." The motivation was widespread, indeed. And so, a Boston hardware wholesaler received a hundred applications in three days for a single clerkship in 1859 while another reported a "swarm" of fifty applicants within just a few hours. "Almost every family has sent here one or more representatives," Joseph Scoville observed of the migration of talent out of the New England countryside in his *Old Merchants of New York City*. "All do not succeed, but some do, and this is quite sufficient to keep the ambition to get a clerkship in New York alive."

Common opinion held that the great majority of America's businessmen had "commenced life behind the desk or the counter." This is where they apparently acquired their "business touch," as twenty-one-year-old William Hoffman rendered that most sublime mercantile quality of all. William, "long . . . abstracted from the desire of making farming" his future, had left home in 1848, hoping to install himself in business. He initially found employment as one of six clerks in a small but aggressive dry goods firm in Albany, New York, sweeping out the premises, brushing off the muslins, and distributing handbill advertisements in neighboring towns and hamlets. After several months he was sent out to collect on bills and to invoice goods destined for country auctions for which William was now listed as "superintendent." But it was "the art of selling" that most excited him. The petty transaction he succeeded in closing while the store's senior clerks were otherwise engaged marked the highlight of his new career, causing "more satisfaction and render[ing] the state of my mind more composed and settled."[22]

Such enthusiasm brought *Hunt's* to observe that clerks would never be satisfied serving as errand boys or a "copying machine." Edward Tailer made that equally clear. Employed by a New York City importer specializing in shawls, Edward was sent around to city firms at the end of the season to collect outstanding debts. "I was compelled to visit about thirteen of our customers in order to quicken their movements in relation to the drawing up and sending in of their notes so that we may close our spring sales and open accounts by note at Eight Months." He also delivered his firm's own notes to creditors. He deposited checks, prepared and shipped out orders, and, as we already saw, waited on line at the Custom House in order to pay duties on goods that needed to be withdrawn from the warehouse. After a year on the job, Edward began complaining about the continued visits to city hotels with pattern cards and about having to deliver parcels, which was the work of a porter. It was a landmark day, therefore, when he was directed to post his first business letter. "The ability to write a good letter—to know just what to say, and how to say it—is an accomplishment second to none which can be possessed by the man of business," as commercial observers acknowledged. But Edward "commenced badly and unpropitiously under my new auspices" when he mistakenly shipped two cases of goods to New Orleans instead of Charleston. "How I could have made this mischievous blunder is beyond my comprehension and has injured me greatly in the estimation of Mr. Alden, who told me 'that it was, a most stupid mistake.'" The merchandise was eventually returned after two months, but then sold well under its original price. This might be why Edward now found himself increasingly engaged in "writing operations," recording the arrival of new goods in the stock book and copying out accounts and receipts.[23]

Meanwhile, William Hoffman continued to pursue a career in sales. He left Albany after nine months in favor of a clerking position in New York City. He quit that job as well after a year for employment in the dry goods house of Gilbert, Prentiss and Tuttle, "a desirable one for any clerk anxious to come up, as every opportunity is offered." The main opportunity that William had in mind was traveling for the firm. Metropolitan jobbers were particularly interested in hiring clerks with provincial experience, hoping that their out-of-town contacts would generate new business for the firm. William consequently began to combine upstate visits to his family with his employers' hunt for hinterland customers. Arriving in Palmyra "with all the grace of a New York Clerk," he set out to convince local storeowners to open accounts with Gilbert, Prentiss, and Tuttle on their next buying trip to New York. "I soon had seen nearly every merchant in town endeavoring to gain their esteem and also to give with my card a lasting impression of my ability to sell them cheap." But there was no guarantee of success; William was not the only city agent promising cut rates. Two months later, with the commencement of the fall season, he waited in vain to reap the fruits of his summertime efforts. "My customer did not come and see me today as he promised, buys his goods elsewhere."[24]

Such setbacks were intrinsic to ambition, of course, which is why failure became a standard, and standardized, event in market society. The Federal Bankruptcy Act of 1841 was just the most acute expression of what was a society-wide effort to address the risks inherent in the systematic pursuit of profit. The ideology of personal mobility was another means of normalizing, or excusing, the proliferation of failure. "In this rich, republican country, no man need be long blaming fortune because he is a subordinate," as the *Whig Review* proclaimed in criticizing a newly formed clerks association that demanded a shorter workday. The *Review* thus sought to make each person singularly responsible for his own fate, the resulting struggle to get ahead then serving to "build a Young Man up," as William Hoffman embraced this emerging ethos of individual mettle. "I must put myself ahead more," a young Boston clerk named Charles French similarly concluded after surveying his chances for promotion. Benjamin Foster, too, testified to an "irresistible impulse for wealth" that had led him to spurn "settling on some farm to some safe, secure, contented, domestic life" in favor of business. Indeed, such personal ambition now replaced property as the common denominator of civic life in the bourgeois republic. "The true proprietors of this continent are those who know how to take advantage of its riches," Tocqueville had declared while the New York Mercantile Library's *Annual Report* announced that "here every one is emphatically the artificer of his own fortune." And so, when Edward Tailer attended a debate sponsored by the Knickerbocker Literary Association over "Which is the greatest incentive to action, Ambition or necessity," the question was decided in favor of the former. There was no better sign of the demise of an economy of pain and its replacement by axioms of growth and plenty.[25]

But growth and plenty were often indistinguishable from conflict and unease. "[I] see other young men gaining in the world and I am almost inclined at times to despond," a young Philadelphia clerk wrote of his life in a rich, republican country where no one need remain subordinate. The commercial order, *Hunt's* itself conceded, offered "the natural selfishness of men . . . its widest range," keeping his acquisitive faculties "in unremitted exertion" and so inciting one and all "to lose sight of the interests of others." Charles French, the clerk from Boston, gave specific expression to the competitive ferment. "Tobin shall not go ahead of me in the store," he resolved after discovering that his rival was getting up a price book, which meant that the latter would soon be going out on his own or, worse yet, would soon be sent out traveling on behalf of the firm. In fact, Charles faced stiff competition. Tobin proved that much one afternoon when he asked for help in taking stock. Charles had no inclination to assist him, of course, and replied that he was otherwise engaged with his own tasks. Tobin went forthwith to Mr. Danforth to complain about the lack of cooperation, prompting the firm's partner to approach Charles and inquire into what was currently occupying his efforts. Nothing in particular, Charles responded, ever eager to take on whatever assignment the boss might have for him. Then go help Tobin, Danforth tersely ordered.[26]

Intraoffice competition occupied William Hoffman, too, and he jealously complained of the "jealous disposition" of the firm's senior clerks who worked less but received a greater portion of the sales. William consequently applauded a reorganization of store responsibilities in which each clerk was assigned his own counter. This seemed a fairer, and certainly more effective, method for preventing the "shirking from the imperative duty incumbent upon each." (William's employer also asked him to keep an eye on any other clerks whom he might suspect of dishonesty. "I assured him I would.") But such management reforms soon yielded less than rational results as William was accused by a fellow clerk named John Boyd of taking away one of his customers. Boyd became so incensed, in fact, that he picked up a board with which to strike William, who successfully dodged the blow but, in so doing, crashed into the counter, sustaining a painful injury.[27]

It was a most tangible expression of the perils of counter-jumping and of the "foolish ambition to see their names over a store door." "Of the crows of hopeful lads who annually find their way from their rural homes into the thronged and busy metropolis," someone typically observed, "how many discover that they have entered upon a race in which the chances of their ultimate defeat are as ten to one?" It was a favorite statistic, although Thoreau typically worsened the odds when writing in *Walden* that "ninety-seven in a hundred, are sure to fail." "They wish to reap before they have ploughed or sown," Henry Ward Beecher criticized the unnatural inversions of the age in his *Lectures to Young Men*, applying the most, and the least, appropriate simile to describe the postagrarian logic that drove so many of the nation's talented youth to almost certain ruin.[28]

Such statistics were, in fact, a nostalgic gesture, alluding to older times when the risks of exchange were confined to a narrow class of traders rather than spread out and practiced by all of society. Edward Tailer, for instance, was harangued by his employer for an overeager sales style that "savored too much of the Chatham St manner of receiving a customer [with] every man in the establishment running out to salute and shake a buyer by the hand." Apprehensions over commercial-driven exuberance also informed an ubiquitous trope concerning the dishonest clerk passing counterfeit bills, removing cash from letters, absconding with the store's merchandise to sell on the black market, or embezzling from the firm, a pattern of criminality that found its ultimate expression in the notorious murder of the prostitute Helen Jewett by a New York clerk named Richard P. Robinson. Employers were consequently urged to transcend narrow business interests and assume paternal control over the situation, "to surround the young mind with counteracting influences and good associations." So much of a man's character "depends on what kind of an employer he had when young," *Hunt's* explained, implicitly assigning the merchant the role of *loco parentis* in relation to his clerk. Only amity and kindness would provide "a solid basis for social order and permanent prosperity." Merchants thus funded Mercantile Library Associations in towns and cities that, in turn, promoted rectitude and propriety through an extensive program of public lectures, evening classes, polite reading, and associational self-government. And they organized mutual aid societies for clerks who otherwise threatened to become one of the city's dangerous classes.[29]

The "ten-to-one" odds of personal defeat were also a form of *caveat emptor* that absolved the employer class of blame for low salaries and delayed promotions. Clerks thought otherwise, however, and they regularly blamed the boss for their personal frustrations, prompting Daniel Haskell to remark on a "strange want of confidence exhibited in the intercourse between merchants and their clerks." Too often, Haskell continued, that intercourse "resembles what may be termed *cross*-examination." Charles Rogers, employed in the embroideries department at A. T. Stewart's Marble Palace, provides a case in point. Offered a raise in 1864 in return for a promise to stay a full year at his new salary, Charles refused to commit. He was consequently put back at his old wage. The failed negotiation left him in a bitter mood. "If I had less scruples about breaking my engagement with a man who I know would break his with me at any time I might have been getting $500." Edward Tailer was no less resentful about his paycheck. "There is not a day which passes," Edward complained about his firm's parsimony while fantasizing about the market's potential to correct the injustice, "during which I do not imagine that I might better my situation as a clerk and receive an ample compensation for services rendered."[30]

Tailer had broached the subject of his salary six months earlier, handing to his employer, Mr. Alden, a letter "in which my views were fully, and most copiously detailed." In response, Alden called Edward into the counting room for a private conversation and offered the twenty-year-old clerk $50 for the year just ended and $100 for the upcoming one. Edward countered that his services were worth at least $150, declaring that it was time he began to support himself and relieve his father of that responsibility. Alden claimed that the city was full of young men willing to enter a store without any salary at all, happy at the opportunity to learn the business before reaching maturity. That might be true, but it stunk of Old World apprenticeship. The two argued to a standstill, with Alden promising to reach a formal decision forthwith, which left Edward complaining about the "mean . . . character" that informed his employer's refusal to make "a faithful and hard working clerk . . . feel happy and independent and inwardly bless the bountiful hand which would thus place him above want."[31]

Edward ended up waiting two and a half months before finally getting a response from Alden, who now agreed to pay him $150 and dangled the possibility of a $50 bonus at year's end, "if I continued to please him." Within a matter of weeks, however, with the firm having grossed $60,000 in the spring season alone, Edward was again voicing his frustration with what he considered to be inadequate remuneration. Indeed, when he eventually left the firm two and a half years later for a sales position with Reimer & Mecke, Alden made sure to tell Edward "that my greatest failing was too strong an anxiety to force myself ahead."[32]

But such "anxieties" were a most common currency. Charles French, for instance, decided to strike for higher wages upon discovering that Tobin was earning more than he. Confident of his value to the firm, Charles worried only that his bashfulness would undermine his position. In fact, it was Charles's very indignation which frustrated his ambition. Nursing his hurt feelings, he added injury to insult by falling into a series of petty confrontations with the office's cashier, even refusing at one point to carry out the latter's explicit instructions. Only after Danforth personally intervened did Charles then agree to undertake the required errand. Upon his return to the office he was summoned into a private room and reprimanded for his obstinance, which left young Charles on the verge of tears, not least because he realized that he would have to wait another half a year before even raising the subject of his salary.[33]

Charles's contrition came much sooner than that. "I shall turn over a new leaf tomorrow at the store," he declared the following day in his diary,

> and from morning until evening Danforth shall not see me henceforth idle, and if I am told to do an errand by anyone above me, will do it, even though I do not wish to, and without showing any temper whatever. Neither do I intend in the future to speak disrespectfully to or of anyone in the store. Though at times I may forget myself, yet in the long run I will and must succeed.

It was a soliloquy worthy of a T. S. Arthur story celebrating the advantages of self-discipline over self-aggrandizement as the key to personal success and, as such, an important moment in the socialization of a self-maximizing citizen. It was also a sober assessment of the practical leverage of the boss. Only Danforth determined which counter or desk to assign to whom and how each would consequently be remunerated. Only Danforth decided who would be sent out traveling, who would be promoted, and who would be invited into the firm as a partner. Only Danforth was in a position to extend credit to clerks wishing to start out in business on their own, or to provide a personal recommendation to others looking for another position, often in another city.[34]

Six months having passed, Charles's anxiety reached a new height. "Now the time approaches that I expect to be spoken to about my salary," he wrote on December 31, and "my doubts begin to arise." He had not seen the partners convene their regular end-of-the-year conference at which they decided on bonuses and raises. Yet another week passed, but still no word was forthcoming. Charles hoped that the silence was an indication of salary increases in the offing. Personally, he wanted to raise his from $300 to $400, and maybe even $500. At that rate, he calculated, he could be earning $800 by the time he turned twenty-one, in two more years. "If they suppose that because I have never found fault with my salary and am or rather have been willing to work hard on a small salary . . . they will find that they have (to use a vulgar expression) 'got the wrong pig by the ear.'" Charles knew very well—for he had access to the books—that the firm had brought in $400,000 over the past year. He thought it only fair that he be allowed to partake in that success since the economy was, after all, a positive-sum game. And so, with still no announcement, he began to toy once again with the possibility of "striking," hoping only that none of the other clerks would beat him to it.[35]

Instead, French plucked up his courage and approached Danforth directly. He opened the conversation by observing that he personally knew other young men in town "who had been in business no longer than I" but who were nevertheless being paid more money. Danforth assured Charles that the firm was entirely satisfied with his job performance, which is why they paid him more than they had ever given anyone else at a comparable age. True, clerks at other firms might be earning $500, and perhaps even more, Danforth conceded. And the rumor regarding Tobin's higher wage was also accurate, he confirmed. But none of these other clerks had much chance for significant advancement. Danforth now took Charles into his confidence by telling him that Tobin, too, though a good worker, lacked those qualities that would move him up the ladder of success. Charles's situation was clearly different. But if he pressed for more money now he would threaten his future prospects with the firm. A raise in salary needed to be based on the clerk's own earnings: whoever generated more business was "worth more" to the firm, Danforth explained. If Charles could bring in $5,000 in sales over the year, for instance, he would be paid accordingly. To that end, Danforth now told Charles that he would be allowed to go around the hotels and pick up custom, for which he would receive a commission. Meanwhile, he insisted, the store's expenses were enormous and profits were consequently smaller than they might seem.[36]

Charles was unappeased. "I fear the firm are growing mean." A trusted friend advised him to get as much as he could now since there was no guarantee that the firm would do "the right thing" when he came of age. "They talk very well but I fear it may be meant for 'salve.'" Only after two more months did Danforth announce to Charles that he would be paid $400, which might be increased to $500 the next year, depending on Charles's performance. Danforth then suggested that Charles use his annual two-week vacation to travel to Connecticut and collect relevant business information among the region's hardware manufacturers. He also urged Charles to develop his acquaintances with city traders since "the amount of custom I carried with me" was the only way to make oneself "useful" to an employer. In fact, Charles was delighted with his success in winning such a significant raise, which was "more than I had reason to hope for." But he also understood that the new salary, and any future increases, now depended on how much he earned for the firm. "I shall also try to sell goods to every customer who enters the store and even go around town to sell odds and ends to the city traders," he resolved.[37]

"Cross-examination" thus proved to be an effective vernacular for the growing numbers of citizens forcing themselves ahead. "Make your views and wishes known," *Hunt's* accordingly advised. "There is no advantage in concealing." Salary negotiations leveled everyone's interest to a common grammar of dollars and sense that heralded the death of all fixed, organic hierarchies. "If you wish anyone to serve you with diligence," a contemporary cliché proclaimed, "you must make it for his interest to do so." Or, as Adam Smith had already explained, one does not talk to others about necessities, but about advantages, for how else was "natural value" or market price to be determined? Subordination itself became negotiable, contingent on a temporary alignment of forces that responded to active intervention. This promotion of everyone into their own best agent overshadowed the dire predictions of invariable failure, which seemed mired in old world truths about scarcity, reflecting a panicky response to modern dynamism and fluidity. This is when the individual became an "ism," that is, a common denominator, if not a unifying force of mutuality, that Tocqueville made sure to distinguish from the far more atavistic "egoism." And this was also why Bartleby, who refused to negotiate, proved so incomprehensible to his employer, and to us: unwilling to play by the universal rules of personal ambition, he was decidedly antisocial.[38]

Hand Work

Charles Rogers, angry after his promotion to the linen department at A. T. Stewart's was rescinded, and repeatedly frustrated in his ongoing attempts to secure a position at Stewart's wholesale store, soon found a better-paying job in 1864 as a copyist for the government. He then joined the Mercantile Library, deposited $25 in the Manhattan Savings Bank, and enrolled in a penmanship course—an enthusiastic demonstration of institutional loyalty to a clerking class. The best-known example of this institutionalization had been founded by H. B. Bryant and H. D. Stratton in 1853, in Cleveland, and then expanded into a "National Chain of Commercial Colleges" that included almost fifty schools by the end of the Civil War. Based on a common curriculum of "commercial science," the chain effectively trained a giant reserve army of clerical labor to figure simple, annual, and compound interest, according to varying state laws, for commission, brokerage, and stock businesses; to make discounts for banks, stock purchases, and merchandise sales; to calculate insurance premiums and insurance-rate percentages; to determine profit and loss ratios in order to establish the most advantageous selling price at a range of costs, as well as estimate the value of inventories; to account for specific or ad valorem duties that included international remittances in foreign currencies; and to arrange a payment schedule for purchases made on various dates, some in cash and some in credit, while plotting the date of maturation of each note and the respective effects of early payment on the firm's general balance.[39]

Such "business arithmetic" belonged to an emerging capitalist pedagogy, a standard corpus of practical knowledge that, like all other important industrial technologies, functioned as an interchangeable set of tools and a highly mobile form of property readily purchased on the open market at competitive prices. The *Annual Register* of Comer's Commercial College in Boston, which claimed to have matriculated 12,000 students in the twenty-five years since opening its doors in 1840, thus described its diploma as "a letter of introduction to the best mercantile houses from Maine to California" which otherwise anonymous young men could then leverage into entrée into the world of business. The bookkeeping course at Comer's—which cost $15 for a month of daily lessons, or $30 for three months (though three months of afternoon or evening classes could be had for only $16)—accordingly offered instruction in personal, partnership, commission, corporate, railroad, shipping, manufacturing, and banking accounts, equipping students for the shifting demands of the labor market.[40]

The business curriculum did not include the art of selling. "Resolution, knowledge, prudence, experience, calculation, and regular method"—these were the recognized foundations of capitalist success, and they rested, first of all, on skilled penmanship. A competent hand, as Bryant and Stratton's *Annual Circular and Catalogue* observed in 1859, "gives currency and real value to every other acquisition in business study. It is the great medium through which thoughts are interchanged, through which commerce speaks." B. F. Foster, too, celebrated the pen's ability "to transmit to others, in places no matter how remote, every species of intelligence, with a secrecy that savors of miracle." Liverpool, New York, and New Orleans sat an inch apart from each other on the written page, making the broad scales of intercontinental trade a far more manageable project. Penmanship also proved essential for building an institutional memory that enhanced the firm's ability to preserve the past in order to better organize the present in hopes of shaping the future. And so, "*business writing* may be said to sway the world!" P. R. Spencer, the dominant authority in the field after the Civil War, declared in what proved not to be a rhetorical flourish.[41]

William Hoffman thus submitted a sample of his handwriting to prospective employers while others brought along their copy-books when searching for a job. Without such training, Comer's *Annual Register* pronounced, no one was properly qualified to take charge of a set of books. Melville's poor handwriting reportedly kept him from finding work in the 1840s while young Charles French, determined to go into a store "as soon as I have learned to write better than I now write," dutifully enrolled in a penmanship course (whose fees included a discounted membership in Boston's Mercantile Library).[42] All now learned a "Bold, Free, and Mercantile style of writing" that emerged as the universal male standard in the nineteenth century. Self-consciously shorn of stylized gesture, business writing embodied the era's functionalist aesthetics. "Use the pen," *Hunt's* advised. "There is no magic in it, but it prevents the mind from staggering about." It was to be compared to other forms of industrial engineering as befitted this tool for the mass production of capitalist knowledge. A mercantile hand was designed to be both attractive and useful. Indeed, it was attractive because it was useful. "Plain to the eye, conveying thought with electric speed to the reader's mind, its perusal gives genuine satisfaction to all to whom it is addressed." Facts could thus speak for themselves by means of a manufacturing technique whose utility was manifest in, both, the standard nature of its production—penmanship systems all claimed to be based on universal principles of physiology—and the standard nature of its product. "Masses of documents now lying in the dead letter office," as P. R. Spencer described the disastrous results of the absence of penmanship standards, "would long since have reached their destination if the address could be deciphered."[43]

The business revolution consequently generated a huge demand for hired penmen capable of operating the office's assembly line of correspondence, contracts, and accounts. As postal rates plummeted in the 1840s and the high costs of the telegraph restricted its use to price quotes and only the most urgent orders, the volume of business letters reached unprecedented levels. "Office, great many letters to copy," George Cayley hurriedly scribbled into his diary, his truncated syntax testifying to commerce's rival demands on his writing hand. "Have much writing to do for store etc and shall find less time for my journal I fear," as Albert Norris likewise discovered that the economy required the most extensive journalizing of all. Robert Graham, a clerk in William Aspinwall's New York City counting room, spent his mornings writing up duplicates of the firm's correspondence until the mail went out at eleven-thirty. His afternoons were then given over to copying accounts current and invoices, or to making duplicates of additional letters into the firm's correspondence book. Edward Tailer was similarly "engaged at the desk," remaining at the store until seven o'clock copying thirty-seven pages of invoice into the stock book, or returning after supper to write up twenty-seven out-of-town accounts that had to be mailed out by the next day. Tailer summed up a busy day at the office: "I finished copying the acc[ount] of stock, posted up all the sales which had been made since the eighth of the month, and carried out all the yards upon the Invoice Book. . . . I had but few moments in which to think about myself or other beings."[44]

The age of capital was consequently overrun with scribbling men, "thousands and tens of thousands, who get their living in one way or another by Penmanship," as B. F. Foster identified the virtually limitless pool of potential clients for his *System of Penmanship*. Edgar Allan Poe accordingly observed the "tribe of clerks" filling up the city's streets and called the phenomenon *deskism*, "for want of a better word." In fact, there was no better word, both because it perspicaciously accorded business administration the status of an "ism," and because it recognized the systematic nature of the labor of those who "bend over a desk and scratch from 'morn till dewey eve' without intermission from day to day," as young Benjamin Foster complained from his raised desk in Bangor. "Ho! The torn coat sleeve to the table. The steel pen to the ink. Write! Write! Be it truth or fable. Words! Words! Clerks never think."[45]

In the absence of effective means of mechanical reproduction, speed became the desideratum of business writing.[46] "As soon as a young man enters the counting-house, he is told that it will never answer to write so slow," B. F. Foster stated the obvious. Rapid penmen could finish thirty words in sixty seconds according to a mid-century statistic, which meant that the quill traveled sixteen and a half feet per minute. It was a suitably industrial measure of work, as was S. A. Potter's warning against applying too much ink to one's pen, for just as "the more dirt a contractor uses in constructing a railroad, the longer it takes to make it," the same calculations were true for the production of written documents. Ironically, perhaps, the ancient quill remained a favored tool of this industrial speed-up. "It is difficult to impart to metal the elasticity of the quill," S. H. Browne observed in his *Manual of Commerce*. After 1820, what's more, ready-made quills, which were thrown away once wearing down, could be purchased in a variety of grades and prices as clerks were no longer expected to be skillful enough to reconfigure the points of their quills with a pen knife. Pen manufacturers, for their part, sought to counteract the continued popularity of quills by promoting an extensive selection of nib styles specifically designed for the use of bankers, merchants, bookkeepers, editorialists, and insurance agents, respectively. What's more, penmanship pedagogues often marketed their own line of pens. Thus, students at Comer's College were urged to buy Comer's pens, together with their own copy of *Comer's Penmanship Made Easy*.[47]

But the effort to relieve the office's production bottleneck focused less on the tools and far more on the techniques of writing itself. James Guild, a Vermont schoolteacher, reported in 1820 that demand by his pupils "to write a business hand" was so great that he had commenced teaching a running style of his own invention. In fact, Benjamin Howard Rand had brought the "running hand" to America a few years earlier in his *New and Complete System of Mercantile Penmanship*. It was characterized by loops and an inclined script that had heretofore been considered effeminate. But now that velocity was a desideratum of writing, and the pen could not be lifted from the page without sacrificing valuable time, loops became unavoidable. By the mid-1830s, B. F. Foster was promoting an "American system" of writing that he adopted from the British innovator Joseph Carstairs, another great champion of speed, that strove to further save on the number of strokes as well as obviate the need to ever lift one's pen from the page. With this same end in mind, P. R. Spencer recommended that *y*'s and *g*'s appearing at the end of words be terminated without a loop: a simple downward line or an easy curve to the left would result in a significant reduction in writing time. Spencer likewise promoted the adoption of simple forms of capital letters that would quicken their execution. And while a protest against systems "which would sacrifice everything to rapidity" was registered in the 1850s, when Foster himself retreated from his earlier Carstairs-ian zealotry and the Boston Mercantile Academy endorsed a "medium" style that sought to strike a happy compromise between an older round-hand and the modern running-hand—"having the legibility of the former with the rapidity of the latter"—the attempts to rationalize, in fact, to industrialize, writing continued apace.[48]

Spencer incorporated a metronome in his stroke exercises and called the system Chirythmography, a neologism constructed from the Greek roots for *time*, *hand*, and *writing* that had reportedly first been developed at Albany's Commercial College. The system's incipient Taylorism was unmistakable. The mechanized uniformity of pen strokes broke the alphabet down into a standard set of basic hand movements. "All the letters, long and short, requiring the same number of motions, are thus executed in precisely the same time." Writing consequently became based on the formal production of interchangeable units that were entirely divorced from the text itself. "Words! Words!" the clerk Benjamin Foster had written. "Be it truth or fable." As such, letters were reduced to form, to pure information, dependent, in turn, on the proper deployment of the penman's physique.[49]

Indeed, writing systems rested on both "philosophical and anatomical principles," as B. F. Foster claimed for his. Otherwise, S. A. Potter noted in *Penmanship Explained*, letters could not be produced in a "free, easy, unconstrained style" and the muscles would fail to fill their rising quotas. Everyone thus sought to anchor writing in the body's own physical disposition. Spencer recommended, for instance, that the initial curves of letters begin well below the line and their terminating curves extend above the height of the short letters since this best accorded with the natural motion of the hand itself. And yet, such "natural motions" could only be acquired by methodical training. Taking up a pen in the counting room, in other words, required an extensive pedagogy because business writers were making new uses of their physiques. The "blots and scrawls" of youth would no longer do. Foster, for his part, attacked those systems that allowed pupils to rest their hands and arms on the paper while writing. This fatigued the fingers, he claimed, slowing down the execution and ruining the parallelism of one's letters. He subsequently designed a series of exercises that organized fingers, hand, and arm into a closely coordinated division of manual labor. Again, Foster adapted his system from Carstairs, who had introduced an instructional method by which the thumb and the first two fingers of the hand were tied together with a ribbon in order to compel the pupil to mobilize his whole arm when writing. The technique was meant to simultaneously achieve the freedom and discipline essential to industrial writing, which were also the defining dyad of the bourgeois personality, proper penmanship serving as "an aid in the work of self-culture," according to Samuel Wells in *How to Do Business*. The fingers would consequently control the finer lines, the forearm supplying the requisite power, and the entire arm directing the writer's broader movements, achieving "bold and free writing."[50]

And so, rather than becoming appendages of the machine, clerks consciously turned their appendages into machines, learning to move "insensibly and without effort" in mass producing for an economy dependent on an exploding amount of information. "Went down with uncle to his office offering him the assistance of my arm," a young clerk wrote in 1838, underscoring Emerson's declaration from the year before that "a man in the view of political economy is a pair of hands." Is this not what distinguished man from the rest of the natural world? "Hands are the instruments most suitable for an intelligent animal," Galen had long ago observed in his survey of human anatomy. "Hand-work" was consequently humanity's signature achievement, the very emblem of the civilizing process, and a foundation of republican culture. This was not, however, that

> strong arm, in its stalwart pride sweeping,
> True as a sunbeam the swift sickle guides.

The clerk's hard-earned "command of hand" represented a wholly different kind of manmade mastery, no longer measured by its productive encounter with the material world but by its very ability to turn that world—including itself—into a tool of abstraction.[51]

10

Soulless Monsters and Iron Horses

The Civil War, Institutional Change, and
American Capitalism

Sean Patrick Adams

The American Civil War was a revolutionary event for many
reasons. Secession from the Union, the abolition of slavery,
and the advent of Reconstruction combined to rend the social
and political fabric of the United States, packing a prodigious
amount of disruption into a short period of time and leaving a
profoundly different nation in their wake. Amid all this rapid
political and social change at the national level, another institutional revolution ripped through Northern statehouses during
these turbulent years. It changed forever the scope and character of the American industrial economy. Corporations—often
disparaged as "soulless monsters" by political critics during the
antebellum era—stood at the center of this change, emerging as
they did from the war years with greater prerogative and more
power than they had ever exercised in the antebellum era. This
constituted a landmark in the history of American capitalism.
The present chapter gives an account of how some of these insti-

tutional changes unfolded and examines their immediate impact upon the American industrial economy.

In contrast to the dramatic break with the past signaled by secession and emancipation, the institutional revolution in the political economy of the North actually corresponded with long- and short-term trends present before the war. This obscures its transformative character. The development of labor relations, consumer markets, and business structures were all well underway in the American North by 1861, and we can easily see how these antebellum trends continued their trajectory into the postwar years. At the same time, in order to earn a "revolutionary" designation, we would expect to see rapid, even sudden, changes occurring in the economy without much warning. This apparent incongruence between the immediate crises of wartime and the on-going evolution of American capitalism can be reconciled by focusing on the impact of the Civil War on state-level institutions. Tracing wartime changes in the environment vis-à-vis such critical institutions as industrial corporations in leading states like Pennsylvania can reconcile the disruptive, extraordinary, and unanticipated challenges provoked by a bloody and costly four-year political, military, and social conflict with the *longue durée* perspective often adopted by historians of capitalism, in which periods of rapid change give way to the forces of equilibrium or inertia. The ways in which the Confederate state grappled with its industrial sector, moreover, offer an alternate perspective on this phe-nomenon, one rooted in a more active state role in the making of industrial policy. Ultimately, the Northern practice of according corporations greater freedom of action prevailed, both on the battlefield and in the economy as a whole. In releasing these "soulless monsters" from formal and informal insti-tutional constraints, state legislatures in the North created a new context for corporate operations that would continue for the rest of the century. As the other chapters in this volume demonstrate, capitalism was liable to unleash unanticipated forces that revolutionized American culture and society. The focus on institutional change illuminates the broader revolutionary effects of the brief but pivotal Civil War years.

The exigencies of war overwhelmed the capacity of individual states to fi-nance the war effort and manage their economies. At the same time, rising prices enhanced prospects for industrial endeavors. Entrepreneurs appraised this new turn of events and responded accordingly. The short-term crisis, in turn, undermined longstanding institutional arrangements in the political economies of the states. Instead of acting as a regulator of industrial activity, they became more of a partner, corporate chartering now serving as the insti-tutional articulation of the relationship between the state policymaker's desire to promote economic growth and the capitalist's need for flexibility and inno-vation. This institutional revolution was hardly bloodless. Numerous groups were left out in the cold; small proprietors, labor, and the advocates of a strong regulatory state all found wartime changes in the state-level political economy to be unsettling, to say the least. Their role in the postwar economy, further-more, would be limited by a new arrangement that gave corporations greater leeway in matters of capital formation, interstate mobility, and their range of responsibilities. As Robert E. Wright shows in this volume, corporations had long been present in the American economy. But the Civil War ensured that they would become the primary engines of the economy, fueling industrial development, boosting state revenues, and building the nation's transporta-tion network. By fusing the interests of many state policymakers to those of corporations, the Civil War can be said to have effected an emancipation of an altogether different kind in the Northern states. It allowed those "soulless monsters" a freedom of action that antebellum policymakers had considered to be, at best, a necessary evil and, at worst, a dire threat to small proprietors, workers, and free markets.

Generations of historians have explored the relationship between American capitalism and the Civil War, often emphasizing the inexorable march of free labor ideology, the modern American state, or of industry's own organic de-velopment in explaining the war's more general significance for the economy. This line of inquiry, pioneered by Charles and Mary Beard in the 1930s and revised over the next seven decades, views the Civil War as a kind of "bourgeois revolution" that necessarily swept away an antiquated slave-labor South.[1] Even as this question of inevitability came under some revision during the 1960s and 1970s, economic and business historians debated the significance of the Civil War by asking whether it had accelerated or retarded the immediate course of American industrialization and, to a larger degree, the nation's "moderniza-tion." Initial research generated by this project tended to revolve around the questions raised by Thomas Cochran's seminal article in the *Mississippi Valley Historical Review* in 1961 in which he posed the "Cochran thesis," which offers the counterintuitive proposition that the war was, in fact, bad for business, at least in the long run.[2]

One assumption undergirds nearly all of the literature: American capitalism had a single course of development that the Civil War either interrupted or ac-celerated. This assumption informs interpretations of both the Northern and Southern economies during the Civil War, even as regional studies tell vastly different stories. Recent scholarship, for example, has done an outstanding job of detailing the ways in which Southern society underwent a great transformation—whether voluntary or not—from a slave society into one based on (relatively) free labor markets. The North experienced dramatic changes during the war years as well. But most models of Northern political and economic development either posit a predetermined course of economic development that was temporarily disrupted or focus on the grand political changes brought about at the national level. Both views promote an instrumental view of state institutions that subjects them to what Marc Egnal recently characterized as the "abstract, disembodied Larger Forces" in his study, *Clash of Extremes: The Economic Origins of the Civil War*.[3]

Egnal focuses on individual agency in his study. This chapter seeks to restore contingency as another important part of economic policymaking. State-level developments in the North suggest that neither temporary distractions nor invariable consolidations were the legacy of the Civil War. In important industrializing states such as Pennsylvania, and in critical industries like the coal trade, the exigencies of crisis brought about significant changes that signaled a break with important aspects of the antebellum relationship between corporations and the state. Rather than signaling a temporary derailment or boost in the course of American capitalist development, state-level corporate policy in the American North underwent a major, qualitative revision in three important areas. The significance of a wartime spike in incorporation, for example, was not so much to be found in the numbers themselves but in the unprecedented range of business possibilities now available to Northern mining and manufacturing companies. Changes in tax policy also showed that individual states actually tied their economic fates to those of corporations during the Civil War. Finally, railroads emerged from the war years not only with record profits, but with far more latitude to build interstate systems that were free of state regulation. The Civil War, in other words, had not only proven the utility of the "iron horse." It also allowed railroads to break free of antebellum regimes of control. The ramifications in these three areas of state economic policy would require another half century to reach full expression. By then it became clear that the Civil War's significance for American capitalism was not as a "bourgeois" or "modern" revolution but as an institutional one.

Economic historians have convincingly shown that the increase in demand triggered by the outbreak of hostilities in 1861 did not result in a massive transformation of American manufacturing techniques, labor productivity, or a significant acceleration of industrialization. The Massachusetts boot and shoe industry, which we might expect to see transformed by military demand, saw average industrial output per worker increase from 578 units in 1855 to only 580 in 1865. National pig iron production actually declined during the first two years of the war from its 1860 level, followed by increases in 1864 and 1865. Major metallurgical innovations such as the use of bituminous or anthracite coal in smelting pig iron, or the Bessemer process for making steel, moreover, which had been introduced in the 1850s, were not significantly diffused during wartime. Even DuPont's explosives industry evidenced few changes in productivity, the manufacturing process, or the size of its labor force. One observer noted in 1864 that the "consumption of powder in time of peace is far greater than during war," as lucrative foreign markets were closed to firms like DuPont. "Far from spurring industrial expansion," Roger Ransom argues in a survey of the war's impact, "the war appears to have produced a period of distinctly *slower* economic growth."[4]

The wartime pressure on prices, however, might have had another, unintended effect upon state-level economic policy that cannot be explained by conventional measures of economic expansion or growth. Here economic contingency becomes an important factor driving institutional change. The Civil War arrived on the heels of a severe economic depression that followed the panic of 1857. While this crisis largely spared the cotton-based export economy of the South, manufacturing in the North and farm production in the West experienced a prolonged, two-year downturn that only brought recovery in late 1859 and early 1860. Labor unrest, particularly the massive strike of shoeworkers in Lynn, Massachusetts, was another effect of economic hardship. For Northern businesses, then, the outbreak of the war would seem to herald yet more uncertainty in an already fragile economy. But the rising prices triggered by the war were actually a cause for business optimism.[5]

What impact would the anticipation of extremely high prices by 1863 and 1864 have upon Northern businesses? In the long run, probably very little. But considering that business prospects had been dull for Northern businesses since 1857, rising prices offered a significant change in the short-term psychological outlook of American capitalists. High prices increased the value of business inventories and spurred hopes that government-generated demand would boost the fortunes of future endeavors. As Glenn Porter and Harold Livesay argue in their comprehensive study of nineteenth-century merchants and manufacturers, "entrepreneurs shed their melancholy for frenzied activity" during wartime. For a certain subset of heavy industries hit especially hard by the panic of 1857, such as coal mining and ironmaking, the war had little impact on technique or productivity but brought a flood of new entrepreneurs into the trades. One study of the iron industry in Pennsylvania notes that the largest, and perhaps the only positive, effect of the war was the entry of new individuals and companies into the market. There is something to be said, then, for the traditional view that wartime conditions spurred optimism among businesses, both large and small.[6]

The prospect of rising prices also brought about a spike in corporate chartering. And this would have lasting repercussions on the economic policies of Northern states. American legislatures had, of course, started chartering corporations very early in the nation's history and the corporation became an ubiquitous presence in a number of economic sectors. As Kenneth Lipartito and David Sicilia argue in a recent anthology devoted to the subject of corporate governance, "the antebellum corporation did not spring up like an insidious capitalist weed in an otherwise pristine republican garden." Instead, its origins are to be found in the social and political institutions of the period. Antebellum benevolent societies, churches, clubs, and businesses all rested on the corporate form of enterprise, an institutional heritage that allowed legislatures to demand a "public service" component in each charter. As a rule, state legislatures created corporate entities with long or indefinite lifespans, limited liability, and the privileges of raising large amounts of capital if this served some public interest. The category that best fit this public interest litmus test included charitable, educational, and philanthropic organizations. Internal improvement companies such as turnpikes, canals, and railroads satisfied this criterion as well since they offered a benefit to the overall economy of the state, obvious even to legislators outside their sphere of influence. Banks were necessary evils in the eyes of Jacksonian policymakers; growth required them, but their ability to make and break fortunes also required eternal vigilance and fairly strict restrictions on their size and behavior. So while all states passed corporate charters for various purposes during the antebellum period, the competitive advantage of this corporate form over individual proprietorships made them suspect in the eyes of many legislators. As "soulless monsters" operated by managers without an ownership stake in the firm, moreover, corporations were incongruous with the "producerist" vision of small-scale stakeholders so prevalent in the political rhetoric of the era. Manufacturing, commercial, and mining firms constituted the most controversial type of charter for legislators, as these entities directly competed with individual proprietors. A Pennsylvania Senate committee thus found in 1834 that in mining and manufacturing, "every charter or act of incorporation, is to a greater or lesser extent an infringement upon the natural rights and liberties of the people—and their natural tendency is to monopoly." And so it was that many antebellum policymakers considered corporations building internal improvements, banks, and large manufacturing and mining concerns a necessary evil at best.[7]

One antebellum solution to this political dilemma was creation of a regime of "general" incorporation. This allowed firms to secure a corporate charter without legislative approval, thus bypassing the log-rolling, vote-swapping, and out-and-out bribery that often accompanied the granting of special charters. In return for making incorporation an administrative process outside of political control, general chartering laws limited the capitalization and business discretion of firms while also creating strict provisions for the corporation's governance structure. New York passed a general incorporation law for manufacturers in 1811, and its constitution of 1846 effectively abolished special incorporation. Indeed, by the outbreak of war in 1861, thirteen states had made general incorporation mandatory. Even in states that still allowed for special charters, policymakers used general incorporation to target certain industries or regions for development, thus exerting control over the pace of chartering and its impact on individual proprietorship. In Pennsylvania's coal trade, for example, legislators passed general incorporation acts in 1849 and 1854 that excluded coal-producing counties with established proprietary interests and that introduced incentives, such as the ability to construct railroad lines, for firms seeking incorporation in less-developed coal regions. And so, whether a state had a special or a general chartering regime or some combination of both methods, the general view was that corporations required oversight and strict rules guiding their creation.[8]

The Civil War tested both these formal and informal restraints on corporations. At the state level, governors and legislatures faced an unprecedented challenge in recruiting, equipping, feeding, and transporting large armies. In this context, the threat of corporations dominating the economic landscape appeared less pressing. Inhibiting the growth of businesses in the face of the national crisis was quite simply not an option. And when businesses needed to raise capital quickly in order to respond to the immediate opportunities offered by wartime demands, they increasingly drew upon corporate charters to do so. Legislators worried about the crisis were less likely to put a halt to chartering as they might have during antebellum decades. As a result, the rate of business incorporations increased in most Northern states, and it remained high following the end of the conflict in 1865. Figure 10.1 presents this upsurge in both special and general chartering that occurred in Connecticut, Maine, Massachusetts, New Jersey, and Ohio, based on the data collected by George Heberton Evans in the 1940s. After observing trends in the nineteenth-century numbers, Evans periodized three long waves of incorporation, from 1800 to 1821, from 1821 to 1843, and from 1843 to 1861. In regards to the Civil War years, Evans concluded that a "fourth long wave may perhaps be said to begin

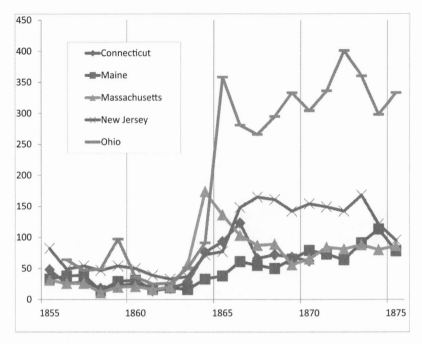

Figure 10.1. Business incorporations in five northern states, 1855–1875. *Source*: George H. Evans, *Business Incorporations in the United States, 1800–1943* (New York: National Bureau of Economic Research, 1948), 12.

with 1861, but its terminal date cannot be marked off." Evans's figures suggest that the real "take-off" for incorporation occurred in the later years of the war and then continued at a high level throughout the 1870s with no significant drop-off coming afterwards either. In other words, a permanent shift in the rate of chartering occurred at some point during the Civil War. Even Illinois, a largely agricultural state with a biennial legislature, witnessed an all-time high in chartering in 1865.

It is difficult to identify a single moment or event that triggered this spike, although the most dramatic increase appears to have occurred in 1864. In that year, for example, Massachusetts authorized more than $43.9 million in capital stock for new corporations—a level that it would not exceed until 1903 and (as shown in fig. 10.2) one that far surpassed any of the surrounding years. To an economist, these numbers might easily be explained by wartime inflation. To state legislators grappling with the wave of laws necessary for equipping, transporting, and feeding an army and keeping their state's economy humming at the same time, the authorization of millions of dollars in new capital was a

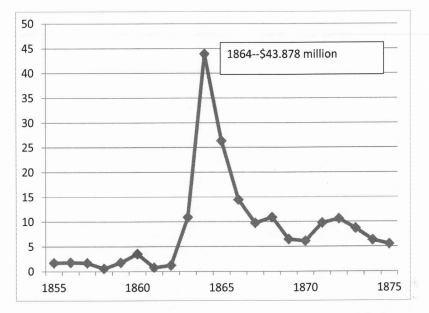

Figure 10.2. Annual authorized capital stock in new incorporations (in millions of dollars), 1855–1875. *Source*: George H. Evans, *Business Incorporations in the United States, 1800–1943* (New York: National Bureau of Economic Research, 1948), 123.

most significant event. Even as those wartime dollars purchased less, the rapid collapse of longstanding political restrictions on capital formation had dramatic implications for the corporate environment. Pro-business Pennsylvania political insider Alexander McClure reflected upon the chartering spike in glowing terms in his memoir.

> Fortunately, the Civil War quickened our industries and invited corporate interests to harvest millions from our oil, our coal, our iron, our lumber and other channels of industry. The battle against the liberal progress then inaugurated, that has since added billions to the wealth of Pennsylvania, was never thereafter seriously renewed.[9]

Certain industries, most notably those that engaged in the extraction of natural resources such as coal, copper, and oil, accounted for much of the wartime spike in charters. "Capital has no bowels or patriotism," C. B. Conant argued as he noted the heightened wartime demand for coal, "and capitalists are instinctive." In this case, their instincts told them to seek corporate charters.

In Ohio mining corporations accounted for 36 of 91 (39.5%) charters that were issued in 1864 and 245 of 358 (68.4%) in 1865. Illinois issued twenty-five charters for mining companies in 1865, a respectable 14 percent for an agricultural state. As the nation's leading coal-mining state, Pennsylvania experienced perhaps the most dramatic spike for both general and special incorporations in coal mining. Strong antichartering interests centered in the southern anthracite region's Schuylkill County had led the antebellum effort to keep corporations out of the state's anthracite fields. Thus, the general chartering laws of 1849 and 1854 applied principally to the state's western bituminous fields. All this changed during the Civil War, when the Pennsylvania legislature passed a liberal general chartering law in 1863 and at the same time continued to issue special charters at an unprecedented rate. Politicians anxious for change would later describe the older, informal restrictions on chartering as a "narrow, illiberal flood-tide of prejudice cherished throughout Pennsylvania" championed by "every demagogic political movement" that had held wealth "in leading strings of ignorance and bigotry." The Civil War saw such longstanding practices overthrown nearly overnight, and not everyone was pleased. "The high price of coal and iron has created a furor among the capitalists amounting almost to a mania, and the files of both houses are filled with bills for chartering new Coal and Iron Companies, and supplements to those already in existence," an exasperated columnist for the Miner's Journal reported in 1864. "These companies are forming in all sections of the State, and the easy manner in which they pass proves that opposition to them would be futile."[10]

Policymakers continued to target certain regions of Pennsylvania for wartime development by loosening restrictions on charters. In 1863 the state's legislature passed an astonishingly liberal general incorporation act. It presented few restrictions on the amount of land companies could hold, fixed capital stock at $5,000 to $500,000 (which was raised to $1 million a year later), and allowed firms to own and mine land outside the Commonwealth's borders. Coal-mining firms comprised about 7 percent of the 1,236 corporations authorized under this act, which was created to accommodate the western bituminous region's need for general charters. Over three-quarters of the coal-mining firms chartered under the 1863 act held lands west of the anthracite region. In fact, the act was originally limited to Allegheny County and initially excluded several anthracite- and bituminous-producing counties. Special charters were still subject to political restrictions during the Civil War, but the volume of general chartering exploded as colliers expressed high hopes for steady or rising prices. And though outrageous amendments to charters might still come under scrutiny, both executive and legislative authorities loosened their grip on the pace of chartering. And so, while on the eve of the Civil War there had been eighty-nine proprietorships and partnerships and one corporation that mined coal in the Monongahela and Youghiogheny bituminous regions in western Pennsylvania, by 1871 those figures for corporations stood at fifty-seven and twenty-five respectively. Even Schuylkill County, a bastion of antebellum anti-chartering rhetoric, was transformed over the course of the Civil War. In 1863 only one mining corporation was to be found in Schuylkill County, and it accounted for a miniscule amount of the region's production. A year later, twenty-five new corporate mining firms were formed. By 1865 that figure had reached fifty-two, and they produced about half of the county's coal. Pennsylvania mining corporations founded just in 1864 accounted alone for over a third of both the number of existing firms and the authorized capital in the state.[11]

With his 1864 veto of a charter supplement to the Lykens Valley Coal Company that would have allowed the firm to quintuple its land holdings to 15,000 acres, Governor Andrew Gregg Curtin announced that he would "approve no bill creating a new monopoly of the kind, or giving one already existing the right of holding a larger quantity of land than they are now authorized to acquire." But at the same time that the *United States Railroad and Mining Register* proudly announced that, with Curtin's veto, "the State now has a *policy,*" corporate consolidation continued its frantic pace. The exigencies of the Civil War had thus eroded many of the political barriers to corporate coal mining in Pennsylvania.[12]

It is important to note that this corporate activity was not accompanied by a significant increase in production. At the same time, the existing constellation of individual proprietorships and corporate mining firms underwent a massive reorganization. While figure 10.3 shows that production in Pennsylvania and in the nation at large did not undergo any dramatic change during the Civil War years, figure 10.4 reveals corporate activity increasing dramatically in the Pennsylvania coal trade. That included supplementary legislation that expanded capitalization and landholding, and allowed certain firms to construct their own short-line railroads. This level of incorporation was unprecedented in Pennsylvania's coal trade and it transformed the industry, even in its most traditional bastions of anticorporate opposition. With access to vast amounts of capital and the right to construct their own linkages to markets, large corporate coal-mining firms began to consolidate control of their respective regions. Protection for individual proprietorships, which had once been the jealously-guarded priority of many legislators, quickly evaporated.

The incorporations of 1864–65 also accelerated the movement of corporate capital across state boundaries. Because corporate charters were created

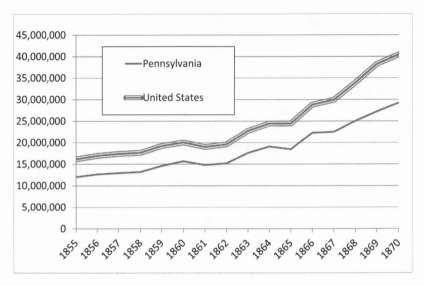

Figure 10.3. Coal production in Pennsylvania and the United States (in tons), 1855–1870. *Source:* Howard Eavenson, *The First Century and a Quarter of American Coal Industry* (Pittsburgh: privately published, 1942), 430–31, 433–34.

by either a legislative or administrative act of a particular state, the legal status of such entities outside its boundaries was that of a "foreign" corporation. The rights of out-of-state corporations in regards to land ownership, liability, and taxation required years of legal wrangling to determine. Suffice it to say that during the antebellum period the ability of corporations chartered in one state to do business in another had not been settled in American law. Few state-level politicians, moreover, had a thorough understanding of the issue's national implications. The wartime incorporation spike now forced the issue of "foreign corporations" to the fore because of an increase in the number of firms that were headquartered in large cities such as Boston, New York, and Philadelphia but did business elsewhere. Thus, while largely bereft itself of deposits of gold, coal, and copper, Massachusetts chartered seventy-three mining firms headquartered in Boston by April 1864. Seventy of them were organized in 1863 and 1864. These firms, variously authorized to mine coal in Pennsylvania, copper in Michigan, and gold in Colorado, raised $21.3 million in capital. Pennsylvania likewise chartered copper-mining firms in Michigan and gold-mining companies in Colorado that were headquartered in Philadelphia and Pittsburgh. This cross-boundary legislation became important for policymakers. Ohio, for example, authorized companies chartered under its own

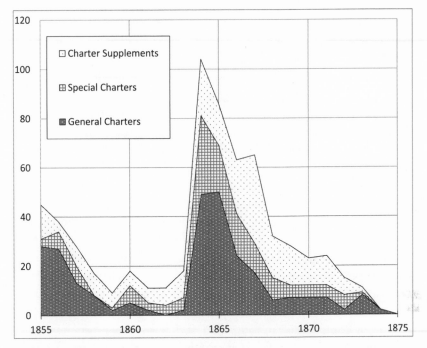

Figure 10.4. Chartering activity in the Pennsylvania coal industry, 1854–1874. *Sources: Laws of Pennsylvania, 1854–1874*; Pennsylvania Corporations Bureau, Letters Patent, 1854–1874, Records of the Department of State, Pennsylvania State Archives, Harrisburg, PA; Sean Patrick Adams, *Old Dominion, Industrial Commonwealth: Coal, Politics, and Economy in Antebellum America* (Baltimore: Johns Hopkins University Press, 2004), 196.

laws to operate "beyond the limits of this state" in 1865 despite the obvious lack of authority to legislate outside its own boundaries. Pennsylvania, on the other hand, limited foreign mining corporations to 300 acres in an act passed in 1863. But it repealed that provision in 1865. When Massachusetts passed a law in 1863 taxing nonresident stockholders at a higher rate, Connecticut governor William Buckingham argued that such an act would "disturb the harmony that now exists between the States by exciting retaliatory legislation." Massachusetts changed the law. The rights and privileges of "foreign corporations" would occupy American courts for decades. But it was already clear that the increased leeway for cross-state business constituted a significant aspect of the corporate "emancipation" from public oversight during the Civil War.[13]

Perhaps the most dramatic example of the chartering spike's imprint on American capitalism occurred in the oil fields of Pennsylvania. The petroleum industry experienced a great boom during the Civil War, transforming the sparsely populated region along the Allegheny River in northwestern Pennsylvania into a hive of economic activity. The need for illuminating and lubricating oil drove prices to unprecedented levels, and production shot up from 1,000 barrels annually in 1859, the year that Colonel Edwin Drake discovered petroleum in the region, to over two million barrels by the end of 1861. Venango County's population doubled in the 1860s, and boomtowns with such evocative names as Pithole, Oil City, Shamburg, and Red Hot sprang up amidst the oil derricks. In 1865–66, fifty-four hotels were operating in Pithole, and the most prominent of them, the Astor House, accommodated over 200 guests in forty rooms, serving 1,000 meals a day. As capital flowed into the region, a guidebook instructed oil entrepreneurs in manipulating Pennsylvania's easy new chartering regime. "The casual observer, or the hasty business man," the author warned, "might be content to assist in the formation of a company under either law, without inquiring as to the effect of being an incorporator." It cost an estimated $15,000 to secure a lease on a small patch of oil land, erect a derrick, and engage in exploratory drilling for a few months, yet many oil companies capitalized themselves at a million dollars and leased less than one-acre sections of Pennsylvania farmland. With such low start-up costs, how could well-capitalized firms avoid the temptation of snatching up competitors? In the oilfields, then, merger and acquisition would characterize growth for corporate firms and limit opportunities for individual proprietors in ways that antebellum policymakers would have found horrifying.[14]

Economic booms were not an unfamiliar phenomenon in the American economy, but the Pennsylvania oil boom during the Civil War diverged from the usual mode. Just a decade earlier the gold rush had transformed California. There, similar to what had previously occurred in Virginia and North Carolina, initial activity was undertaken by individual proprietors who were then replaced by corporate mining concerns. Small-scale prospecting with pick, shovel, and sluice gave way to the hydraulic mining of more highly organized corporations. And yet, California's legislature remained ambivalent enough toward the chartering process to build in numerous restrictions on corporate behavior. Thus, for instance, the General Incorporation Act of 1850 made charters available to mining firms but authorized state officials to investigate companies at any time, prohibited the disbursement of stock dividends until a firm reached profitability, and held stockholders entirely liable for the company's debts. In Pennsylvania's oilfields a decade later, in contrast, corporations with few financial constraints spearheaded development. The legislature's wartime revisions of existing laws, together with a generous 1863 general incorporation law, provided the institutional impetus for an orgy of

corporate formation in the oil region. Earlier legislatures had limited capitalization of mining and manufacturing companies to $500,000, but Pennsylva-
nia's wartime policymakers doubled that amount. The response of coal-trade
insiders suggests that these actions were undertaken in order to spur interest
in the state's coalfields rather than to keep up with inflation. In May of 1865,
for example, legislators further loosened restrictions on the sale of land between corporations and allowed firms to borrow money equal to their capital
stock and issue bonds with interest rates reaching 7 percent. "Every week new
companies are organized," one journalist reported in February of 1864, "very
many of them giving promise of unusually favorable results. Dividends of from
3 to 5 per cent per month are by no means uncommon." In 1865 Philadelphia
directories listed the offices of eighty-six companies operating in the oil region.
They represented $48.5 million in capital. Pittsburgh hosted eleven new cor-
porations with $2.32 million in capital. All ninety-seven of these companies
were formed in 1864. Ultimately, the oil region would witness the creation of
innumerable corporations—some actual, some existing only on paper—with
massive capital authorizations from New York ($350 million), Massachusetts
($160 million), and Pennsylvania ($145 million).[15]

The accelerated reliance upon corporate actors was not inevitable, nor was
it the only option available to American policymakers. As Confederate officials demonstrated, a method of managing industrial resources by a more activist state was deeply rooted in American political economy. The South's commitment to statist policies during the Civil War appears paradoxical to many
historians, who dismiss it as the product of wartime necessity and being at
odds with the "states' rights" doctrine of secessionists. John Majewski's recent
study of Confederate visions of economic growth, however, traces the numerous continuities between antebellum and Confederate political economy in
the South, arguing that "the strong Confederate state was not a radical disjuncture but a natural outgrowth of southern attitudes established during the
antebellum period." State officials in both the antebellum North and South,
for example, demonstrated a willingness to boost economic development by
means of internal improvement networks, specifically targeted corporate charters, and scientific surveys, among other policies. And, of course, the massive
effort to protect the institution of slavery signaled the intention of Southern
political authorities to proactively maintain the distinct economic character
of their region. State interventions during times of great national crisis, then,
seem a continuation rather than a break with state-level political economy.
Rather than loosen constraints on corporations, Southern authorities sought
to boost production by other methods. Certainly, the Southern economy's

dependence on cotton and its stunted antebellum manufacturing sector offered good reasons for the Confederacy's active management of industrial production. Nonetheless, the coordination of public and private interests in the
South during the Civil War presents a distinct alternative to the institutional
path taken by Northern states.[16]

The effort to spur pig-iron production is an excellent example of the Confederacy's statist methods. Shortages plagued the Confederate War Department early in the struggle. "Our contractors are many of them at a dead stand
for lack of Iron," Chief of Ordnance General Josiah Gorgas wrote to Secretary
of War James Seddon in November of 1862, "and it will be impossible to supply projectiles for the new guns now in the field, unless it can be had." Gorgas
went so far as to recommend a state confiscation of iron stocks. The Confederacy did not pursue this strategy but worked, rather, through a contracting
system and the use of interest-free loans to private firms in lieu of out-and-
out state control. Eastern Virginia's Catharine Furnace, for example, received
a contract for 2,000 tons of pig iron at very lucrative terms. W. L. Sanders, an
Alabama ironmaster, received a $50,000 advance in Confederate bonds on a
1863 contract and a Smythe County, Virginia, iron furnace secured free passage on canals and railroads courtesy of the Confederate Mining and Nitre
Bureau. By 1864 a kind of partnership had developed in which Confederate
officials paid for iron in advance but then only requisitioned between 50 to 83
percent of the produce so as "to stimulate production by private interest, and
to throw up on the market an additional quantity of iron for agriculture and
the rail roads." And so, in the case of pig iron, military necessity provoked a
statist response from Confederate authorities who were effectively managing
the South's ironmaking capacity by the final years of the war.[17]

Unlike their counterparts in the North, who chose to work through corporate chartering, many state-level officials in the Confederacy became directly involved in encouraging industrial production. In Georgia the governor
authorized a bonus of $10,000 to "any person or company who shall erect a
foundry in this State for the casting of cannon." Georgia officials continued to
encourage manufacturing with bonuses, conscription exemptions, and other
incentives. Georgia's legislature also passed a "Monopoly and Extortion Bill"
to insure that private firms could not take advantage of wartime shortages.
This law against "exorbitant, unjust, or unreasonable prices" provided fines
ranging up to $5,000 for guilty "monopolists." As the war progressed, both
state and Confederate officials stepped up their efforts to manage industrial
production. This occasionally included the confiscation of private property in
service of the war effort. When David Yulee's Florida Railroad refused to allow

Confederate troops to confiscate its iron rails in 1863, Florida's governor, John
Milton, reminded him that

> gentlemen whose distinguished resources from wealth and social or political posi-
> tion—and especially those who have enjoyed public confidence and public favors,
> should not permit themselves to be wedded to schemes of personal ambition—or
> particular local and selfish interests—at the peril of the political existence of the
> State and the lives, and property of their fellow citizens.

In the end, though, Southern officials resorted to the carrot as much as the
stick. In Texas state officials not only contracted for military supplies but also
offered lucrative incentives for industrial production. The statist Confederate
economy thus represented an alternative path that was highly consistent with
antebellum policies. Northern states by and large spurned such an activist approach, preferring instead to work through other channels.[18]

Since the North witnessed such a dramatic proliferation of corporations,
many officials began to take an interest in how they were being taxed and, more
specifically, how corporations could help with the chronic funding shortages
caused by the war. One of the most striking economic aspects of the American
Civil War was its immense cost, which threatened to swamp the traditional
funding structure—tariffs, excise taxes, and the sale of public lands—of the
federal government. The US Army, which had approximately 16,000 men under arms at the beginning of 1861, swelled to over 700,000 by the end of the
same year. Keeping these soldiers fed, clothed, and armed strained the Treasury Department beyond all expectations. The National Banking Act of 1863,
the brief appearance of a national income tax, and federal "greenback" notes
were all emergency innovations created to meet this crisis. They were put into
place to satisfy the unprecedented demand for government spending, which
was estimated to have reached $1.8 billion by the end of the war. This was more
money than the federal government had spent in the previous eighty years of
its existence. The war brought fiscal crisis to the states as well. Pennsylvania,
New York, and Massachusetts, for example, all floated $3-million bond issues
in the early years of the war though these states respectively expended $2.157,
$2.495, and $3.327 million in 1861 alone. Even when federal authorities took
over most of the military procurement duties, wartime conditions strained
state treasuries, which relieved heavily on property taxes for revenues. Another
source of state-level funding was clearly necessary and, like the incorporation
spike, wartime changes in state taxing regimes constitute yet another way in
which short-term solutions rearranged the institutional framework in which

American capitalists operated. And like the new pattern of corporate chartering in the postwar economy, the changes initiated in state-level taxing policies
would continue to develop over the next half century.[19]

The fiscal emergency forced many states to examine antiquated systems that
relied upon local officials to assess values for the purpose of a general property
tax. The usual practice of most states was to levy taxes on banks and insurance
companies. However, this was largely a regulatory rather than a revenue policy.
The property of many railroad, manufacturing, and mining companies was
subject to property taxes, but assessment was scandalously uneven, with local or
state assessors absolving well-connected firms from taxation while shamelessly
skinning others. New York's legislature commissioned a survey of assessments
and exemptions in 1862. The composite portrait presented by James Bell to
his legislative colleagues the following year revealed a set of highly subjective
real estate and personal property assessments and a crazy quilt of exemptions.
These were characteristic of state-level taxation across the nation. The byzan-
tine structure, need for political capital, and lack of overall clarity resembled
antebellum corporate chartering. The Civil War forced many states to come
to grips with this system's inadequacies. Illinois, for example, found itself ex-
pending nearly $4 million with the onset of the war. Although the federal gov-
ernment reimbursed much of that sum, Governor Richard Yates judged the
assessments on Illinois property to be "absurdly low" in 1863 and called for
an equalization of the system. Revenues did increase, probably as the result of
the governor's scolding, but true reform only came in the immediate aftermath
of the war. Ohio altered its assessment of railroad property in 1862 so as to
distribute revenues among a route's counties in proportion to valuations. In
1863 Ohio redefined its concept of "private property" to include a railroad's
profits or unallocated funds. Iowa also changed its system of assessing the value
of railroads, moving from a makeshift regime that taxed the capital stock of
shareholders to one that directly taxed the gross receipts of railroads and then
distributed the revenues to counties based on their railroad mileage.[20]

Pennsylvania enacted one of the most ambitious taxation reforms during
the Civil War. Corporate revenues were the reform's main target. Firms already
paid a direct tax based on the value of their capital stock, but their corporate
property was exempted from local property tax valuations. In order to address
the war's financial challenges, the Pennsylvania legislature now levied a number of new taxes on the income of private brokers and bankers in 1861 and a
tax on the net earnings and loans of corporations in 1864. The most innovative
of these new measures was a tonnage tax passed in a special legislative session
in 1864 that required all transport companies to pay a rate of two cents per

mile for carrying "the products of mines." Although this new system of taxation would not last into the 1870s, it did signal several new trends that would become important after the war. First of all, Pennsylvania's wartime policy remade corporate taxes into a major source of state revenue. In 1856, the last year of prosperity before the war, corporate taxes constituted 4.7 percent of the state's revenue. In the first full year of the Civil War, 1862, that figure had increased to 8.1 percent. Corporate taxes continued to fill a growing proportion of the state's treasury. In 1863 this amounted to 10.2 percent, in 1864 13.5 percent, and in 1865 the figure reached 19.9 percent. In the first full year after the war, corporate taxes constituted 21 percent of the state's revenues, and for the first time in Pennsylvania's history, corporate tax revenues exceeded those of the old fiscal standby, the personal property and real estate tax. Second, while the tax on tonnage provided only 6.3 percent of Pennsylvania's revenue in its first full year of existence, 1865, it constituted a most valuable precedent, for state authorities were now directly taxing economic activity rather than property values, in marked contrast to antebellum practices. Such taxes had been used in the past in Pennsylvania and other states, but that was usually for purposes of regulation rather than revenue. Pennsylvania's wartime measures, despite their origins in a temporary problem, provided a new range of options for policymakers who were searching for ways to benefit from an increasingly industrial, railroad-based, and corporate economy in the postwar years. These wartime taxation policies linked state-level fiscal policies to corporations, for better or worse, in the postbellum decades.[21]

Massachusetts likewise raised direct revenue from corporations during the Civil War. But while corporate capital stock was subject to Massachusetts' property tax, assessment was uneven and enforcement notoriously lax. C. K. Yearly estimated that two-thirds of the $225 million in capital stock that should have been subject to taxation in the first year of the war avoided assessment. Rather than simply clamp down on assessors, as was done in Ohio and Illinois, Massachusetts passed a new general corporation tax in 1864 that allowed both the state and local authorities to tax corporations directly instead of assessing the value of individual stockholdings under the property tax provision. The state would now retain tax revenues in proportion to the corporation's percentage of out-of-state stockholders — thus resolving the thorny problem of "foreign" stockholders — while distributing the remaining income to the localities. Like Pennsylvania, Massachusetts thus emerged from the Civil War far more dependent on corporate taxes for financing state government.[22]

Railroads also emerged from the Civil War with an enhanced status, both among public policymakers and private economic actors. Railroad companies,

the most vibrant corporations of the late antebellum period—famously referred to by the business historian Alfred Chandler as the "pioneers in the
management of modern business enterprise"—began the war in uncertain condition. Historians influenced by the Cochran thesis regarding the war's dismal
influence on the economy cite the decline in track construction, the absence
of any significant technical innovation, and the railroads' own self-proclaimed
financial difficulties. An alternative view points to the extraordinary success of
Northern railroads in transporting men and material throughout the struggle,
the high dividends paid out to stockholders, and the sharp increase in shipping capacity that resulted from double-tracking and other wartime necessities. This was evidence of the Civil War's positive impact on the nation's railroad system. Like the larger argument regarding the conflict's general impact
on the American economy, this debate will probably never be definitively resolved. It is certainly too large to address in detailed fashion in the present
chapter. Nonetheless, the significance of railroads to postwar markets requires
a discussion of the wartime changes in the institutional framework in which
they operated.[23]

Railroads across the North benefited from the unique circumstances of the
Civil War and finished the conflict in strong economic condition. In Pennsylvania changes in state oversight of the rail system offered firms a golden business
opportunity. As relatively late arrivals in the antebellum legislative landscape,
railroad corporations had fewer "public service" encumbrances than other charters. Nonetheless, before the war legislators had placed several limitations on
railroad charters in the interest of maintaining competition and restricting the
consolidation of power. Over the course of the conflict, Pennsylvania's legislature loosened many of these restrictions. This began with an 1861 law allowing
railroad firms to purchase the stock or bonds of other railroads and corporations.
As happened in the state's coal and oil fields, liberalization of railroad legislation
likewise spurred mergers and consolidations, immediately and in the long term.
The legislated changes in railroading were dizzying. Pennsylvania standardized
merger proceedings (1861), authorized lateral lines in central Pennsylvania's bituminous region (1862), extended the authority to build lateral roads (1863),
authorized the railroads to hire private police forces (1865), increased the authorized capital stock of railroads without a special act (1865), standardized the
"one share, one vote" governance structure among railroad stockholders (1865),
and allowed large railroad corporations to purchase branch lines (1865). The
cumulative effect of this legislation was a system that allowed railroads to expand with little state oversight and pursue a policy of consolidation, much like
the mining industry was doing. Railroads often touted the reduced public scru-

tiny to investors. "It is believed that no charter more favorable for stockholders was ever passed by the Pennsylvania Legislature than that of the Summit Branch Railroad Company," one 1863 prospectus bragged. In order to drive this point home, the Summit Branch Railroad Company not only published its large authorized capital and generous provisions but also provided investors with a summary of the restrictions that had been in place in Pennsylvania before the war but which no longer applied.[24]

While Pennsylvania freed railroads from many antebellum restrictions, the Union war effort pulled the federal government into the affairs of railroads. Gilded Age reformers knew that the federal state offered the best hope for railroad regulation, but early decisions taken by federal policymakers during the Civil War would make their reform strategy more difficult. Simply stated, railroads evaded federal oversight at every turn. Corporate executives remembered the era of state canal boards when legislatures could easily intervene to alter their charters. What's more, limited links between the federal and state governments, together with the fact that the Baltimore and Ohio Railroad controlled virtually all the connections between Washington and the rest of the loyal states, created strong incentives for government action. When the B&O's president, John Garrett, announced that his railroad was a "Southern line" on the eve of the war, the need for federal action seemed all the more pressing.[25]

But though the circumstances might seem to invite government intervention, Northern railroads avoided such actions by seeking a profitable partnership with federal and state policymakers. The first step, as in industrial production as well, revolved around the authority of the corporate charter. Thomas Scott of the Pennsylvania Railroad convened a meeting with several railroad administrators in the governor's office in June 1861 and began with a question: "Is there any provision in the charter of your company making special rates of fare and freight for the transportation of troops and munitions of war, whenever called upon, for the purpose of insurrections or repelling invasions?" When the twenty-one railroad directors claimed that there was no such a provision, Scott authored a resolution that would set the rates for transporting military personnel at a discounted rate, while keeping freight rates at prewar levels. Although eight of the railroad executives balked at his proposal, Scott negotiated a plan for the government to pay railroads two cents per mile for transporting passengers. Since costs averaged 1.8 cents per mile at the outbreak of war, this was a favorable deal for the railroads. Scott served as assistant secretary of war until the summer of 1862. During this period he established a strong precedent of cooperation between railroads and the War Department that avoided any significant regulation of the railroads. When the US House Committee on Government Contracts challenged his policies, Scott argued that wartime traffic strained railroad capacity and disrupted regular service, justifying generous compensation for these companies. Secretary of War Edwin Stanton revised Scott's original toll downward by about 10 percent, but railroads nevertheless retained their favorable rate structure and, more important, their independence throughout the Civil War. As John Clark recently argued, this relationship created "level playing fields with favorable slopes" for Northern railroads.[26]

Even when operating under federal authority, railroad companies found ways to expand and consolidate their economic position. For example, when the War Department assumed control of the middle sections of the Baltimore and Ohio Railroad in 1862 it reconstructed bridges, repaired track, and replaced rolling stock that had been destroyed in several Confederate military actions. As the major east-west trunkline straddling the border between the Union and the Confederacy, the B&O suffered the wrath of Confederate raids throughout the war. Federal seizure was no hardship in this instance. In fact, B&O president John Garrett complained bitterly in 1861 that Secretary of War Simon Cameron neglected his railroad so as to boost traffic on a rival east-west trunkline, the Pennsylvania Railroad. When federal protection of the B&O began in earnest in 1862, the company saw its net receipts grow from $1.8 million in 1861 to $4.4 million, increasing its stock dividends from 6 percent to 7 percent in 1864 and to 8 percent by 1865. More important, the B&O was able to move ahead in several strategic expansion projects. President Garrett embarked upon ambitious plans to build a bridge over the Ohio River, to secure control of the Central Ohio Railroad, which linked the B&O to Columbus, and to pursue a link westward to Chicago. Thomas Scott also used his position as assistant secretary of war and, later, as an informal advisor to the War Department to further the interests of his own railroad. While traveling to appraise western railroad lines for military purposes, Scott met with the presidents of potential acquisitions for the Pennsylvania Railroad and evaluated their postwar potential. One of Scott's biographers noted that "it was no accident that the Pennsylvania Central was the first eastern road to gain control of the tributary lines in the Ohio Valley during the race for railroad empire in reconstruction days," referring to Scott's wartime career not as public service but as an "investment."[27]

Northern railroads of all sizes emerged from the war in generally fantastic shape. One quantitative study of the performance of Northern railroads during the Civil War found that fifty-one of seventy-eight under examination paid high dividends in the war, fifty-one of sixty-seven posted positive gross earnings per mile, and thirty-five of sixty-seven demonstrated an increase in net earnings. Overall, sixty-eight of eighty-seven railroads demonstrated "favorable responses" to the unique conditions of wartime. Most of them never caught a whiff of federal regulation. Those that did benefited from the experience. The Louisville and Nashville Railroad spent much of the Civil War under the effective control of the federal government, proving essential to the success of Sherman's invasion of Georgia in 1864. Serving as an agent of the War Department paid dividends, literally, for the stockholders of the L&N. They earned an impressive 14 percent cash dividend in 1865 as the L&N more than quadrupled its net earnings relative to 1861. More important, the L&N engaged in several strategic expansions during the Civil War and emerged as one of the leaders in reshaping the devastated Southern railroad network. This trend was not lost on industry insiders. "The companies have got out of debt or largely reduced their indebtedness, their earnings are increasing, their dividends have become regular and inviting," the *American Railroad Journal* announced in early 1864. "The past year has been, therefore, the most prosperous ever known to American railways."[28]

Not all economic actors thrived during the Civil War. In Pennsylvania, for example, workers discovered that state-level policy during the war did not work to their benefit. Public officials had rarely intervened in industrial relations in the antebellum years. Any willingness to intercede on behalf of wage earners waned even more so during the Civil War. In 1849 Pennsylvania passed the first in a series of laws that defined miners' wages as the first debts to be paid in the event of a mine operator's bankruptcy, thus placing a "worker's lien" on the mining venture's land, lease, improvements, and property. The lien signaled a willingness to provide some relief for miners in the volatile coal trade. However, attempts to draw the legislature into the cause of mine safety, hospitals for injured miners, or the injustices of the company store system all failed during the 1850s. A pattern evolved by which popular agitation and a barrage of petitions led to a number of rectifying legislative initiatives that were killed by mining interests either outright or in committee. Pennsylvania's public officials, in short, appeared to be sympathetic but were reluctant to undertake action to protect the health and rights of miners. A change of antebellum economic policy might, thus, be a welcome development for Pennsylvania miners. The wartime campaign to raise wages and prohibit mining firms from charging exorbitant rates to workers at company-owned stores marked a distinct divergence from the former refusal to intercede, one that issued from the same emergency contingencies that also released corporate charters from antebellum restrictions.

However, in his annual message to the legislature in January 1863, Governor Curtin argued that "it would be most unwise for the State to interfere at all with the rate of wages" even while he also denounced the company store system as a system "most unwise and unjust" and in need of legislative correction. A bill to eliminate these practices subsequently passed both houses in January of 1864, but Curtin vetoed the law. The veto favored the new mining corporations at the expense of their workers. Wartime institutional contingency, in other words, broke in a different direction vis-à-vis the rights of labor.[29]

When strikes broke out in Pennsylvania's anthracite regions in 1862 and 1863, state officials again sided with corporate interests, effectively using the war to undermine labor organization in the coalfields. Mine operators, many of them newly organized under Pennsylvania's liberal wartime chartering regime, cited violent resistance to the military draft established by the Conscription Act of 1863 to demand that state and federal officials quell the rising power of the miners. Federal provost marshals, together with regular army troops, imposed martial law in mining regions, ostensibly in order to suppress draft rioters. In fact, the presence of federal troops broke the back of the burgeoning miners' unions. This pattern continued after the war as well, state officials often citing wartime precedents to justify their support for large corporations at the expense of working-class organizations. Mine operators sponsored the Coal and Iron Police Act in 1866, for example, which created a quasi-public enforcement agency designed to break strikes and repress labor organization under the pliant guidelines of "protection of private property" and "safeguarding the interests." And just as draft resistance provided the wedge for undermining collective action, the Coal and Iron Police protected property in ways that frustrated the attempts to organize workers at the same pace that corporations were being organized. Even seemingly worker-friendly acts favored the coal companies after the war. In 1868 the legislature passed an eight-hour workday but included a loophole that excluded contracted workers—the vast majority of mine laborers—from the provisions of the act.[30]

How pervasive was corporate power during the Civil War? The creation of the state of West Virginia provides a rare insight into the conventional wisdom guiding wartime policymakers. Western Virginians had long complained that their interests were marginalized in the state's planter-dominated legislature. Old Dominion's secession in April 1861 gave them the chance to change that situation. Unionist politicians gathered at Wheeling in the summer in order to form the "Reorganized Government of Virginia," which denounced the legitimacy of secession, declared loyalty to the Union, and seated members in both the federal House of Representatives and the Senate. In August 1861 the

Reorganized Government passed "An Ordinance to Provide for the Formation of a New State Out of a Portion of the Territory of This State," which would allow Congress to recognize West Virginia two years later when the issue of emancipation was settled. Fifty-three delegates from thirty-nine western Virginia counties met in Wheeling in November of 1861 to draft a constitution for the new state. Hoping to develop long-dormant resources, West Virginia attempted, in the words of one historian, to "borrow an Ohio broom to sweep away Virginian cobwebs." In doing so, they revealed just how much those brooms were under corporate control.[31]

Corporations played a large role in West Virginia's economy from the get-go. At the state's constitutional convention one delegate considered corporations "essential as the sun or the changing seasons almost to our national existence, to our institutions—a part and parcel of our society," which worked for "the benefit of the community" and were therefore undeserving of strict oversight. West Virginia adopted a chartering system modeled on Pennsylvania's blend of general and special charters. General charters were made mandatory for mining and manufacturing operations, but special charters—with a requisite public disclosure of their application in the legislature—were allowed in the case of internal improvements. By 1865 West Virginia was well on its way toward emulating its Northern neighbors, forming corporations with investors from both inside and outside the state. Of the fifty-two general coal-mining charters granted in 1865, forty-four originated in other states. Investors from Philadelphia created twenty of these firms, and Baltimore investors accounted for seven charters, while capitalists from Pittsburgh, Boston, Cincinnati, and Chicago applied for coal-mining charters as well. The median capitalization of the forty-four foreign firms was $300,000, compared to $150,000 for firms organized by West Virginia investors, with the average stock subscription for the former being $5,000 and the latter $2,000. This was not only an indication of the new flexibility given corporations crossing state lines but signaled the reliance of resource-rich, capital-poor states on the financial assets of outside interests. In states hoping to quickly develop their resources at the war's conclusion, there was an important role for out-of-state corporate actors, which would have been highly unlikely in the antebellum decades.[32]

West Virginia also discovered that railroads were central to its postwar economic development. Indeed, they formed the very boundaries of the new state. West Virginia's constitutional convention drew delegates from thirty-nine counties west of the Allegheny Mountains, which constituted the traditional definition of "western Virginia." The Committee on Boundary recommended the addition of thirty-one more counties, including several situated east of the

274 Sean Patrick Adams

Alleghenies. The most controversial of these were Morgan, Berkeley, and Jefferson, which make up West Virginia's "Eastern Panhandle" through which the Baltimore and Ohio Railroad ran. In fact, Waitman Willey claimed that the future of the new state depended upon the B&O Railroad. "It conveys into our center," Willey argued, "or by its ramifications of necessity infuses through the entire body politic of this new State the life-blood of its existence." Keeping the B&O within West Virginia's boundaries became a leading state aim, as did the creation of a friendly environment for further corporate investment. A convention delegate from Parkersburg exhorted in 1861:

> Make a good constitution, under which capital will feel safe, under which capital and enterprise will be encouraged and protected, omitting all this wild folly of trying to use the credit of the State to build railroads into country that can offer them no business until it has been created.

Capital did indeed feel safe in West Virginia, particularly the Baltimore and Ohio Railroad. Henry Gassaway Davis, a Democratic state senator, was appointed to a legislative committee in 1869 charged with negotiating a tax settlement between West Virginia and the B&O Railroad. Davis had sold supplies to both the B&O and the federal government during the war and he ran for office with the railroad's financial support. By keeping B&O president John Garrett updated on the negotiations and distributing free passes to friendly state officials, Davis helped expedite an extremely friendly settlement for the B&O which allowed them to evade paying taxes to West Virginia until the 1880s.[33]

This was a most tangible example of the relationship between states and American capitalism during the Civil War, of policymakers' drive to construct an institutional framework that would attract investment from across the nation, maintain strong ties with important railroads, and abdicate significant regulatory prerogative in the interests of keeping their states "capital-friendly." It also demonstrated how much corporate enterprise now stood at the forefront of American capitalism. Of those Southern states later following West Virginia back into the Union, many explicitly recognized the rights and privileges of corporations. North Carolina, Florida, Texas, and Tennessee all warned against the power of "perpetuities and monopolies" in their postwar constitutions and reserved the right to tax corporations at the same rate as individuals. But even though such antebellum anticorporate rhetoric found some expression in the new wave of constitution-making, regulating provisions limiting the actions of corporate actors were now largely toothless. In fact, the status of corporations in the postbellum South was enhanced. Some states offered limited liability to corporate stockholders for the first time in their history during Reconstruction. Explicitly rejecting their wartime policies, Southern states now generally prohibited state financial support for corporations. Southern policymakers worked to disentangle their states from directly supplying economic aid at the same time that they encouraged industrial development by both domestic and out-of-state corporations, interstate investment made possible by the liberalizations established by Northern states during the Civil War. As Eric Foner notes, "The desire to attract outside capital doomed the Radicals' demand for an ab initio Reconstruction that would wipe away existing state debt and all laws, including corporate charters and railroad land grants, dating from the Confederacy." Providing more leeway for corporations thus became a priority of Southern legislatures during Reconstruction, just as it had been for Northern policymakers during the war.[34]

What was the general significance of the wartime spike in incorporations, the wedding of state treasuries to corporate taxes, and the renewed power and independence of the railroads? This is difficult to summarize in a brief space. The impact of these developments on the next half-century of American capitalism is manifest in the greater size and scope of corporate enterprise and the willingness of states to give those corporations wide latitude in exchange for tax revenue. Railroads, in particular, emerged from the Civil War as a main engine of capitalist development. Wartime events all but guaranteed that they would now function without public oversight. "Capture" best characterizes the relationship between railroads and state governments in Gilded Age America. Charles Francis Adams bemoaned this trend in 1871 when he wrote that several Northern states have "notoriously been controlled by their railroad corporations" and that New York, New Jersey, Pennsylvania, and Maryland had all succumbed to corporate rather than public interests. "Not one of these States owns a mile of railroad," Adams wrote, "and yet it is difficult to conceive of any form of State ownership which would entail greater scandals or political evils than those which now spring from the system in use in them." This system might have had its origins in the rise of corporate capital over the long course of the nineteenth century but it owed much of its distinct institutional shape to the exigencies of the Civil War.[35]

Wartime institutional change at the state level set the stage for the rise of large corporate enterprise in the late nineteenth and early twentieth centuries. Without a doubt, the "producerist" vision of small-scale proprietors continued to resonate with large numbers of Americans throughout the period. Corporations still threatened the political sensibilities of many, as Charles Francis

Adams's remarks suggest. And yet the corporation kept growing in size and strength. When caricaturists and critics depicted Standard Oil as a grasping octopus, for instance, they were simply recycling Jackson's view of the Second Bank as a "many-headed hydra." Both monsters, in the eyes of contemporaries, required a political check on their behavior. Postbellum "monsters," however, dominated the economy, a domination born of wartime circumstances. Railroads needed a few more years to consolidate a national network, but the Civil War years served as an excellent launching point for this endeavor. Even though, as Gerald Berk has convincingly demonstrated, many policymakers continued to favor a regional alternative to the nationally integrated marketplace dominated by interstate railroad corporations, the latter vision would prevail.[36]

This chapter has shown how the Civil War helped put into place the institutional underpinnings of the "bigness" that would come to define the nineteenth century's Era of Big Business. Policymakers at all levels of government had a hand in this process. But for the corporate economy, state-level changes in the North were of the most significance. With our historical vision clouded by the excesses of Gilded Age industrial capitalism, it is difficult to imagine a period when the corporation did not hold sway over the nation's economy. The important institutional changes in wartime state-level political economy, however, suggest that the "soulless monsters" and "iron horses" improved their position in the postwar economy because of the unique challenges faced by states fighting the Civil War.

Acknowledgments

The author would like to thank R. Scott Huffard Jr., Matthew Hall, and Brenden E. Kennedy for their invaluable research assistance on this project, and the fellow authors in this collection for their many helpful hints in revising an early draft of this work. Special thanks go out to Michael Zakim and Gary Kornblith for their energy, vision, and above all, patience, in organizing this volume.

Afterword

Anonymous History

Jean-Christophe Agnew

Capitalism Takes Command is a memorable formulation: striking and appropriately economical. Each word amplifies the con-
notations of force contained in the others: capitalism, takes,
command. A rhetorical multiplier effect, so to speak. But what
kind of capitalism is it that takes command in America's sprawling nineteenth century? And what might "command" mean in
the context of capitalism's tumultuous ascendency during those
years? These are large questions, to which the editors offer their
own provocative answers in the introduction, answers that contributors flesh out in equally striking and original ways. The volume surprises, illuminates, and delights at every turn, and the
turns are many.

Still, a reader stumbling upon a book titled *Capitalism Takes
Command* might be forgiven for thinking immediately of the
speculators, industrialists, and investment bankers who have
swaggered their way through the pages of countless popular and
populist histories of American business, from Charles Francis

Adams's *Chapters of Erie* (1886) through Matthew Josephson's *The Robber Barons* (1934) to H. W. Brands's *American Colossus: The Triumph of Capitalism, 1865–1900* (2010). Vanderbilt, Gould, Rockefeller, Carnegie, and Morgan still cast long shadows in the economic and social history that our textbooks have left us. Yet none of them—or anyone like them—appears in the dramas that animate this volume, not even in cameo. The capitalism that takes command in this volume, we are told, does so invisibly, anonymously.

Here, a reader of a more institutionalist frame of mind would likely turn to another kind of capitalist colossus: the corporation. The modern corporation emerged in the latter half of the nineteenth century, we know, and with it came the strategy and structures its newly minted managerial class devised to reorganize and rationalize resource, labor, and distributive markets. This "managerial revolution" was largely anonymous and invisible, too, at least until the publication of Alfred D. Chandler's *The Visible Hand* in 1977. But while Robert Wright and Sean Adams dramatically recast and reperiodize the history of incorporation in America, they also take care to detach their story, causally speaking, from any post–Civil War transformation in corporate form and function or from any postwar spike in industrial productivity. Whatever impact the war had on sectional economies, it had more to do with the accumulation and disposition of capital than with the logistical or organizational transformation of enterprise itself. The wartime mix of state exigency and business opportunism did not add up to a managerial or a "bourgeois" revolution.

What might "capitalism" and "command" mean, then, in a volume that so conspicuously avoids the classical components of capitalism's story, whether in its entrepreneurial, managerial, or Marxist variants? What, for example, of the separation of labor from the land and of the formation of a working class with nothing to sell but its labor? What of the arrival of a class of *industrial* capitalists ready to take labor on, break its associations, and subject it to the discipline of the machine, the clock, and the factory? What of the active resistance—social, political, cultural—of wage workers, their households, and their communities? What of the labor movement? And what of the courts, the National Guard, and the deputized private police forces of the Gilded Age— state actors dedicated to enforcing the new concepts of property embodied in corporate charters? American labor history in the latter half of the nineteenth century was a conspicuously violent history, one of the bloodiest in the record of industrial capitalism. Yet the din of class conflict is, at most, a distant thunder in what we read here about the coal patches of Civil War Pennsylvania or the muted grumbling of ambitious counter-jumpers in the mercantile houses of New York. Where is the *action* of capitalism, we wonder, and where the commanding heights from which it was directed?

The answer, I suspect, is that there are no heights in this new economic and cultural geography of capitalism. Instead, we are shown something closer to a flatland of ordinary material practices that habituated Americans to the new, systemic rules of capitalism as a market form of life and that did so in ways of which most Americans at the time were only dimly and bemusedly aware. *Capitalism Takes Command*, the editors tell us, takes its inspiration from architectural historian Siegfried Giedion's pathbreaking design history (and prehistory) of industrial capitalism, *Mechanization Takes Command* (1948). And the parallel works brilliantly for this volume as a whole, regardless of whether any particular contributors understood themselves to be writing under the Giedion Aegis.

Giedion subtitled his book "A Contribution to Anonymous History," by which he meant a history that looked past famous architects, engineers, or inventors (the Colossi of Design) in order to understand the impact of quite ordinary devices like bread ovens, washing machines, and barber chairs, the production of which has come to define what we now commonly call the Fordist age. *Mechanization* was a study of the cumulative cultural consequences of "humble things, things not usually granted earnest consideration, or at least things not valued for their historical import." Thanks in part to Giedion's example, though, historians no longer take the vernacular technologies of industrial and consumer capitalism for granted. To the contrary, we now find ourselves awash in cultural biographies of particular consumer devices and technologies.

What we lack, as the editors remind us, are equally attentive, equally nuanced, equally researched social and cultural histories of the financial devices and technologies—the credit, commercial, and corporate "instruments"—by which Americans adapted (and were adapted to) the intensifying capitalization of land, labor, and goods of the nineteenth century. Here is where the contributions to this volume—each one rich and rewarding in its own right— converge to provide a fascinating *tour d'horizon* of what we might call the Great Collateralization: a catchall category for the multifarious legal and commercial instruments that eased the transformation of the United States from a mosaic of familial, proprietary, and conspicuously "landed" capitalisms to a national *system* of industrial capitalism.

To speak of a Great Collateralization is not to point to an event in the conventional sense but to invoke a much longer and complicated historical process—analogous to the iconic epoch of English enclosures, perhaps, yet far more various, creative, and occulted. From Edward Baptist and Jonathan Levy we learn that it was a process as critical to the last years of chattel slavery as it was to the last years of the mixed-farming freehold. If, at moments of panic, collateralization "demolished communities, friendships, relationships, and families" in the slave world, it also remapped kin and familial obligations in modest farm households in the West and in affluent, white Northern communities, where (in Elizabeth Blackmar's words) it steadily "siphoned off a share of family property to corporate investors." The securitization of familial estates and family farms helped spell the end of family capitalism in city and countryside.

Securitization spelled even more than that, though. It also furnished a guilt-edged primer in market epistemology, tutoring its beneficiaries and victims alike in the calculation of opportunity costs. There is, for example, the young Kansas farmwife profiled so memorably in Jonathan Levy's essay. Squeezed by the mortgage and her husband's precarious health, Rosie Ise learned to assess the world inside and outside her farmhouse in terms of the shadow prices of its maintenance. Other farmwives might have been tempted to add their husband's actuarial prospects into their mental calculations. Why? Because, as Levy notes, a single insurance company could end up holding a farm household's mortgage *and* its life insurance policy, a double indemnity for the firm on those occasions when a despairing policyholder took his own life.

How did nineteenth-century Americans express the affective side of these lived contradictions of leverage and loss in the Great Collateralization? The specter of dispossession that haunts Will Carleton's mordant 1881 poem of the farmer-turned-tramp suggests at first a precocious, literary mixture of the gothic and the hard-boiled, with its ghostly figure of the "dark-browed, scowling mortgage" working "the hardest and steadiest of us all." But this reading would miss the poem's moral and sentimental attachment to a patrimonial self, the same manly model of yeoman and householder "independence" that the free-market polemicist of Jeffrey Sklansky's essay—William Leggett—was in earnest to protect a half century earlier.

Will Carleton's farmer, though, has compromised that honor by *allowing* his wife to "die of mortgage." His remorse fuels, even as it hedges, the impotent rage that wells up as he lives and labors before the unflinching, baleful gaze of the mortgage: "It watched us every minute, and it ruled us right and left." Carleton somehow manages to capture just that which escaped Leggett's melodramatic devices and imaginative resources: the cognitive and emotional distillation of a systemic contradiction. What makes Carleton's poem so poignant and so prescient is his pitch-perfect use of the familiar ballad form to express a farmer's experience of defamiliarization: a world turned upside down, a home turned inside out.

Put another way, Carlton's farmer has stumbled upon an economic *system* at work in his life, at work *on* his life. It is a system, to paraphrase Levy, of intermediated obligation as indifferent to kin and community as to the circadian and seasonal rhythms of farm life, yet a system also increasingly exposed to the vicissitudes of an abstracted, national, and international market in commodity and credit capital. Home has become for Carleton's beleaguered husbandman an uncanny space—uncanny, that is, in Freud's sense of *Unheimlich*: a space where the mortgage is at once unfathomably distant and imperiously present, where the debt is both introjected as moral judgment and anthropomorphized as a rogue farmhand, an avatar of the Invisible Hand. The mortgage that came to dinner. The mortgage *who* came to dinner. "It settled down among us, and it never went away."

And of course, "it" never did go away, as this volume attests and as our own experience confirms. So, when Elizabeth Blackmar refers to new, juridically enforced, probate investment models operating as "engines of accumulation," or when Jonathan Levy refers to the farm mortgage as "commanding" the farmer's labor, there is nothing hyperbolic about their metaphors. Quite the contrary, they are figures of thought that capture both the experientially empowering and coercive features of the enforceable testaments, bonds, and other securities that judges, attorneys, bankers, insurance agents, and brokers were thrusting—often in fractal form—into the expanding circuits of commercial capital during America's long nineteenth century. As Levy quotes Rosie Ise on the condition of plains farming: "Nobody's responsible." Anonymous history indeed.

Bankers and brokers, attorneys and accountants—these bland and anonymous historical figures, together with their obliging or insolent clerks—are the captains of consciousness in the sprawling, composite story that this volume tells. Through their good offices—and the material infrastructure of banks, insurance companies, telegraph offices, bonded warehouses, and so on— issued a continuous stream of newly refined property rights, commercial instruments, and economic personae, the sum of which instituted a commercial and financial capital*ism* as the disciplinary and tutelary *system* into which nineteenth-century Americans of all classes were drawn and made over into market subjects.

For most economic historians, the archive is but the warehoused record of behavior and institutions already coded as "economic." But in keeping with the spirit of Siegfried Giedion, Michael Zakim insists that we see this "paperwork"—

and the apparatus that produced it—as something more than the mere detritus of otherwise opaque economic forces, that we see it as a constitutive force of its own. Capitalism, in this account, did not *leave* a trail of these documents; it blazed a trail by means of them: accommodation loans, warehouse notes, slave-based bonds, mortgages, yes, but also penmanship manuals, audit rulebooks, probate instructions, and corporate charters. All of these instruments turn out to have been the utilities, the software or killer apps, so to speak, through which generations of nineteenth-century farmers, workers, merchants, and manufacturers were schooled to a new ideological schema of marketization.

Even before the arrival of business schools and a business press at the turn of the century, then, the institutions of commercial and financial capital had formed a cultural apparatus of their own, an apparatus capable of putting its own scrip(t)s into performance, giving those performances the color of the law, and then (according to Tamara Plakins Thornton) aestheticizing the whole structure—its awesome volatility and order, "chaos and control"—in the romantic idiom of the sublime. To borrow a term from the sociologist Michel Callon, collateralization *reformatted* a society with markets to operate as a market society.

Capital takes command in this account by producing (and performing) the cultural codes in which commands themselves come to be translated into the morally charged vernacular of a transactional lifeworld—partible land, labor, and selfhood. No assembly lines here, then, just the office desk and chair. No time-clocks either, just the mortgage and the metronome. These devices compose what might be called, in Giedion's terms, the "constituent furniture of the nineteenth century." Accordingly, capitalism's arsenal of power—its catalogue of command—looks quite different from our conventionally industrialist views of it. We are no longer talking of the exiguousness of the wage, for example, but of the exigencies of the debt. Not the lockout but the foreclosure. Not the strike but the crash. Not the loud and menacing threats of strikebreakers, but the quiet, almost subliminal maturity dates of securitization. Again: not *industrial* capitalism, but *commercial and financial* capitalisms—the capitalisms that underwrote and eventually overrode the Fordist epoch.

Or did they? Rich and revelatory as these essays are, they do not take up the connections—the articulations, as anthropologists would say—between commercial or credit capital and industrialization as such. This silence might strike a reader of *Mechanization Takes Command* as a bit ironic, considering that the interwar period of the twentieth century (the apogee of Fordism and Bauhaus) was for Siegfried Giedion the historical moment when mechanization finally did take command. But in another, more methodological sense—the sense of anonymous history—this volume keeps faith with Giedion's project: a history of "humble things" in their conjoint and cumulative impact. Humble objects, he wrote, "have shaken our mode of living to its very roots. Modest things of daily life, they accumulate into forces acting upon whoever moves with the orbit of our civilization."

And so it has been with the "paperwork," the office supplies, and the warehouses that have been as much the agents in the history written here as the nameless brokers, bankers, auditors, and clerks who made use of them. By clearing the historiographical landscape of nineteenth-century capitalism of its iconic landmarks and its familiar cast of heroes and villains, *Capitalism Takes Command* enables us to see the systemic and socializing features of commercial and financial capitalism as that system was lived and understood—or misunderstood. A landscape flattened in this manner brings the invisible wiring of a network, a system, and, perhaps, even a culture, into view—like a schematic diagram or flow chart. In its own non-programmatic way, this volume suggests intriguing affinities with recent sociological and ethnographic studies of market machinery and practices produced under the auspices of so-called Actor Network Theory.

Why should scholars in such different disciplines be converging on the same territory and on the same mechanisms of market-making? The "banal objects" and practices of marketization, securitization, financialization? And why is it that our own metaphorical taxonomy of software and hardware or of virtual worlds seems so well fitted to the "constituent furniture" of nineteenth-century credit and capital markets? "History is a magical mirror," Giedion wrote in 1948. "Who peers into it sees his own image in the shape of events and developments." Do we, too, not see and feel the credit collapse of our own moment in nineteenth-century embryo? Edward Baptist's chapter on the financialization of chattel slavery is the only essay to acknowledge this almost spectral sense of continuity with the present crisis or to reflect at any length on the "devastating" damage wrought upon slave "collateral" by an earlier paroxysm in capital markets: the panic of 1837. His reminder could not be more timely, at a moment when Americans are expected to write the collateral damage of market collapse off as mere externalities or neighborhood effects. A perfect storm. A tsunami.

As of this writing, Americans (among others) are still wandering dazedly around the wreckage of the so-called credit bubble, still unwinding their mortgages, still struggling to understand the math and metaphysics of a credit default swap in much the same way that William Leggett and Will Carleton did more than a century ago. Our cultural apparatus—the business press and the cable channel pundits—assures us that "there's enough blame to go around." As a drive-by observation on system failure, the pundits' bromide is unexceptional; but as a historical evaluation of the "asymmetries" of power and responsibility, it is no more than a moral hedge—a self-forgiving translation of Rosie Ise's despairing judgment on the agricultural economy: "Nobody's responsible."

Anonymous history brings into view precisely that which William Leggett's melodramas could not: namely, how economic, social, and cultural practice coalesce into identifiable patterns, structures, and traditions and, at the same time, how those same practices forge the optic through which they become alternately visible or invisible as a system. Mechanization was for Giedion "an agent, like water, fire, light . . . blind and without direction of its own." Capital-ism of whatever kind—mercantile, industrial, financial—cannot be described in the same way, for its blind spots are fitted to the social and political powers served by them; they are part of the cultural formatting, if you will. So, at moments when that formatting goes haywire and a market regime comes into question, we should not be surprised to find the scarcity postulate temporarily suspended in order to effect an equal distribution of blame. What remains to be seen—now as in the nineteenth century—is who will get the credit.

Contributors

Sean Patrick Adams is an associate professor of history at the University of Florida. He is the author of *Old Dominion, Industrial Commonwealth: Coal, Politics, and Economy in Antebellum America* (Baltimore: Johns Hopkins University Press, 2004) and editor of *The Early American Republic: A Documentary History* (Boston: Wiley-Blackwell, 2008), and has published articles in the *Journal of American History*, *Journal of Policy History*, Common-place.org, and other journals. He is currently writing a book on energy transitions and home heating in nineteenth-century America.

Jean-Christophe Agnew is professor of American studies and history at Yale University. He is the author of *Worlds Apart: The Market and the Theater in Anglo-American Thought, 1550–1750* (New York: Cambridge University Press, 1986) and of numerous articles on capitalism and culture.

Edward E. Baptist received his PhD from the University of Pennsylvania. He is the author of *Creating an Old South: Middle Florida's Plantation Frontier Before the Civil War* (Chapel Hill: University of North Carolina Press, 2002), and the coeditor of *New Studies in the History of American Slavery* (Athens: University of Georgia Press, 2006). He is currently writing a history of the expansion of slavery in the United States, titled *The Half That Has Never Been Told*. He teaches in the Department of History at Cornell University.

Elizabeth Blackmar is professor of history at Columbia University and author of *Manhattan for Rent, 1789–1850* (Ithaca. NY: Cornell University Press, 1989) and coauthor, with Roy Rosenzweig, of *The Park and the People: A History of Central Park* (Ithaca, NY: Cornell University Press, 1992). She is currently writing a book on the relation of capital and land in the United States in the nineteenth and twentieth centuries.

Christopher Clark is a professor of history at the University of Connecticut. Among his publications are *The Roots of Rural Capitalism: Western Massachusetts, 1780–1860* (Ithaca: Cornell University Press, 1990), *The Communitarian Moment: The Radical Challenge of the Northampton Association* (Amherst: University of Massachusetts Press, 2003), and *Social Change in America: From the Revolution through the Civil War* (Chicago: Ivan R. Dee, 2006).

Gary J. Kornblith is professor of history at Oberlin College, where he has taught since 1981. He is the author of *Slavery and Sectional Strife in the Early American Republic, 1776–1821* (Lanham, MD: Rowman and Littlefield, 2010), editor of *The Industrial Revolution in America* (Boston: Houghton Mifflin, 1998), and coeditor of *Teaching American History: Essays Adapted from the* Journal of American History, *2001–2007* (Boston: Bedford/St. Martin's, 2009). He has published articles in the *Journal of American History, Journal of the Early Republic,* and *Business History Review,* among other journals, and he has contributed essays to several scholarly collections. With Carol Lasser, he is currently working on *Elusive Utopia: A History of Race in Oberlin, Ohio.*

Jonathan Levy is assistant professor of history at Princeton University. He received his PhD from the University of Chicago and is the author of "Contemplating Delivery: Futures Trading and the Problem of Commodity Exchange in the United States, 1875–1905," *American Historical Review* (2006). He is currently completing *The Ways of Providence: Capitalism, Risk, and Freedom in America, 1840–1920.*

Jeffrey Sklansky is an associate professor of history at the University of Illinois at Chicago. He is the author of *The Soul's Economy: Market Society and Selfhood in American Thought, 1820–1920* (Chapel Hill: University of North Carolina Press, 2002) and editor of the series New Studies in American Intellectual and Cultural History from Johns Hopkins University Press. He is currently writing a book on the "money question"—the long struggle over what should serve as money and how it should be created and controlled—in eighteenth- and nineteenth-century America.

Amy Dru Stanley, a historian at the University of Chicago, is the author of *From Bondage to Contract: Wage Labor, Marriage, and the Market in the Age of Slave Emancipation* (Cambridge: Cambridge University Press, 1998). She is currently working on a book titled "The Passions and the Will in the Age of Slavery and Abolition" (forthcoming, Harvard University Press). Her articles have appeared in the *American Historical Review*, the *Journal of the Early Republic*, and the *Journal of American History*. Ongoing and recent projects explore law, culture, and commodity relations; emancipation and human rights; and American photography after World War II.

Tamara Plakins Thornton is professor of history at the State University of New York, Buffalo. She is the author of *Cultivating Gentlemen: The Meaning of Country Life among the Boston Elite, 1785–1860* (New Haven: Yale University Press, 1989) and *Handwriting in America: A Cultural History* (New Haven: Yale University Press, 1996). Her article, "A 'Great Machine' or a 'Beast of Prey': A Boston Corporation and Its Rural Debtors in an Age of Capitalist Transformation," appeared in the *Journal of the Early Republic* in 2007. She is currently at work on a biography of Nathaniel Bowditch, capitalist and scientist.

Robert E. Wright is the Nef Family Chair of Political Economy at Augustana College in South Dakota, director of the college's Thomas Willing Institute for the Study of Financial Markets, Institutions, and Regulations, and the author of fourteen books on financial history and public policy including, most recently, *The WSJ Guide to the 50 Economic Indicators (That Really Matter)* (New York: HarperCollins, 2011); *Fubarnomics* (Amherst, NY: Prometheus, 2010); *Bailouts* (New York: Columbia University Press, 2009); and *One Nation Under Debt* (New York: McGraw-Hill, 2008).

Michael Zakim teaches history at Tel Aviv University. He is the author of *Ready-Made Democracy: A History of Men's Dress in the American Republic, 1760–1860* (Chicago: University of Chicago Press, 2003) and of a forthcoming study of the business clerk in the nineteenth century entitled *Accounting for Capitalism*.

Notes

Introduction

1. Karl Marx and Friedrich Engels, "Communist Manifesto," in *The Marx-Engels Reader*, ed. Robert C. Tucker, 2nd ed. (New York: Norton, 1978), 477; Ezekiel Bacon, *Recollections of Fifty Years Since* (Utica, NY: R. W. Roberts, 1843), 15, 24–25.

2. "Disorganized" is a paraphrase of Claus Offe, *Disorganized Capitalism: Contemporary Transformations of Work and Politics* (Cambridge, MA: MIT Press, 1985). "Fast property" from Charles Frederick Briggs, *The Adventures of Harry Franco, a Tale of the Great Panic* (New York: F. Saunders, 1839), 16; Alexis de Tocqueville, *Democracy in America*, ed. J. P. Mayer (Garden City, NY: Anchor Books, 1969), 536.

3. Edward Everett, "Accumulation, Property, Capital, and Credit," *Hunt's Merchant's Magazine* 1, no. 1 (1839): 24; Joseph Hopkinson, *Lecture upon the Principles of Commercial Integrity* (Philadelphia: Carey and Lea, 1832), 6–7.

4. John Adams could not have agreed more. In a letter to James Warren in 1777, he wrote that "the medium of trade ought to be as unchangeable as truth, as immutable as morality. The least variation in its value does injustice to multitudes." Paine and Adams in James L. Huston, *Securing the Fruits of Labor: The American Concept of Wealth Distribution* (Baton Rouge: Louisiana

State University Press, 1998), 45. Geoffrey Ingham, "On the Underdevelopment of the 'Sociology of Money,'" *Acta Sociologica* 41, no. 1 (1998): 10–11.

5. "Origins of Industrial Capitalism in Europe" (1920), in *Max Weber: Selections in Translation* (Cambridge: Cambridge University Press, 1978), 333; A. R. Bridbury, "Markets and Freedom in the Middle Ages," in *The Market in History*, ed. B. L. Anderson and A.J.H. Latham (London: Croom Helm, 1986), 105–10; Karl Polanyi, "Our Obsolete Market Mentality," in *Primitive, Archaic, and Modern Economies*, ed. George Dalton (Boston: Beacon Press, 1968), 65.

6. Joyce Appleby has consistently argued against this tendency. See, for instance, *Capitalism and a New Social Order: The Republican Vision of the 1790s* (New York: NYU Press, 1984) and, more recently, *The Relentless Revolution: A History of Capitalism* (New York: Norton, 2010). Significantly, too, social and labor histories that emphasized gender dynamics consistently revealed a more complex, and ambivalent, relationship between class consciousness and progressive politics. See, for instance, Mary Blewett, *Men, Women, and Work: Class, Gender, and Protest in the New England Shoe Industry, 1780–1910* (Urbana: University of Illinois Press, 1988), and Elizabeth Blackmar, *Manhattan for Rent, 1785–1850* (Ithaca, NY: Cornell University Press, 1989).

7. Charles Grier Sellers, *The Market Revolution: Jacksonian America, 1815–1846* (New York: Oxford University Press, 1991).

8. Ibid., 4. For an exemplary study of capital as a historical subject, see William Cronon, *Nature's Metropolis: Chicago and the Great West* (New York: Norton, 1991).

9. Siegfried Giedion, *Mechanization Takes Command: A Contribution to Anonymous History* (New York: Oxford University Press, 1948), 14, 42–43, 714, 716.

10. George Simmel, *The Philosophy of Money*, ed. David Frisby (London: Routledge, 1990), 103.

Chapter 1

1. Alan L. Olmstead, "Introduction," chapter Da of *Historical Statistics of the United States, Earliest Times to the Present: Millennial Edition,* ed. Susan B. Carter et al. (Cambridge: Cambridge University Press, 2006), http://dx.doi.org/10.1017/ISBN-9780511132971.Da.ESS.01; for number of farms, series Da 93. James Belich, *Replenishing the Earth: The Settler Revolution and the Rise of the Anglo-World, 1783–1939* (Oxford: Oxford University Press, 2009).

2. Farmers adapting to markets did not necessarily "specialize" in fewer crops; sometimes the variety increased. See Mary Eschelbach Gregson, "Rural Response to Increased Demand: Crop Choice in the Midwest, 1860–1880," *Journal of Economic History* 53 (1993): 332–45.

3. Bruce L. Gardner, *American Agriculture in the Twentieth Century: How It Flourished and What It Cost* (Cambridge: Harvard University Press, 2002).

4. On farm productivity after the 1920s see Sally H. Clarke, *Regulation and the Revolution in United States Farm Productivity* (Cambridge: Cambridge University Press, 1994), 3–6, 50–82. Carter et al., eds., *Historical Statistics of the United States*, series Da1144, shows that it took 2.61 times longer to produce a bushel of corn in 1800 than it did in 1915–19, but 44 times as long in 1915–19 than it would in 1982–86.

5. David Danbom, *Born in the Country: A History of Rural America* (Baltimore: Johns Hopkins University Press, 1995), 42–44, notes that "it is important to remember that, while they participated in markets, farmers were not market driven in the way their modern counterparts are." On twentieth-century agricultural change, see Paul K. Conkin, *A Revolution Down on the Farm: The Transformation of American Agriculture since 1929* (Lexington: University Press of Kentucky, 2008), chap. 1.

6. Susan A. Mann, *Agrarian Capitalism in Theory and Practice* (Chapel Hill: University of North Carolina Press, 1990), discusses the constraints upon wage labor in farming.

7. William Appleman Williams, *The Roots of the Modern American Empire: A Study of the Growth and Shaping of Social Consciousness in a Marketplace Society* (New York: Random House, 1969), argues that the nineteenth century's rural majority was a key force behind US territorial expansion, the development of markets, and, subsequently, the search for overseas influence to sustain markets.

8. Richard White, *The Middle Ground: Indians, Empires and Republics in the Great Lakes Region, 1650–1815* (Cambridge: Cambridge University Press, 1991), chap. 3.

9. Quoted by Alan Taylor, "Land and Liberty on the Post-Revolutionary Frontier," in *Devising Liberty: Preserving and Creating Freedom in the New American Republic*, ed. David Thomas Konig (Stanford, CA: Stanford University Press, 1995), 83. On popular demand for land, see Allan Kulikoff, *From British Peasants to Colonial American Farmers* (Chapel Hill: University of North Carolina Press, 2000); on unequal access to it, see Charles Post, "The Agrarian Origins of US Capitalism: The Transformation of the Northern Countryside before the Civil War," *Journal of Peasant Studies* 22 (1995): 415–19, 423–27; David F. Weiman, "Peopling the Land by Lottery?: The Marketing of Public Lands and the Regional Differentiation of Territory on the Georgia Frontier," *Journal of Economic History* 51 (1991): 835–60.

10. Arturo Warman, *Corn and Capitalism: How a Botanical Bastard Grew to Global Dominance*, trans. Nancy L. Westrate (Chapel Hill: University of North Carolina Press, 2003), 192.

11. *Baltimore Sun*, September 30, 1871.

12. George R. Wickham, *Sixty-Two Years of the Homestead Law*, 68th Cong. 1st. Sess., Senate Doc. No. 113 (Washington, DC, 1924).

13. Russell R. Menard, "Colonial America's Mestizo Agriculture," in *The Economy of Early America: Historical Perspectives and New Directions*, ed. Cathy Matson (University Park: Pennsylvania State University Press, 2006), chap. 3. See also Lorena S. Walsh, *Motives of Honor, Pleasure, and Profit: Plantation Management in the Colonial Chesapeake, 1607–1763* (Chapel Hill: University of North Carolina Press, 2010).

14. Timothy R. Mahoney, *River Towns in the Great West: The Structure of Provincial Urbanization in the American Midwest, 1820–1870* (Cambridge: Cambridge University Press, 1990); David L. Carlton, "Antebellum Southern Urbanization," in *The South, the Nation, and the World: Perspectives on Southern Economic Development*, ed. David L. Carlton and Peter A. Coclanis (Charlottesville: University of Virginia Press, 2003), 35–48. Contrast Christopher Morris, *Becoming Southern: The Evolution of a Way of Life: Warren County and Vicksburg, Mississippi, 1760–1860* (New York: Oxford University Press, 1995), on Vicksburg's growth as a commercial center, with David F. Weiman, "Urban Growth on the Periphery of the Antebellum Cotton Belt: Atlanta, 1847–1860," *Journal of Economic History* 48 (1988): 259–72, on the constraints upon Atlanta's emergence as a regional metropolis.

15. On small farmers in plantation regions, see Stephanie McCurry, *Masters of Small Worlds: Yeoman Households, Gender Relations, and the Political Culture of the Antebellum South Carolina Low Country* (New York: Oxford University Press, 1995). On nonplantation regions, see Steven Hahn, *The Roots of Southern Populism: Yeoman Farmers and the Transformation of the Georgia Upcountry* (New York: Oxford University Press, 1983), part 1; and David F. Weiman, "Farmers and the Market in Antebellum America: A View from the Georgia Upcountry," *Journal of Economic History* 47 (1987): 627–47.

16. John D. Majewski, *A House Dividing: Economic Development in Pennsylvania and Virginia before the Civil War* (Cambridge: Cambridge University Press, 2000).

17. Carville Earle and Ronald Hoffman, "The Foundation of the Modern Economy: Agriculture and the Costs of Labor in the United States and England, 1800–1860," *American Historical Review* 85 (1980): 1055–94.

18. Christopher Clark, "Social Structure and Manufacturing before the Factory: Rural New England, 1750–1830," in *The Workplace before the Factory: Artisans and Proletarians, 1500–1800*, ed. Thomas Max Safley and Leonard N. Rosenband (Ithaca, NY: Cornell University Press, 1993), chap. 1.

19. David R. Meyer, *The Roots of American Industrialization* (Baltimore: Johns Hopkins University Press, 2003), chaps. 2, 3, and 6.

20. Richard Perren, *Taste, Trade, and Technology: The Development of the International Meat Industry since 1840* (Aldershot: Ashgate, 2006).

21. Tamara Plakins Thornton, "'A Great Machine' or a 'Beast of Prey': A Boston Corporation and Its Rural Debtors in the Age of Capitalist Transformation," *Journal of the Early Republic* 27 (2007): 567–97. See also Glenn H. Miller Jr., "The Hawkes Papers: A Case Study of a Kansas Mortgage Brokerage Business, 1871–1888," *Business History Review* 32 (1958): 293–310.

22. William Cronon, *Nature's Metropolis: Chicago and the Great West* (New York: W. W. Norton, 1991); Jonathan Ira Levy, "Contemplating Delivery: Futures Trading and the Problem of Commodity Exchange in the United States, 1875–1905," *American Historical Review* 111 (2006): 307–35; David S. Jacks, "Populists versus Theorists: Futures Markets and the Volatility of Prices," *Explorations in Economic History* 44 (2007): 342–62.

23. Eric Rauchway, *Blessed Among Nations: How the World Made America* (New York: Hill and Wang, 2006).

24. Avner Offer, *The First World War: An Agrarian Interpretation* (Oxford: Oxford University Press, 1989), part 2.

25. Price V. Fishback et al., eds., *Government and the American Economy: A New History* (Chicago: University of Chicago Press, 2007); Donald J. Pisani, *Water and American Government: The Reclamation Bureau, National Water Policy, and the West, 1902–1935* (Berkeley: University of California Press, 2002).

26. William H. Bergmann, "'A Commercial View of This Unfortunate War': Economic Roots of an American National State in the Ohio Valley, 1775–1795," *Early American Studies* 6 (2008): 137–64.

27. On European land hunger and early American expansion, see Kulikoff, *From British Peasants to Colonial American Farmers*, and Williams, *The Roots of the Modern American Empire*.

28. Francois Furstenberg, "The Significance of the Trans-Appalachian Frontier in Atlantic History," *American Historical Review* 113 (2008): 643–77; Alan Taylor, *The Divided Ground: Indians, Settlers, and the Northern Borderland of the American Revolution* (New York: Knopf, 2006).

29. On regional distinctions, see W. T. Easterbrook, *North American Patterns of Growth and Development: The Continental Context* (Toronto: University of Toronto Press, 1990); Marc Egnal, *Divergent Paths: How Culture and Institutions Have Shaped North American Growth* (New York: Oxford University Press, 1996); Peter A. Coclanis, "The Paths before Us/US: Tracking the Economic Divergence of the North and the South," in *The South, the Nation, and the World*, ed. Carlton and Coclanis, 12–23.

30. Gavin Wright, *Slavery and American Economic Growth* (Baton Rouge: Louisiana State University Press, 2006).

31. Jan Lewis, "The Problem of Slavery in Southern Political Discourse," in *Devising Liberty*, ed. Konig, 278; Alexis de Tocqueville, *Democracy in America*, trans. Henry Reeve, 3rd ed., 2 vols. (Cambridge, MA, 1863), 1:464–67; Alfred Tischendorf and E. Taylor Parks, eds., *The Diary and Journal of Richard Clough Anderson, Jr., 1814–1826* (Durham, NC: Duke University Press, 1964), 68.

32. Robin L. Einhorn, *American Taxation, American Slavery* (Chicago: University of Chicago Press, 2006).

33. Michael Merrill, "Cash Is Good to Eat: Self-Sufficiency and Exchange in the Rural Economy of the United States," *Radical History Review* 3 (1977): 42–71; James A. Henretta, "Families and Farms: *Mentalité* in Pre-Industrial America," *William and Mary Quarterly* 35 (1978): 3–32; Post, "Agrarian Origins of US Capitalism," reviews the ensuing literature. See also Richard Lyman Bushman, "Markets and Composite Farms in Early America," *William and Mary Quarterly* 55 (1998): 351–74.

34. Samuel G. Goodrich, *Recollections of a Lifetime, Or Men and Things I Have Seen* (New York, 1856), 1:75–76; Hans Huth and Wilma J. Pugh, eds., *Talleyrand in America as a Financial Promoter, 1794–96: Unpublished Letters and Memoirs* (1942; reprint ed., New York: DaCapo Press, 1971).

35. Daniel Vickers, "Competency and Competition: Economic Culture in Early America," *William and Mary Quarterly* 47 (1990): 3–29; Vickers, *Farmers and Fishermen: Two Centuries of Work in Essex County, Massachusetts, 1630–1830* (Chapel Hill: University of North Carolina Press, 1994).

36. Vickers, "Competency and Competition"; Christopher Clark, *The Roots of Rural Capitalism: Western Massachusetts, 1780–1860* (Ithaca, NY: Cornell University Press, 1990), chap. 2; Martin Bruegel, "Uncertainty, Pluriactivity, and Neighborhood Exchange in the Rural Hudson Valley in the Late Eighteenth Century," *New York History* (July 1996): 245–72; Christopher Clark, "The Ohio Country in the Political Economy of Nation Building," in *The Center of a Great Empire: The Ohio Country in the Early Republic*, ed. Andrew R. L. Cayton and Stuart D. Hobbs (Athens: Ohio University Press, 2005), 147, 151, 153–55; Richard F. Nation, *At Home in the Hoosier Hills: Agriculture, Politics, and Religion in Southern Indiana, 1810–1870* (Bloomington: Indiana University Press, 2005); Melvin Patrick Ely, *Israel on the Appomattox: A Southern Experiment in Black Freedom from the 1790s through the Civil War* (New York: Knopf, 2004); Timothy J. Lockley, "Trading Encounters between Non-Elite Whites and African Americans in Savannah, 1790–1860," *Journal of Southern History* 66 (2000): 25–48.

37. Alan L. Olmstead and Paul W. Rhode, "Beyond the Threshold: An Analysis of the Character and Behavior of Early Reaper Adopters," *Journal of Economic History* 55 (1995): 27–57.

38. Anthony E. Kaye, *Joining Places: Slave Neighborhoods in the Old South* (Chapel Hill: University of North Carolina Press, 2007), chap. 4.

39. Nancy Beadie, "Education and the Creation of Capital, Or What I Have Learned from Following the Money," *History of Education Quarterly* 48 (2008): 1–29; J. M. Opal, *Beyond the Farm: National Ambitions in Rural New England* (Philadelphia: University of Pennsylvania Press, 2008); Johann N. Neem, *Creating a Nation of Joiners: Democracy and Civil Society in Early National Massachusetts* (Cambridge: Harvard University Press, 2008).

40. On "market discipline," see Post, "Agrarian Origins of US Capitalism," 394–95, 415–23, 426–28.

41. Tony Freyer, *Producers versus Capitalists: Constitutional Conflict in Antebellum America* (Charlottesville: University Press of Virginia, 1994); B. Zorina Khan, "'Justice of the Market-

place': Legal Disputes and Economic Activity on America's Northeastern Frontier, 1700–1860," *Journal of Interdisciplinary History* 39 (2008): 1–35; Naomi R. Lamoreaux, "Rethinking the Transition to Capitalism in the Early American Northeast," *Journal of American History* 90 (2003–4): 437–61.

42. Martin Bruegel, *Farm, Shop, Landing: The Rise of a Market Society in the Hudson Valley, 1780–1860* (Durham, NC: Duke University Press, 2002), 67–68, discusses market regulations. On bankruptcy, see Edward Balleisen, *Navigating Failure: Bankruptcy and Commercial Society in Antebellum America* (Chapel Hill: University of North Carolina Press, 2001), especially chaps. 3 and 4.

43. "The Travel Diary of James Guild," *Proceedings of the Vermont Historical Society* 5 (1937): 250–313.

44. Tischendorf and Parks, ed., *Diary and Journal of Richard Clough Anderson*, 42–43; Naomi R. Lamoreaux, *Insider Lending: Banks, Personal Connections, and Economic Development in Industrial New England* (Cambridge: Cambridge University Press, 1994); Thornton, "'A Great Machine.'"

45. A. Glenn Crothers, "Banks and Economic Development in Post-Revolutionary Northern Virginia," *Business History Review* 73 (1999): 1–39.

46. Ruth Wallis Herndon and John E. Murray, eds., *Children Bound to Labor: The Pauper Apprentice System in Early America* (Ithaca, NY: Cornell University Press, 2009); Carol Shammas, *A History of Household Government in America* (Charlottesville: University of Virginia Press, 2002), 31, estimates the proportion of "dependents" in the colonial population.

47. Evsey D. Domar, "The Causes of Slavery or Serfdom: A Hypothesis," *Journal of Economic History* 30 (1970): 18–32.

48. Theodore Rosengarten, *All God's Dangers: The Life of Nate Shaw* (New York: Avon, 1974), 39, 55. On sharecroppers' children's labor: Dylan C. Penningroth, "The Claims of Slaves and Ex-Slaves to Family and Property: A Transatlantic Comparison," *American Historical Review* 112 (2007): 1039–69; Amy Dru Stanley, *From Bondage to Contract: Wage Labor, Marriage, and the Market in the Age of Slave Emancipation* (Cambridge: Cambridge University Press, 1998).

49. Donald Worster, *A Passion for Nature: The Life of John Muir* (New York: Oxford University Press, 2008), 55.

50. *Philadelphia Inquirer*, September 28, 1878.

51. Harriet Friedmann, "World Market, State, and Family Farm: Social Bases of Household Production in the Era of Wage Labor," *Comparative Studies in Society and History* 20 (1978): 545–86, discusses the continued importance of family labor. See also Anne B. W. Effland, "Agrarianism and Child Labor Policy for Agriculture," *Agricultural History* 79 (2005): 281–97.

52. Gavin Wright, "American Agriculture and the Labor Market: What Happened to Proletarianization?" *Agricultural History* 62 (1988): 182–209.

53. Victoria Saker Woeste, *The Farmer's Benevolent Trust: Law and Agricultural Cooperation in Industrial America, 1865–1945* (Chapel Hill: University of North Carolina Press, 1998).

54. Robert B. Campbell, "Newlands, Old Lands: Native American Labor, Agrarian Ideology, and the Progressive-Era State in the Making of the Newlands Reclamation Project, 1902–1926," *Pacific Historical Review* 71 (2002): 203–38; Kate Brown, "Gridded Lives: Why Kazakhstan and Montana Are Nearly the Same Place," *American Historical Review* 106 (2001): 17–48.

55. Lee A. Craig and Thomas Weiss, "Hours at Work and Total Factor Productivity Growth

in Nineteenth-Century U.S. Agriculture," *Advances in Agricultural Economic History* 1 (2000): 1–30; Alan L. Olmstead and Paul W. Rhode, *Creating Abundance: Biological Innovation and American Agricultural Development* (Cambridge: Cambridge University Press, 2008).

56. Terry Bouton, *Taming Democracy: "The People," the Founders, and the Troubled Ending of the American Revolution* (New York: Oxford University Press, 2007); Woody Holton, *Unruly Americans and the Origins of the Constitution* (New York: Hill and Wang, 2007); Robert A. Gross, "A Yankee Rebellion: The Regulators, New England, and the New Nation," *New England Quarterly* 82 (2009): 112–35.

57. Stuart Banner, *How the Indians Lost Their Land: Law and Power on the Frontier* (Cambridge: Harvard University Press, 2005).

58. Brendan McConville, *These Daring Disturbers of the Public Peace: The Struggle for Property and Power in Early New Jersey* (Ithaca, NY: Cornell University Press, 1999); Alan Taylor, *Liberty-Men and Great Proprietors: The Revolutionary Settlement on the Maine Frontier, 1760–1820* (Chapel Hill: University of North Carolina Press, 1990); Reeve Huston, *Land and Freedom: Rural Society, Popular Protest and Party Politics in Antebellum New York* (New York: Oxford University Press, 2000); Thomas Summerhill, *Harvest of Dissent: Agrarianism in Nineteenth-Century New York* (Urbana: University of Illinois Press, 2005).

59. Taylor, "Land and Liberty on the Post-Revolutionary Frontier," in *Devising Liberty*, ed. Konig, 83, 87.

60. Abraham Lincoln to Henry L. Pierce and others, April 6, 1859, in *The Collected Works of Abraham Lincoln*, ed. Roy P. Basler, 8 vols. (New Brunswick, NJ: Rutgers University Press, 1953), 3:375. See Eric Foner, *Free Soil, Free Labor, Free Men: The Ideology of the Republican Party before the Civil War* (New York: Oxford University Press, 1970).

61. Mathew Carey, *Essays on Political Economy* (1822; reprint ed., New York: A. M. Kelley, 1968), 72, 97–98; Henry C. Carey, *The Past, the Present, and the Future* (Philadelphia, 1847); Henry Carey, *The North and the South* (New York, 1854). In January 1861 Henry Carey wrote to President-elect Abraham Lincoln urging him to pass a tariff law and criticizing the proposed Homestead bill as an antiprotectionist policy; Abraham Lincoln Papers, Library of Congress.

62. Michael A. Morrison, *Slavery and the American West: The Eclipse of Manifest Destiny and the Coming of the Civil War* (Chapel Hill: University of North Carolina Press, 1997).

63. James L. Huston, *Calculating the Value of the Union: Slavery, Property Rights, and the Economic Origins of the Civil War* (Chapel Hill: University of North Carolina Press, 2003), 26–30.

64. David W. Blight, *Race and Reunion: The Civil War in American Memory* (Cambridge: Harvard University Press, 2001).

65. Frederick Jackson Turner, "The Significance of the Frontier in American History," paper presented to the American Historical Association, Chicago, July 12, 1893, inspired by population density data reported from the 1890 federal census.

66. Zeynep K. Hansen and Gary D. Libecap, "The Allocation of Property Rights to Land: US Land Policy and Farm Failure in the Northern Great Plains," *Explorations in Economic History* 41 (2004): 103–29.

67. "Free Homesteads for Settlers," *Report of Frank M. Eddy*, 56th Cong. 1st. Sess., House Report No. 195 (Washington, DC, 1900).

68. Silvana R. Siddali, "'Must We Not *Punish* to *Conquer*?': The Militant Northern Home Front and the Early Development of Hard War Ideas," *North and South* 8 (2005): 46–56; Siddali, *From Property to Person: Slavery and the Confiscation Acts, 1861–1862* (Baton Rouge: Louisiana State University Press, 2005).

69. Steven Hahn, *A Nation Under Our Feet: Black Political Struggles in the Rural South from Slavery to the Great Migration* (Cambridge: Harvard University Press, 2003), 127–46; Eric Foner, *Forever Free: The Story of Emancipation and Reconstruction* (New York: Knopf, 2005). See also Elizabeth D. Leonard, *Men of Color to Arms! Black Soldiers, Indian Wars, and the Quest for Equality* (New York: W. W. Norton, 2010).

70. "Homesteads—Report of Mr Julian," 40th Cong. 2nd Sess., House Report no. 25 (1868); "Resolution of the Legislature of Kansas," 40th Cong., 3rd Sess., Senate Misc. Doc. no. 35 (1869); "Memorial of the Legislature of Minnesota Relating to Homestead Entries," 41st Cong., 2nd Sess., House Misc. Doc. no. 117 (1870); "Petition of Citizens of the Des Moines Valley, Iowa," 41st Cong. 3rd Sess., Senate Misc. Doc. no. 49 (1871); "Memorial of the Legislature of Minnesota Relating to Soldiers' Homesteads," 42nd Cong., 2nd Sess., House Misc. Doc. no. 162 (1872); "Resolution of the Legislature of Iowa," 43rd Cong. 1st Sess., Senate Misc. Doc. no. 72 (1874); "Settlers on the Public Lands," 45th Cong. 2nd Sess., House Report no. 704 (1878).

71. James Bradford Olcott, "Third Prize Paper, No. 25," in Committee on Better Roads, *A Move for Better Roads: Essays on Roadmaking and Maintenance and Road Laws*, comp. Lewis M. Haupt (Philadelphia, 1891), 141.

72. Matthew Hild, *Greenbackers. Knights of Labor, and Populists: Farmer-Labor Insurgency in the Late-Nineteenth-Century South* (Athens: University of Georgia Press, 2007); Charles Postel, *The Populist Vision* (New York: Oxford University Press, 2007); Robert C. McMath et al., "Roundtable on Populism," *Agricultural History* 82 (2008): 1–35.

73. Jim Bissett, "Socialism from the Bottom Up: Local Activists and the Socialist Party of Oklahoma, 1900–1920," *Chronicles of Oklahoma* 82 (2004–5): 388–411; William C. Pratt, "Historians and the Lost World of Kansas Radicalism," *Kansas History* 30 (2007–8): 270–91.

74. Naomi R. Lamoreaux, Daniel M. G. Raff, and Peter Temin, "Beyond Markets and Hierarchies: Towards a New Synthesis of American Business History," *American Historical Review* 108 (2003): 404–33; Louis D. Johnston, "The Growth of the Service Sector in Historical Perspective: Explaining Trends in US Sectoral Output and Employment, 1840–1990," paper presented at the Economic History Association, New Brunswick, NJ, September 1997.

75. Roy V. Scott, *The Reluctant Farmer: The Rise of Agricultural Extension to 1914* (Urbana: University of Illinois Press, 1971).

76. Jane H. Adams, "The Decoupling of Farm and Household: The Differential Consequences of Capitalist Development on Southern Illinois and Third World Family Farms," *Comparative Studies in Society and History* 30 (1988): 453–82.

77. On migration: Patricia Kelly Hall and Steven Ruggles, "'Restless in the Midst of Their Prosperity': New Evidence on the Internal Migration of Americans, 1850–2000," *Journal of American History* 91 (2004–5): 829–46; Robert L. Boyd, "'A Migration of Despair': Unemployment, the Search for Work, and Migration to Farms during the Great Depression," *Social Science History* 83 (2002): 554–67; Luther Adams, "'Headed for Louisville': Rethinking Rural-Urban Migration in the South, 1930–1950," *Journal of Social History* 40 (2006–7): 407–30. On nonfarm employment see Shane L. Hamilton, *Trucking Country: The Road to America's Wal-Mart Economy* (Princeton, NJ: Princeton University Press, 2008).

Chapter 2

1. On the western farm mortgage market, see Kenneth A. Snowden, "The Evolution of Interregional Mortgage Lending Channels, 1870–1940: The Life Insurance-Mortgage Company Connection," in *Coordination and Information: Historical Perspectives on the Organization*

of Enterprise, ed. Naomi Lamoreaux and Daniel Raff (Chicago: University of Chicago Press, 1996), 209–47; Snowden, "Mortgage Securitization in the U.S.: 20th Century Developments in Historical Perspective," in *Anglo-American Financial Systems: Institutions and Markets in the Twentieth Century,* ed. M. Bordo and R. Sylla (New York: New York University Press, 1995), 261–98; Allan G. Bogue, *Money at Interest: The Farm Mortgage on the Middle Border* (Ithaca, NY: Cornell University Press, 1955); Lance Davis and Robert Gallman, *Evolving Financial Markets and International Capital Flows: Britain, the Americas, and Australia, 1865–1914* (Cambridge: Cambridge University Press, 2001), chap. 2; Lance E. Davis, "The Investment Market, 1870–1914: The Evolution of a National Market," *Journal of Economic History* 25, no. 3 (September 1965): 355–99; Robert F. Stevenson et al., "Mortgage Borrowing as Frontier Development," *Journal of Economic History* 36 (1966): 147–68; H. Peers Brewer, "Eastern Money and Western Mortgages in the 1870s," *Business History Review* 50, no. 3 (Autumn 1976): 356–80.

2. *Report on Real Estate Mortgages in the United States at the Eleventh Census: 1890* (Washington, DC, 1895), 315–23, table 104.

3. This sense is confirmed by economic historians. See Jeremy Atack, Fred Bateman, and William N. Parker, "The Farm, the Farmer, and the Market," in *The Cambridge Economic History of the United States,* ed. Stanley L. Engerman and Robert E. Gallman, vol. 2, *The Long Nineteenth Century* (New York: Cambridge University Press, 2000), 254–84. William Parker elsewhere wrote that after 1870 a "bridge was burned" in American agriculture. William N. Parker, "The True History of the Northern Farmer," in *Europe, America and the Wider World: Essays on the History of Western Capitalism,* vol. 2, *America and the Wider World* (New York: Cambridge University Press, 1991), 172. Gavin Wright adds that after 1870 "American farmers were increasingly constrained by market forces." Gavin Wright, "American Agriculture and the Labor Market: What Happened to Proletarianization?" *Agricultural History* 62, no. 3 (Summer 1998): 185.

4. See Clarence Danhoff, *Change in Agriculture: The Northern United States, 1820–1870* (Cambridge: Harvard University Press, 1969). The subsequent debate concerning the relative commercial orientation of antebellum American farmers is extensive and too lengthy to fully cite. Something like a consensus on the liminal state emphasized by Danhoff, somewhere between a way of life and a capitalist enterprise, is evident in a convergence in the works of economists Jeremy Atack and Fred Bateman, *To Their Own Soil: Agriculture in the Antebellum North* (Ames: Iowa State University Press, 1987) and the historian Alan Kulikoff, *The Agrarian Origins of American Capitalism* (Charlottesville: University of Virginia Press, 1992). See also, and for a review of the literature, Naomi R. Lamoreaux, "Rethinking the Transition to Capitalism in the Early Northeast," *Journal of American History* 90, no. 2 (September 2003): 437–61.

5. B. C. Keeler, *Where to Go to Become Rich* (Chicago, 1880). See also Charles Postel, *The Populist Vision* (New York: Oxford University Press, 2007), 24–44. Parker refers to the prototype of the "Yankee" versus the "peasant." Parker, "True History of the Northern Farmer," 161.

6. On the immigrant experience and western farming, see Kathleen Neils Conzen, *Making Their Own America: Assimilation Theory and the German Peasant Pioneer* (New York: Berg, 1990); Conzen, "Immigrants in Nineteenth-Century Agricultural History," in *Agriculture and National Development,* ed. Lou Ferleger (Ames: Iowa University Press, 1990), 303–42; Walter D. Kamphoefner, *The Westfalians: From Germany to Missouri* (Princeton, NJ: Princeton University Press, 1987); John Gjerde, *The Minds of the West: Ethnocultural Evolution in the Rural Middle West, 1830–1917* (Chapel Hill: University of North Carolina, 1997).

7. Ise published his memoir in dramatized form, in the third person, constructed from

three sources: his own memory, a series of oral histories taken from his mother, and research he conducted between 1924 and 1932 on central western Kansas in the late nineteenth century. Ises's contemporary editor, Von Rothenberger, has researched and confirmed the factual outline of the account, including such details as the 1887 mortgage. After researching John Ise's papers at the University of Kansas and verifying the "authenticity of Ise's notes and sources," Rothenberger concludes that *Sod and Stubble* is a "work of astonishing historical accuracy." See John Ise, *Sod and Stubble: The Story of a Kansas Homestead* (Lawrence: University Press of Kansas, 1996), xvii.

8. Ise, *Sod and Stubble*, 229, 268, 53.

9. *Report on Real Estate Mortgages*, 26.

10. See Tamara Plakins Thornton, "'A Great Machine' or a 'Beast of Prey': A Boston Corporation and Its Rural Debtors in an Age of Capitalist Transformation," *Journal of the Early Republic* 27, no. 4 (Winter 2007): 567–97.

11. Ise, *Sod and Stubble*, 254.

12. Barry Eichengreen, "Interest Rates in the Populist Era," *American Economic Review* 74, no. 5 (December 1984): 995–1015.

13. On land values, see Peter H. Lindert, "Long-Run Trends in American Farmland Values," *Agricultural History* 62 (1988): 45–85. For a positive account of the western farmer's market position, see Douglass North, *Growth and Welfare in the American Past* (New York: Prentice-Hall, 1966), chap. 8.

14. The touchstone work for an interpretation that centers on populist farmers' discomfort with market uncertainty is Anne Mayhew, "A Reappraisal of the Causes of Farm Protest Movements in the United States, 1870–1900," *Journal of Economic History* 32 (June 1972): 464–75. See also Robert McGuire, "Economic Causes of Late Nineteenth-Century Agrarian Unrest: New Evidence," *Journal of Economic History* 41 (December 1981): 835–52; James A. Stock, "Real Estate Mortgages, Foreclosures, and Midwestern Agrarian Unrest, 1865–1920," *Journal of Economic History* 44 (March 1984): 89–106.

15. According to H. W. Chaplin in 1890: "As it reads upon the records in Boston and in Portland, so it read in England in the thirteenth century." H. W. Chaplin, "The Story of Mortgage Law," *Harvard Law Review* 4, no. 1 (1890): 9. Robert C. Allen, *Enclosure and the Yeoman: The Agricultural Development of the South Midlands, 1450–1850* (Oxford: Clarendon Press, 1992); Allan Kulikoff, *From British Peasants to Colonial American Farmers* (Chapel Hill: University of North Carolina Press, 2000).

16. On land banks and resistance to specialization, see Mary M. Schweitzer, *Custom and Contract: Household, Government, and the Economy in Colonial Pennsylvania* (New York: Columbia University Press, 1987), chap. 4 and p. 65.

17. See Thornton, "'Great Machine' or 'Beast of Prey'"; Benjamin Hibbard, *A History of Public Land Policies* (New York, 1924).

18. Henry David Thoreau, *Walden: Or, Life in the Woods* (1854; New York: Knopf, 1992), 29, 5, 50. It was no accident Thoreau inquired at the tax assessor's. The need for cash to pay taxes was a powerful reason to mortgage a farm, which, in turn, increased the scope not only of the market but also state power. Thoreau was fearful of both. On Concord, see Robert A. Gross, "Culture and Cultivation: Agriculture and Society in Thoreau's Concord," *Journal of American History* 69, no. 1 (June 1982): 42–61; Brian Donahue, *The Great Meadow: Farmers and Land in Colonial Concord* (New Haven: Yale University Press, 2007), chap. 9.

19. George S. Boutwell, *Address Before the Middlesex Society of Husbandmen and Manufacturers* (Boston, 1850), 6, 15, 17, 18.

20. Thoreau, *Walden*, 7; *Transactions of the Agricultural Societies in the State of Massachusetts for the Year 1849* (Boston, 1849), 368.

21. Atack and Bateman, *To Their Own Soil*, 203, 267, 273. See also Danhoff, *Change in Agriculture*, 21.

22. Lacy K. Ford, "Frontier Democracy: The Turner Thesis Revisited," *Journal of the Early Republic* 13, no. 2 (Summer 1993): 155.

23. On age of wealth transfer, see Atack and Bateman, *To Their Own Soil*, and for a review of farmers and old-age security strategies, and on the pull of urban labor markets, see William A. Sundstrom and Paul A. David, "Old-Age Security Motives, Labor Markets, and Farm Family Fertility in Antebellum America," *Explorations in Economic History* 25 (1988): 164–97. On land shortages, see Christopher Clark, *The Roots of Rural Capitalism: Western Massachusetts, 1780–1860* (Ithaca, NY: Cornell University Press, 1990). On the soil, Steven Stoll, *Larding the Lean Earth: Soil and Society in Nineteenth-Century America* (New York: Hill and Wang, 2002). On agrarian laments, see, for instance, Horace Bushnell, *An Address Delivered Before the Hartford Agricultural Society* (Hartford, 1847).

24. Edwin Freedley, *Practical Treatise on Business* (Philadelphia, 1853), 71, 74; Boutwell, *Address*, 6; Frederick Butler, *The Farmer's Manual* (Hartford, 1819), 108, 129.

25. James L. Huston, *Securing the Fruits of Labor: The American Concept of Wealth Distribution, 1765–1900* (Baton Rouge: Louisiana State University Press, 1998), and Allan Kulikoff, "The Transition to Capitalism in Rural America," *William and Mary Quarterly* 46 (January 1989): 140.

26. On the connection between the more familiar history of eastern proletarianization and more recent histories of commercial failure, see Edward Balleisen, *Navigating Failure: Bankruptcy and Commercial Society in Antebellum America* (Chapel Hill: University of North Carolina Press, 2001); Scott A. Sandage, *Born Losers: A History of Failure in America* (Cambridge: Harvard University Press, 2005).

27. "Mixed Husbandry," *The Genoese Farmer and Gardner's Journal* (January 6, 1838). See also, for instance, Nathaniel Gage, *Address before the Essex Agriculture Society at Topsfield, September 27, 1837* (Salem, 1838); Josiah T. Marshall, *An Address, delivered before an agricultural meeting at Jefferson County, N.Y. on the 26th September, 1838* (Watertown, 1838).

28. On bankrupted farmers, Clark, *Roots of Rural Capitalism*, 280. On homestead laws, see Paul Goodman, "The Emergence of Homestead Exemption in the United States: Accommodation and Resistance to the Market Revolution, 1840–1880," *Journal of American History* 80, no. 2 (September 1993): 470–98.

29. U.S. Congress 47:2, House Miscellaneous Document, 13:3, *Report on the Production of Agriculture (10th Census),* 1880, 25; W. F. Mappin, "Farm Mortgages and the Small Farmer," *Political Science Quarterly* 4, no. 3 (September 1889): 436; U.S. Congress 49:1, House Executive Document 378, *Report of the Commissioner of Agriculture,* 1886, 423; James Willis Gleed, "Western Mortgages," *Forum* (March 1890): 180.

30. With the Homestead Act of 1862 households needed only file an application, improve the land for five years, and then refile for the deed to claim a quarter. Railroads and eastern speculators also offered land for sale. In general on the disposal of western lands, see Paul Wallace Gates, Allan G. Bogue, and Margaret Beattie Bogue, *The Jeffersonian Dream: Studies in the History of American Land Policy and Development* (Albuquerque: University of New Mexico Press, 1996).

31. On this ecological logic, see Donahue, *Great Meadow*.

32. When grain prices plummeted, it was not uncommon for plains farmers to burn their products for fuel.

33. The story is told by William Cronon, *Nature's Metropolis: Chicago and the Great West* (New York: Norton, 1991).

34. On wealth holding and distribution see Lee Soltow, *Men and Wealth in the United States, 1850–1870* (New Haven: Yale University Press, 1975).

35. Keeler, *Where to Go to Become Rich*, 43. Most estimates are for a slightly earlier time period. Clarence H. Danhoff, "Farm Making Costs and the Safety Valve," *Journal of Political Economy* 49 (1941): 317–59; Jeremy Atack, "Farm and Farm-Making Costs Revisited," *Agricultural History* 56 (1982): 663–76.

36. In 1880, nationwide, 25 percent of farmers were tenants. Paul W. Gates made much of this fact. Recently, the literature sees tenancy as a life-cycle phenomenon. See Paul W. Gates, *Landlords and Tenants on the Prairie Frontier* (Ithaca, NY: Cornell University Press, 1973); Jeremy Atack, "Tenants and Yeomen in the Nineteenth Century," *Agricultural History* 62, no. 3 (Summer 1998): 6–32. On wage labor and the ladder see Wright, "American Agriculture and the Labor Market."

37. In a sample of 219,291 households. *Report on Real Estate Mortgages*, 278.

38. A growing tendency in the literature is to see new consumer opportunities as impetuses for late nineteenth-century agricultural commercialization. See David B. Danbom, *Born in the Country: A History of Rural America*, 2nd ed. (Baltimore: Johns Hopkins University Press, 2006), 131–61, and Rebecca Edwards, *New Spirits: Americans in the Gilded Age, 1865–1905* (New York: Oxford University Press, 2006), 81–104.

39. Atack, Bateman, and Parker, "The Farm, the Farmer, and the Market," 259.

40. See Wright, "American Agriculture and the Labor Market," 194.

41. See *Willis A. Olmsted and Mary E. Olmsted v. The New England Mortgage Security Company*, 11 Neb. 487 (1881).

42. See Erling A. Erickson, "Money and Banking in a 'Bankless' State: Iowa, 1846–1847," *Business History Review* 43, no. 2 (Summer 1969): 171–91.

43. Sections 8 and 28. The 1884 Supreme Court case *Fortier v. New Orleans National Bank* held that mortgage loans were not violations of the act. But national banks still largely avoided owning mortgages. See Richard H. Keehn and Gene Smiley, "Mortgage Lending by National Banks," *Business History Review* 51, no. 4 (Winter 1977): 474–91.

44. See Larry McFarlane, "British Investment in Midwestern Farm Mortgages and Land, 1875–1900: A Comparison of Iowa and Kansas," *Agricultural History* 48, no. 1 (January 1974): 183.

45. "The Late Austin Corbin's Buffalo," *New York Times*, December 12, 1897; A. N. Harbert, "Austin Corbin," *Iowa Historical Record* 14, no. 1 (January 1898): 193–201. Corbin consolidated the Long Island Railroad; *Olmsted v. New England Mortgage Security*.

46. A sense confirmed by Thornton, "A Great Machine."

47. Ise, *Sod and Stubble*, 199; See Alison D. Morantz, "There's No Place Like Home: Homestead Exemption and Judicial Constructions of Family in Nineteenth-Century America," *Law and History Review* 24, no. 2 (Summer 2006); Goodman, "Emergence of Homestead Exemption," 470–98; Edward Darrow, *A Treatise on Mortgage Investments* (Minneapolis, 1892), 8.

48. Corbin claimed to never mortgage above one-third. See *Ten Per Cent First Mortgages on Improved Farms in Iowa and Kansas, Negotiated by the Corbin Banking Company* (New York, 1872).

49. See "The Usury Laws of the United States," *The Bankers' Magazine*, March 1861.

50. *Report on Real Estate Mortgages*, 259, 170.

51. Richard H. Dana Jr., *Speech . . . On the Repeal of Usury Laws* (New York, 1872), 20, 10. For examples, see James Avery Webb, *A Treatise on the Law of Usury* (St. Louis, 1899), 14. On interest rates, see Bogue, *Money at Interest*; Eichengreen, "Interest Rates in the Populist Era," which holds that regional variance of rates was rational adjustment to the risk of repayment. Snowden is skeptical: Kenneth A. Snowden, "Mortgage Rates and American Capital Market Development in the Late Nineteenth Century," *Journal of Economic History* 47, no. 3 (September 1987): 671–91.

52. This is the gist of Webb, *Treaty on the Law of Usury*. Brokers often kicked backed commissions to eastern principals.

53. Ise, *Sod and Stubble*, 199.

54. Davis and Gallman, *Evolving Financial Markets and International Capital Flows*, 20.

55. "Western Mortgages," *Boston Daily Advertiser*, November 13, 1877.

56. Jane Addams, "The Snare of Preparation" (1912), in *The Jane Addams Reader*, ed. Jean Bethke Elshtain (New York: Basic Books, 2002), 108.

57. Darrow, *Treatise on Mortgage Investments*, 38, 43.

58. Gleed, "Western Mortgages," 96; *The Independent*, April 4, 1889; *Ten Per Cent First Mortgages on Improved Farms in Iowa and Kansas*; *The Independent*, May 31, 1889; Snowden, "Evolution of Interregional Mortgage Lending Channels," 227.

59. Gleed, "Western Mortgages," 102.

60. *The Congregationalist*, April 21, 1887; See Beers, "Eastern Money." Maturities varied from one to twenty years; D. M. Frederiksen, "Mortgage Banking in America," *Journal of Political Economy* 2, no. 2 (March 1894): 212–13; Mappin, "Farm Mortgages and the Small Farmer," for instance, claimed Kansas and Nebraska had 134 incorporated companies, with another 200 companies chartered out of state doing business there.

61. Darrow, *Treatise on Mortgage Investments*, 25; See Snowden, "Mortgage Securitization in the U.S" on mortgage brokers' lack of skin in the game; *Teal v. Walker* 111 US 242 (1882).

62. It seems farmers also succeeded politically in acquiring the right to prepayment, making bonds far more difficult to price. See Samuel Armstrong Nelson, *The Bond Buyer's Dictionary* (New York, 1907), 129. Not until the 1980s did Wall Street develop mathematical models to price bonds that accurately reflected prepayment risk.

63. Not since this episode has there been widespread private individual investment in mortgage-backed securities. Wall Street has subsequently reserved that honor for institutional investors.

64. Snowden, "Evolution," 220. "Western" includes here the states of IA, MN, NE, ND, SD, WY, and MT.

65. Nelson, *Bond Buyer's Dictionary*, 129.

66. After the land bust of the panic of 1873, New York state barred its savings banks from investing in mortgages. Connecticut and Wisconsin firms most heavily invested in the western market: Aetna Insurance Company, the Connecticut Mutual Insurance Company, the Travelers Insurance Company, and the Northwestern Mutual Insurance Company in particular.

67. On antebellum life insurance see Viviana A. Rotman Zelizer, *Morals and Markets: The Development of Life Insurance in the United States* (New York: Columbia University Press, 1983); Sharon Ann Murphy, *Investing in Life: Life Insurance in Antebellum America* (Baltimore: Johns Hopkins University Press, 2010).

68. "Life Insurance: A Way to Save a Mortgage," *Christian Union*, April 22, 1874.

69. *Seventh Biennial Report of the Bureau of Labor, Census and Industrial Statistics State of Wisconsin, 1895–1896* (Madison, 1896), 110.

70. See Harold Williamson and Orange Smally, *Northwestern Mutual Life: A Century of Trusteeship* (Evanston, IL: Northwestern University Press, 1957).

71. See M. Friedberger, "The Farm Family and the Inheritance Process: Evidence from the Corn Belt, 1870–1950," *Agricultural History* 57, no. 1 (1983): 1–13. More traditional practices were manifest in ethnic enclaves; see Kathleen Neils Conzen, "Peasant Pioneers: Generational Succession among German Farmers in Frontier Minnesota," in *The Countryside in the Age of Capitalist Transformation: Essays in the Social History of Rural America*, ed. Steven Hahn and Jonathan Prude (Chapel Hill: University of North Carolina Press, 1985), 259–92.

72. See the tongue-and-cheek story of a North Carolina man who tried: "A Man Who Mortgaged Himself," *Cleveland Herald*, March 31, 1884.

73. *The Advocate*, April 23, 1890. The *Advocate* was the Topeka Kansas Farmer's Alliance newspaper.

74. See "Examples Accident Losses Paid," Box 17, Collection 60, Warshaw Collection of Business Americana, Insurance Collection, Smithsonian National Museum of American History.

75. Bruce M. Pritchett, *A Study of Capital Mobilization: The Life Insurance Industry of the Nineteenth Century* (New York: Arno Press, 1977), 290; *Seventeenth Annual Report of the Superintendent of Insurance of the State of Kansas, for the Year ending December 31, 1897* (Topeka, 1887), 329, 330; *Twenty-Eighth Annual Report of the Superintendent of Insurance of the State of Kansas, for the Year ending December 31, 1897* (Topeka, 1898), xvi–xix.

76. *First Biennial Report of the Bureau of Labor and Industrial Statistics of Nebraska, 1887 and 1888* (Omaha, 1888); *Seventh Biennial Report*, 116–19.

77. *Seventh Biennial Report*, 117.

78. Ibid., 114; *First Biennial Report*, 208, 210.

79. Ise, *Sod and Stubble*, 217.

80. Ibid., 217, 209.

81. A.H.J., "Paying the Mortgage," *Michigan Farmer*, August 22, 1882; Ise, *Sod and Stubble*, 215.

82. Will Carleton, *Farm Festivals* (New York, 1881), 118–21.

83. Like "The Clock" in Herbert G. Gutman, *Work, Culture, and Society in Industrializing America: Essays in American Working-Class and Social History* (New York: Vintage, 1976), 23.

84. Ise, *Sod and Stubble*, 229.

85. *Stone v. United States Casualty Company* (1871), 34 NJL 371; The Travelers Insurance Companies, *Accident Department, The Travelers Insurance Company* (Hartford, 1871), sec. 19; William C. Niblack, *The Law of Voluntary Societies, Mutual Benefit Insurance and Accident Insurance* (Chicago, 1894), sec. 363.

86. See, for instance, Henry C. Taylor, *The Story of Agricultural Economists in the United States, 1840–1932* (Ames: Iowa State College Press, 1952).

87. "Western Farm Mortgages," *The Daily Inter Ocean* (October 30, 1888).

88. All quoted in Edward Atkinson, "The True Meaning of Farm Mortgage Statistics," *Forum* (May 1895). See also John Gjerde, *The Minds of the West: Ethnocultural Evolution in the Rural Middle West, 1830–1917* (Chapel Hill: University of North Carolina, 1997), 146.

89. *Seventh Biennial Report*, 117.

90. The classic work on regional specialization remains Allan G. Bogue, *From Prairie to Corn Belt: Farming on the Illinois and Iowa Prairies in the Nineteenth Century* (1963; Ames: Iowa State University Press, 1994), although Bogue cautions that multiple combinations of crops and livestock were still possible. See also Mary Eschelbach Gregson, "Specialization in

Late-Nineteenth Century Midwestern Agriculture," *Agricultural History* 67 (Winter 1993): 16–35, which argues for an increase of market diversification. See also Eugene V. Robinson, *Early Economic Conditions and the Development of Agriculture in Minnesota* (Minneapolis, 1915).

91. Winifred B. Rothenberg, *From Market-Places to a Market Economy: The Transformation of Rural Massachusetts, 1760–1850* (Chicago: University of Chicago Press, 1992), 98.

92. C. Knick Harley, "Transportation, and the World Wheat Trade, and the Kuznets Cycle," *Explorations in Economic History* 17 (1980): 246–47.

93. *Fourth Annual Report of the Bureau of Labor Statistics of the State of Connecticut, for the Year Ending 1888* (Hartford, 1889), 140–44.

94. George S. Boutwell, "Feeding Cattle," *Massachusetts Ploughman and New England Journal of Agriculture* (January 19, 1878). On changes in northeastern farming, see Hal S. Barron, *Mixed Harvest: The Second Great Transformation in the Rural North, 1870–1930* (Chapel Hill: University of North Carolina Press, 1997).

95. On freedpeople's desire for landed independence, see Gerald David Jaynes, *Branches Without Roots: Genesis of the Black Working Class in the American South, 1862–1882* (New York: Oxford University Press, 1986); Julie Saville, *The Work of Reconstruction: From Slave to Wage Laborer in South Carolina, 1860–1870* (New York: Cambridge University Press, 1994). On the postbellum southern credit market Roger L. Ransom and Richard Sutch, *One Kind of Freedom: The Economic Consequences of Emancipation* (New York: Cambridge University Press, 2001); Steven Hahn, *The Roots of Southern Populism: Yeoman Farmers and the Transformation of the Georgian Upcountry, 1850–1890* (New York: Oxford University Press, 1983).

96. Hamilton (GA) *Weekly Visitor*, February 7, 1893, quoted in Gavin Wright, *Old South, New South: Revolutions in the Southern Economy Since the Civil War* (New York: Basic Books, 1986), 114. On corn versus cotton see Gavin Wright and Howard Kunreuther, "Cotton, Corn, and Risk in the Nineteenth Century," *Journal of Economic History* 35, no. 3 (September 1975): 526–51; Robert A. McGuire, "A Portfolio Analysis of Crop Diversification and Risk in the Cotton South," *Explorations in Economic History* 17 (October 1980): 342–71.

97. Jonathan Ira Levy, "Contemplating Delivery: Futures Trading and the Problem of Commodity Exchange in the United States, 1875–1905," *American Historical Review* 111, no. 2 (April 2006): 307–35.

98. See Elizabeth Sanders, *Roots of Reform: Farmers, Workers, and the American State, 1877–1917* (Chicago: University of Chicago Press, 1999).

99. See ibid., and Postel, *Populist Vision*.

100. Ise, *Sod and Stubble,* 276, 254.

101. Ibid., 228; George H. Hepworth, "Old Badger's Mortgage," *The Independent*, October 22, 1896; Carleton, *Farm Festivals*, 118.

102. George K. Holmes, "Mortgage Statistics," *Publications of the American Statistical Association* 2, no. 9 (1890): 20.

103. Ise, *Sod and Stubble*, 254.

104. "Some Remarks about Mortgages," *Michigan Farmer*, July 6, 1889; Keeler, *Where to Go to Become Rich*, 39.

105. See *The Advocate*, November 9, 1889; Holmes, "Mortgage Statistics," 13.

106. *Report on Real Estate Mortgages*, 301, 309, 76, 170, 311, 310, 312.

107. Holmes, "Mortgage Statistics," 21.

108. *Atchison Daily Champion*, October 25, 1888; *Daily Inter Ocean,* May 5, 1893; *Milwaukee Journal,* May 8, 1893; *Daily Picayune*, August 6, 1891.

109. In the 1887 Nebraska survey disgruntled mortgaged farmers called themselves "white slaves" and "serfs." The western Kansas populist newspaper *The Farmer's Advocate* called the western mortgage market "the most stupendous landlord system ever known on earth."

110. Mappin, "Farm Mortgages and the Small Farmer," 451.

111. Atkinson, "True Meaning of Farm Mortgage Statistics."

112. See Willie Lee Rose, *Rehearsal for Reconstruction: The Port Royal Experiment* (New York: Oxford University Press, 1964), 226.

113. Daniel R. Goodloe, "Western Mortgages," *Forum* (November 1890).

114. A line running, to name but a few examples, from John Hicks, *The Populist Revolt* (Lincoln: University of Nebraska Press, 1931), to Lawrence Goodwyn, *Democratic Promise: The Populist Movement in America* (New York: Oxford University Press, 1976), to Scott G. McNall, *The Road to Rebellion: Class Formation and Kansas Populism, 1865–1900* (Chicago: University of Chicago Press, 1988). A much more balanced view, centered on the issue of business cooperation and incorporation, is presented by Postel, *Populist Vision*.

115. A revisionist interpretation against Hicks was presented by Fred A. Shannon, *The Farmer's Last Frontier* (New York: Rinehart, 1945), which was then taken up by the cliometric historians of the 1960s and, afterwards, culminating in the question posed by one 1994 cliometric textbook that asked whether "farmers' complaints were real or imagined?" See Jeremy Atack and Peter Passell, *A New Economic View of American History from Colonial Times to 1940* (New York: Norton, 1994), 424, and 425 for further cites concerning this view.

116. The interpretive spirit of Postel, *Populist Vision*.

117. *Annual Report of the U.S. Department of Agriculture* (Washington, DC, 1908), 151–52.

Chapter 3

1. Alan Greenspan, speech to the Federal Reserve Board, January 26, 2004, http://www.federalreserve.gov/boarddocs/speeches/2004/20040126/default.htm (accessed October 30, 2010).

2. Robert Solow, "Hedging America," *New Republic*, January 12, 2010.

3. Joseph Bieller to Jacob Bieller, June 1, 1828, Alonzo Snyder Papers, Lower Louisiana and Mississippi Valley Collections, Hill Special Collections Library, Louisiana State University, Baton Rouge (hereinafter abbreviated as LLMVC).

4. Ibid., April 7, 1829, and Joseph Bieller to Jacob Bieller, November 11, 1827, Alonzo Snyder Papers.

5. Arthur Schlesinger Jr., *The Age of Jackson* (Boston: Little, Brown, 1945), 18; Bray Hammond, *Banks and Politics in America: From the Revolution to the Civil War* (Princeton, NJ: Princeton University Press, 1957). Though more recent studies have pointed at other causes, Hammond's charge—one originally made by contemporary Whigs—that the Specie Circular brought on the panic has been incorporated into many general accounts of the period. Cf. Daniel Walker Howe, *What Hath God Wrought: The Transformation of America, 1815–1848* (New York: Oxford University Press, 2007).

6. John Cassidy, *How Markets Fail: The Logic of Economic Calamities* (New York: Farrar, Strauss, and Giroux, 2009).

7. Michael Lewis's *The Big Short: Inside the Doomsday Machine* (New York: W. W. Norton, 2010) may have the most succinct explanation of this.

8. Histories of the 2007–9 crash include Cassidy, *How Markets Fail*; Andrew Ross Sorkin, *Too Big to Fail: The Inside Story of How Washington and Wall Street Fought to Save the Financial System from Crisis—and Themselves* (New York: Viking, 2009); Lewis, *The Big Short*; Robert

Shiller, *The Subprime Solution: How Today's Global Financial Crisis Happened, and What to Do about It* (Princeton: Princeton University Press, 2008). For sensible introductions to the etiology of financial crises and panics, see Cassidy, *How Markets Fail*; also the work of Hyman Minsky and Charles Kindleberger, *Manias, Panics, and Crashes: A History of Financial Crises* (New York: Basic Books, 1978).

9. Bieller vs. Bieller, Petition for Divorce, 1835, Folder 1/15, Bieller Papers, LLMVC.

10. Here is a process that has probably been described more frequently than almost any other in the history of the rise of the West. Kenneth Pomeranz, *The Great Divergence: China, Europe, and the Making of the Modern World Economy* (Princeton, NJ: Princeton University Press, 2000), contains a nice synopsis of varying etiologies of this particular episode in the rise of the West. Some will argue that the Netherlands achieved these levels of growth before Britain, but it is fair to say that they did not sustain and expand upon them in the same fashion.

11. Ibid., 264–97. Nor could British colonies match the quantity, quality, and low cost of cotton produced by slaves in North America.

12. Ibid. I discuss cotton-picking in more depth in my forthcoming book, Edward E. Baptist, *The Half That Has Never Been Told: The Slave Migration that Shaped African America, the United States, and the Modern World* (New York: Basic Book, forthcoming). This fact has numerous implications, but has gone unnoticed for a very long time. A recent attempt by two economists to measure the increase in productive efficiency assembled a vast quantity of data that revealed that such increases existed. They credited it entirely to planters' prowess at improving the quality of the cotton plant. Something that apparently never came to mind was the possibility that enslaved people were picking faster (Alan Olmstead and Paul Rohde, "Biological Innovation and Productivity Growth in the Antebellum Cotton Economy," *Journal of Economic History* 69 [2008]: 1123–71). Enslaved people, as I detail in my chapter, tell a very different story.

13. George Green to John Minor, February 1, 1819 (Folder 20), January 6, 1819 (Folder 18), and August 2, 1826 (Folder 31), Minor Family Papers, Southern Historical Collection, Wilson Special Collections Library, University of North Carolina, Chapel Hill, NC (hereafter abbreviated as SHC).

14. George Green to John Minor, August 2, 1826, Folder 31, Minor Family Papers.

15. Larry Neal, "The Financial Crisis of 1825 and the Restructuring of the British Financial System," *Federal Reserve Bank of St. Louis Review* 80 (May–June 1998): 53–76; Peter Temin, *The Jacksonian Economy* (New York: Norton, 1969).

16. Matt Taibbi, "The Great American Bubble Machine," *Rolling Stone* 1082/1083 (July 9, 2009): 52–101, Academic Search Premier, EBSCOhost (accessed May 3, 2010).

17. Ralph C. H. Catterall, *The Second Bank of the United States* (Chicago: University of Chicago Press, 1903), 93–113; Richard H. Kilbourne Jr., *Slave Agriculture and Financial Markets in Antebellum America: The Bank of the United States in Mississippi, 1831–1852* (London: Pickering and Chatto, 2006), 1–56.

18. Isaac Franklin to R. C. Ballard, January 9, 1832, Folder 4, R. C. Ballard Papers, SHC; cf. Steven Deyle, *Carry Me Back: The Domestic Slave Trade in American Life* (New York: Oxford University Press, 2005); Wendell Stephenson, *Isaac Franklin: Slave Trader and Planter of the Old South, With Plantation Records* (Baton Rouge: Louisiana State University Press, 1938); Baptist, "'Cuffy,' 'Fancy Maids,' and 'One-Eyed Men': Rape, Commodification, and the Domestic Slave Trade in the United States," *American Historical Review* 106 (December 2001): 1619–50.

19. Richard Roeder, "New Orleans Merchants, 1790–1837," PhD diss., Harvard University,

1959; Ralph W. Hidy, *The House of Baring in American Trade and Finance: English Merchant Bankers at Work, 1763–1861* (Cambridge: Harvard University Press, 1949); Kilbourne, *Slave Agriculture and Financial Markets.*

20. Joseph Bieller to Jacob Bieller, June 15, 1827, Folder 1/2; A. Fisk to Jacob Bieller, February 17, 1826, Folder 2/9; Alvarez Fisk to Jacob Bieller, May 15, 1828, Folder 2/10, Alonzo Snyder Papers.

21. Daniel Draffin to Jacob Bieller, August 9, 1833, Folder 1/6, Alonzo Snyder Papers; estimate from Michael Tadman, *Speculators and Slaves: Masters, Traders, and Slaves in the Old South,* (Madison: University of Wisconsin Press, 1989), 12–13; "Statement of Slaves' Deaths on Ste Sophie Plantation during Ownership by J. J. Coiron"; "Act Passed By Judge De Flechier Netween Laurent Millaudon and Jos. François Coiron and family," 1824; Certified Statement of the Number of Slaves Who Died on Ste Sophie Plantation, April 1, 1829, all in Ste. Sophie/Live Oak Plantation Records, Louisiana Research Collection, Howard-Tilton Memorial Library, Tulane University. In later years, insurance corporations would sell thousands of policies to both slave traders and more stationary enslavers, but in the 1830s this practice was still in its infancy: cf. Sharon Murphy, *Investing in Life: Insurance in Antebellum America* (Baltimore: Johns Hopkins University Press, 2010).

22. James P. Franklin to Mssrs. R. C. Ballard and Co., March 4, 1832 (Folder 5); Isaac Franklin to R. C. Ballard, December 8, 1832 (Folder 8) and June 11, 1833 (Folder 11), R. C. Ballard Papers. Cf. Charles E. Rosenberg, *The Cholera Years: The United States in 1832, 1849, and 1866* (Chicago: University of Chicago Press, 1962). For death rates in the Southwest, see Richard H. Steckel, *The Economics of U.S. Slave and Southern White Fertility* (New York: Garland Publishing, 1985).

23. Bieller vs. Bieller, Petition for Divorce; Will of Jacob Bieller, December 1835, Alonzo Snyder Papers.

24. Louisiana State Supreme Court Case Report (notes), in ibid.

25. Jacob Bieller Purchases, Folder 2/15, Alonzo Snyder Papers.

26. Nancy Bieller to Jacob Bieller, August 18, 1836, Folder 1/7, Alonzo Snyder Papers.

27. Undated note, Folder: 1824, A. P. Walsh Papers, Louisiana State University.

28. Irene Neu, "J. B. Moussier and the Property Banks of Louisiana," *Business History Review* 35 (Winter 1961): 550–57; Fritz Redlich, *The Molding of American Banking: Men and Ideas*, vol. 1, *1781–1840* (New York: Hafner, 1951), 206–7.

29. Reginald C. McGrane, *Foreign Bondholders and American State Debts* (New York: Macmillan, 1935); Neu, "J. B. Moussier and the Property Banks of Louisiana," 550–57; H. Lavergne to Manuel Andry, September 6, 1828, Folder 1A/Box 2, the Consolidated Association of the Planters of Louisiana (CAPL) Papers, LLMVC; George D. Green, *Finance and Economic Development in the Old South: Louisiana Banking, 1804–1861* (Stanford, CA: Stanford University Press, 1972), 113–16; Roeder, "New Orleans Merchants."

30. Baring Brothers was the major lender to the Second Bank of the United States, but they were increasingly resentful of Biddle's penchant for borrowing too much in order to maintain his control over US financial markets. By the early 1830s at the latest they were signaling that they would like an end run around Biddle. This point is from Hidy, *The House of Baring in American Trade and Finance*, 95–98.

31. McGrane, *Foreign Bondholders and American State Debts.*

32. H. Lavergne to Manuel Andry, September 14, 1828, Folder 1A/1, CAPL Papers.

33. Ironically British investors were thus becoming slaveowners in new ways even as the British empire was entering a formal process of emancipation within its own borders, beginning

in 1834. Baring Brothers helped market the loan by which the empire compensated its West Indian planters for "their" slaves.

34. McGrane, *Foreign Bondholders and American State Debts*, remains the best account of these proceedings, though he does not discuss Tennessee or Alabama. Cf. R. W. Hidy, "The Union Bank of Louisiana Loan, 1832: A Case Study in Marketing," *Journal of Political Economy* 47 (April 1939): 232–53.

35. *Times of London*, October 27, 1832; Thomas C. Holt, *The Problem of Freedom: Race, Labor, and Politics in Jamaica, 1832–1938* (Baltimore: Johns Hopkins University Press, 1992).

36. Hugues Lavergne and Alexander Gordon to Thomas Baring, August 19, 1828, in the Baring Manuscripts in the Canadian National Archives in Ottawa, quoted in McGrane, *Foreign Bondholders and American State Debts*, 176.

37. Forstall, quoted in McGrane, *Foreign Bondholders and American State Debts*, 171; *Times of London*, February 16, 1835. Cf. Irene D. Neu, "Edmond Jean Forstall and Louisiana Banking," *Explorations in Economic History* 7 (Autumn–Winter 1969): 383–98.

38. Andrew Jackson, "Veto Message Regarding the Bank of the United States," July 10, 1832, http://avalon.law.yale.edu/19th_century/ajveto01.asp (accessed April 29, 2010).

39. The Bank War has been the subject of hundreds of articles, dissertations, and books over the years. Recent treatments include Sean Wilentz, *The Rise of American Democracy: Jefferson to Lincoln*, (New York: W. W. Norton, 2005); and the many books and articles he cites. For the pet banks and politics, see Frank Gathell, "Spoils of the Bank War: Political Bias in the Selection of the Pet Banks," *AHR* 70 (October 1964): 35–58; Harry N. Scheiber, "The Pet Banks in Jacksonian Economy and Finance, 1833–1841," *Journal of Economic History* 23 (June 1963): 196–214.

40. Cassidy, *How Markets Fail*, 239.

41. W. H. Dorsey to Jacob Bieller, April 15, 1835, Folder 1/7. Alonzo Snyder Papers; Green, *Finance and Economic Development in the Old South*, 22–23.

42. McGrane, *Foreign Bondholders and American State Debts*.

43. Fabius J. Haywood to Alfred Williams, February 20, 1836, Folder 146, and P. A. Bolling to Edmund Hubard, February 24, 1837, Folder 72, Hubard Family Papers, SHC.

44. Source of that number is Tadman, *Speculators and Slaves*, chap. 1; Bacon Tait to R. C. Ballard, August 2, 1836 (Folder 19) and May 2, 1838 (Folder 24), R. C. Ballard Papers.

45. Henry Watson to Henry Watson Sr., December 15, 1836, Henry Watson Jr. Papers, and Robert Carson to Henderson Forsyth, December 3, 1836, John A. Forsyth Papers, Perkins Library Special Collections, Duke University, Durham, NC.

46. McGrane, *Foreign Bondholders and American State Debts*; Thomas Harrison to James Harrison, August 28, 1836, Folder 5, James Thomas Harrison Papers, SHC.

47. *New Orleans Price-Current*, August 20, 1836, in Folder 5, Jackson, Riddle, and Co. Papers, SHC, predicted that the short-term debts of Louisiana residents, which they accounted at $23 million, would be erased by the revenues accruing to them of the incoming crops of the Mississippi Valley, which the writer predicted would total $60 million. The collapse in commodity prices would invalidate that calculation.

48. P. A. Bolling to Edmund Hubard, February 24, 1837, Folder 72, Hubard Family Papers.

49. Stephen Duncan to William N. Mercer, August 7, 1837, William N. Mercer Papers, August Records of Ante-Bellum Southern Plantations from the Revolution to the Civil War, Series H, Reel 24; cf. John Elliott to "My Dear Lucy," April 8, 1837, Samuel Bryarly Papers, Duke University, Durham, NC.

50. McGrane, *Foreign Bondholders and American State Debts*; for the collapse in slave prices, cf. virtually every letter about slave prices from the Southwest in this period, e.g., Robert Carson to "Dear Sir," August 20, 1839, John A. Forsyth Papers.

51. Key exceptions include Jessica Lepler, "1837: Anatomy of a Panic," PhD diss., Brandeis University, 2008.

52. Case File of John Richardson, no. 112, ELA37/Bankruptcy Act of 1841 Case Files; Book 2, 47, E36, Bankruptcy Act of 1841 Dockets, both in Record Group 21, Records of the U.S. District and Bankruptcy Courts, National Archives, Fort Worth Branch, Fort Worth, TX.

53. George Rawick, ed., *The American Slave: A Composite Autobiography* (Westport, CT: Greenwood Press, 1972–77), vol. 11.2, MO, Dave Harper, 163; ibid., Supplement, Series 2, vol. 2.1, TX, John Bates, 213.

54. See Kilbourne, *Slave Agriculture and Financial Markets*; New Orleans Office Ledger, 1844–45, vol. 124, Brown Brothers and Co. Papers, New York Public Library; Neu, "Edmond Forstall and Louisiana Banking."

Chapter 4

1. *Report of the Trial by Impeachment of James Prescott* (Boston: Office of the Daily Advertiser, 1821), 73.

2. Eileen Spring, "Landowners, Lawyers, and Land Law Reform in Nineteenth-Century England," *American Journal of Legal History* 21, no. 1 (January 1977): 50.

3. Alice Hanson Jones, *Wealth of a Nation to Be: The American Colonies on the Eve of the Revolution* (New York: Columbia University Press, 1980), 48.

4. In 1732 Parliament passed the Debt Recovery Act, making land in the colonies answerable for commercial debt; Claire Priest, "Creating an American Property Law: Alienability and its Limits in American History," *Harvard Law Review* 120, no. 385 (December 2006), which perhaps too quickly attributes the whole of the nineteenth-century American property regime to Parliament's action.

5. The reliance on enslaved rather than waged labor kept the South out of the emerging capitalist order, of course, but personal proprietorship and the household as the site of labor made families the primary economic institution in both regions.

6. For the "widening and thickening" of credit networks, see Winifred Barr Rothenberg, *From Market-Places to a Market Economy: The Transformation of Rural Massachusetts, 1750–1850* (Chicago: University of Chicago Press, 1992), esp. 126–30, and Christopher Clark, *The Roots of Rural Capitalism: Western Massachusetts, 1780–1860* (Ithaca, NY: Cornell University Press, 1990).

7. Carole Shammas, Marylynn Salmon, and Michel Dahlin, *Inheritance in America: From Colonial Times to the Present* (New Brunswick, NJ: Rutgers University Press, 1987), 64–65, summarizes state inheritance laws in 1790. See also Stanley Katz, "Republicanism and the Law of Inheritance in the American Revolutionary Era," *Michigan Law Review* 76, no. 1 (1977). For a local study, see Toby Ditz, *Property and Kinship: Inheritance in Early Connecticut, 1750–1820* (Princeton, NJ: Princeton University Press, 1986).

8. Shammas, Salmon, and Dahlin, *Inheritance in America*, 67–69.

9. For a riveting account of the indebted estates of Virginia planters, see Herbert Sloan, *Principle and Interest: Thomas Jefferson and the Problem of Debt* (New York: Oxford University Press, 1995).

10. Thomas D. Morris, *Southern Slavery and the Law, 1619–1860* (Chapel Hill: University of North Carolina Press, 1996), chap. 3.

11. David Parker to William Minot, September 3, 1831, Box 6, William Minot Papers (hereafter Minot Papers), Massachusetts Historical Society, Boston.

12. Minot to Jacob Parker, October 11, 1833, and September 30, 1834, William Minot Letterbook (1812–1835) (hereafter Minot Letterbook); "Memorandum of Agreement," February 16, 1835, Box 6, both in Minot Papers.

13. Jacob Parker, memo, January 1831, Box 6 ($22,000), and Minot to David Parker, July 14, 1831, William Minot Letterbook (1812–1835), Minot Papers.

14. Minot to David Parker, July 14, 1831, Minot Letterbook.

15. Minot to Charlotte Parker, July 7, 1834, Minot Letterbook.

16. Joseph Brown Estate Papers, Box 6, Folder 6, Series I (Papers of estates administered by Nathan Brooks), Nathan Brooks Family Papers, Special Collections, Concord Free Public Library, Concord, MA.

17. Samuel Burr Estate Papers, Box 7, folder 5; Box 8, folder 2, Series I, Nathan Brooks Family Papers.

18. Adam Rothman, *Slave Country: American Expansion and the Origins of the Deep South* (Cambridge: Harvard University Press, 2005).

19. Edward Balleisen, *Navigating Failure: Bankruptcy and Commercial Society in Antebellum America* (Chapel Hill: University of North Carolina Press, 2001).

20. James G. Smith, *Trust Companies in the United States* (New York: Thomas Holt and Company, 1928), 232, citing *25th Annual Report of the Massachusetts Bureau of Statistics of Labor* (March 1895), 265.

21. In 1819 a lawyer noted that the widow of an impoverished housewright "has a small amount of furniture (say $100 worth) which she fears will be taken by some of her husband's creditors." By going through probate, she could claim a recently mandated widow's right to up to $200 in personal furnishings, J. W. Gane to William Minot, October 31, 1819, Carton 2, Minot Family Business and Financial Records, 1810–1939, Massachusetts Historical Society.

22. See, for example, Will of Joseph Coolidge, September 29, 1820, in Carton 3, Minot Family Business and Financial Records.

23. Peter Dobkin Hall, "What the Merchants Did with Their Money: Charitable and Testamentary Trusts in Massachusetts, 1780–1880," in *Entrepreneurs: The Boston Business Community, 1700–1850*, ed. Conrad Edick Wright and Katheryn P. Viens (Boston: Massachusetts Historical Society, 1997), 365–421.

24. Thomas D. Russell, "South Carolina's Largest Auctioneering Firm," *Chicago-Kent Law Review* 68, no. 1241 (1993).

25. Robert Gordan, "Paradoxical Property," in *Early Modern Conceptions of Property*, ed. John Brewer and Susan Staves (New York: Routledge, 1994), 95–110.

26. *John Holland v. Edward Cruft, et al.*, 69 Mass. 162 (1855). For Pennsylvania deliberations over the relation of real to personal property, see *M'Coy v. Scott*, 2 Rawle 222 (1828) and Morrow, for the heirs of *Isett v. Brenizer*, 2 Rawle 185 (1828).

27. Lawrence Friedman, "The Dynastic Trust," *Yale Law Journal* 73, no. 547 (1964). Shammas, Salmon, and Dahlin, *Inheritance in America*, 56–57, note the widespread use of trusts in the colonial South. See also Peter Dobkin Hall, *The Organization of American Culture, 1700–1900* (New York: New York University Press, 1982), 114–24. In England, trusts fell under equity rather than common law; in the United States those states that did not have equity courts (for example, courts of chancery) generally granted equity powers, including oversight of trusts, to probate courts, subject to review by the regular courts of appeal.

28. Schieffelin v. Stewart, 1 Johnson Ch. 620 (1815).

29. James King to State Chancellor of New York, August 29, 1839, in Injunction Master's Annual Report on Accounts of Guardians, Committees, and Receivers, J-2076–82, New York State Archives, Albany (hereafter NYSA). See also *Rules and Orders of the Court of Chancery of the State of New York* (New York: W and A Gould, 1839).

30. In re William Van Aldtyne; In re Edward Price, In re John P. Barrainger, all in King to the State Chancellor, August 29, 1831, in Injunction Master's Annual Report, NYSA.

31. King to State Chancellor, October 2, 1832, and August 15, 1835, in Injunction Master's Annual Report, NYSA.

32. In re Hiram Fowler in King to State Chancellor, August 29, 1931; In re Maria W. Bradley in Charles A. Mann to State Chancellor, March 7, 1831; In re Hiram Fowler in King to State Chancellor, September 21, 1833; In re Helen Sanford, et al., King to State Chancellor, October 2, 1832; September 21, 1833; In re Emily Sandford et al., in King to State Chancellor, December 31, 1834 (guardian's protest), in Injunction Master's Annual Report, NYSA.

33. In re Mary Allen and Margaret Allen, A23, Box 1, In Re Papers (1800–1847), J0057–82, New York Court of Chancery, NYSA.

34. *Frederick de Peyster v. Mathew Clarkson, Jr., et al., Case on the part of the Appellant* (New York: Geo. F. Hopkins, 1828), 4, 9, 11, 27, Box 2, Frederick De Peyster, Master in Chancery Papers, New York Historical Society.

35. *De Peyster v. Clarkson*, 2 Wend. at 106 (1829).

36. *Manning et al. v. Executors of Manning*, 1 Johnson Chancery at 236 (1815).

37. *Pusey v. Clemson*, 9 Serg. and Rawle at 209 (1823). See also *Nimmo's Executor v. the Commonwealth*, 14 Va 57 (1809).

38. See, for example, petitions from Thomas Ash, Anton Artois, and John B. Coles, Box 1, DePeyster, Master in Chancery Papers.

39. Examples can be found in the Minot Office Papers and letterbooks, for instance, in transactions of the estate of Governor Thomas L. Winthrop in Minot Letterbook (1840–47), passim.

40. See, for example, *Stewart's Administrator v. Stewart's Heirs*, 31 Ala. 207 (1857), noting the 1835 Alabama law. For probate in Alabama more generally, see John A. Cuthbert, *Compendium of the Law of Executors, Administrators, Guardians, and Dower in Force in Alabama* (Mobile, AL.: Thomas J. Carver and Co., 1850).

41. Deed, Benjamin Brown to Benjamin Comstock, August 15, 1792, Box 1, Comstock Family Papers, American Antiquarian Society, Worcester, MA.

42. Benjamin Comstock Will, September 6, 1824, Comstock Family Papers.

43. David Putnam to William Comstock, January 28, 1833, Comstock Family Papers.

44. Putnam to Comstock, February 8, 1838, and September 12, 1839, Comstock Family Papers.

45. Heirs of Benjamin Comstock in account with David Putnam, November 6, 1843, Comstock Family Papers.

46. William Comstock, Memo on "Father's Estate," n.d.; Douglas Putnam to William Comstock, January 24, 1854, Comstock Family Papers.

47. William Minot to Jacob Slade, June 19, 1849, Minot Letterbook (1847–53).

48. For the use of brokers to liquidate mortgages, see, for example, William Minot to W. L. Tiffany, February 28, 1848, Minot Letterbook (1847–53).

49. Elizabeth Blackmar, *Manhattan for Rent, 1785–1850* (Ithaca, NY: Cornell University Press, 1989), 202.

50. Gerald T. White, *A History of the Massachusetts Hospital Life Insurance Company* (Cambridge: Harvard University Press, 1955), 38.

51. Ibid., 41, 55; Hall, "What the Merchants Did with Their Money," 379–88. See also Tamara Plakins Thornton, "'A Great Machine' or a 'Beast of Prey': A Boston Corporation and Its Rural Debtors in an Age of Capitalist Transformation," *Journal of the Early Republic* 27 (Winter 2007): 567–97. On the number of banks, Naomi R. Lamoreaux, *Insider Lending: Banks, Personal Connections and Economic Development in Industrial New England* (New York: Cambridge University Press, 1994), 14.

52. New York Life Insurance and Trust, Monthly Report to the Board of Trustees Statement Book, V. AB-1 Baker Library, Harvard University. See also Accounts of Infants with New York Life Insurance Company, J0056–82, New York Chancery Court, NYSA.

53. Lamoreaux, *Insider Lending*; Robert F. Dalzell Jr., *Enterprising Elite: The Boston Associates and the World They Made* (Cambridge: Harvard University Press, 1987), 79–112.

54. *Harvard College and Massachusetts General Hospital v. Amory*, 26 Mass. at 461.

55. Ibid.

56. Guardianship and trust papers, Box 2, Folder 11, Flint Family Papers, American Antiquarian Society.

57. Simpson Estate Papers, Box 2, Folder 10, Flint Family Papers.

58. Titus Welles Estate, and Simpson Estate Papers, in Flint Family Papers.

59. *Worrell's Appeal*, 23 Pa. at 48 (1854) and the doctrine's development in *Worrell's Appeal*, 9 Pa. 508 (1848); *Hemphill's Appeal*, 18 Pa. 303 (1852).

60. *Pray's Appeal*, 34 Pa. 100 (1859).

61. *King v. Talbot*, 40 NY at 88, 89 (1869).

62. *Allen v. Gaillard*, 1 SC at 279 (1870); *Womack v. Austin*, 1 SC 421 (1870).

63. Jairus Ware Perry, *A Treatise on the Law of Trusts and Trustees* (Boston: Little, Brown, 1872). 408–28, 412 (quote). Mississippi, Maryland, Kentucky, and Ohio continued to permit trustees' investments in bank stocks. For courts' reliance on Perry, see, for example, *Tucker v. Indiana*, 72 Ind. 242 (1880), *White v. Sherman*, 168 Ill. 589 (1897), *Simmons v. Olicer*, 74 Wis. 633 (1889). For a review of the states adopting the "liberal" Massachusetts doctrine, see *Willis v. Braucher*, 79 Ohio St. at 300 (1909).

64. *Staples & al. v. Staples & al.*, 65 Va. at 249 (1874).

65. *Mills & al. v. Mills' Executors & al.*, 69 Va at 497 and 498 (1877).

66. Alfred Robinson to Abel Stearns, May 11, December 5, 1870, Box 56, Abel Stearns Papers, Collection I, Huntington Library, San Marino, CA

67. See accounts of Arcardia Bandini Baker estate in the Cave J. Couts Papers, Boxes 41 and 74, Huntington Library. For the fate of the rancheros see *The Decline of the Californios: A Social History of the Spanish-Speaking Californians, 1846–1890* (Berkeley: University of California Press, 1966).

68. Clay Herick, *Trust Companies: The Organization, Growth, and Management* (New York: Bankers Publishing Company, 1915), 20.

69. Shammas, Salmon, and Dahlin, *Inheritance in America,* 19, arguing for a national pattern based on a sample from Bucks County, Pennsylvania. The proportion of household wealth in real property increased slightly in the second half of the twentieth century as home ownership increased to more than 60 percent of households.

70. National Banking Act, June 3, 1864, sec. 28, in *Documentary History of Banking and Currency in the United States*, ed. Herman E. Krooss (New York: Chelsea House Publishers, 1969), 2:1395. Richard H. Kehen and Gene Smilely, in "Mortgage Lending by National Banks,"

Business History Review 15 (Winter 1977): 474–91, note that national banks continued to hold mortgages.

71. Frank McKinney, *Trust Investments: General Principles* (New York: Press of Trust Companies Magazine, 1927), provides a state-by-state list of approved investments for corporate trustees, which many state courts took as guidelines for private trustees. Nine states permitted investment in corporate stocks (37). For the development of lists of approved investments, see Friedman, "Dynastic Trust," 557–62.

72. Richard Bensel, *Yankee Leviathan: The Origins of Central State Authority in America, 1859–1877* (New York: Cambridge University Press, 1990), 226–74.

73. See, for example, the Homans Real Estate Trust Deed, quoted in Priestley v. Burrill, 230 Mass. 452 (1918).

74. The use of real estate trusts as alternatives to either incorporated real estate companies or standard business partnerships in Massachusetts took off in the 1880s following two decisions, *Gleason v. McKay*, 134 Mass. 419 (1883), and *Phillips v. Blatchford*, 137 Mass. 510 (1894), ruling that such "associations," or "partnerships with transferable shares," having been formed under common law, were not subject to the state's excise tax on corporations. These cases laid the foundation for what came to be known nationwide as the "Massachusetts association," a business organized through trust agreements. In 1923 (*Hecht et al. v Malley, et al.*, 265 US 1444), after Congress revised a 1909 law, the Supreme Court ruled that such trusts were business associations subject to federal excise taxes. Massachusetts business trusts should not be confused with trusts organized as holding companies, the object of antimonopoly trust-busting. For an example of one early commercial real estate trust, see the Boston Real Estate Trust Agreement of 1886, organized by twenty Bostonians and capitalized at $2 million, quoted in *Priestly v. Burrill*, 230 Mass. 452.

75. For the formation of commercial real estate trusts out of practices learned in managing family trusts, see the career of Richards M. Bradley, who in the late 1880s became his mother's trustee. His mother's suit against her uncles, *Williams v. Bradley*, 85 Mass. 270 (1861), established the principle that trustees could not withhold trust income from the beneficiaries. Bradley joined prominent Bostonians in directing investments of the Boston Ground Rent Trust and the Western Real Estate Trustees; and with his brother-in-law, Owen F. Aldis, he established the Chicago Real Estate Trustees and the City Real Estate Trustees. For just one example of the process of organizing Boston investment in western cities, see John H. Storer to Richards M. Bradley, July 27, 1892, Bradley Family Papers, Series II, Box 20, Schlesinger Library, Radcliffe College, Cambridge, MA.

76. Massachusetts Tax Commissioner, *Report on Voluntary Associations*, January 17, 1812, House Document No. 1646, Massachusetts Assembly.

77. See accounts of the Adams Real Estate Trust in Adams Office Papers, cartons 2, 3, 8 and 69, Massachusetts Historical Society. For a parallel story of the Adams family investment in the state-chartered Riverbank Improvement Company for family land along Commonwealth Avenue, see cartons 4, 10, and 76.

78. Morton Keller, *Life Insurance Enterprise, 1885–1910: A Study in the Limits of Corporate Power* (Cambridge: Harvard University Press, 1963). By 1914, 84 percent of mortgages from banks and trust companies and 60 percent from life insurance companies were in non-farm property; Kingman Nott Robins, *The Farm Mortgage Handbook* (New York: Doubleday, Page, 1916), 223.

79. Chicago Real Estate Daily, April 16, 2009, http://www.chicagorealestatedaily.com/cgi-bin/news.pl?id=33713 (accessed August 10, 2009). See also Elizabeth Blackmar, "Of REITs

and Rights: Absentee Ownership at the Periphery," in *City, Country, Empire: Landscapes in Environmental History*, ed. Jeffrey M. Diefendorf and Kurk Dorsey (Pittsburgh: University of Pittsburgh Press, 2005).

80. George E. Marcus with Peter Dobkin Hall, *Lives in Trust: The Fortunes of Dynastic Families in Late Twentieth-Century America* (Boulder, CO: Westview Press, 1992).

Chapter 5

1. Address of Frederick Douglass in *American Slavery. Report of a public meeting held at Finsbury Chapel, Moorfields, to receive Frederick Douglass, the American slave, on Friday, May 22, 1846* (London, 1846), 11; address of Howell Cobb, in "Cotton Planters' Convention," *The American Cotton Planter* 2, no. 11 (1858): 331; Karl Marx, "The British Cotton Trade," *New-York Daily Tribune*, October 14, 1861. On the slave ship, see Marcus Rediker, *The Slave Ship: A Human History* (New York: Viking, 2007); on cotton, see Sven Beckert, "Emancipation and Empire: Reconstructing the World of Cotton Production in the Age of the American Civil War," *American Historical Review* 109, no. 5 (2004): 1405–38. While controversy continues over the link between New World slavery and the early modern emergence of capitalism— between the slave trade and capital accumulation, and between slave-produced sugar and metropolitan consumption—the link between slave-produced cotton and industrial capitalism in the nineteenth century is not disputed. Some landmark contributions to the debate over slavery and capitalism include Eric Williams, *Capitalism and Slavery* (Chapel Hill: University of North Carolina Press, 1944); D. B. Davis, *The Problem of Slavery in the Age of Revolution, 1770–1823* (Ithaca, NY: Cornell University Press, 1975); Eugene D. Genovese and Elizabeth Fox-Genovese, *Fruits of Merchant Capital: Slavery and Bourgeois Property in the Rise and Expansion of Capitalism* (New York: Oxford University Press, 1983); Sidney Mintz, *Sweetness and Power: The Place of Sugar in Modern History* (New York: Viking, 1985); Barbara L. Solow and Stanley L. Engerman, eds., *British Capitalism and Caribbean Slavery: The Legacy of Eric Williams* (Cambridge: Cambridge University Press, 1987); David Eltis, *Economic Growth and the Ending of the Transatlantic Slave Trade* (New York: Oxford University Press, 1987); Robin Blackburn. *The Making of New World Slavery: From the Baroque to the Modern 1492–1800* (New York: Verso, 1997); David Eltis and Stanley L. Engerman, "The Importance of Slavery and the Slave Trade to Industrializing Britain," *Journal of Economic History* 60 (March 2000): 123–44.

2. Ulrich B. Phillips, *American Negro Slavery* (New York: D. Appleton, 1918), 360–62; Du Bois review of Phillips in *W.E.B. Du Bois: A Reader*, ed. David L. Lewis (New York: H. Holt and Co., 1995), 193–96; Frederic Bancroft, *Slave-Trading in the Old South* (Baltimore: J. H. Furst Company, 1931), 67–87; Robert W. Fogel and Stanley L. Engerman, *Time on the Cross: The Economics of American Negro Slavery* (Boston: Little, Brown, 1974), 78–86, 107–57; Richard Sutch, "The Breeding of Slaves for Sale," in *Race and Slavery in the Western Hemisphere: Quantitative Studies*, ed. Stanley L. Engerman and Eugene D. Genovese (Princeton, NJ: Princeton University Press, 1975), 173–210; Herbert G. Gutman, *The Black Family in Slavery and Freedom, 1750–1925* (New York: Pantheon Books, 1976), 75–86, 80–84; Richard Lowe and Randolph B. Campbell, "The Slave-Breeding Hypothesis: A Demographic Comment on the 'Buying' and 'Selling' States," *Journal of Southern History* 42, no. 3 (1976): 401–12; Darlene Clark Hine, "Female Slave Resistance: The Economics of Sex," *Western Journal of Black Studies* 3, no. 2 (1979): 123–27; Deborah Gray White, *Ar'n't I a Woman?: Female Slaves in the Plantation South* (New York: Norton, 1985), 68, 103; Michael Tadman, *Speculators and Slaves: Masters, Traders, and Slaves in the Old South* (Madison: University of Wisconsin Press, 1989),

121–32; Robert W. Fogel and Stanley L. Engerman, "The Slave-Breeding Thesis," in *Without Consent or Contract: The Rise and Fall of American Slavery, Conditions of Slave Life and the Transition to Freedom: Technical Papers,* vol. 2, ed. Robert W. Fogel and Stanley L. Engerman (New York: Norton, 1992), 455–72.

    3. See Ira Berlin, *Generations of Captivity: A History of African-American Slaves* (Cambridge, MA: Belknap Press., 2003); Gavin Wright, *Slavery and American Economic Development* (Baton Rouge: Louisiana State University Press, 2006); Fogel and Engerman, *Time on the Cross,* 25–29; Allan Kulikoff, "A 'Prolifick' People: Black Population Growth in the Chesapeake Colonies, 1700–1790," *Southern Studies* 16 (1977): 391–428; Tadman, *Speculators and Slaves;* Philip D. Morgan, *Slave Counterpoint: Black Culture in the Eighteenth-Century Chesapeake and Lowcountry* (Chapel Hill: University of North Carolina Press, 1998), 75–95; Steven Deyle, *Carry Me Back: The Domestic Slave Trade in American Life* (New York: Oxford University Press, 2005); Adam Rothman, *Slave Country: American Expansion and the Origins of the Deep South* (Cambridge: Harvard University Press, 2005); James L. Huston, *Calculating the Value of the Union: Slavery, Property Rights, and the Economic Origins of the Civil War* (Chapel Hill: University of North Carolina Press, 2003),28; Robert W. Fogel, *Without Consent or Contract: The Rise and Fall of American Slavery* (New York: Norton, 1989), 106.

    4. Phillips, *American Negro Slavery,* 360–62; Bancroft, *Slave-Trading in the Old South,* 81, 67, 80, 84, 67; W.E.B. Du Bois, *Black Reconstruction in America, 1860–1880* (1935; New York: The Free Press, 1998), 11. Along with the scholarship cited in n. 2, see also for studies that explicitly join the argument over slave breeding and/or more generally address the subject of forcible sex, reproduction, and love under slavery: Kenneth M. Stampp, *The Peculiar Institution: Negro Slavery in the American South* (1956; reprint, London: Vintage Books, 1964), 245; John Hope Franklin, *From Slavery to Freedom: A History of American Negroes* (New York: Knopf, 1947), 131, 198; Winthrop D. Jordan, *White Over Black: American Attitudes Toward the Negro, 1550–1812* (New York: Norton, 1968), 32–40, 136–67; Eugene D. Genovese, *Roll, Jordan, Roll: The World the Slaves Made* (New York: Pantheon, 1974), 414–31; Herbert G. Gutman and Richard Sutch, "Victorians All? The Sexual Mores and Conduct of Slaves and Their Masters," in *Reckoning with Slavery: A Critical Study in the Quantitative History of American Slavery,* ed. Paul A. David et al. (New York: Oxford University Press, 1976), 134–62; Fogel, *Without Consent or Contract,* 116–53, 392; Brenda E. Stevenson, *Life in Black and White: Family and Community in the Slave South* (New York: Oxford University Press, 1996), 226–57; Berlin, *Generations of Captivity,* 168–69, 214–30; Roger L. Ransom, "Was It Really All That Great to Be a Slave? A Review Essay," *Agricultural History* 48, no. 4 (1974): 578–81; Kathleen M. Brown, *Good Wives, Nasty Wenches, and Anxious Patriarchs: Gender, Race, and Power in Colonial Virginia* (Chapel Hill: University of North Carolina Press, 1996); Jennifer L. Morgan, *Laboring Women: Reproduction and Gender in New World Slavery* (Philadelphia: University of Pennsylvania Press, 2004); Emily West, *Chains of Love: Slave Couples in Antebellum South Carolina* (Urbana: University of Illinois Press, 2004); Deyle, *Carry Me Back,* 46–51; Marie Jenkins Schwartz, *Birthing a Slave: Motherhood and Medicine in the Antebellum South* (Cambridge: Harvard University Press, 2006); Anthony W. Neal, *Unburdened by Conscience: A Black People's Collective Account of America's Ante-Bellum South and the Aftermath* (Lanham, MD: University Press of America, 2009), 71, 78; Annette Gordon-Reed, *The Hemingses of Monticello: An American Family* (New York: Norton, 2008).

    5. On chattel slavery and capitalist market relations in antebellum America, see Eugene D. Genovese, *The Political Economy of Slavery: Studies in the Economy and Society of the Slave South* (New York: Pantheon, 1965); Genovese, *Roll, Jordan, Roll;* Elizabeth Fox-Genovese,

Within the Plantation Household: Black and White Women of the Old South (Chapel Hill: University of North Carolina Press, 1989); Tadman, *Speculators and Slaves*; Roger Ransom and Richard Sutch, "Capitalists without Capital: The Burden of Slavery and the Impact of Emancipation," *Agricultural History* 62, no. 3 (1988): 133–60; James Oakes, *Slavery and Freedom: An Interpretation of the Old South* (New York: Knopf, 1990); Walter Johnson, *Soul by Soul: Life Inside the Antebellum Slave Market* (Cambridge: Harvard University Press, 1999); Walter Johnson, "The Pedestal and the Veil: Rethinking the Capitalism/Slavery Question," *Journal of the Early Republic* 24, no. 2 (2004): 299–308; Lacy Ford, "Reconsidering the Internal Slave Trade: Paternalism, Markets, and the Character of the Old South," in *The Chattel Principle: Internal Slave Trades in the Americas*, ed. Walter Johnson (New Haven: Yale University Press, 2004), 143–64; Edward E. Baptist, "'Cuffy,' 'Fancy Maids,' and 'One-Eyed Men': Rape, Commodification, and the Domestic Slave Trade," *American Historical Review* 106, no. 5 (2001): 1619–50; Robert H. Gudmestad, *A Troublesome Commerce: The Transformation of the Interstate Slave Trade* (Baton Rouge: Louisiana State University Press, 2003); Deyle, *Carry Me Back*, 94–183. On commodity relations and abolition of the Atlantic slave trade, see Philip Gould, *Barbaric Traffic: Commerce and Antislavery in the Eighteenth-Century Atlantic World* (Cambridge: Harvard University Press, 2003).

6. On capitalism, bourgeois asceticism, social reform, and antislavery, see Max Weber, *The Protestant Ethic and the Spirit of Capitalism*, trans. Talcott Parsons (London: G. Allen and Unwin, 1930); E. P. Thompson, "Time, Work-Discipline, and Industrial Capitalism," *Past and Present* 38 (1967): 56–97; Nancy F. Cott, "Passionlessness: An Interpretation of Victorian Sexual Ideology, 1790–1850," *Signs* 4, no. 2 (1978): 219–36; Ben Barker-Benfield, "The Spermatic Economy: A Nineteenth-Century View of Sexuality," *Feminist Studies* 1, no. 1 (1972): 45–74; Ronald G. Walters, "The Erotic South: Civilization and Sexuality in American Abolitionism," *American Quarterly* 25, no. 2 (1973): 177–201; Carol Lasser, "Voyeuristic Abolitionism: Sex, Gender, and the Transformation of Antislavery Rhetoric," *Journal of Early Republic* 28, no. 1 (2008): 83–114. But on desire see Edmund S. Morgan, "The Puritans and Sex," *New England Quarterly* 15 (1942): 597–602; Colin Campbell, *The Romantic Ethic and the Spirit of Modern Consumerism* (London: B. Blackwell, 1987); Karen Halttunen, "Humanitarianism and the Pornography of Pain in Anglo-American Culture," *American Historical Review* 100, no. 2 (1995): 303–34; Ann Fabian, *Card Sharps and Bucket Shops: Gambling in Nineteenth-Century America* (Ithaca, NY: Cornell University Press, 1990); Jackson Lears, *Something for Nothing: Luck in America* (New York: Viking, 2003). And on love as a subject of historical analysis, see, for example, "Special Issue on the History of Love," *Journal of Social History* 15, no. 3 (1982); Jan Lewis, *The Pursuit of Happiness: Family and Values in Jefferson's Virginia* (New York: Cambridge University Press, 1983), 169–208; Karen Lystra, *Searching the Heart: Women, Men, and Romantic Love in Nineteenth-Century America* (New York: Oxford University Press, 1989); Ruth H. Bloch, "Changing Conceptions of Sexuality and Romance in Eighteenth-Century America," *William and Mary Quarterly* 60 (January 2003), 13–42; Gordon-Reed, *The Hemingses of Monticello*.

7. John Quincy Adams, *Memoirs of John Quincy Adams, Comprising Portions of His Diary from 1795 to 1848*, ed. Charles Francis Adams, 12 vols. (Philadelphia, 1876), 11:50, and see 54, 65, 158, 342, 408. On the implications for slave households of westward expansion, see Berlin, *Generations of Captivity*, 14–18, 112–13, 157–93, 214–30.

8. Henry Clay, *Speech of Mr. Clay, of Kentucky, on the Measures of Compromise, Delivered in the Senate of the United States, July 22, 1850* (Washington, DC, 1850), 14, 13.

9. Ibid., 13; *Cong. Globe*, 31st Cong., 1st Sess., Appendix, 881.

10. Thaddeus Stevens, *Speech of the Hon. Thaddeus Stevens of Pennsylvania, On the Subject of the Admission of Slavery in the Territories, Delivered in the House of Representatives at Washington, Wednesday, February 20, 1850* (Harrisburg, PA, 1850), 3; *Speech of Hon. R. K. Meade, to his Constituents of the 2d Congressional District of Virginia, on the Subject of Restricting Slavery in the Territories of the United States. August 1849* (n.p., 1849), 2.

11. *Cong. Globe*, 31st Cong., 1st Sess., Appendix, 701, 703, 704.

12. *Speech of John Quincy Adams of Massachusetts, upon the Right of the People, Men and Women, to Petition on the Freedom of Speech and of Debate in the House of Representatives of the United States* (Washington, DC, 1838), 83; Adams, *Address of John Quincy Adams, to his Constituents of the Twelfth Congressional District, at Braintree, September 17th, 1842* (Boston, 1842), 16; William E. Channing, *A Letter to the Hon. Henry Clay, on the Annexation of Texas to the United States* (Boston, 1837), 36; *Cong. Globe*, 33rd Cong., 2nd Sess., Appendix, 231; *Cong. Globe*, 28th Cong., 1st Sess., Appendix, 532; *Cong. Globe*, 27th Cong., 3rd Sess., Appendix, 197, 195; Joshua R. Giddings, *Speech of Mr. J. R. Giddings, of Ohio, on the Annexation of Texas, Delivered in the House of Representatives, US, in Committee of the Whole on the State of the Union. May 21, 1844* (Washington, DC, n.d.), 3; Joshua R. Giddings, *Speech of Mr. J. R. Giddings, of Ohio, on the Annexation of Texas, Delivered in the House of Representatives, US, in Committee of the Whole on the State of the Union. Jan. 22, 1845* (n.p., n.d.), 4; Joshua R. Giddings, *Speeches in Congress* (Boston, 1853), 125, 98. See also Henry Wilson, *History of the Rise and Fall of the Slave Power in America*, 3 vols. (Boston, 1875), 1:42 and chap. 8; Oakes, *Slavery and Freedom*, 103, 143.

13. *Hansard's Parliamentary Debates*, 3rd ser., vol. 71 (London, 1843), 916–17; John Tyler, *Message from the President of the United States*, 28th Cong., 1st Sess. (June 6, 1844), 367; *Cong. Globe*, 28th Cong., 1st Sess., Appendix, 524; *Cong. Globe*, 28th Cong, 2nd Sess., 169; Giddings, *Speech of Mr. J. R. Giddings, of Ohio, on the Annexation of Texas*, 1. And see "The Economist's Library. Import Duties," *The Economist* (1844): 1138–39; "Parliamentary Intelligence," *The Times of London*, August 19, 1843, 3; "British Parliament," *Civilian and Galveston Gazette*, October 7, 1843, 2; "Texas," *New Englander* 2, no. 7 (1844): 453–69; *Cong. Globe*, 28th Cong., 1st sess., Appendix, 532, 169; John C. Calhoun, *The Works of John C. Calhoun*, ed. Richard K. Cralle, vol. 5, *Reports and Public Letters of John C. Calhoun* (New York, 1855), 311–35; Harriet Smither, "English Abolitionism and the Annexation of Texas," *Southwestern Historical Quarterly* 32, no. 3 (1929): 193–205; "The United States and Texas," *The Economist*, August 2, 1845, 717; Francis Wayland, "Slavebreeding in America: The Stevenson-O'Connell Imbroglio of 1838," *Virginia Magazine of History and Biography* 50, no. 1 (1942): 47–54; John Niven, *John C. Calhoun and the Price of Union: A Biography* (Baton Rouge: Louisiana State University Press, 1988), 268–82.

14. Horace Mann, *Slavery: Letters and Speeches* (Boston, 1853), 555; Charles Sumner, *The Barbarism of Slavery: Speech of Hon. Charles Sumner, on the Bill for the Admission of Kansas as a Free State, in the United States Senate, June 4, 1860* (New York, 1863), 39; Thomas Babington Macaulay, "A Speech Delivered in the House of Commons on the 26th of February, 1845," *The Miscellaneous Writings Speeches and Poems of Lord Macaulay*, 4 vols. (London, 1889), 3:276 (and quoted in *Cong. Globe*, 33rd Cong., 2nd sess., Appendix, 232); B. Gratz Brown, *Emancipation as a State Policy. Letter of B. Gratz Brown to the "Palmyra Courier"* (n.p., 1862), 14. See also Eric Foner, *Free Soil, Free Labor, Free Men* (New York: Oxford University Press, 1970), esp. 219–20.

15. *Cong. Globe*, 28th Cong., 2nd Sess., 91; *Cong. Globe*, 33rd Cong., 2nd Sess., Appendix, 233, 231; *Cong. Globe*, 31st Cong., 1st Sess., Appendix, 340, 341.

16. *Cong. Globe*, 31st Cong., 1st Sess., Appendix, 701, 702.

17. *Cong. Globe*, 30th Cong., 2nd Sess., Appendix, 319, 320, 321; Horace Mann, *Speech of Mr. Horace Mann, of Mass., on the Subject of Slavery in the Territories, and the Consequences of the Threatened Dissolution of the Union. Delivered in the House of Representatives, February 15, 1850* (Washington, DC, 1850), 12, 4, 3; Mann, *Slavery*, 58, 67–68, 555. See also Karen Sanchez-Eppler, *Touching Liberty: Abolition, Feminism, and the Politics of the Body* (Berkeley: University of California Press, 1993), 21–49; Amy Dru Stanley, "The Right to Possess All the Faculties that God Has Given: Possessive Individualism, Slave Women, and Abolitionist Thought," in *Moral Problems in American Life*, ed. Lewis Perry and Karen Halttunnen (Ithaca, NY: Cornell University Press, 1999); Pamela D. Bridgewater, "Un/Re/Dis Covering Slave Breeding in Thirteenth Amendment Jurisprudence," *Washington and Lee Race and Ethnic Ancestry Law Journal* 7 (2001): 11–43; Michael D. Pierson, *Free Hearts and Free Homes: Gender and American Antislavery Politics* (Chapel Hill: University of North Carolina Press, 2003); Lasser, "Voyeuristic Abolitionism"; Amy Dru Stanley, "Instead of Waiting for the Thirteenth Amendment: The War Power, Slave Marriage, and Inviolate Human Rights," *American Historical Review* 115, no. 3 (2010): 732–65. On masters' sale of children and slavery as prostitution, see, for example, "The Conflict between Religious Truth and American Infidelity. Speech of Hon. J. R. Giddings," *The Liberator*, March 19, 1858; Stevens, *Speech of the Hon. Thaddeus Stevens of Pennsylvania*.

18. Thomas Smallwood, *A Narrative of Thomas Smallwood (Coloured Man): Giving an Account of His Birth—The Period He Was Held in Slavery—His Release—and Removal to Canada, etc. Together With an Account of the Underground Railroad. Written by Himself* (Toronto, 1851), 52, 53.

19. Frederick Douglass, "Reception Speech at Finsbury Chapel, Moorsfield, England, May 12, 1846," in Douglass, *My Bondage and My Freedom* (New York, 1855), 411–12; Douglass, *My Bondage and My Freedom*, 217–19. See also "Letter from Frederick Douglass," *The Liberator*, June 26, 1846, 103; Douglass, "What, to the Slave, is the Fourth of July," in *Lift Every Voice: African American Oratory 1787–1900*, ed. Philip S. Foner and Robert James Branham (Tuscaloosa: University of Alabama Press, 1998), 259.

20. *Minutes of the Proceedings of a Convention of Delegates from the Abolition Societies Established in different Parts of the United States, Assembled at Philadelphia* (Philadelphia, 1794), in *American Convention for Promoting the Abolition of Slavery, and Improving the Condition of the African Race, Minutes, Constitution, Addresses, Memorials, Resolutions, Reports, Committees and Anti-Slavery Tracts*, 3 vols. (New York: Bergman Publishers, 1969), 1:24, 25; *The Abolitionist: Or Record of the New England Anti-Slavery Society* (Boston, 1833), 147; *Proceedings of the New-England Anti-Slavery Convention, Held in Boston on the 27th, 28th and 29th of May, 1834* (Boston, 1834), 65. Convention delegates came mainly from New England, but included abolitionists from New York, Ohio, and Kentucky. On the absence of attention to slave breeding in early antislavery protest, see, for example, an 1817 compilation of antislavery writings, which includes no protests against slave breeding, but, conversely, the observation that, in the West Indies, buying slaves was more profitable than the expense of propagating them, John Kendrick, *Horrors of Slavery: In Two Parts* (Cambridge, 1817), 24. On the rise of protest against slave breeding, see William Hillhouse, *Pocahontas: A Proclamation, with Plates* (New Haven, 1820); Alice Dana Adams, *The Neglected Period of Anti-Slavery in America (1808–1831)* (Boston, 1908), 196–98. See also Ulrich B. Phillips, ed., *Plantation and Frontier Documents: 1649–1863*, 2 vols. (1910; reprint New York: B. Franklin, 1969), 2:54–58, 1:109.

21. *Proceedings of the New-England Anti-Slavery Convention*, 60, and see 65, 31. On the reduction of slaves to the status of animals, see David Brion Davis, *Inhuman Bondage: The Rise and Fall of Slavery in the New World*, 28–64, 160, 178–79; Jordan, *White Over Black*, 28–38.

22. Wendell Phillips Garrison and Francis Jackson Garrison, *William Lloyd Garrison, 1805–1879: The Story of His Life Told by His Children*, 4 vols., vol. 3: *1841–1860* (New York, 1889), 289; William Goodell, *The American Slave Code in Theory and Practice: Its Distinctive Features Shown by Its Statutes, Judicial Decisions, and Illustrative Facts* (New York,1853), 61; Harriet Beecher Stowe, *Uncle Tom's Cabin, Or, Life among the Lowly* (Boston, 1851), 240, 268; Frances Ellen Watkins Harper, "Could We Trace the Record of Every Human Heart," *National Anti-Slavery Standard*, May 23, 1857. See also George Bourne, *Slavery Illustrated in Its Effects upon Woman and Domestic Society* (Boston, 1837), 33–94, 119; Harriet Beecher Stowe, *A Key to Uncle Tom's Cabin: Presenting the Original Facts and Documents upon which the Story Is Founded. Together with Corroborative Statements Verifying the Truth of the Work* (Boston, 1853), 151, 152; "A Moral Crusader," *Macmillan's Magazine* 62 (1890): 21; Archibald H. Grimké, *William Lloyd Garrison: The Abolitionist* (New York, 1891), 343; William Goodell, *Slavery and Anti-Slavery: A History of the Great Struggle in Both Hemispheres; With a View of the Slavery Question in the United States* (New York, 1852), 273; William Wells Brown, *Clotel; or, The President's Daughter: A Narrative of Slave Life in the United States* (London, 1853), 86, 62; Austin Steward, *Twenty-Two Years a Slave, and Forty Years a Freeman; Embracing a Correspondence of Several Years, While President of Wilberforce Colony, London, Canada West* (Rochester, NY, 1857), 131; Henry Clarke Wright, *No Rights, No Duties: Or, Slaveholders, as Such, Have No Rights; Slaves, as Such, Owe No Duties. An Answer to a Letter from Hon. Henry Wilson., Touching Resistance to Slaveholders, Being the Right and Duty of the Slaves, and of the People and States of the North* (Boston, 1860), 11; Frederick Law Olmstead, *A Journey in the Seaboard Slave States; With Remarks on Their Economy* (New York, 1856), 56–57, 281.

23. Theodore Dwight Weld, *American Slavery as It Is: Testimony of a Thousand Witnesses* (New York, 1839), 175, 110, 183, 182; Theodore Dwight Weld, *Slavery and the Internal Slave Trade in the United States of North America; Being Replies to Questions Transmitted by the Committee of the British and Foreign Anti-slavery Society, for the Abolition of Slavery and the Slave Trade throughout the World* (London, 1841), 32; "Mount Vernon a Human Stock Farm!" *Frederick Douglass' Paper*, October 29, 1852. See also, for example, "Letter from Mr. Child," *The Liberator,* August 13, 1836; "Thaddeus Stevens," *The Emancipator*, September 18, 1837; "A Stevenson and Slave Breeding Virginia," *Genius of Universal Emancipation*, March 8, 1839.

24. "The Late Annual Meeting," *The Emancipator*, May 29, 1840; *Influence of the Slave Power* (Boston, 1843), 2; John Stuart Mill, *The Subjection of Women* (London, 1869), 17, 16; *Report of the British and Foreign Anti-Slavery Society*, quoted in W. E. Adams, *The Slaveholders' War: An Argument for the North and the Negro* (London, 1863), 22; "The Impending Crisis in the Southern States of America," *The Economist,* December 24, 1859, 1429; "Cultivation of Cotton in India, and Slavery in America," *The Economist*, February 12, 1859, 167. See also Harriet Martineau, *Society in America*, 3 vols. (Paris, 1837), 2:118; Ebenezer Davies, *American Scenes, and Christian Slavery: A Recent Tour of Four Thousand Miles in the United States* (London, 1849), 80; Frances Anne Kemble, *Journal of a Residence on a Georgian Plantation in 1838–1839* (New York, 1864), 122, 60; J. E. Cairnes, *The Slave Power: Its Character, Career, and Probable Designs: Being an Attempt to Explain the Real Issues Involved in the American Contest* (New York, 1862), xiv, 76, 78; "The Political Economist," *The Economist,* August 2, 1845, 717; "Expedition against Cuba," *The Economist,* September 22, 1849, 10, 48; "A Thousand Chances to Make Money," *The Economist*, April 16, 1859, 426; "The Bearings of American Disunion," *The Economist,* January 12, 1861, 30. See also an 1838 letter from the Irish abolitionist Daniel O'Connell to the *London Morning Chronicle*, cited in William Lloyd Garrison, *Letter to Louis Kossuth, Concerning Freedom and Slavery in the United States* (Boston, 1852), 27.

25. William Ellery Channing, *Emancipation* (London, 1841), 40; Mann, *Slavery*, 555 (in particular, Mann was attacking the fugitive slave provision of the 1850 Compromise); Edward Atkinson, *Cheap Cotton by Free Labor: By a Cotton Manufacturer* (Boston, 1861), 29; *Minutes of Proceedings of the Requited Labor Convention, Held in Philadelphia, on the 17th and 18th of the Fifth Month, and, by Adjournment, on the 5th and 6th of the Ninth Month, 1838* (Philadelphia, 1838), 12. See also *Proceedings of the Anti-Slavery Convention of American Women, Held in the City of New York, May 9th, 10th, 11th, and 12th, 1837* (New York, 1837), 13; *Annual Report of the American and Foreign Anti-Slavery Society, Presented at New-York, May 6, 1851, with the Addresses and Resolutions* (New York, 1851), 95–96, 82; Lawrence Glickman, "'Buy for the Sake of the Slave': Abolitionism and the Origins of American Consumer Activism," *American Quarterly* 56, no. 4 (2004): 889–912; Carol Faulkner, "The Root of Evil: Free Produce and Radical Antislavery, 1820–1860," *Journal of the Early Republic* 27, no. 3 (2007): 377–405. On allegations of northern merchants' more general complicity with Southern slavery, see William Jay, *Miscellaneous Writings on Slavery* (Boston, 1853), 217–18; *Report of the Board of Managers of the Free Produce Association of Friends* (New York, 1850); Richard H. Abbott, *Cotton and Capital: Boston Businessmen and Antislavery Reform, 1854–1868* (Amherst: University of Massachusetts Press, 1991).

26. William E. Channing, *Slavery* (Boston, 1835), 81, 80, 81, 77, 79, 85, 92–93.

27. Weld, *Slavery and the Internal Slave Trade,* 42–43, 44, 42. And see Weld, *American Slavery as It Is,* 15, 115.

28. Weld, *American Slavery as It Is,* 182, 183; Martineau, *Society in America,* 328; William Jay, *A View of the Action of the Federal Government in Behalf of Slavery,* in Jay, *Miscellaneous Writings on Slavery,* 265, and see 258, 232; William I. Bowditch, *Slavery and the Constitution* (Boston, 1849), 75–76; Thomas R. Dew, *Review of the Debate in the Virginia Legislature of 1831 and 1832* (Richmond, VA, 1832), 49. See also, for example, "Slavery and the Slave-Trade under the Authority of Congress," *The Anti-Slavery Record* 3, no. 11 (1837): 9; Theodore Parker, *A Letter to the People of the United States Touching the Matter of Slavery* (Boston, 1848), 36–37; *The Letters of William Lloyd Garrison*, vol. 4, *From Disunionism to the Brink of War, 1850–1860* (Cambridge, MA: Belknap Press, 1976), 173; Joseph Sturge, *A Visit to the United States in 1841* (Boston, 1842), 97; Goodell, *Slavery and Anti-Slavery,* 248; "Abolition of Slavery. Speech of Hon. William Slade," *Niles' Register,* November 6, 1841, 154; Stowe, *A Key to Uncle Tom's Cabin,* 147–49; Wilson Armistead, ed., preface to *Five Hundred Thousand Strokes for Freedom: A Series of Anti-Slavery Tracts* (London, 1853), 6; Wilson, *History of the Rise and Fall of the Slave Power,* 1:100; John Jay, *Caste and Slavery in the American Church* (New York, 1843), 34; Wright, *No Rights, No Duties,* 5.

29. George Fitzhugh, *Cannibals All! Or, Slaves Without Masters* (Richmond, VA, 1857), 236, 237.

30. James Henry Hammond, "Hammond's Letters on Slavery," in *The Pro-Slavery Argument, as Maintained by the Most Distinguished Writers of the Southern States: Containing the Several Essays, on the Subject, of Chancellor Harper, Governor Hammond, Dr. Simms, and Professor Dew* (Charleston, SC, 1852), 161, 163, 165, 164; William Harper, "Harper's Memoir on Slavery," in ibid., 32, 33. On Southerners' denial of slave breeding, see also *Annual Report of the American and Foreign Anti-Slavery Society,* 82. Southern journals sometimes reprinted tirades against slave breeding; see, for example, D. Lee, "Plantation and Farm Economy," *Southern Cultivator* 10 (October 1852): 289. And see Fogel, *Without Consent or Contract,* 119–21; Deyle, *Carry Me Back,* 46–51.

31. Hammond, "Hammond's Letters on Slavery," 161, and see 32, 33, 160, 161, 163, 162.

See Elizabeth Fox-Genovese and Eugene D. Genovese, *The Mind of the Master Class: History and Faith in the Southern Slaveholders' Worldview* (New York: Cambridge University Press, 2005).

32. Fitzhugh, *Cannibals All!*, 318, 22; George Fitzhugh, *Sociology for the South, or the Failure of Free Society* (Richmond, VA, 1854), 248, 46, 200, 246.

33. Fitzhugh, *Cannibals All!*, 141, 52, 197, xviii–xix, 314–15, 141.

34. "A Voice from Africa. No. 3," *The Liberator*, January 2, 1836, 2; Parker, *A Letter to the People of the United States*, 37. The phrase "free love" was not used by abolitionists, but see its appearance in a quoted passage on the fundamental importance of the institution of marriage as the framework for the relation between the sexes, Bowditch, *Slavery and the Constitution*, 56–57. See Leslie M. Harris, *In the Shadow of Slavery: African Americans in New York City, 1626–1863* (Chicago: University of Chicago Press, 2003), 219–23; Hal Sears, *The Sex Radicals: Free Love in High Victorian America* (Lawrence, KS: Regents Press of Kansas, 1977); John C. Spurlock, *Free Love: Marriage and Middle-Class Radicalism in America, 1825–1860* (New York: New York University Press, 1990).

35. Gerrit Smith, *Letter of Gerrit Smith to Hon. Henry Clay* (New York, 1839). On Smith, see John Stauffer, *The Black Hearts of Men: Radical Abolitionists and the Transformation of Race* (Cambridge:: Harvard University Press, 2002).

36. "Letter from Jeremiah Holt to Thomas Ruffin," in *The Papers of Thomas Ruffin*, 4 vols., ed. G. De Roulhac Hamilton (Raleigh, NC: Edwards & Broughton, 1920), 3:175; *The State v. John Mann*, 13 NC 263 (1829), 266.

37. Petition of William Hickman to the Circuit Court of Bourbon County, Kentucky, June 6, 1829, Records of the Circuit Court, Case Files, box 718–722, packet 722, Bourbon County Courthouse, Paris, KY; Petition of Frederick Broaders and Laurent Dursse et al. to the Equity Court of the District of Charleston, South Carolina, February 24, 1820, Records of the Equity Court, Petitions, no. 1820-4, box 4, South Carolina Department of Archives and History (hereafter SCDAH), Columbia, SC; Petition of John Fettmelz et al. to the Equity Court of the District of Richland, South Carolina, January 21, 1832, Records of the Equity Court, Bills, roll 340, box 42, SCDAH. See also Johnson, *Soul by Soul*, 78–116; Gutman, *The Black Family in Slavery and Freedom*, 76.

38. Petition of Elizabeth Mills et al. to the Equity Court of Craven County, North Carolina, ca. 1836, John H. Bryan Collection, Slaves and Emancipation, North Carolina Department of Archives and History, Raleigh, NC; Petition of Robert Wade et al. to the Chancery Court of Maury County, Tennessee, January 28, 1832, Records of the Chancery Court, Case Files, Maury County Courthouse, Columbia, TN; Petition of the grandchildren of William Smiley to the Equity Court of the District of Richland, South Carolina, December 21, 1846, Records of the Equity Court, Bills, box 62, folder 2, SCDAH.

39. Petition of William Robinson to the Circuit Court of Chesterfield County, Virginia, ca. 1858, Chancery Court Causes, box 464, folder R-21858, Library of Virginia, Richmond; Petition of Daniel Brunson to the Equity Court of the District of Edgefield, South Carolina, January 15, 1859, Records of the Equity Court, Petitions, microfilm reel 3, MD163, frame 149, SCDAH; Petition of Lewis and John Featherston to the Equity Court of the District of Anderson, South Carolina, June 9, 1859, Records of the Equity Court, Bills, no. 1860-303, box 7, SCDAH; Petition of William Botkin Jr. et al. to the Circuit Court of Harrison County, Kentucky, March 28, 1831, Records of the Circuit Court, Case Files, no. 6080, box 221–224, Harrison County Courthouse, Cynthiana, KY.

40. Petition of William Owens to the Circuit Court of Albemarle County, Virginia,

March 14, 1856, Chancery Court Suits, box 644, Library of Virginia, Richmond; Petition of C. D. Melton to the Equity Court of the District of Chester, South Carolina, July 2, 1859, Records of the Equity Court, Petitions, no. 423, SCDAH; Petition of William E. Cameron to the Hustings Court of the City of Petersburg, Virginia, February 18, 1864, Ended Chancery Court Causes, packet 19, box 18–21, Circuit Court Clerk's Office, Petersburg, VA; Petition of Willis Wallace and Kitty Goodman to the Equity Court of the District of Laurens, South Carolina, May 16, 1864, Records of the Equity Court, Petitions, no. 1864–99, box 2, SCDAH.

41. See "Cotton Planters' Convention," 331; "Management of Slaves," *Southern Cultivator* 4 (March 1846): 43; T. E. Blunt, "Rules for the Government of Overseers," *Southern Cultivator* 5 (April 1847): 61; "Rules of the Plantation," *Southern Cultivator* 7 (July 1849): 103; "Management of Negroes upon Southern Estates," *Debow's Review* 10 (June 1851): 621. And see also Gutman, *The Black Family in Slavery and Freedom*. On field labor and the decline of fertility, see Richard Follett, "Heat, Sex, and Sugar: Pregnancy and Childbearing in the Slave Quarters," *Journal of Family History* 28 (October 2003): 510–39.

42. Petition of John Winston to the Virginia Legislature, December 11, 1820, Legislative Petitions, Henrico County, Library of Virginia, Richmond.

43. On slavery, love, sexuality, and marriage, see John W. Blassingame, *The Slave Community: Plantation Life in the Antebellum South* (New York: Oxford University Press, 1972), 149–91; Genovese, *Roll, Jordan, Roll*, 458–501; Stevenson, *Life in Black and White*, 226–57; Gutman, *The Black Family in Slavery and Freedom*, pt. 1; West, *Chains of Love*; Norrece T. Jones Jr., "Rape in Black and White: Sexual Violence in the Testimony of Enslaved and Free Americans," and Jan Lewis, "Commentary," in *Slavery and the American South*, ed. Winthrop D. Jordan (Jackson: University Press of Mississippi, 2003), 93–116. On slave narratives as historical source and cultural production, see John Blassingame, "Using the Testimony of Ex-Slaves," in *The Slave's Narrative*, ed. Charles T. Davis and Henry Louis Gates Jr. (New York: Oxford University Press, 1985); Ann Fabian, *The Unvarnished Truth: Personal Narratives in Nineteenth-Century America* (Berkeley: University of California Press, 2000); Charles J. Heglar, *Rethinking the Slave Narrative: Slave Marriage and the Narratives of Henry Bibb and William and Ellen Craft* (Westport, CT: Greenwood Press, 2001).

44. J. D. Green, *Narrative of the Life of J. D. Green, a Runaway Slave, from Kentucky, Containing an Account of His Three Escapes, in 1839, 1846, and 1848* (Huddersfield, Eng, 1864), 15, 16, 18, 22.

45. Andrew Jackson, *Narrative and Writings of Andrew Jackson, of Kentucky; Containing an Account of His Birth, and Twenty-Six Years of His Life While a Slave; His Escape; Five Years of Freedom, Together with Anecdotes Relating to Slavery; Journal of One Year's Travels, Sketches, etc. Narrated by Himself; Written by a Friend* (Syracuse, NY, 1847), 8.

46. Charles Ball, *Slavery in the United States: A Narrative of the Life and Adventures of Charles Ball, a Black Man, Who Lived Forty Years in Maryland, South Carolina and Georgia, as a Slave Under Various Masters, and was One Year in the Navy with Commodore Barney, During the Late War* (New York, 1837), 70, 72.

47. William Wells Brown, *Narrative of William W. Brown, a Fugitive Slave. Written by Himself* (Boston, 1847), 86, 88, 87, 81.

48. Henry Bibb, *Narrative of the Life and Adventures of Henry Bibb, an American Slave, Written by Himself* (New York, 1849), 33–35, 40, 35. See also Israel Campbell, *An Autobiography. Bond and Free: Or, Yearnings for Freedom, from My Green Brier House. Being the Story of My Life in Bondage, and My Life in Freedom* (Philadelphia, 1861), 57. And see Heglar, *Rethinking the Slave Narrative*, 33–78.

49. Harriet Jacobs, *Incidents in the Life of a Slave Girl. Written by Herself* (Boston, 1861), 76, 122, 31, 60, 29, 45, 61–62, 58, 85. On slavery, love, and female volition, see Gordon-Reed, *The Hemingses of Monticello*; Liese M. Perrin, "Resisting Reproduction: Reconsidering Slave Contraception in the Old South," *Journal of American Studies* 35 (2001): 255–74; Claudia Tate, *Domestic Allegories of Political Desire: The Black Heroine's Text at the Turn of the Century* (New York: Oxford University Press, 1992); Thelma Jennings, "'Us Colored Women Had to Go Through a Plenty': Sexual Exploitation of African-American Slave Women," *Journal of Women's History* 1 (Winter 1990): 45–66.

50. Douglass, *My Bondage and My Freedom*, 86, 87, 86, 88.

51. Ibid., 87, 86.

52. Charles Grandison Finney, "Lecture IV: True and False Religion," *The Oberlin Evangelist: A Semi-Monthly Periodical Devoted to the Promotion of Religion,* February 13, 1839, 34.

Chapter 6

1. William Duane, *Observations on the Principles and Operation of Banking with Strictures on the Opposition to the Bank of Philadelphia* (Philadelphia: Helmbold, 1804), 8–9.

2. A fourth type of capital, equity capital or owner equity, is simply an accounting term that refers to the difference between the value of a business's assets and its liabilities.

3. Use of the term "capitalist" in America dates to at least 1791, but it shared time with phrases like "moneyed men" well into the nineteenth century. "Capitalist," *Oxford English Dictionary Online*; Alexander Hamilton, *Report of the Secretary of the Treasury of the United States, on the Subject of Manufactures,* December 5, 1791; Tench Coxe, *A View of the United States of America in a Series of Papers, Written at Various Times, Between the Years 1787 and 1794* (Philadelphia: Wrigley and Berriman, 1794), 381.

4. Egerton argued that "*the* key ingredient in producing a robust capitalist economy above the Mason-Dixon was the rise of a fluid, free labor force, an ingredient notably absent in the South" (Douglas Egerton, "Markets Without a Market Revolution: Southern Planters and Capitalism," *Journal of the Early Republic* 16 [Summer 1996]: 207–21, 211). Rather than viewing free labor as a cause, a veritable sine qua non, of capitalism, I see its rise as an effect of capitalism. In any event, firm labor choices North and South can be explained with a simple cost-benefit model. Robert E. Wright, *Fubarnomics: A Lighthearted, Serious Look at America's Economic Ills* (Buffalo, NY: Prometheus, 2010).

5. Robert E. Wright, *Origins of Commercial Banking in America, 1750–1800* (Lanham, MD: Rowman and Littlefield, 2001); Robert E. Wright, *The First Wall Street: Chestnut Street, Philadelphia, and the Birth of American Finance* (Chicago: University of Chicago Press, 2005); Robert E. Wright and David J. Cowen, *Financial Founding Fathers: The Men Who Made America Rich* (Chicago: University of Chicago Press, 2006).

6. Robert E. Wright, *One Nation Under Debt: Hamilton, Jefferson, and the History of What We Owe* (New York: McGraw-Hill, 2008). The data underlying these assertions can be downloaded here: http://eh.net/databases/govtbond/.

7. Those published prices can be downloaded here: http://eh.net/databases/early-us-securities-prices.

8. For a similar argument using different examples, see [William Bard?], *An Inquiry Into the Nature and Utility of Corporations, Addressed to the Farmers, Mechanics, and Laboring Men of Connecticut* ([New York?], [1835?]), 2–3.

9. Robert E. Wright, *The Wealth of Nations Rediscovered: Integration and Expansion in American Financial Markets, 1780–1850* (New York: Cambridge University Press, 2002);

Robert E. Wright, *Hamilton Unbound: Finance and the Creation of the American Republic* (Westport, CT: Praeger, 2002).

10. Thomas Cochran, "The Business Revolution," *American Historical Review* 79 (December 1974): 1449–66, quotations at 1456, 1457. For information on corporations, see, for example, John Eilert, "Illinois Business Incorporations, 1816–1869," *Business History Review* 37 (Autumn 1963): 169–81.

11. "Manufacturing Corporations," *American Jurist* (July 1829): 94.

12. Robert E. Wright, "Rise of the Corporation Nation," in *Founding Choices: American Economic Policy in the 1790s*, ed. Douglas Irwin and Richard E. Sylla (Chicago: University of Chicago Press, 2011), 217–58; James Taylor, *Creating Capitalism: Joint-Stock Enterprise in British Politics and Culture, 1800–1870* (Woodbridge: Boydell, 2006), 6; Joseph Angell and Samuel Ames, *A Treatise on the Law of Private Corporations Aggregate* (Boston: Hilliard, Gray, Little and Wilkins, 1832), v–vi, 35.

13. Jonathan Fairplay, *Distributing the Surplus Revenue: Equal Rights Against Monopoly* (New York: Henry Ludwig, 1837), 7. See also *Letter on the Use and Abuse of Corporations* (New York: C and G Carvill, 1827), 35.

14. Richard Sylla, Jack Wilson, and Robert E. Wright, "Early U.S. Securities Prices," EH.NET, based on National Science Foundation, grant no. SES-9730692, "America's First Securities Markets, 1787–1836: Emergence, Development, Integration."

15. Nathan Appleton, *Introduction of the Power Loom and Origin of Lowell* (Lowell, MA: B. H. Penhallow, 1858), 30; [Bard?], *An Inquiry Into the Nature and Utility of Corporations*, 3; *What Is a Monopoly?: Or Some Considerations Upon the Subject of Corporations and Currency* (New York: George P. Scott and Co., 1835), 12.

16. Limited liability came to Britain much later, presumably because wealthy elites did not need it and did not wish to empower economic competitors who might later rival them politically as well. Douglass North, John Wallis, and Barry Weingast, *Violence and Social Orders: A Conceptual Framework for Recorded Human History* (New York: Cambridge University Press, 2009).

17. Adam Smith, *An Inquiry Into the Nature and Causes of the Wealth of Nations* (New York: Modern Library, 1937), 700.

18. Paul Paskoff, *Industrial Evolution: Organization, Structure, and Growth of the Pennsylvania Iron Industry, 1750–1860* (Baltimore: Johns Hopkins University Press, 1983), 91–131; Lucius Ellsworth, "Craft to National Industry in the Nineteenth Century: A Case Study of the Transformation of the New York State Tanning Industry," *Journal of Economic History* 32 (1972): 399–402.

19. Robert E. Wright, Wray Barber, Matthew Crafton, and Anand Jain, *History of Corporate Governance: The Importance of Stakeholder Activism*, 6 vols. (London: Pickering and Chatto, 2004); "Manufacturing Corporations," 114; Wilbur Dreikorn, "The History and Development of Banking in New Jersey," master's thesis, Rutgers-ABA, 1949, 31.

20. C. H. Lee, "Corporate Behaviour in Theory and History: I. The Evolution of Theory," *Business History* 32 (January 1990): 17–31.

21. Appleton, *Introduction of the Power Loom*, 14; Paskoff, *Industrial Evolution*, 91–131.

22. Engineers Annual Report to the President and Stockholders of the Cincinnati Gas Light and Coke Co., January 1847, Box 7, Folder 56, John Jeffrey Papers, Filson Historical Society, Louisville, KY; Appleton, *Introduction of the Power Loom*, 8–11, 26, 32.

23. C. G. Haines, *Arguments Against the Justice and Policy of Taxing the Capital Stock of Banks and Insurance Companies in the State of New York* (New York: Hopkins, 1824), 20.

24. *Letter on the Use and Abuse of Corporations*, 36–37. As early as 1765 Americans knew that "an increase in price, and falling in the goodness of quality, is the usual effect of monopolies." *Considerations on the Propriety of Imposing Taxes in the British Colonies* . . . (New York: John Holt, 1765), 43.

25. George Taylor, *Effect of Incorporated Coal Companies Upon the Anthracite Coal Trade of Pennsylvania* (Pottsville, PA: Benjamin Bannan, 1833), 22–25; *Observations on the Principles and Operation of Banking with Strictures on the Opposition to the Bank of Philadelphia* (Philadelphia: Helmbold, 1804), 18; John L. Sullivan, *The Answer of Mr. Sullivan to the Letter and Mis-statements of the Hon. Cadwallader D. Colden* (Troy, NY: William S. Parker, 1823), 24–25; *Letter on the Use and Abuse of Corporations*, 16–19; Jeremiah O'Callaghan, *Usury, Funds, and Banks* (Burlington, VT: For the author, 1834), 159–66; *Letters to the People of New Jersey on the Frauds, Extortions, and Oppressions of the Railroad Monopoly* (Philadelphia: Carey and Hart, 1848), 3–4; *Beauties of the Monopoly System of New Jersey* (Philadelphia: C. Sherman, 1848), 2.

26. *What Is a Monopoly?*, 18. See also *Letters to the People of New Jersey*, 8, 11.

27. William Alexander Duer, *A Reply to Mr. Colden's Vindication of the Steam-Boat Monopoly* (Albany: E. and E. Hosford, 1819), 14. Duer claimed that his definition of monopoly was "of common use and known import." See also *What Is a Monopoly?*, 12.

28. Taylor, *Effect of Incorporated Coal Companies*, 11.

29. *Cause of, and Cure for, Hard Times* (New York, 1818), 25. See also page 41, which discusses how merchants and speculators (both plural) "enhance the price to an extravagant amount, double or treble their real worth, or what they would be had at without monopoly, thus compelling their fellow men, who cannot do without them, to give those exorbitant prices."

30. [Bard?], *An Inquiry Into the Nature and Utility of Corporations*, 1.

31. Taylor, *Effect of Incorporated Coal Companies*, 15–16, 19–22.

32. *Letter on the Use and Abuse of Corporations*, 36; Taylor, *Effect of Incorporated Coal Companies*, 4.

33. On marine insurance, see Christopher Kingston's papers on the subject: http://www.amherst.edu/~cgkingston/Research.html. See also *What Is a Monopoly?*, 18, and David and Philip Grimm to Watson and Paul, February 4, 1799, Historical Society of Pennsylvania. Newark meeting as quoted in Daniel Walker Howe, *What Hath God Wrought: The Transformation of America, 1815–1848* (New York: Oxford University Press, 2007), 558.

34. Appleton, *Introduction of the Power Loom*, 15–16.

35. Ibid., 30; *Letters to the People of New Jersey*, 51–57; *Beauties of the Monopoly System of New Jersey*, 3; Taylor, *Effect of Incorporated Coal Companies*, 5.

36. Taylor, *Effect of Incorporated Coal Companies*, 5; O'Callaghan, *Usury, Funds, and Banks*, 157. "The insolvency of corporations arises from similar causes to that of individuals. Among the most important, are, a fall in the price of manufactured articles; an improvident expenditure which renders the cost of the manufactured article higher than it can be sold for; losses by the failure of agents and factors, or other persons indebted to them; a fraudulent division of the property among the stockholders." "Manufacturing Corporations," 116.

37. "Manufacturing Corporations," 94.

38. Taylor, *Effect of Incorporated Coal Companies*, 9–14.

39. Pauline Maier, "The Revolutionary Origins of the American Corporation," *William and Mary Quarterly*, 3rd ser., 50, no. 1 (January 1993): 51–84; G.H.E., "Harrison's 'Shuttlecock,'" *Radical, in Continuation of Working Man's Advocate* (April 1841); *Letter on the Use and Abuse of Corporations*, 11, 41–45; "Chenango Bank Stopped," Diary of Henry Van Der Lyn, 1:213–14, New York Historical Society.

40. *A View of Certain Proceedings in the Two Houses of the Legislature, Respecting the Incorporation of the New State Bank* (Albany, NY: Daniel and Samuel Whiting, 1803), 23; *What Is a Monopoly?*, 29–30; *Letters to the People of New Jersey*, 8; *Beauties of the Monopoly System of New Jersey*, 3. Douglas Arner, "Development of the American Law of Corporations to 1832," *SMU Law Review* 55 (2002): 47–48; Taylor, *Effect of Incorporated Coal Companies*, 16.

41. *Letter on the Use and Abuse of Corporations*, 7–10; Sullivan, *The Answer of Mr. Sullivan*, 20; "Chenango Bank Stopped," 1:214.

42. *Cause of, and Cure for, Hard Times*, 44.

43. Ibid., 16. See also O'Callaghan, *Usury, Funds, and Banks*, 158.

44. *Letter on the Use and Abuse of Corporations*, 3–4, 54; Taylor, *Effect of Incorporated Coal Companies*, 16; *What Is a Monopoly?*, 13.

45. Andrew Schocket, *Founding Corporate Power in Early National Philadelphia* (DeKalb: Northern Illinois University Press, 2007); *Letter on the Use and Abuse of Corporations*, 3; Taylor, *Effect of Incorporated Coal Companies*, 26.

46. *Cause of, and Cure for, Hard Times*, 67.

47. John F. Watson, *Annals of Philadelphia* (Philadelphia: E. L. Carey and A. Hart, 1830), 219.

48. Taylor, *Effect of Incorporated Coal Companies*, 25; Asa Martin, "Lotteries in Pennsylvania Prior to 1833," *Pennsylvania Magazine of History and Biography* 47 (1923): 307–27; 48 (1924): 66–93, 159–76.

49. *Can the Camden and Amboy Monopoly Be Lawfully Abolished?* (Burlington, NJ: 1855), 14–15; Arner, "Development of the American Law of Corporations to 1832," 48–50.

50. As quoted in Taylor, *Effect of Incorporated Coal Companies*, 12.

51. *View of Certain Proceedings in the Two Houses of the Legislature*, 6; Jonas Platt, *Mr. Platt's Speech on the Bill for Establishing the Western District Bank* (n.p, 1811), 5.

52. There is no easy way to demonstrate this claim in short compass. See Wright, *Wealth of Nations Rediscovered*, Wright, *Hamilton Unbound*, and Wright, *One Nation Under Debt*, for evidence, which entails reporting the number of stockholders and describing the distribution of holdings (minimum, maximum, mean, median, and mode holdings) for a sample of corporations at a moment in time.

53. This claim often is, but should not be, confused with political terms like "democratic." Just as no law barred white men from voting in most states by the Jacksonian period, no law barred them, or women or free blacks for that matter, from owning corporate securities. Early and widespread limited liability also lowered entry barriers for investors, especially smallholders whose entire net worth could be easily wiped out otherwise. But simply because someone has the legal right to vote or own securities, however, does not mean that he or she will do so at every opportunity. Corporations were certainly not a means of significant elite political control. See Robert E. Wright, review of Andrew M. Schocket, *Founding Corporate Power in Early National Philadelphia*, in *Register of the Kentucky Historical Society* (Spring 2007): 295–97. The large number of corporations suggests that they were also not a means of elite economic control in most instances either, except as discussed in the text.

54. [Bard?], *An Inquiry Into the Nature and Utility of Corporations*, 2; Henry Ashmead, *History of the Delaware County National Bank* (Chester, PA: The Chester Times, 1914), 13, 168–70; John A. Patterson, "Ten and One-Half Years of Commercial Banking in a New England Country Town: Concord, Massachusetts, 1832–1842," Old Sturbridge Village, Sturbridge, MA, 1971, 14–25; Harvey Tuckett, *Practical Remarks on the Present State of Life Insurance in the United States* (Philadelphia: Smith and Peters, 1850), 28.

55. Alan Olmstead, "Investment Constraints and New York City Mutual Savings Bank

Financing of Antebellum Development," *Journal of Economic History* 32 (December 1972): 811–40. For the good done by the Hartford Savings Bank, see Bard?, *An Inquiry Into the Nature and Utility of Corporations*, 9–10.

56. [Bard?], *An Inquiry Into the Nature and Utility of Corporations*, 5.

57. Ibid., 4.

58. Maier, "Revolutionary Origins of the American Corporation," 75; "Manufacturing Corporations," 94; Achille Murat, *A Moral and Political Sketch of the United States of North America* (London: Effingham Wilson, 1833), 337–38; *What Is a Monopoly?*, 9; Samuel Breck, *Sketch of the Internal Improvements Already Made by Pennsylvania* (Philadelphia: J. Maxwell, 1818), 11.

59. John P. Jackson, *A General Railroad System for New Jersey, by Free Legislation for Local Railroads for Every Part of the State and a Main Trunk Double-Track Railway for the Nation, and an Examination of the Alleged Monopoly of the Camden and Amboy Railroad Company* (Newark, NJ: A. Stephen Holbrook, 1860); Breck, *Sketch of the Internal Improvements*, 11–12.

60. Joseph Saltar, "Among the causes that contributed to the growth and prosperity of Buffalo, was the establishment in the year 1829 of a Branch of the Bank of the United States" (July 1862). See also Platt, *Mr. Platt's Speech*, 6.

61. Breck, *Sketch of the Internal Improvements*, 21; *View of Certain Proceedings in the Two Houses of the Legislature*, 11. Richard Sylla, John Wallis, and John Legler, "Banks and State Public Finance in the New Republic: The United States, 1790–1860," *Journal of Economic History* 47 (June 1987): 391–403.

62. Maier, "Revolutionary Origins of the American Corporation," 51–84.

63. Ronald Seavoy, *The Origins of the American Business Corporation, 1784–1855: Broadening the Concept of Public Service during Industrialization* (Westport, CT: Greenwood Press, 1982), 3–7, 149–75; L. Ray Gunn, *The Decline of Authority: Public Economic Policy and Political Development in New York State, 1800–1860* (Ithaca, NY: Cornell University Press, 1988), 222–45.

64. Taylor, *Effect of Incorporated Coal Companies*, 26; *What Is a Monopoly?*, 13, 18–19.

65. *The Doctrine of Anti-Monopoly in an Address to the Democracy of the City of New York* (New York, 1835).

66. John J. Wallis, "The National Era," in Price Fishback et al., *Government and the Economy: A New History* (Chicago: University of Chicago Press, 2007), 179.

67. "General incorporations are now in force in nearly every State in the Union." Victor Morawetz, *Treatise on the Law of Private Corporations* (1886), 27, 38. But in many states corporations could still apply for special charters if organizers did not wish to form under existing general incorporation statutes. Special chartering did not begin to fade in absolute terms until after 1904. Presumably, a special charter was not deemed a grant of special privilege if largely the same terms were available via general incorporate laws. Susan Pace Hamill, "From Special Privilege to General Utility: A Continuation of Willard Hurst's Study of Corporations," *American University Law Review* (October 1999): 82–180.

68. *Letters to the People of New Jersey*, 14; *Can the Camden and Amboy Monopoly Be Lawfully Abolished?*; Jackson, *General Railroad System for New Jersey*; John Cadman, *The Corporation in New Jersey: Business and Politics, 1791–1875* (Cambridge: Harvard University Press, 1949), 59, 174, 437.

69. *Speech of Charles C. Bonney, of Peoria, Against an Act Entitled an Act to Incorporate the Illinois River Improvement Company* (St. Louis, 1857).

70. William C. Barney, *The Ocean Monopoly and Commercial Suicide* (New York, March 1856).

71. Burton Folsom, *The Myth of the Robber Barons*, 3rd ed. (Herndon, VA: Young America's Foundation, 1996), 1–15.

72. As quoted in Seavoy, *Origins of the American Business Corporation*, 183.

73. Luther Kauffman, *Kauffman's Manual for Stock Companies, Organized Under the Laws of Colorado* (Denver: Whipple and Pierson, 1882), in *History of Corporate Governance: The Importance of Stakeholder Activism*, ed. Robert E. Wright et al. (London: Pickering and Chatto, 2004), 5:81–82; George H. Evans, *Business Incorporations in the United States, 1800–1943* (Cambridge, MA: National Bureau of Economic Research, 1948), 10–12, 31.

74. Henry G. Manne, "Our Two Corporation Systems: Law and Economics," *Virginia Law Review* 53 (March 1967); Henry Hitchcock, "Annual Address," *Annual Report of the American Bar Association* (1887), 233–60.

75. John Majewski, *A House Dividing: Economic Development in Pennsylvania and Virginia before the Civil War* (New York: Cambridge University Press, 2000), 85–86.

76. *What Is a Monopoly?*, 32–34.

77. *Answer and Remonstrance of the American Telegraph Company to the Memorial of the Magnetic Telegraph Company and the New England Union Telegraph Company* (1858); Josiah Quincy, *Public Interest and Private Monopoly: An Address Delivered Before the Boston Board of Trade, October 16, 1867* (Boston: J. H. Eastburn, 1867), 12.

78. Henry Wood, *The Long-Suffering Shareholder, Railroad Directorial Mismanagement, and Governmental Oppression* (Boston: W. B. Clarke, 1889), in *History of Corporate Governance*, ed. Wright et al., 5:284.

79. All in Wright et al., eds., *History of Corporate Governance*: Minnesota Electoral Reform Association, *Minority Representation in Stock Companies* (Minneapolis: Minnesota Electoral Reform Association, 1874) , 4:353–60; *Arguments of the New York Cheap Transportation Associations in Favor of . . . Minority Representation in Boards of Direction of Railroad Companies* (Albany, NY, 1874), 4:364–84; Henry Wood, *The Long-Suffering Shareholder, Railroad Directorial Mismanagement, and Governmental Oppression* (Boston: W. B. Clarke, 1889), 5:285–90.

80. Wood, *Long-Suffering Shareholder*, 5:290.

81. Colleen A. Dunlavy, "Social Conceptions of the Corporation: Insights from the History of Shareholding Voting Rights," *Washington and Lee Law Review* 63, no. 1 (Fall 2006): 353, 361; Lee, "Corporate Behaviour in Theory and History," 17–31; Adolf Berle and Gardiner Means, *The Modern Corporation and Private Property* (New York: Harcourt, Brace and World, 1932; New Brunswick, NJ: Transaction Publishers, 1991).

82. Gardiner Means, "Implications of the Corporate Revolution in Economic Theory," in Berle and Means, *The Modern Corporation and Private Property*, xlii.

83. Thomas Navin and Marian Sears, "The Rise of a Market for Industrial Securities, 1887–1902," *Business History Review* 29 (1955): 105–39; Naomi Lamoreaux, *The Great Merger Movement in American Business, 1895–1904* (New York: Cambridge University Press, 1988).

Chapter 7

1. John Lowell (hereafter JL) to Francis Cabot Lowell, January 16, 1805, in Francis Cabot Lowell Papers (hereafter FCL), Massachusetts Historical Society, Boston; [JL], "Original Letters; from an American Traveller in Europe," *Monthly Anthology, and Boston Review* 4 (January 1807): 29 and 5 (February 1809): 90; "Observations by J. Lowell Esq. in his passage to Europe

1803," FCL; JL to Rebecca Lowell, December 17, 1804, FCL; JL to Samuel P. Gardner, September 22, 1804, FCL. On the culture of refinement, see Richard L. Bushman, *The Refinement of America: Persons, Houses, Cities* (New York: Knopf, 1992).

2. [JL]," "Original Letters," *Monthly Anthology, and Boston Review* 5 (September 1808): 10; JL to Francis Cabot Lowell, March 29, 1804, FCL.

3. The word "dock," as opposed to wharf, quay, pier, or slip, was usually reserved for just these commercial complexes.

4. Diary of Mary B. Thompson, October 7, 1817, William B. Thompson Collection, Historical Society of Pennsylvania, Philadelphia; diary of Charles E. Cathrall, May 13 (Liverpool) and 23 (London), 1834, Historical Society of Pennsylvania; *England Described: or, the Traveller's Companion* (London, 1788), 231; "Miscellaneous Paragraphs," *The Port-Folio*, September 17, 1803, 301; S.W., *A Visit to London Containing a Description of the Principal Curiosities in the British Metropolis* (Philadelphia, 1817), 88–92; [S. G. Goodrich], *Peter Parley's Rambles in England, Wales, Scotland and Ireland* (New York, 1839), 9, 97–99; Heman Humphrey, *Great Britain, France, and Belgium*, 2 vols. (New York, 1838), 1:192; Orville Dewey, *The Old World and the New*, 2 vols. (New York, 1836), 1:20; "London—Its Docks—Shipping—and Tunnel," *The New-Yorker*, November 12, 1836, 2. This essay is based almost entirely on American sources: unpublished diaries and letters written by Americans, works by Americans published in America, and articles appearing in American newspapers and magazines (some of them reprinted from British publications). I am not arguing that American responses were unique. The reprinting of English material in American periodicals, for example, indicates otherwise, as do the urban guidebooks published in England. Outside the Anglo-American world, responses to the docks among the educated may have been similar. See, for example, Karl Friedrich Schinkels's diary entries regarding the London and West India docks in L. Ettlinger, "A German Architect's Visit to England in 1826," *Architectural Review* 91 (May 1945): 182.

5. John Malham, *The Naval Gazetteer; or, Seaman's Complete Guide* (Boston, 1797), 49–50; *The Liverpool Guide; Including a Sketch of the Environs* (Liverpool, 1797), 54; F. W. Simms, ed., *Public Works of Great Britain*, 2 vols. (London, 1838), 2:29–32; James Wallace, *A General and Descriptive History of the Antient and Present State, of the Town of Liverpool* (Liverpool, 1797), 90–107; Joshua Montefiore, *A Commercial Dictionary Containing the Present State of Mercantile Law and Custom* (Philadelphia, 1804), 57–63; "Docks, Edifices, and Commerce of Liverpool," *Mechanics' Magazine* 1 (January 1833): 37; J. R. McCulloch, *A Dictionary, Practical, Theoretical, and Historical, of Commerce and Commercial Navigation*, 2 vols. (London, 1854), 1:515–25.

6. Simms, ed., *Public Works of Great Britain*, 2:34–39; McCulloch, *Dictionary*, 1:491–511; Joseph G. Broodbank, *History of the Port of London*, 2 vols. (London: D. O'Connor, 1921), 1:77–162; Gareth Stedman Jones, *Outcast London: A Study of the Relationship between Classes in Victorian London* (Oxford: Oxford University Press, 1971), 111–24, 163–64; Alex Werner, "The Port of London, 1750–1806," in *North Sea Ports and Harbours: Adaptations to Change*, ed. Paul Holm and John Edwards (Esbjerg, Denmark: Fiskeri- og Søfartsmuseet, 1992), 39–61; Walter M. Stern, "The First London Dock Boom and the Growth of the West India Docks," *Economica* 73 (February 1952): 59–77; John Christopher Lovell, *Stevedores and Dockers: A Study of Trade Unionism in the Port of London, 1870–1914* (London: Macmillan, 1969), 12–18. I use "London Docks" to denote those owned by the London Dock Company in Wapping, and "London docks" to indicate the series of docks along the Thames.

7. P[atrick] Colquhoun, *A Treatise on the Commerce and Police of the River Thames* (London, 1800); William Vaughan, *A Treatise on Wet Docks, Quays, and Warehouses, for the Port of*

London (London, 1794); Peter Linebaugh, *The London Hanged: Crime and Civil Society in the Eighteenth Century* (Cambridge: Cambridge University Press, 1993), 416–35; Peter D'Sena, "Perquisites and Casual Labour on the London Wharfside in the Eighteenth Century," *London Journal* 14, no. 2 (1989): 130–47.

8. Montefiore, *Commercial Dictionary*, 73–84; Edward Sargent, "The Planning and Early Building of the West India Docks," *The Mariner's Mirror* 77 (May 1991): 119–41; Linebaugh, *London Hanged*, 425; George Pattison, "The Coopers' Strike at the West India Dock, 1821," *The Mariner's Mirror* 55 (May 1969): 163–84. For a firsthand account of work at the docks, see Pat Hudson and Lynette Hunter, eds., "The Autobiography of William Hart, Cooper, 1776–1857: A Respectable Artisan in the Industrial Revolution. Part II," *London Journal* 8, no. 1 (1982): 66–75.

9. S.W., *Visit to London*, 91; Benjamin Silliman, *A Journal of Travels in England, Holland and Scotland* (New York, 1810), 136; [From the *Boston Chronicle*], "London Docks," *Berkshire County Whig*, August 1, 1844, 22. On the expiration of the requirement for tickets, see "A Looking-Glass for London.—No. XVII. Commerce—The Docks," *Penny Magazine of the Society for the Diffusion of Useful Knowledge*, July 1, 1837, 254, and "Commercial Docks," *Hunt's Merchant's Magazine and Commercial Review* (hereafter *Hunt's*) 5 (September 1841): 248.

10. "Homeward Bound," in *The Oxford Book of Sea Songs*, ed. Roy Palmer (Oxford: Oxford University Press, 1986), 187. The Blackwall Dock refers to that owned by the East India Company in 1806. Palmer dates this ballad to the 1820s, and notes that British variants refer to other docks and American variants to American port cities (188), indicating that the location is incidental.

11. Records of the London Criminal Courts, at http://www.oldbaileyonline.org, reference numbers t18000917-139 (Robins), t18210718-72 (Salter), t18081126-54 (Darrett, 1808), t18021027-22 (Rawey), t18021027-69 (Williams), t18091101-92 (Carter, Wood). For a description of casual laborers pressing for work at the docks, see Henry Mayhew, *London Labour and the London Poor*, 4 vols. (London, 1861–62), 3:303–5.

12. Terry Eagleton, *The Ideology of the Aesthetic* (London: Blackwell, 1990), 20; Kenneth John Myers, "On the Cultural Construction of Landscape Experience: Contact to 1830," in *American Iconology: New Approaches to Nineteenth-Century Art and Literature*, ed. David C. Miller (New Haven: Yale University Press, 1993), 72–79; Michel Foucault, "The Eye of Power," in *Power/Knowledge: Selected Interviews and Other Writings, 1972–1977*, ed. Colin Gordon, trans. Colin Gordon et al. (New York: Pantheon, 1980), 146–65; Carole Fabricant, "The Aesthetics and Politics of Landscape in the Eighteenth Century," in *Studies in Eighteenth-Century British Art and Aesthetics*, ed. Ralph Cohen (Berkeley: University of California Press, 1985), 49–81; Stephan Oettermann, *The Panorama: History of a Mass Medium* (New York: Zone, 1997), 5–47; Alan Wallach, "Wadsworth's Tower: An Episode in the History of American Landscape Vision," *American Art* 10 (Autumn 1996): 9–27.

13. For representative examples of these terms, see Nathaniel S. Wheaton, *Journal of a Residence during Several Months in London* (Hartford, 1830), 144 (vast); Silliman, *Journal of Travels*, 133 (immense); C. S. Stewart, *Sketches of Society in Great Britain and Ireland*, 2 vols. (Philadelphia, 1834), 1:14 (magnificent); "London—Its Docks—Shipping," 126 (stupendous); Nathaniel H. Carter, *Letters from Europe* (New York, 1827), 50 (gigantic); John Griscom, *A Year in Europe* (Philadelphia, 1823), 30 (prodigious); William Cullen Bryant, *Letters of a Traveller*, 3rd ed. (New York, 1851), 146 (massive).

14. See, for example, "From a London Paper. West-India Docks," *Albany Gazette*, December 17, 1804, 2, and *Mechanics' Magazine* 1 (January 1833): 37.

15. A. G. Carlsund, quoted in Simms, ed., *Public Works of Great Britain*, 2:47–48; Calvin Colton, *Four Years in Great Britain, 1831–1835*, 2 vols. (New York, 1835), 1:153.

16. For an overview of the development of the Sublime in eighteenth-century Britain, see Samuel H. Monk, *The Sublime: A Study of Critical Theories in XVIII–Century England* (New York: Modern Language Association of America, 1935). Edward J. Nygren reviews the American usage of eighteenth-century aesthetic categories in "From View to Vision," in *Views and Visions: American Landscape before 1830*, ed. Nygren and Bruce Robertson (Washington, DC: Corcoran Gallery of Art, 1986), 3–81.

17. Edmund Burke, *A Philosophical Enquiry into the Origin of Our Ideas of the Sublime and Beautiful*, ed. J. T. Boulton (1757; London: Routledge and Paul, 1958), 124, 39–40, 51–52, 70, 40.

18. Ibid., pt. 2 (quotations 124, 74); Silliman, *Journal of Travels*, 133; Henry B. McLellan, *Journal of a Residence in Scotland, and a Tour through England, France, Germany, Switzerland, and Italy* (Boston, 1834), 95; "The London Docks," *Spirit of the Times*, July 23, 1859, 284; "London Docks," *Berkshire Whig*, 1.

19. On the Picturesque, see Malcolm Andrews, *The Search for the Picturesque: Landscape Aesthetics and Tourism in Britain, 1760–1800* (Aldershot, England: Scolar, 1989), and Bruce Robertson, "The Picturesque Traveler in America," in *Views and Visions*, ed. Nygren and Robertson, 189–211.

20. *Liverpool Guide*, 45; Carter, *Letters from Europe*, 53, 106; Stewart, *Sketches of Society*, 1:95.

21. On the natural advantages of America's harbors see, for example, James Birket, *Some Cursory Remarks Made by James Birket in His Voyage to North America, 1750–1751* (New Haven: Yale University Press, 1916), 22–23, 29, 43, 64; William Priest, *Travels in the United States of America: Commencing in the Year 1793 and Ending in 1797* (London, 1802), 164; *Blunt's Strangers' Guide to the City of New-York* (New York, 1817), 205; and "The Harbors of North America," *Hunt's* 2 (April 1840): 317–29.

22. *Blunt's Strangers' Guide*, 205; John Melish, *Travels through the United States of America, in the Years 1806 & 1807, and 1809, 1810, & 1811* (London, 1818), 79.

23. On the Sublime in America, see Barbara Novak, *Nature and Culture: American Landscape and Painting, 1825–1875*, 3rd ed. (New York: Oxford University Press, 2007); Elizabeth McKinsey, *Niagara Falls: Icon of the American Sublime* (Cambridge: Cambridge University Press, 1985); and John F. Sears, *Sacred Places: American Tourist Attractions in the Nineteenth Century* (Amherst: University of Massachusetts Press, 1998).

24. Arthur Young, *Tours in England and Wales* (London, 1784), excerpted in *"The Most Extraordinary District in the World": Ironbridge and Coalbrookdale*, ed. Barrie Trinder, 3rd ed. (Chichester, England: Phillimore, 2005), 44; diary of Katherine Plymley, June 4, 1794, excerpted in Henry Skrine, *Two Successive Tours through the Whole of Wales, with Several of the English Counties* (1798), and Charles Didbin, *Observations on a Tour through Almost the Whole of England* (1801–2), in *"Most Extraordinary District,"* ed. Trinder 64, 74, 82. See also Francis D. Klingender, *Art and the Industrial Revolution* (London: N. Carrington, 1947), 71–80.

25. John F. Kasson, *Civilizing the Machine: Technology and Republican Values in America, 1776–1900* (New York: Penguin, 1976), 161–80; David E. Nye, *American Technological Sublime* (Cambridge, MA: MIT Press, 1994), esp. chaps. 3, 5; Leo Marx, *The Machine in the Garden: Technology and the Pastoral Ideal* (New York: Oxford University Press, 1964), chap. 4.

26. "London Docks," *Berkshire Whig*, 1; Griscom, *Year in Europe*, 1:85.

27. "Description of the Wapping Docks near London," *The Literary Magazine, and American Register*, August 1805, 146.

28. Joshua E. White, *Letters on England: Comprising Descriptive Scenes with Remarks on the State of Society, Domestic Economy, Habits of the People, and Condition of the Manufacturing Classes Generally* (Philadelphia, 1816), 8–9.

29. Burke, *Philosophical Enquiry*, 57.

30. Roger B. Stein, *Seascape and the American Imagination* (New York: C. N. Potter, 1975), 3–6.

31. Burke characterized the Sublime as a passion related to self-preservation, turning on pain and danger, and the Beautiful as a passion related to society, including "the Society of the Sexes" and "society in general," both sources of pleasure. Burke, *Philosophical Enquiry*, 38–43. In her commentary on Burke, Frances Ferguson comments that "the beautiful has been defined as what we love because it submits to us and the sublime as what we admire for its power over us." Ferguson, *Solitude and the Sublime: Romanticism and the Aesthetics of Individuation* (New York: Routledge, 1992), 48.

32. "West India Docks," *Daily Advertiser* (New York), October 19, 1802, 2.

33. Alexander Slidell Mackenzie, *The American in England*, 2 vols. (New York, 1835), 2:236; White, *Letters on England*, 316; "Kirwan," *Men and Things as I Saw Them in Europe* (New York, 1854), 16. "Kirwan" is a pseudonym for Nicholas Butler, a Presbyterian minister.

34. Jacob Green, *Notes of a Traveller, during a Tour through England, France, and Switzerland, in 1828* (Philadelphia, 1830), 79; "Wapping Docks," *Daily Advertiser*, November 3, 1802, 2; "From a London Paper. West-India Docks," 2; "From a London Paper. Docks," *New-England Palladium* (Boston), June 22, 1804, 4; Burke, *Philosophical Enquiry*, 71.

35. William Buell Sprague, *Letters from Europe, in 1828* (New York, 1828), 131; *Liverpool Guide*, 72; "Description of the Wapping Docks," 146; JL to Francis Cabot Lowell, March 29, 1804.

36. John Brewer, *The Sinews of Power: War, Money and the English State* (London: Unwin, Hyman, 1989), 34–36; Miles Ogborn, *Spaces of Modernity: London's Geographies, 1609–1780* (New York: Guilford, 1998), 158–200.

37. William J. Ashworth, "'System of Terror': Samuel Bentham, Accountability and Dockyard Reform during the Napoleonic Wars," *Social History* 23 (January 1996): 63–79 (quotations 64, 65, 67, 68, 78). See also Linebaugh, *London Hanged*, chap. 11, and Simon Schaffer, "'The Charter'd Thames': Naval Architecture and Experimental Spaces in Georgian Britain," in *The Mindful Hand: Inquiry and Invention from the Late Renaissance to Early Industrialization*, ed. Lissa Roberts, Simon Schaffer, and Peter Dear (Amsterdam : Koninkliijke Nederlandse Akademie van Wetenschappen, 2007), 279–305. The naval facilities administered by Bentham, termed "dockyards," were not docks as described in this essay but facilities for building ships.

38. "From a London Paper. West India Docks," 2; L[ouis] Simond, *Journal of a Tour and Residence in Great Britain during the Years 1810 and 1811* (New York, 1815), 29.

39. Burke, *Philosophical Enquiry*, 58, 64.

40. Mayhew, *London Labour and the London Poor*, 3:303.

41. Fabricant, "Aesthetics and Politics of Landscape," 73. Kevin L. Nevers makes a similar point in "Immovable Objects, Irresistible Forces: The Sublime and the Technological in the Eighteenth-Century," *Eighteenth-Century Life* 19 (February 1995): 18–38.

42. Bushman, *Refinement of America*, 148; Stein, *Seascape and the American Imagination*, 55–66; Nygren, "From View to Vision," 10–12; John Wilmerding, *A History of American Marine Painting* (Salem, MA: Peabody Museum, 1968), 89–142. The following are examples of these modes of representation in both England and America. "Over-the-water" prospects: Johannes Kip, "A Prospect of the City of London," 1724, and William Burgis, "A South Prospect

of ye Flourishing City of New York in the Province of New York in America, 1719–21" (New-York Historical Society); Commercial activity: Henry Freeman James, "A View of Liverpool," 1823 (National Museums, Liverpool), and Robert Salmon, "Wharves of Boston," 1829 (The Bostonian Society); Genre scenes, bustle: Henry Moses, "Sketches of Shipping," 1824 (National Maritime Museum, Greenwich [hereafter NMM]), and William James Bennett, "South St. from Maiden Lane," 1828 (Metropolitan Museum of Art); Genre scenes, immorality: Louis Philippe Boitard, "The Imports of Great Britain from France," 1757 (British Museum), and John Carlin, After a Long Cruise," 1857 (Metropolitan Museum of Art).

43. Samuel Owen, "West India Docks," 1811 (NMM); Matthews and J. T. Neale, "The West India Docks," 1815 (NMM).

44. Oettermann, *Panorama*, 8–12, 120–21; John Kasson, *Rudeness and Civility: Manners in Nineteenth-Century Urban America* (New York: Hill and Wang, 1990), 72–73.

45. The series is reproduced in Broodbank, *Port of London*, illustrations opp. 1:70, 92, 113, 121, 131. With George Dance, Daniell also published *Views of the London Docks* (London, 1800–1808), but his engraving of the London Docks at Wapping enjoyed a second life when it was reproduced as a full page in "New Tea Warehouses at the London Docks," *Illustrated London News* 7 (September 27, 1845): 204. In 1837 a similar, though not identical, unattributed bird's-eye view of the London Docks appeared in an American magazine ("The Docks," *Penny Magazine*, 253). Daniell is best known for his views of India, executed with his uncle, Thomas Daniell, based on their travels in India between 1786 and 1794. These were published in a series of books titled *Oriental Scenery* (1795–1808). The East India Company may have provided a connection to the dock series. While the images of India were not bird's-eye views, they exhibited some characteristics suggestive of the dock series, namely an "atmosphere of quiet composure" and a "meticulous and precise" style. William Foster, "British Artists in India, 1760–1820," *Annual Volume of the Walpole Society* 19 (1930–31): 20–23, and Pratapaditya Pal and Vidya Dehejia, *From Merchants to Emperors: British Artists and India, 1757–1930* (Ithaca, NY: Cornell University Press, 1986), 15–16, 104–10 (quotations 109).

46. "London Docks," *Berkshire Whig*, 1.

47. *Liverpool Guide*, 34. But note that an individual is credited with acting impartially, rather than crediting an impartial system. For London docks and commercial bustle, see, for example, the 1827 engraving of the Commercial Docks in George Cooke, *Views of London and Its Vicinity* (London, 1834), plate 42.

48. There is a large literature on the ideal of quantification, related technologies such as accounting and statistics, and their relation to state and corporate power. See, for example, Theodore M. Porter, *Trust in Numbers: The Pursuit of Objectivity in Science and Public Life* (Princeton, NJ: Princeton University Press, 1995), and William Ashworth, "The Calculating Eye: Baily, Herschel, Babbage and the Business of Astronomy," *British Journal for the History of Science* 27 (December 1994): 409–41.

49. Simond, *Journal of a Tour*, 29.

50. "The London Docks," *Hunt's* (June 1847): 639; "London Docks," *Berkshire Whig*, 1; "London Docks," *Spirit of the Times*, 284; "The Queen's Tobacco-Pipe," *Friends' Review* 4 (April 12, 1851): 30.

51. Kasson, *Rudeness and Civility*, 73.

52. Malachy Postlethwayt, *The Universal Dictionary of Trade and Commerce*, 4th ed., 2 vols. (London, 1774), 2: n.p. [s.v. "Madder"]; McCulloch, *Commercial Dictionary*, 347.

53. Mayhew, *London Labour and the London Poor*, 3:302, 303; "The British Tobacco Warehouse at Liverpool," *Hunt's* 16 (April 1847): 396; "Wine Vaults of the London Docks,"

Hunt's 33 (August 1855): 227; Wheaton, *Journal of a Residence*, 144; "London Docks," *Spirit of the Times*, 384.

54. Alain Corbin, *The Foul and the Fragrant: Odor and the French Social Imagination* (Cambridge: Harvard University Press, 1986); Constance Classen, David Howes, and Anthony Synott, *Aroma: The Cultural History of Smell* (London: Routledge, 1994), 3–5 (quote on 5). See also Lissa Roberts, "The Death of the Sensuous Chemist: The 'New' Chemistry and the Transformation of Sensuous Technology," in *Empire of the Senses: The Sensual Culture Reader*, ed. David Howes (Oxford: Berg, 2005), 106–27.

55. "London Docks," *Spirit of the Times*, 284; McLellan, *Journal*, 229; Wheaton, *Journal of a Residence*, 144; "London Docks," *Berkshire Whig*, 1; Mackenzie, *American in England*, 2:236.

56. "The Poetry of Trade," *Hunt's* 13 (November 1845): 405, 406–7; Daniel D. Barnard, "Commerce, as Connected with the Progress of Civilization," *Hunt's* 1 (July 1839): 14, 13; "The American Merchant," *Hunt's* 2 (June 1840): 511.

57. "London Docks," *Berkshire Whig*, 1; Simond, *Journal of a Tour*, 29. On the alphabetized organization of merchants' bureaus and the order it represented, see David Hancock, *Citizens of the World: London Merchants and the Integration of the British Atlantic Community, 1735–1785* (Cambridge, England: Cambridge University Press, 1997), 101–2. At the West India Docks, the warehouses were designated by numbers (Sargent, "West India Docks," passim).

58. Frederick Law Olmsted, *Walks and Talks of an American Farmer* (New York, 1852), 79, 68, 69; Frederick Law Olmsted to the Board of Commissioners of the Central Park, January 22, 1861, and Olmsted to John Olmsted, January 14, 1858, in *The Papers of Frederick Law Olmsted*, vol. 3, *Creating Central Park, 1857–1861*, ed. Charles E. Beveridge and David Schuyler (Baltimore: Johns Hopkins University Press, 1983), 314, 113. See also Roy Rosenzweig and Elizabeth Blackmar, *The Park and the People: A History of Central Park* (Ithaca, NY: Cornell University Press, 1992), 139–40, 147–49.

59. On the utopian aesthetics of the royal dockyards, see Schaffer, "Charter'd Thames," 282.

Chapter 8

1. On the conception of "the market," see Jean-Christophe Agnew, *Worlds Apart: The Market and the Theater in Anglo-American Thought, 1550–1750* (Cambridge: Cambridge University Press, 1986), 17–56.

2. On Leggett as the acme of Jacksonian laissez-faire ideology, see Richard Hofstadter, "William Leggett, Spokesman of Jacksonian Democracy," *Political Science Quarterly* 58 (1943): 581–94; Marvin Meyers, "A Free-Trade Version: William Leggett," in *The Jacksonian Persuasion: Politics and Belief* (Stanford, CA: Stanford University Press, 1957), 141–56; John Ashworth, *"Agrarians" and "Aristocrats": Party Political Ideology in the United States, 1837–1846* (London: Royal Historical Society, 1983), 94–97. But see also, on Leggett as an advocate of "proletarian" politics, Harry Ammon, "William Leggett: Equal Rights Editor," MA thesis, Georgetown University, 1940; on Leggett as "the leading exponent of a simple agrarian economy and way of life," Lester Harvey Rifkin, "William Leggett: Journalist-Philosopher of Agrarian Democracy in New York," *New York History* 32, no. 1 (January 1951): 45–60; and on Leggett as a "precapitalist" "economic conservative," Stanley Nelson Worton, "William Leggett, Political Journalist (1801–1839): A Study in Democratic Thought," PhD diss., Columbia University, 1954. Edward K. Spann, *Ideas and Politics: New York Intellectuals and Liberal Democracy, 1820–1880* (Albany: State University of New York Press, 1972), 64–78, describes Leggett as a "born loser" who voiced the dismay of those left behind by metropolitan development. For reappropriations of Leggett as a precursor of the twentieth-century libertari-

anism of Friedrich Hayek, Ayn Rand, and Murray Rothbard, see Steven K. Beckner, "Leggett: Nineteenth-Century Libertarian," *Reason* 8, no. 10 (February 1977): 32–34; and Lawrence H. White, "William Leggett: Jacksonian Editorialist as Classical Liberal Political Economist," *History of Political Economy* 18, no. 2 (1986): 307–24.

3. Sean Wilentz, *Chants Democratic: New York City and the Rise of the American Working Class, 1788–1850* (New York: Oxford University Press, 1984), 107–42; Edward B. Mittelman, "Trade Unionism," in *History of Labour in the United States*, vol. 1, ed. John R. Commons et al. (New York: Macmillan, 1919), 347–49; John B. Clark, "Introduction," in *A Documentary History of American Industrial Society*, vol. 5, ed. John R. Commons et al. (Cleveland: Arthur H. Clark Co., 1910), 19–20.

4. On the lower-middle-class political tradition that the workingmen's movement inaugurated, see Bruce Laurie, "'Spavined Ministers, Lying Toothpullers, and Buggering Priests': Third-Partyism and the Search for Security in the Antebellum North," in *American Artisans: Crafting Social Identity, 1750–1850*, ed. Howard B. Rock, Paul A. Gilje, and Robert Asher (Baltimore: Johns Hopkins University Press, 1995), 98–119.

5. On the ideological distinction between gambling and speculation, see Ann Fabian, *Card Sharps and Bucket Shops: Gambling in Nineteenth-Century America* (New York: Routledge, 1999). On the close relationship between counterfeiting and banking, see Stephen Mihm, *A Nation of Counterfeiters: Capitalists, Con Men, and the Making of the United States* (Cambridge: Harvard University Press, 2007).

6. The only extended treatment of Leggett's early writings is Page S. Procter Jr., "The Life and Works of William Leggett (1801–1839)," PhD diss., Yale University, 1949, but it focuses on the artistic merits and weaknesses of this work by mid-twentieth-century standards. See also, on Leggett's sea stories, Hester Blum, *The View from the Masthead: Maritime Imagination and Antebellum American Sea Narratives* (Chapel Hill: University of North Carolina Press, 2008), 79–81; on his relation to James Fenimore Cooper and Edgar Allan Poe, John D. Seelye, "Buckskin and Ballistics: William Leggett and the American Detective Story," *Journal of Popular Culture* 1, no. 1 (Summer 1967): 52–57; and on his relation to Herman Melville, John D. Seelye, "'Spontaneous Impress of Truth': Melville's Jack Chase: A Source, an Analogue, a Conjecture," *Nineteenth-Century Fiction* 20, no. 4 (March 1966): 367–76.

7. See also Jeffrey Sklansky, "The Moneylender as Magistrate: Nicholas Biddle and the Ideological Origins of Central Banking in the United States," *Theoretical Inquiries in Law* 11, no. 1 (January 2010): 319–59.

8. "Address to the Mechanics and Working Men of the State of New York," *New York Evening Post*, July 23, 1836, quoted in Mittelman, "Trade Unionism," 462.

9. *Plaindealer*, December 3, 1836, 1.

10. On the spread of chartered corporations for municipal, eleemosynary, and business purposes in the early United States, see Pauline Maier, "The Revolutionary Origins of the American Corporation," *William and Mary Quarterly*, 3rd ser., 50, no. 1 (January 1993): 51–84; John Lauritz Larson, *Internal Improvement: National Public Works and the Promise of Popular Government in the Early United States* (Chapel Hill: University of North Carolina Press, 2001).

11. Leggett, "The Monopoly Banking System," *Evening Post*, December 1834, in *A Collection of the Political Writings of William Leggett*, vol. 1, ed. Theodore Sedgwick Jr. (New York: Taylor and Dodd, 1840), 103.

12. On commercial banks' assumption of the sovereign power to create currency in the early United States, see Christine Desan, "The Market as a Matter of Money: Denaturalizing Economic Currency in American Constitutional History," *Law and Social Inquiry* 30, no. 1

(January 2005): 1–60; James Willard Hurst, *A Legal History of Money in the United States, 1774–1970* (Lincoln: University of Nebraska Press, 1973), 152.

13. Edward Kellogg, *Labor and Other Capital: The Rights of Each Secured and the Wrongs of Both Eradicated. Or, An Exposition of the Cause Why Few Are Wealthy and Many Poor, and the Delineation of a System, Which, Without Infringing the Rights of Property, Will Give to Labor Its Just Reward* (New York: Edward Kellogg, 1849), xxxv.

14. William Leggett, "Rich and Poor," *Evening Post*, December 6, 1834, in *Political Writings*, ed. Sedgwick, 1:110 (italics added).

15. For a fine overview of the "banking question" as it figured in the Jacksonian labor movement, see Walter Hugins, *Jacksonian Democracy and the Working Class: A Study of the New York Workingmen's Movement, 1829–1837* (Stanford, CA: Stanford University Press, 1960), 172–202.

16. See David M. Henkin, *City Reading: Written Words and Public Spaces in Antebellum New York* (New York: Columbia University Press, 1998), 137–66.

17. See James Steven Rogers, *The Early History of the Law of Bills and Notes: A Study of the Origins of Anglo-American Commercial Law* (Cambridge: Cambridge University Press, 1995).

18. Hanna Fenichel Pitkin, *The Concept of Representation* (Berkeley: University of California Press, 1967). On the dual discourse of literary and political representation in the early republic, see Carolyn Eastman, *A Nation of Speechifiers: Making an American Public after the Revolution* (Chicago: University of Chicago Press, 2009); Jay Fliegelman, *Declaring Independence: Jefferson, Natural Language, and the Culture of Performance* (Stanford, CA: Stanford University Press, 1993); Christopher Looby, *Voicing America: Language, Literary Form, and the Origins of the United States* (Chicago: University of Chicago Press, 1996); Thomas Gustafson, *Representative Words: Politics, Literature, and the American Language, 1776–1865* (Cambridge: Cambridge University Press, 1992); Michael Warner, *The Letters of the Republic: Publication and the Public Sphere in Eighteenth-Century America* (Cambridge: Harvard University Press, 1990); Larzer Ziff, *Writing in the New Nation: Prose, Print, and Politics in the Early United States* (New Haven: Yale University Press, 1991).

19. Jeffrey L. Pasley, *"The Tyranny of Printers": Newspaper Politics in the Early American Republic* (Charlottesville: University Press of Virginia, 2001), 1–23; Edward Pessen, *Most Uncommon Jacksonians: The Radical Leaders of the Early Labor Movement* (Albany: State University of New York Press, 1967), 57.

20. On the problem of representation in early American religion, science, and fashion and etiquette, see, respectively, James E. Block, *A Nation of Agents: The American Path to a Modern Self and Society* (Cambridge: Belknap Press of Harvard University Press, 2002); James Delbourgo, *A Most Amazing Scene of Wonders: Electricity and Enlightenment in Early America* (Cambridge: Harvard University Press, 2006), 129–64; and Karen Halttunen, *Confidence Men and Painted Women: A Study of Middle-Class Culture in America, 1830–1870* (New Haven: Yale University Press, 1982).

21. Gary A. Richardson, "Plays and Playwrights: 1800–1865," in *The Cambridge History of American Theatre*, vol. 1, *Beginnings to 1870*, ed. Don B. Wilmeth and Christopher Bigsby (Cambridge: Cambridge University Press, 1998), 258; David Grimsted, *Melodrama Unveiled: American Theater and Culture, 1800–1850* (Chicago: University of Chicago Press, 1968); Bruce A. McConachie, *Melodramatic Formations: American Theatre and Society, 1820–1870* (Iowa City: University of Iowa Press, 1992).

22. Peter Brooks, *The Melodramatic Imagination: Balzac, Henry James, Melodrama, and the Mode of Excess* (New Haven: Yale University Press, 1976), 85, 14; Allardyce Nicoll, *A History*

of Early Nineteenth-Century Drama, 1800–1850, vol. 1 (Cambridge: Cambridge University Press, 1930), 101–2.

23. In many respects, melodrama recalls what the literary theorist Erich Auerbach has called the "Homeric style" of the *Odyssey* and its descendants, which aims "to represent phenomena in a fully externalized form, visible and palpable in all their parts." Erich Auerbach, *Mimesis: The Representation of Reality in Western Literature*, trans. Willard R. Trask (Princeton, NJ: Princeton University Press, 1953), 6. But modern melodrama brings the Homeric style to bear on commonplace experience.

24. On the melodramatic elements of the Declaration of Independence, see Michael T. Gilmore, *Surface and Depth: The Quest for Legibility in American Culture* (Oxford: Oxford University Press, 2003), 43–45. On the defining role of melodrama in framing continual conflicts over the relationship between the state and civil society in France since the Revolution, see James R. Lehning, *The Melodramatic Thread: Spectacle and Political Culture in Modern France* (Bloomington: Indiana University Press, 2007).

25. Joseph A. Schumpeter, *History of Economic Analysis*, ed. Elizabeth Moody Schumpeter (New York: Oxford University Press, 1954), 264–65, 277, 282; D. Foley, "Money in Economic Activity," in *The New Palgrave: A Dictionary of Economics*, ed. John Eatwell, Murray Milgate, and Peter Newman (London: Macmillan, 1987), 519–25; Ronald L. Meek, *Studies in the Labor Theory of Value*, 2nd ed. (New York: Monthly Review Press, 1956).

26. On the popularity of Shakespeare in nineteenth-century America, see Lawrence Levine, *Highbrow/Lowbrow: The Emergence of Cultural Hierarchy in America* (Cambridge: Harvard University Press, 1988), 11–81.

27. Cf. James L. Rosenberg, "Melodrama," in *Tragedy: Vision and Form*, ed. Robert W. Corrigan (San Francisco: Chandler Publishing Co., 1965), 232–44.

28. For an aesthetic critique along these lines of one major product of nineteenth-century political economy, see Wylie Sopher, "Aesthetic of Revolution: The Marxist Melodrama," in *Tragedy*, ed. Corrigan, 258–67. For a more recent response, see Jane Gaines, "The Melos in Marxist Theory," in *The Hidden Foundation: Cinema and the Question of Class*, ed. David E. James and Rick Berg (Minneapolis: University of Minnesota Press, 1996), 56–71.

29. See Susan Gillman, *Blood Talk: American Race Melodrama and the Culture of the Occult* (Chicago: University of Chicago Press, 2003), 14–16, 21–23; and Jacky Bratton, Jim Cook, and Christine Gledhills, eds., *Melodrama: Stage, Picture, Screen* (London: British Film Institute, 1994).

30. Cf. Gordon S. Wood, "Conspiracy and the Paranoid Style: Causality and Deceit in the Eighteenth Century," *William and Mary Quarterly*, 3rd ser., 39, no. 3 (July 1982): 402–41.

31. William Cullen Bryant, "William Leggett," *United States Magazine and Democratic Review* 6, no. 19 (July 1839): 20.

32. Leggett suffered from serious but amorphous infirmities for much of his life, and the precipitating cause of his early death is unclear, variously attributed to rheumatism and "high grade bilious fever." Worton, "William Leggett," 18–20.

33. Records of General Courts Martial and Courts of Inquiry of the Navy Department, 1799–1867, National Archives Microfilm Publications, Microcopy no. 273, roll 19, vol. 17, Cases 430¼–434, June 21–September 5, 1825, 0098, 0100, 0121, 0134; James E. Valle, *Rocks and Shoals: Order and Discipline in the Old Navy, 1800–1861* (Annapolis, MD: Naval Institute Press, 1980), 3, 259–60.

34. Records of Courts Martial, 0076-0077, 0078, 0065.

35. Records of Courts Martial, 0148-0149, 0124-0125, 0090-0094, 0076-0077, 0078, 0171.

36. Records of Courts Martial, 0149.

37. See Andrew Lawson, "Downwardly Mobile: American Literary Realism and the Lower Middle Class," unpublished manuscript.

38. Procter, "Life and Works of William Leggett," 1–9; Ammon, "William Leggett," 6–9.

39. Procter, "Life and Works of William Leggett," 10, 14–33; Solon J. Buck, *Illinois in 1818*, 2nd ed., rev. ed. (1917; Urbana: University of Illinois Press, 1967), 90, 149–52.

40. The newspaper notice of Leggett's supposedly last recitation in Edwardsville lists the following selections: "Collins' Ode on Music. Cassius' Speech instigating Brutus to join the conspiracy against Caesar. Mark Antony's Oration over the dead body of Caesar. Cato's Soliloquy on the immortality of the soul. The Dagger Scene from Macbeth. Othello's Apology for his Marriage. The Soliloquy of Dick the apprentice. The Sailor-boy's Dream. The Soldier's Dream. Hamlet's Soliloquy on Death. The Battle of Hohenlinden. The Speech of Logan to the white men. The fall of Poland, & c." *Edwardsville Spectator*, April 24, 1821.

41. *Leisure Hours at Sea: Being a Few Miscellaneous Poems. By a Midshipman of the United States Navy* (New York: George C. Morgan, and E. Bliss & E. White, 1825).

42. Carolyn Eastman, "'A Nation of Speechifiers': Oratory, Print, and the Making of a Gendered American Public, 1780–1830," PhD diss., Johns Hopkins University, 2001, 15–17, 24, 32–33, 59–60; Noah Webster, *An American Selection of Lessons in Reading and Speaking; Calculated to Improve the Minds and Refine the Taste of Youth. To Which Are Prefixed, Rules in Elocution, and Directions for Expressing the Principal Passions of the Mind*, 4th ed. (Philadelphia: David Hogan, 1809), x.

43. Bruce McConachie, "American Theatre in Context, from the Beginnings to 1870," in *Cambridge History of American Theatre*, 1:127–32.

44. Ammon, "William Leggett," 25; Procter, "Life and Works of William Leggett," 117, 119–20.

45. See McConachie, "American Theatre," 152; Joseph Roach, "The Emergence of the American Actor," in *Cambridge History of American Theatre*, 1:352–56; Jill Lepore, "The Curse of Metamora," in *The Name of War: King Philip's War and the Origins of American Identity* (New York: Alfred A. Knopf, 1998), 194, 198–99. For Forrest's biography, see William Rounseville Alger, *Life of Edwin Forrest, The American Tragedian*, 2 vols. (Philadelphia: Lippincott and Co., 1877).

46. Christopher Bigsby and Don B. Wilmeth, "Introduction," in *Cambridge History of American Theatre*, 1:15–16.

47. Procter, "Life and Works of William Leggett," 137–38, 231.

48. *Tales and Sketches* (New York: J. and J. Harper); *Naval Stories* (New York: G. and C. and H. Carrill).

49. On the "fear of falling," see Laurie, "Spavined Ministers," 119; Lawson, "Downwardly Mobile."

50. Seelye, "Buckskin and Ballistics," 54.

51. Procter, "Life and Works of William Leggett," 139, 152, 177; Ammon, "William Leggett," 29; *The Critic* 2, no. 7 (June 20, 1829): 89.

52. Kendall B. Taft, *Minor Knickerbockers: Representative Selections, with Introduction, Bibliography, and Notes* (1947; Freeport, NY: Books for Libraries Press, 1970), xli; M. H. Abrams, *The Mirror and the Lamp: Romantic Theory and the Critical Tradition* (New York: Oxford University Press, 1953), 14; Michael T. Gilmore, "Letters of the Early Republic," *The Cambridge History of American Literature*, vol. 1, *1590–1820*, ed. Sacvan Berkovitch (Cambridge: Cambridge University Press, 1994), 542–44.

53. *The Critic* 1, no. 25A (April 26, 1829): 396, 397.

54. Ibid., no. 7 (December 13, 1828): 107; no. 2 (November 8, 1828): 19–20; and no. 5 (November 29, 1828): 65. On addiction as a metaphor for "the annulment of the bourgeois subject's autonomy, willpower, and self-mastery," and on the relevance of that concept to the money question in the Gilded Age, see Timothy A. Hickman, "'Mania Americana': Narcotic Addiction and Modernity in the United States, 1870–1920," *Journal of American History* 90, no. 4 (March 2004): 1269–94, esp. 1289–93.

55. *The Critic* 1, no. 9 (December 27, 1828): 138.

56. Allan Nevins, *The Evening Post: A Century of Journalism* (New York: Boni and Liveright, 1922), 141.

57. See Gilmore, "Letters of Early Republic," 541–57.

58. *Plaindealer*, December 10, 1836, 19. On "middling rhetoric," see Kenneth Cmiel, *Democratic Eloquence: The Fight over Popular Speech in Nineteenth-Century America* (New York: William Morrow, 1990), 56–63.

59. *Political Writings*, ed. Sedgwick, 1:127–28, 303, 261–62, 94–95.

60. Ibid., 1:257, 91–92, 103, 21; Meyers, *Jacksonian Persuasion*, 146.

61. Wilentz, *Chants Democratic*, 64–66, 76–77, 219–21; Helen L. Sumner, "Citizenship," in *History of Labour*, ed. Commons et al., 1:177, 232–33, 274–77; Mittelman, "Trade Unionism," 381–82, 402–10; Dixon Ryan Fox, *The Decline of Aristocracy in the Politics of New York* (New York: Longmans, Green and Co., 1919), 391–93.

62. F. Byrdsall, *The History of the Loco-Foco or Equal Rights Party. Its Movements, Conventions and Proceedings, with Short Characteristic Sketches of Its Prominent Men* (New York: Clement and Packard, 1842), 26, 27, 46. "Loco Focos" were the matches that the equal-rights partisans used to light candles at a tumultuous 1835 meeting in Tammany Hall after Democratic Party regulars departed and turned out the gas lamps.

63. *The Critic* 1, no. 22 (April 4, 1829): 355; emphasis in original.

64. Ibid., 2, no. 7 (June 20, 1829): 89.

65. Frank Luther Mott, *American Journalism: A History of Newspapers in the United States Through 250 Years, 1690 to 1940* (New York: Macmillan, 1941), 215–16, 241–43; Michael Schudson, *Discovering the News: A Social History of American Newspapers* (New York: Basic Books, 1978), 12–60.

66. Nevins, *Evening Post*, 135–36, 153, 166–167; Hugins, *Jacksonian Democracy*, 38; Arthur Schlesinger Jr., *The Age of Jackson* (Boston: Little, Brown, 1945), 191; William Leggett to Robert Montgomery Bird, New York City, November 8, 1836, Robert Montgomery Bird Papers, Folder 84, Special Collections, Rare Book and Manuscript Library, University of Pennsylvania.

67. Alger, *Life of Edwin Forrest*, 1:373.

68. *Plaindealer*, February 4, 1837, 149–50.

69. On the flour riot, see Byrdsall, *History of the Loco-Foco*, 99–107; *Plaindealer*, February 18, 1837, 190; Joshua R. Greenberg, *Advocating the Man: Masculinity, Organized Labor, and the Household in New York, 1800–1840* (New York: Columbia University Press, gutenberg<e>book, 2006), "Conclusion—The Loco Foco Party"; Edwin G. Burrows and Mike Wallace, *Gotham: A History of New York City* (New York: Oxford University Press, 1999), 609–11; J. T. Headley, *The Great Riots of New York, 1712 to 1873* (New York: E. B. Treat, 1873), 97–110.

70. *Plaindealer*, February 25, 1837, 194.

71. Recently, Leggett has been the subject of a little revival among historians focused on his role as a leading Democratic abolitionist. See Jonathan H. Earle, *Jacksonian Antislavery and*

the Politics of Free Soil, 1824–1854 (Chapel Hill: University of North Carolina Press, 2004), 17–26; J. David Greenstone, *The Lincoln Persuasion: Remaking American Liberalism* (Princeton, NJ: Princeton University Press, 1993), 124–39; Sean Wilentz, "Jacksonian Abolitionist: The Conversion of William Leggett," in *The Liberal Persuasion: Arthur Schlesinger Jr. and the Challenge of the American Past*, ed. John Patrick Diggins (Princeton, NJ: Princeton University Press, 1997), 84–106.

72. Leonard L. Richards, *"Gentlemen of Property and Standing": Anti-Abolition Mobs in Jacksonian America* (New York: Oxford University Press, 1970), 7, 16, 48–52, 62–70, 72–73, 168.

73. *Political Writings*, ed. Sedgwick, 1:30, 207–9; 2:24, 33–34.

74. Ibid., 2: 14, 16. On Leggett's reaction to the abolitionist mails controversy and on his related advocacy of privatizing the postal service, see Richard R. John, *Spreading the News: The American Postal System from Franklin to Morse* (Cambridge: Harvard University Press, 1995), 278, 252–55.

75. *Plaindealer*, December 3, 1836, 1–2. In 1838 Leggett's outspoken abolitionism narrowly prevented his nomination for Congress on the Democratic ticket. Bryant, "William Leggett," 24–25.

76. *Plaindealer*, December 24, 1836, 54.

77. Wilentz, "Jacksonian Abolitionist."

78. *Political Writings*, ed. Sedgwick, 1:106.

79. Ibid., 1:83–84, 106, 143; *Plaindealer*, January 14, 1837, 100–101, and February 18, 1837, 178–79.

80. *Plaindealer*, May 13, 1837, 369, and July 29, 1837, 546.

81. On religious and political radicalism sparked by the panic of 1837, see John Stauffer, *The Black Hearts of Men: Radical Abolitionists and the Transformation of Race* (Cambridge: Harvard University Press, 2002), 114–17.

82. *Political Writings*, ed. Sedgwick, 1:248, 2:86.

83. *Plaindealer*, August 5, 1837, 564.

84. *Political Writings*, ed. Sedgwick, 1:228.

85. Ibid., 43.

86. *Plaindealer*, August 12, 1837, 579; *Political Writings,* ed. Sedgwick, 1:105.

87. See David Laidler, "Bullionist Controversy," in *New Palgrave*, ed. Eatwell, Milgate, and Newman 289–93; Lloyd W. Mints, *A History of Banking Theory in Great Britain and the United States* (Chicago: University of Chicago Press, 1945), 5, 9–10, and passim; Rogers, *Early History of the Law of Bills and Notes*, 228–32.

88. *Political Writings*, ed. Sedgwick, 1:21.

89. Fritz Redlich, *The Molding of American Banking: Men and Ideas*, pt. 1 (New York: Hafner Publishing Co., 1947), 10–11; Naomi R. Lamoreaux, *Insider Lending: Banks, Personal Connections, and Economic Development in Industrial New England* (Cambridge: Cambridge University Press, 1994), 2.

90. See Hugins, *Jacksonian Democracy*, 191–93.

91. William M. Gouge, *A Short History of Paper Money and Banking in the United States* (New York: Augustus M. Kelley, 1968).

92. William Cullen Bryant to Frances F. Bryant, New York, May 23, 1836, in *The Letters of William Cullen Bryant*, vol. 2, ed. William Cullen Bryant II and Thomas G. Voss (New York: Fordham University Press, 1977), 23.

93. Gouge, *Short History*, 118, 41.

94. Hugins, *Jacksonian Democracy*, 191.

95. On the oversights in the "real bills doctrine," see Laidler, "Bullionist Controversy"; Mints, *History of Banking Theory*, 30 and passim.

96. Raymond Williams, *Modern Tragedy*, ed. Pamela McCallum (1966; Toronto: Broadview Press, 2006), 94–95.

Chapter 9

1. "On becoming educated by judicious application of leisure hours . . . men can better fit themselves to be good citizens." *Hunt's Merchant's Magazine* 11 (December 1844): 573. On clerking demands for early closing, see *New York Tribune*, August 12, 16, 20, 31, and September 1, 11, 1841; December 14 and 24, 1846; January 12, 23, February 28, March 1, May 15, 20, and July 12, 1850.

2. "'Money makes money' is a vulgar but true adage." *Hints to Young Tradesmen, and Maxims for Merchants* (Boston: Perkins and Marvin, 1838), 29; *Journal of the Geographic and Statistical Society*, July 1859, 213; W. and R. Chambers, *Treasury of Knowledge* (New York: A. S. Barnes and Co., 1849), 75; Georg Simmel, *Simmel on Culture: Selected Writings*, ed. David Frisby and Mike Featherstone (London: Sage Publications, 1997), 235.

3. *Hunt's* 1 (October 1839): 291; "Chapters from the Experiences of a Merchant," *Hunt's* 15 (October1846): 343–44, 347; Edward N. Tailer, Diaries, New-York Historical Society, entry dated January 15, 1850; James D. McCabe, *Lights and Shadows of New York Life* (Philadelphia: National Publishing Company, 1872), 843–47.

4. *Putnam's Monthly*, June 1855, 578; Virginia Penny, *The Employments of Women: A Cyclopaedia of Woman's Work* (Boston: Walker, Wise and Co., 1863), 126; *Vermont Watchman and State Journal*, June, 24, 1852; *American Phrenological Journal* 10, no. 8 (August 1848): 254; Theodore Parker, "Thoughts on Labor" *The Dial*, April 1841, 497; Henry David Thoreau, "Life without Principle," *Atlantic Monthly*, October 1863, 488; Karl Marx and Friedrich Engels, "Manifesto of the Communist Party," in *The Marx-Engels Reader*, ed. Robert C. Tucker, 2nd ed. (New York: Norton, 1978), 476. See, generally, Andrew Lyndon Knighton, "Idle Threats: The Limits of Productivity in Nineteenth-Century America," PhD, University of Minnesota, 2004.

5. Charles H. Foster, ed., *Down East Diary by Benjamin Browne Foster* (Orono: University of Maine at Orono Press, 1975), 15, 16, 121, 219, 220–21, 229, 297, 287–88; [Herman Melville], "Bartleby, the Scrivener," *Putnam's*, November 1853, 550; *New York Star*, quoted in Box 6, Commonplace Book, Daniel F. Child Papers, Massachusetts Historical Society, Boston; Manuel Castells, *Rise of the Network Society* (Oxford: Blackwell Publishers, 2000), esp. 77–162; James H. Madison, "The Evolution of Commercial Credit Reporting Agencies in Nineteenth-Century America," *Business History Review* 48, no. 2 (Summer 1974); *Hunt's* 24 (January 1851): 46–51; Thomas Cochran, "The Business Revolution," *American Historical Review* 79 (December 1974): 1450.

6. *Hunt's* 1 (July 1839): 77; "Basis of Prosperity," quoted in Scott A. Sandage, *Born Losers: A History of Failure in America* (Cambridge: Harvard University Press, 2005), 163; Edward J. Balleisen, *Navigating Failure: Bankruptcy and Commercial Society in Antebellum America* (Chapel Hill: University of North Carolina Press, 2001), 27; *Hunt's* 15 (November 1846),483. On railroads and telegraphs, see, for instance, Richard John, "Recasting the Information Infrastructure for the Industrial Age," in *A Nation Transformed by Information: How Information Has Shaped the United States from Colonial Times to the Present*, ed. Alfred D. Chandler Jr. and James W. Cortada (New York: Oxford University Press, 2000), 68–86; James R. Beniger, *The*

Control Revolution: Technological and Economic Origins of the Information Society (Cambridge: Harvard University Press, 1986), 11–12, 123–27, 130–31, 132–44, 153–68, 173–77; Thomas Cochran, *Frontiers of Change: Early Industrialism in America* (New York: Oxford University Press, 1981), 10, 24–25, 37–39.

7. Spencer in *Hunt's* 37 (December 1857): 702; "capital of mind" in Granville Sharp, *Prize Essay* (London: Banker's Magazine, 1852), 1; *Hunt's* 15 (October 1846): 383, 384.

8. Weber, quoted in Sandage, *Born Losers*, 163; Balleisen, *Navigating Failure*, 51–52.

9. Bryant & Stratton Commercial School, *Annual Circular and Catalogue* (Boston, 1859), 26–30.

10. Frederick Beck, *Young Accountant's Guide* (Boston: Stimpson and Clapp, 1831), 10; Karl Marx, *Capital* (Moscow: Foreign Language Publishing House, 1957–62), 3:400; Sidney Pollard, *The Genesis of Modern Management: A Study of the Industrial Revolution in Great Britain* (1965; Hampshire: Gregg Revivals, 1993), 209–19, 221–22; Frederick Michael E. Hobart and Zachary S. Schiffman, *Information Ages: Literacy, Numeracy, and the Computer Revolution* (Baltimore: Johns Hopkins University Press, 1998), 148–50. Thomas Cochran, "The Business Revolution," *American Historical Review* 79 (December 1974): 1454–55; N.S.B. Gras, *Business and Capitalism: An Introduction to Business History* (1939; New York: Augustus M. Kelley, 1971), 116–19; G. A. Lee, "The Concept of Profit in British Accounting, 1760–1900," *Business History Review* 49, no. 1 (Spring 1975): 10–17, 29–32.

11. C. W. Moore, Diary, Special Collections, New York Public Library, 218–19; Charles Edward French Diaries, Massachusetts Historical Society, Journal No. 2, entries dated October 1, 2, 3, and 6, 1851; *Hunt's* 15 (October 1846): 384; Hobart and Schiffman, *Information Ages*, 90–91, 103; Onno De Wit, January Van Den Ende, Johan Schot, and Ellen Van Oost, "Innovation Junctions: Office Technologies in the Netherlands, 1880–1980," *Technology and Culture* 43 (January 2002): 54; Yoneji Masuda, *Managing in the Information Society: Releasing Synergy Japanese Style* (Oxford: Basil Blackwell, 1990), 34–35; James C. Scott, *Seeing like a State: How Certain Schemes to Improve the Human Condition Have Failed* (New Haven: Yale University Press, 1998), 77–78, 82–83, 93; *Duties of Employers and Employed, Considered with Reference to Principals and Their Clerks or Apprentices* (New York: J. S. Redfield, 1849), 23.

12. Lois S. Severini, *Architecture of Finance: Early Wall Street* (Ann Arbor, MI: UMI Research Press, 1983), 24–26, 52–59; *New York Journal of Commerce*, July 10, 1849; *New York Times*, March 15, 1854; Deborah S. Gardner, "The Architecture of Commercial Capitalism: John Kellum and the Development of New York, 1840–1875," PhD diss., Columbia University, 1979, 101–19; William M. Thayer, *The Poor Boy and Merchant Prince; or, Elements of Success* (Boston: Gould and Lincoln, 1857), 121–23; Sharp, *Prize Essay*, 5–7, 15, 41–43; Siegfried Giedion, *Mechanization Takes Command: A Contribution to Anonymous History* (1948; New York: W. W. Norton, 1969), 56.

13. Giovanni Arrighi, *The Long Twentieth Century: Money, Power, and the Origins of Our Times* (New York: Verso, 1994), 33–34; F. R. R[eed], *Experience of a New York Clerk* (New York: F. R. Reed, 1877), 27–37, 75–82.

14. JoAnne Yates, *Control Through Communication: The Rise of System in American Management* (Baltimore: Johns Hopkins University Press, 1989), 2–3; Frazar Kirkland, *Cyclopaedia of Commercial and Business Anecdotes* (New York: D. Appleton, 1864 and 1865). 2:672, 677; Glenn Porter and Harold C. Livesay, *Merchants and Manufacturers: Studies in the Changing Structure of Nineteenth-Century Marketing* (Baltimore: Johns Hopkins Press, 1971), 5–6.

15. Porter and Livesay, *Merchants and Manufacturers*, 9, 17–18; Pierre Gervais, "Background Discussion: What Is the 'Industrial Revolution'?" manuscript in author's possession, 26;

Freedley quoted in Harvey J. Wexler, "Business Opinion and Economic Theory, 1840–1860," in *Explorations in Entrepreneurial History* 1, no. 3 (March 1949): 15; James Kimball, *The Dry-Goods Jobbers* (Boston: Commercial Agency, 1870), 7; Michael Pryke and John Allen, "Monetized Time-Space: Derivatives—Money's 'New Imaginary'?" *Economy and Society* 29, no. 2 (May 2000): 269–70, 180–81.

16. Kimball, *Dry-Goods Jobbers*, 22, 24–25; *Hunt's* 24 (January 1851), 51.

17. *Hunt's* 1 (July 1839); 39 (October 1858), 412–14; B. F. Foster, *Prospectus of the Commercial Academy* (New York, 1837); *125 Years of Education for Business: The History of Dyke College, 1848–1973*, n.p. (chap. 2). For writing masters see *New-York as It Is, in 1833* (New York: J. Disturnell, 1833), 224; Benjamin R. Haynes and Harry P. Jackson, *A History of Business Education in the United States* (Cincinnati: Southwestern Pub. Co., 1935), 21–22; Jones in *New York Tribune*, August 31, 1841; *New York Herald*, September 30, 1839; *Gem* (1844): 7; Leverett S. Lyon, *Education for Business* (Chicago: University of Chicago Press, 1922), 233–34, 235, 237–39; William H. Eaton, *Eaton's Self-Instructing Counting-Room Arithmetic* (Boston, 1866); Bryant, Stratton & Co., in Warshaw Collection of Business Paraphernalia, Box 2, Business Colleges, Smithsonian Institution, Washington, DC.

18. *Hunt's* 4 (February 1841), 142; Hobart and Schiffman, *Information Ages*, 4–6, 90–91, 103; Bruno Latour, "Visualization and Cognition: Thinking with Eyes and Hands," in *Knowledge and Society: Studies in the Sociology of Culture Past and Present*, 6:22–23 (New York: Jai Press, 1986).

19. Wm. P. M. Ross, *The Accountant's Own Book and Business Man's Manual*, 2nd ed. (Philadelphia: Thomas, Cowperthwait and Co., 1852), 11. On the market's flattening of space, see Elizabeth Blackmar, *Manhattan for Rent, 1785–1850* (Ithaca, NY: Cornell University Press, 1989), 94–100.

20. Karl Marx, *Grundisse* (New York: Penguin, 1993), 142; Karl Polanyi, "Our Obsolete Market Mentality," in Polanyi, *Primitive, Archaic, and Modern Economies*, ed. George Dalton (Boston: Beacon Press, 1968).

21. Jackson, quoted in Charles Sellers, *The Market Revolution: Jacksonian America, 1815–1846* (New York: Oxford University Press, 1991), 325.

22. Spencer in *Hunt's* 37 (December 1857): 702; Gary J. Kornblith, "Self-Made Men: The Development of Middling-Class Consciousness in New England," *Massachusetts Review* 26, nos. 2/3 (1985): 469; Horatio Alger Jr. *Ragged Dick, or, Street Life in New York with Boot Blacks* (1868; New York: Norton, 2008), 77, 86; *Phrenological Journal* 17 (1853): 75; French diary, Journal 6, 6, 15–16; Joseph Scoville, *The Old Merchants of New York City. By Walter Barrett, Clerk* (New York: Carleton, 1863), 56–57; William Hoffman, Diary, New-York Historical Society, entries March 30, July 12, and October 28, 1848.

23. *Hunt's* 24 (May 1851), 533; Bryant and Stratton, *Catalogue*, 37; Tailer diary, entries dated March 22, June 3, December 5 and 17, 1849; January 19 and 21, February 11 and 28, April 30, March 27, and May 3 and 25, 1850.

24. Hoffman diary, entries dated March 9, 1849; March 4, June 21, July 3, 7, September 19, 24, and November 1, 1850.

25. *Whig Review*, May 1852, 473; Hoffman diary, entry dated August 31, 1850; French diary, Journal No. 3, entry dated March 5, 1855; Colin Gordon, "Governmental Rationality: An Introduction," in *The Foucault Effect: Studies in Governmentality*, ed. Graham Burchell, Colin Gordon, and Peter Miller (Chicago: University of Chicago Press, 1991), 28, 33; debate in Sandage, *Born Losers*, 124; Tocqueville quoted in G. J. Barker-Benfield, *The Horrors of the Half-Known Life: Male Attitudes toward Women and Sexuality in Nineteenth-Century America*

(New York: Routledge, 2000), 5; New York Mercantile Library, *Annual Report*, vol. 17 (New York, 1838), 7; Foster, ed., *Down East Diary*, 109, entry dated May 13, 1848.

26. *Whig Review*, 472; anonymous diary, 1834–36, Special Collections, Bryn Mawr College, Bryn Mawr, PA, entry dated August 29, 1836; "Maxims for Merchants and Business Men," in *Hunt's* 15 (November 1846): 483; French diary, entries dated March 3, 4, and June 24, 1856.

27. Hoffman diary, entries dated August 31, 1850, and September 4, 1848.

28. Thoreau quoted in Sandage, *Born Losers*, 7–8; "Crows" in Daniel A. Cohen, "Arthur Mervyn and His Elders: The Ambivalence of Youth in the Early Republic," *William and Mary Quarterly* 43, no. 3 (July 1986): 369; Daniel Wise, *The Young Man's Counsellor* (New York: Carlton and Phillips, 1853), 100; *Herbert Tracy; or the Trials of Mercantile Life, and the Morality of Trade, by a "Counting-House Man"* (New York: John C. Riker, 1851), 5–6; Henry Ward Beecher, *Lectures to Young Men, on Various Important Subjects*, 3rd ed. (New York: J. C. Derby, 1856), 28.

29. Tailer diary, entry dated January 15, 1852. On the dishonest clerk see, for instance, "The Value of a Clerkship in New York," *Hunt's* 20 (May 1849), 570; "Counsel to Merchants' Clerks," *Hunt's* 29 (August 1853), 264; "The Merchant's Clerk and His Duties," *Hunt's* 41 (October 1859), 522–23, 26–29; Daniel N. Haskell, *An Address Delivered before the Boston Mercantile Library Association* (Boston: Dutton and Wentworth, 1848), 20; *Duties of Employers and Employed*, 3, 18; James W. Alexander, "The Merchant's Clerk Cheered and Counselled," in Alexander et al., *The Man of Business, Considered in his Various Relations* (New York: Anson D. F. Randolph, 1857), 8; Thomas Augst, *The Clerk's Tale: Young Men and Moral Life in Nineteenth-Century America* (Chicago: University of Chicago Press, 2003); *A sketch of the life of R. P. Robinson, the alleged murderer of Helen Jewett, containing copious extracts from his journal* (New York, 1836); Patricia Cline Cohen, *The Murder of Helen Jewett: The Life and Death of a Prostitute in Nineteenth-Century New York* (New York: Knopf, 1998).

30. Haskell, *Address*, 20; Charles E. Rogers, Diary, Special Collections, New York Public Library, entries dated March 2 and 3, 1864; Tailer diaries, entry dated June 8, 1850.

31. Tailer diary, entry dated December 12, 15, 1849. On no compensation paid in the first year see *New York Journal of Commerce*, August 7, 1849.

32. Tailer diary, entries dated January 7, February 16, 28, June 8, 1850; October 19 and November 1, 1852.

33. French diary, Journal No. 4, entries dated February 29 and March 1, 1856.

34. Ibid., entry dated March 2, 1856.

35. Ibid., entries dated December 31, 1856, and January 4 and 9, 1857.

36. Ibid., entry dated January 17, 1857.

37. Ibid., entries dated January 28 and March 14, 1857.

38. "Maxims for Merchants and Business Men," in *Hunt's* 15 (November 1846), 483; Alexis de Tocqueville, *Democracy in America* ed. J.P. Mayer (New York: Harper and Row, 1988), 506; Koenraad W. Swart, "'Individualism' in the Mid-Nineteenth Century (1826–1860)," *Journal of the History of Ideas* 23, no. 1 (1962).

39. Rogers diary, entries dated July 11, 27, September 6, 8, and December 2, 1864; Bryant and Stratton, *Catalogue* (1859), 26–30; 11–13; Samuel Lyman Munson, Diary, New-York Historical Society, May 8, August 26, and September 9, 1862; "Commercial Colleges—Their Nature and Object," *Hunt's* 39 (October 1858): 412.

40. Comer's Commercial College, *Annual Register* (1866), n.p. (front of pamphlet); *Annual Register* (1865), 4, 6, 8.

41. Bryant and Stratton, *Catalogue*, 30; Platt R. Spencer, *Spencerian Key to Practical*

Penmanship (New York: Ivison, Phinney, Blakeman and Co., 1869), 89, 93; B. F. Foster, *Foster's System of Penmanship: or, the Art of Rapid Writing Illustrated and Explained, to which is added the Angular and anti-Angular Systems* (Boston: Perkins, Marvin and Co., 1835), 10–11. Latour, "Visualization and Cognition," 28–29. On privileging writing over speaking in the modern move from rhetoric to statistics, see Mary Poovey, *A History of the Modern Fact: Problems of Knowledge in the Sciences of Wealth and Society* (Chicago: University of Chicago Press, 1998).

42. Hoffman diary, 179–80, entry dated March 8, 1849; Comer's Commercial College, *Annual Register* (1865), 7; Frazar Kirkland, *Cyclopaedia of Commercial and Business Anecdotes*, vol. 2 (New York: D. Appleton, 1865), 688; Augst, *The Clerk's Tale*, 219; French diary, entries dated July 30, and August 6 and 22, 1851.

43. Tamara Plakins Thornton, *Handwriting in America: A Cultural History* (New Haven: Yale University Press, 1996), 37, 43; Foster, *Down East Diary*, 12; Foster, *System of Penmanship*; Stanley Morison, *American Copybooks: An Outline of Their History from Colonial to Modern Times* (Philadelphia: Wm. F. Fell Co., 1951), 26–31; Thomson H. Littlefield, "Before Spencerian: A Development of B. F. Foster and the American System," *Print* 3, no. 4 (1945): 39; Spencer, *Spencerian Key*, 24; Rogers diary, entries dated July 27, September 6 and 8, and December 2, 1864; French diary, vol. 1, entries dated July 30 and August 6 and 27, 1851; Margery W. Davies, *Woman's Place Is at the Typewriter: Office Work and Office Workers, 1870–1930* (Philadelphia: Temple University Press, 1982), 13; Francis Barker, *The Tremulous Private Body: Essays on Subjection* (Ann Arbor: University of Michigan Press, 1995), 3–4; *New York Herald*, September 30, 1839.

44. Hobart and Schiffman, *Information Ages*, 30; *Hunt's* 15 (November 1846), 483–85; Sharp, *Prize Essay*, 28; David M. Henkin, *The Postal Age* (Chicago: University of Chicago Press, 2006), 42–53; JoAnne Yates, "Investing in Information: Supply and Demand Forces in the Use of Information in American Firms, 1850–1920," in *Inside the Business Enterprise: Historical Perspectives on the Use of Information*, ed. Peter Temin (Chicago: University of Chicago Press, 1991), 133–34; Tailer diary, entry dated May 25, 1850; Keith Robson, "Accounting Numbers as 'Inscription': Action at a Distance and the Development of Accounting," *Accounting, Organizations and Society* 17, no. 7 (1992); George John Child, Papers, 1:151; Albert Lane Norris, Journal, Special Collections, Winterthur Library, entry dated July 9, 1858; Cayley diary, entry dated January 16, 1844, New-York Historical Society; Robert Graham, Journal of Passing Events, New-York Historical Society, entries dated January 16, 1844, and February 13, March 25, April 20, and May 5 and 9, 1848; Tailer diary, entries dated December 18, 19, 20, 1849, and February 11, May 25, and May 28, 1850.

45. Foster, *System of Penmanship*, iii; Edgar A. Poe, *Man of the Crowd*, in Nina Baym et al., compilers, *Norton Anthology of American Literature* (New York, Norton, 1985), 1382; Foster, *Down East Diary*, 12, 121.

46. Attempts were accordingly made to mechanize all the writing, that is, to find "easy combinations of chemical and mechanical skill" by which the production of multiple copies would "scarcely [demand] more time and apparatus than is now required to write a single copy." An early version of carbon paper became available in the early nineteenth century. However, it smelled bad—a result of the oxidation of the oils with which it was prepared—and could only be used with a pencil. Meanwhile, James Watt, Christopher Wrenn, Thomas Jefferson, and Benjamin Franklin were only some of those trying to build a copying machine. The resulting manifold letter writers and letter presses could not, however, keep up with the escalating demands of the paper office. Government departments in Washington, DC, for instance, were hiring extra copyists at ten cents per hundred words in the 1850s in order to process their grow-

ing volume of documentation. *Hunt's* 15 (November 1846): 483–85; Barbara Rhodes, *Before Photocopying: the Art and History of Mechanical Copying, 1780–1938* (New Castle, DE: Oak Knoll Press, 1999), 4, 8–10, 12, 18–21, 24 (quote); Cindy Sondik Aron, *Ladies and Gentlemen of the Civil Service: Middle-Class Workers in Victorian America* (New York: Oxford University Press, 1987); Silvio A. Bedini, *Thomas Jefferson and His Copying Machines* (Charlottesville: University Press of Virginia, 1984).

47. Foster, *System of Penmanship*, 41, 89–104; S. A. Potter, *Penmanship Explained* (New York: Schermerhorn, Bancroft and Co.,1864), 22, 25–26; S. H. Browne, *The Manual of Commerce* (Springfield, MA: Bill, Nichols and Co., 1871), 313; Comer's Commercial College, *Annual Register* (Boston: Geo. C. Rand & Avery, 1866), inside back cover.

48. "From Turnbridge, Vermont, to London, England," *Proceedings of the Vermont Historical Society* 3 (1937): 287; Benjamin H. Rand, *The American Penman* (Philadelphia, 1840), n.p.; Morison, *American Copybooks*, 24–26; Benjamin Franklin Foster, *Writing and Writing Masters* (New York: Mason Brothers, 1854), n.p.; Littlefield, "Before Spencerian," 33–40; Charles Carpenter, *History of American Schoolbooks* (Philadelphia, University of Pennsylvania Press, 1963), 184. See the polemic in *Massachusetts Teacher*, April 1855, 113–17; July 1855, 213–18; November 1855, 332–37; Ben Kafka, "The Demon of Writing: Paperwork, Public Safety, and the Reign of Terror," *Representations* 98 (2007): 4–5.

49. Warshaw Collection, penmanship, box 1; Spencer, *Spencerian Key*, 143; Thornton, *Handwriting in America*, 47–55; Carpenter, *History of American Schoolbooks*, 189; Foster, *Prize Essay*, 50; Adam Wm. Rapp, *A Complete System of Scientific Penmanship* (Philadelphia: M. Fithian, 1832); Warren P. Spencer, *Origin and History of the Art of Writing* (New York: Ivison, Phinney, Blakeman and Co., 1869), 27; Spencer, *Spencerian Key*, 92–93. "Chirhythmography" also received a prominent place in the handbill announcing the opening of Folsom's Mercantile College in Cleveland in 1851; see *125 Years*; Friedrich Kittler, *Gramophone, Film, Typewriter* (Stanford, CA: Stanford University Press, 1999), 198–99, 230–31. Friederich Kittler has forcibly argued that it was the typewriter that effected this "destruction of the word," ushering in a "modern loop of endless replication" that turned the keyboard into a site of industrial alienation and robbed language of its defining content. But his claim assigns too much agency to the machine. The typewriter, like so many other mechanical apparatuses at this stage of "capitalization," enhanced a process that was already well under way, driven by the logic of capital rather than technology, and patently manifest in the era's intensifying applications of the pen.

50. Potter, *Penmanship Explained*, 29–32; Samuel Roberts Wells, *How to Do Business: A Pocket Manual of Practical Affairs* (New York: Fowler and Wells, 1857), 31; George W. Winchester, *Theoretical and Practical Penmanship, in Four Books*, rev. ed. (New York: Pratt, Oakley and Co., 1855); Foster, *System of Penmanship*, vii; Benjamin Franklin Foster, *Prize essay on the best method of teaching penmanship* (Boston : Clapp and Broaders, 1834), 24–25, 33; Littlefield, "Before Spencerian," 34; Rapp, *Complete System of Scientific Penmanship*, 14; Morison, *American Copybooks*, 26–27.

51. Jonathan Goldberg, *Writing Matter: From the Hands of the English Renaissance* (Stanford, CA: Stanford University Press, 1990), 86–89, 311–13; anon. diary, 1834–36, June 19, 1838; R. W. Emerson, "Doctrine of the Hands" (1837), quoted in Wai Chee Dimock, "Class, Gender, and a History of Metonymy," in *Rethinking Class: Literary Studies and Social Formations*, ed. Wai Chee Dimock and Michael T. Gilmore (New York: Columbia University Press, 1994), 58; "Labor," *American Phrenological Journal* 12, no. 9 (September 1850): 293–94; Barker, *Tremulous Private Body*, 70–80.

Chapter 10

1. Charles A. Beard and Mary R. Beard, *The Rise of American Civilization*, vol. 2, new rev. ed. (New York: Macmillan, 1935), 98–121; Louis M. Hacker, *The Triumph of American Capitalism: The Development of Forces in American History to the End of the Nineteenth Century* (New York: Columbia University Press, 1940), 339–73; Barrington Moore, *Social Origins of Dictatorship and Democracy: Lord and Peasant in the Making of the Modern World* (Boston: Beacon Press, 1966), 112; Raimondo Luraghi, "The Civil War and the Modernization of American Society: Social Structure and Industrial Revolution in the Old South Before and During the War," *Civil War History* 8 (1972): 230–50; Eric McKitrick, "Party Politics and the Union and Confederate War Efforts," from *American Party Systems: Stages of Political Development*, ed. William Nesbit Chambers and Walter Dean Burnham (New York: Oxford University Press, 1967); Leonard Curry, *Blueprint for Modern America: Non-Military Legislation of the First Civil War Congress* (Nashville: Vanderbilt University Press, 1968); William Shade, "'Revolutions May Go Backwards': The American Civil War and the Problem of Political Development," *Social Science Quarterly* 55 (1974): 763; Richard Bensel, *Yankee Leviathan: The Origins of Central State Authority in America, 1859–1877* (New York: Cambridge University Press, 1990); Heather Cox Richardson, *The Greatest Nation on Earth: Republican Economic Policies during the Civil War* (Cambridge: Harvard University Press, 1997); Mark R. Wilson, *The Business of Civil War: Military Mobilization and the State, 1861–1865* (Baltimore: Johns Hopkins University Press, 2006).

2. W. W. Rostow, *The Stages of Economic Growth: A Non-Communist Manifesto*, 3rd ed. (New York: Cambridge University Press, 1990), 95; Thomas Cochran, "Did the Civil War Retard Industrialization?" *Mississippi Valley Historical Review* 48 (1961): 197–210; Pershing Vartanian, "The Cochran Thesis: A Critique in Statistical Analysis," *Journal of American History* 51 (1964): 77–89; David T. Gilchrist and W. David Lewis, eds., *Economic Change in the Civil War Era* (Greenville, DE: The Eleutherian Mills–Hagley Foundation, 1965); Harry Scheiber, "Economic Change in the Civil War Era: An Analysis of Recent Studies," *Civil War History* (1965): 396–411; Stanley Engerman, "The Economic Impact of the Civil War," *Explorations in Entrepreneurial History* 3 (1966): 176–99; Ralph Andreano, ed., *The Economic Impact of the American Civil War* (New York: Schenckman, 1967); Claudia Goldin and Frank Lewis, "The Economic Cost of the American Civil War: Estimates and Implications," *Journal of Economic History* 35 (1975): 299–326; Stephen J. DeCanio and Joel Mokyr, "Inflation and Wage Lag during the American Civil War," *Explorations in Economic History* 14 (1977): 311–36; Saul Engelbourg, "The Economic Impact of the Civil War on Manufacturing Enterprise," *Business History* 21 (1979): 148–62.

3. Marc Egnal, *Clash of Extremes: The Economic Origins of the Civil War* (New York: Hill and Wang, 2009), 15. Examples of creative scholarship on the war's larger impact alluded to in this paragraph include J. Matthew Gallman, *Mastering Wartime: A Social History of Philadelphia during the Civil War* (New York: Cambridge University Press, 1990); Roger Ransom, "The Economic Consequences of the Civil War," in *The Political Economy of War and Peace*, ed. Murray Wolfson (Boston: Kluwer Academic Publishers, 1998): 49–74; Drew Gilpin Faust, *Mothers of Invention: Women of the Slaveholding South in the American Civil War* (Chapel Hill: University of North Carolina Press, 1996); Amy Dru Stanley, *From Bondage to Contract: Wage Labor, Marriage, and the Market in the Age of Slave Emancipation* (New York: Cambridge University Press, 1998); LeeAnn Whites, *The Civil War as a Crisis in Gender: Augusta, Georgia, 1860–1890* (Athens: University of Georgia Press, 2000); Marc Egnal, "The Beards Were Right: Parties in the North, 1840–1860," *Civil War History* 47 (2001): 30–56.

4. Engelbourg, "Economic Impact of the Civil War," 151–52, 155; James Moore Swank, *History of the Manufacture of Iron in All Ages: and Particularly in the United States from Colonial Time to 1891* (Philadelphia: American Iron and Steel Association, 1892), 376; Robert Gordon, *American Iron, 1607–1900* (Baltimore: Johns Hopkins University Press, 1996), 220–31; Ransom, "The Economic Consequences of the American Civil War," 49–50; Ross Thompson, "The Continuity of Innovation: The Civil War Experience," *Enterprise and Society* 11 (2010): 128–65.

5. James Huston, *The Panic of 1857 and the Coming of the Civil War* (Baton Rouge: Louisiana State University Press, 1987), 210–30; David Hackett Fischer, *The Great Wave: Price Revolutions and the Rhythm of History* (New York: Oxford University Press, 1996), 157; DeCanio and Mokyr, "Inflation and Wage Lag during the American Civil War," 315.

6. Huston, *The Panic of 1857*, 29; Gallman, *Mastering Wartime*, 266–71; Glenn Porter and Harold Livesay, *Merchants and Manufacturers: Studies in the Changing Structure of Nineteenth-Century Marketing* (Baltimore: Johns Hopkins Press, 1971), 119–25, quote is from p. 120; Keith Edward Wagner, "Economic Development in Pennsylvania during the Civil War, 1861–1865," PhD thesis, Ohio State University, 1969, 155; Robert Sharkey, *Money, Class and Party: An Economic Study of Civil War and Reconstruction* (Baltimore: Johns Hopkins Press, 1959), 144.

7. Kenneth Lipartito and David B. Sicilia, *Constructing Corporate America: History, Politics, Culture* (New York: Oxford University Press, 2004), 344; S. J. Packer, *Report of the Committee of the Senate of Pennsylvania Upon the Subject of the Coal Trade* (Harrisburg, PA: Henry Welsh, 1834), 24.

8. George Heberton Evans Jr., *Business Incorporations in the United States, 1800–1943* (New York: National Bureau of Economic Research, 1948), 11; L. Ray Gunn, *The Decline of Authority: Public Economic Policy and Political Development in New York, 1800–1860* (Ithaca, NY: Cornell University Press, 1988), 222–45; Sean Patrick Adams, *Old Dominion, Industrial Commonwealth: Coal, Politics, and Economy in Antebellum America* (Baltimore: Johns Hopkins University Press, 2004), 170–78.

9. Evans, *Business Incorporations in the United States*, 10; John Eilert, "Illinois Business Incorporations, 1861–1869," *Business History Review* 37 (1963): 171; Alexander K. McClure, *Old Time Notes of Pennsylvania: A Connected and Chronological Record of the Commercial, Industrial and Educational Advancement of Pennsylvania, and the Inner History of All Political Movements Since the Adoption of the Constitution of 1838*, vol. 1 (Philadelphia: John C. Winston, 1905), 536.

10. Evans, *Business Incorporations in the United States*, 19; Eilert, "Illinois Business Incorporations," 179; C. B. Conant, "Coal Fever," *The Merchants' Magazine and Commercial Review* 52 (May 1865): 350; Adams, *Old Dominion, Industrial Commonwealth*, 196–202; McClure, *Old Time Notes*, 535; *Miner's Journal* (Pottsville, PA), March 26, 1864.

11. George H. Thurston, *Directory of the Monongahela and Youghiogheny Valleys: Containing Brief Historical Sketches of the Various Towns Located on Them; With a Statistical Exhibit of the Collieries Upon the Two Rivers* (Pittsburgh: A. A. Anderson, 1859), 253–66; James Macfarlane, *The Coal-Regions of America: Their Topography, Geology, and Development* (New York: D. Appleton, 1875), 664–65; Adams, *Old Dominion, Industrial Commonwealth*, 196–202; Isaac Costa, comp., *Gopsill's Pennsylvania State Business Directory: Containing the Names and Addresses of Merchants, Manufacturers, Professional Men, and Over 70,000 Farmers. With an Appendix Giving a Complete List of Banks, Insurance Companies, Railroads, Corporations, Newspapers, and other Useful Information* (Jersey City, NJ: James Gopsill, 1865), 911–14.

12. Macfarlane, *Coal-Regions of America*, 662; *Laws of Pennsylvania, 1863*, 1102–9; *Penn-*

sylvania Senate Journal, 1863, 567; *United States Railroad and Mining Register* (Philadelphia, PA), May 21, 1864.

13. "A Tabular List of All the Coal and Mining Companies Organized Under General Laws," Massachusetts House Document No. 270, April 18, 1864; Costa, comp., *Gopsill's Pennsylvania State Business Directory*, 911–14; *General and Local Laws and Joint Resolutions Passed by the Fifty-Sixth General Assembly of the State of Ohio, at its Second Session, Begun and Held in the City of Columbus, January 3, 1865 and in the Sixty-Third Year of Said State* (Columbus: Richard Nevins, 1865), 37; E. Cooper Shapley Jr., *Legal Guide for Oil Companies and Stockholders; Including a Digest of the Mining Laws of Pennsylvania* (Philadelphia: Fowler and Moon, 1865), 24; *New Hampshire Statesman* (Concord, NH), May 1, 1863; *Boston Daily Advertiser*, May 4, 1863; *New Haven* (CT) *Daily Palladium*, May 4, 1864.

14. Shapely, *Legal Guide for Oil Companies and Stockholders*, 3; Brian Black, *Petrolia: The Landscape of America's First Oil Boom* (Baltimore: Johns Hopkins University Press, 2000), 114, 150–57.

15. Gerald D. Nash, *State Government and Economic Development: A History of Administrative Policies in California, 1849–1853* (Berkeley, CA: Institute of Governmental Studies, 1964), 81–96; Maureen A. Jung, "Capitalism Comes to the Diggings: From Gold-Rush Adventure to Corporate Enterprise," in *A Golden State: Mining and Economic Development in Gold Rush California*, ed. James J. Rawls and Richard Orsi (Berkeley: University of California Press, 1999), 62; Shapley, *Legal Guide for Oil Companies and Stockholders*, 4–5, 11–15; *The Merchants' Magazine and Commercial Review* 51 (December 1864):485; Costa, comp., *Gopsill's Pennsylvania State Business Directory*, 914–18; Black, *Petrolia*, 150–52.

16. John Majewski, *Modernizing a Slave Economy: The Economic Vision of the Confederate Nation* (Chapel Hill: University of North Carolina Press, 2009), 7.

17. Charles Dew, *Ironmaker to the Confederacy: Joseph Reid Anderson and the Tredegar Iron Works* (New Haven: Yale University Press, 1966), 140–43; Gorgas, quoted in Frank Vandiver, *Ploughshares into Swords: Josiah Gorgas and Confederate Ordnance* (Austin: University of Texas Press, 1952), 147; Mining and Nitre Bureau, *Message of the President, Feb. 15, 1865 [and Communication from the Secretary of War Transmitting a Report from the Chief of the Nitre and Mining Bureau]* (Richmond: n.p., 1865), 2, 7–10, 11–13. CI 1322, Confederate Imprint Collection, Virginia Historical Society, Richmond.

18. "An Ordinance to Encourage the Manufacture of Cannon in this State" (1861), in U.S. War Department, *Official Records of the Union and Confederate Navies in the War of the Rebellion*, ser. 4, vol. 1 (Washington, DC: Government Printing Office, 1900), 170; Chad Morgan, *Planters' Progress: Modernizing Confederate Georgia* (Gainesville: University Press of Florida, 2005), 56–57; John Milton to David Yulee, June 8, 1863, John Milton Letterbook, Florida Historical Society, Cocoa, FL; P. Murrah to Gen. J. B. Magruder, April 7, 1864, in US War Department, *Official Records*, ser. 1, 34:748.

19. James Bell, *Report on the State Assessment Laws* (Albany, NY: Weed, Parsons, and Company, 1863); C. K. Yearley, *The Money Machines: The Breakdown and Reform of Governmental and Party Finance in the North, 1860–1920* (Albany: State University of New York Press, 1970), 37–42; Wilson, *The Business of Civil War*, 7–23.

20. Robert Murray Haig, *A History of the General Property Tax in Illinois* (Champaign, IL: Flanigan-Pearson, 1914), 112–13; Ernest L. Bogart, "Financial History of Ohio," in *University of Illinois Studies in the Social Sciences*, vol. 1 (Champaign-Urbana: University of Illinois Press, 1912), 317–19; Yearley, *The Money Machines*, 160–62, 198; Robin Einhorn, *American Taxation, American Slavery* (Chicago: University of Chicago Press, 2006), 207–50.

21. Frank Marshall Eastman, *Taxation for State Purposes in Pennsylvania* (Philadelphia: Kay and Brother, 1898), xiii; Frederic Garver, *The Subvention in the State Finances of Pennsylvania* (Mensasha, WI: George Banta Publishing Company, 1919), 86, 140–41; Yearley, *The Money Machines*, 198–99; R. Rudy Higgens-Evenson, *The Price of Progress: Public Services, Taxation, and the American Corporate State, 1877 to 1929* (Baltimore: Johns Hopkins University Press, 2003), 15; Adams, *Old Dominion, Industrial Commonwealth*, 205. Statistics on state revenues come from the Pennsylvania Auditor General's Annual Reports, 1856, 1862–66.

22. *Boston Daily Advertiser*, February 7, 1862; Yearley, *The Money Machines*, 61; Higgens-Evenson, *Price of Progress*, 15–17.

23. Alfred D. Chandler Jr., *The Visible Hand: The Managerial Revolution in American Business* (Cambridge, MA: Belknap Press, 1977), 80. Like every facet of the American Civil War, the role of Northern railroads in the struggle has generated a huge literature. Most of these works focus on the military value of railroads and do not deal with the larger question of the conflict's significance to the long-term development of railroad networks. See, for example, Edwin Pratt, *The Rise of Rail Power in War and Conquest, 1833–1914* (Philadelphia: J. B. Lippincott, 1916); George E. Turner, *Victory Rode the Rails: The Strategic Place of Railroads in the Civil War* (Indianapolis: Bobbs-Merrill, 1953); George Rogers Taylor and Irene D. Neu, *The American Railroad Network, 1861–1890* (Cambridge: Harvard University Press, 1956); James A. Ward, *That Man Haupt: A Biography of Herman Haupt* (Baton Rouge: Louisiana State University Press, 1973); John Westwood, *Railways at War* (San Diego: Howell-North Books, 1980); Benjamin Bacon, *Sinews of War: How Technology, Industry, and Transportation Won the Civil War* (Novato, CA: Presidio, 1997). Some notable exceptions to this trend are Thomas Weber, *The Northern Railroads in the Civil War* (New York: King's Crown, 1952); Peter Harold Jaynes, "The Civil War and the Northern Railroads: A Test of the Cochran Thesis," PhD thesis, Boston University, 1973; John E. Clark, *Railroads in the Civil War: The Impact of Management on Victory and Defeat* (Baton Rouge: Louisiana State University Press, 2001).

24. George W. I. Ball, comp., *General Railroad Laws of the State of Pennsylvania and Acts Relative to Corporations Affecting Railroad Companies* (Philadelphia: Allen, Lane, and Scott, 1875), 98–100, 101–2, 110, 118–19, 123–27, 128–30; *Summit Branch Railroad Company and the Bear Valley Coal Company: Charter, Capital Stock, &C., &C. October 24, 1863* (Boston, 1863), 6.

25. Weber, *Northern Railroads in the Civil War*, 28–29.

26. *Philadelphia Inquirer*, June 7, 1861; Samuel Richey Kamm, "The Civil War Career of Thomas A. Scott," PhD thesis, University of Pennsylvania, 1940, 70–75; Clark, *Railroads in the Civil War*, 35–36, 39.

27. John F. Stover, *History of the Baltimore and Ohio Railroad* (West Lafayette, IN: Purdue University Press, 1987), 99–117; Kamm, "The Civil War Career of Thomas A. Scott," 191, 192.

28. Jaynes, "The Civil War and Northern Railroads," 296–98; Maury Klein, *History of the Louisville and Nashville Railroad*, rev. ed. (Lexington: University of Kentucky Press, 2003), 40–43; *American Railroad Journal*, January 2, 1864.

29. Alexander Trachtenberg, *The History of Legislation for the Protection of Coal Miners in Pennsylvania, 1824–1915* (New York: International Publishers, 1942), 12–16; Anthony F. C. Wallace, *St. Clair: A Nineteenth-Century Coal Town's Experience with a Disaster-Prone Industry* (New York: Alfred A. Knopf, 1987), 276–81; *Pennsylvania Archives, Papers of the Governors, 1858–1871*, 4th ser., vol. 8 (Harrisburg, PA: W. Stanley Ray, 1902), 466–67, 544–45.

30. J. Walter Coleman, *Labor Disturbances in Pennsylvania, 1850–1880* (Washington, DC: Catholic University of America Press, 1936), 40–49; Arnold Shankman, "Draft Riots in Civil

War Pennsylvania," *Pennsylvania Magazine of History and Biography* 101 (1977): 190–204; Grace Palladino, *Another Civil War: Labor, Capital, and the State in the Anthracite Regions of Pennsylvania, 1840–68* (Urbana: University of Illinois Press, 1990), 140–62; Kevin Kenny, *Making Sense of the Molly Maguires* (New York: Oxford University Press, 1998), 87–102; Priscilla Long, *Where the Sun Never Shines: A History of America's Bloody Coal Industry* (New York: Paragon House, 1989), 98–99; William A. Russ Jr., "The Origin of the Ban on Special Legislation in the Constitution of 1873," *Pennsylvania History* 11 (1944): 260–75; J. P. Shalloo, *Private Police: With Special Reference to Pennsylvania* (Philadelphia: The American Academy of Political and Social Science, 1933), 58–65.

31. Quote is from John Alexander Williams, "The New Dominion and the Old: Antebellum and Statehood Politics as the Background of West Virginia's 'Bourbon Democracy,'" *West Virginia History* 33 (1972): 342; Richard Orr Curry, *A House Divided: A Study of Statehood Politics and the Copperhead Movement in West Virginia* (Pittsburgh: University of Pittsburgh Press, 1964), 52–68, and Curry, "Crisis Politics in West Virginia, 1861–1870," in *Radicalism, Racism, and Party Realignment: The Border States during Reconstruction,* ed. Richard O. Curry (Baltimore: Johns Hopkins Press, 1969), 80–114.

32. Charles H. Ambler, Frances Hanoi Atwood, and William B. Mathews, eds., *Debates and Proceedings of the First Constitutional Convention of West Virginia,* 3 vols. (Huntington, WV: Gentry Brothers, 1939), 2:38–39. Statistics drawn from the list of charters granted in 1865 as reported by the West Virginia Secretary of State. *Laws of West Virginia, 1866* (Wheeling, WV: John Frew, 1866), 141–266.

33. Charles H. Ambler and Festus P. Summers, *West Virginia, the Mountain State,* 2nd ed. (Englewood Cliffs, NJ: Prentice-Hall, 1958), 232; Ambler, Atwood, and Mathews, eds., *Debates and Proceedings of the First Constitutional Convention of West Virginia,* 1:438, 3:133–34; Henry Gassaway Davis (HGD) to John King, August 3, 1868; HGD to William E. Stevenson, May 7, 1869; HGD to Nathan Goff, May 7, 1869; HGD to J. W. Garrett and John King, May 27, 1869; all in Henry Gassaway Davis Papers, West Virginia University, Morgantown.

34. Eric Foner, *Reconstruction: America's Unfinished Revolution, 1863–1877* (New York: Harper and Row, 1988), 325; *Constitution of the State of North Carolina, Together With the Ordinances and Resolutions of the Constitutional Convention* (Raleigh, NC: Joseph W. Holden, 1868), 27.

35. Charles Francis Adams, "The Railroad System," in *Chapters of Erie and Other Essays,* ed. Henry Adams and Francis Amasa Walker (New York: Henry Holt, 1886), 418.

36. Gerald Berk, *Alternative Tracks: The Constitution of American Industrial Order, 1865–1917* (Baltimore: Johns Hopkins University Press, 1994); Charles Postel, *The Populist Vision* (New York: Oxford University Press, 2007), 137–71.

Index

Page numbers in italics refer to illustrations.

102, 109, 111–13, 114–16, 117. *See also* probate courts; probate laws
insurance companies, 41, 52–55, 109, 113, 116, 158, 280
interest rates, 49–50, 64, 263
internal slave trade, 77, 90–91, 123, 127, 137–39. *See also* slave-breeding debate
Ise family, 40, 41, 46–47, 54–57, 61–63, 281, 284, 297–98n7; mortgage of, 40, 41, 47–50, 56, 61, 280

Jackson, Andrew (escaped slave), 140
Jackson, Andrew (president), 7, 84, 86, 87, 208, 276; and Second Bank of the United States, 7, 8, 71, 84, 233; and state banks, 84, 85
Jacksonians, 160, 199–200, 203, 208, 254; and abolitionism, 214, 215; and monetary issues, 216, 218, 219, 233. *See also* Leggett, William
Jacobs, Harriet, 141–42
Jefferson, Thomas, 44
Johnston, David Claypoole, *197*
Jones, Thomas, 231–32
Josephson, Matthew, 279

Kansas, 45, 54–55, 63, 125, 154; farm mortgages in, 45, 49, 54–55, 59, 62, 64, 280 (*see also* Ise family: mortgage of)
Kasson, John, 192
Keeler, B. C., 63
Kellogg, Edward, 202
Kent, James, 104–5
Kentucky, 22, 30, 87, 151, 153; sale of slaves from, 77, 81
Keynes, John Maynard, 76
Khan, B. Zorina, 24
Kindleberger, Charles, 85
King, James, 103
Knight, Richard Payne, 177
knowledge economy, 226

labor activism, 253, 271–72. *See also* unions; workingmen's movement
labor historians, 6, 7, 12, 225, 290n6
Lamoreaux, Naomi, 25
landed independence, 16–17, 40, 44–46, 66; African Americans' exclusion from, 32–33, 36, 60; and inheritance, 93–94, 96–97; loss of, 19, 34–35, 42, 54, 61, 63, 66, 94–95, 99, 225, 247

landownership, extent of, 16–17, 21, 94
Latour, Bruno, 232
Lavergne, Hugues, 80–81
lawyers, 105. *See also* probate courts
Leggett, William, 10–11, 199–203 208–13, 221, 280, 336n32; and abolitionism, 214–15, 339n75; background of, 200, 205–8; economic views of, 10–11, 199–200, 202, 211, 213–14, 215–21; and melodrama, 10, 200, 203, 211, 284; and panic of 1837, 200, 216–17; and workingmen's movement, 200, 211–12
Lenin, V. I., 27
leverage, 73
Liberty Party, 130–31
life estates, 102, 114
life insurance policies, 41, 53–54, 113
"limitation of risk," 58
limited liability, 148, 155, 160, 274–75, 323n16, 325n53
Lincoln, Abraham, 31, 33
Lipartito, Kenneth, 254
Liverpool: docks in (*see* docks, British); and international cotton trade, 75, 77, 78, 80, 87
Livesay, Harold, 253
lobbyists, 159
Loco Focos, 212, 213–14, 338n62
London: as banking center, 83, 87; docks in (*see* docks, British)
lotteries, 160
Louisiana: corporations in, 151, 153, 165; slaveholders in, 78, 80–84 (*see also* Bieller, Jacob). *See also* New Orleans
Lowell, Francis Cabot, 156, 171, 196
Lowell, John, 169–70, 171, 182, 196

Macauley, Thomas, 125–26
Madison, James, 133
Maine, 23, 24, 107, 225–26; corporations in, 150, 152, 255
Majewski, John, 263
Mann, Horace, 127, 131
manufacturing, 17–18, 60, 155, 156–57, 158, 228; in Civil War, 252–53, 264; and slavery, 131. *See also* textile industry
Mappin, W. F., 65
Marx, Karl, 35–36, 119, 233. See also *Communist Manifesto*
Marxian tradition, 14